Security and the War on Terror

The terrorist attacks of 11 September 2001 marked a turning point in international politics, representing a new type of threat that could not easily be anticipated or prevented through state-based structures of security alone. Opening up interdisciplinary conversations between strategic, economic, ethical and legal approaches to global terrorism, this edited book recognises a fundamental issue: while major crises initially tend to reinforce old thinking and behavioural patterns, they also allow societies to challenge and overcome entrenched habits, thereby creating the foundations for a new and perhaps more peaceful future.

The objective of this volume is to address the issues that are at stake in this dual process of political closure, and to therefore rethink how states can respond to terrorist threats. The contributors offer a unique combination, being drawn from leading conceptual theorists to policy-oriented analysts, from senior academics to junior researchers. The book explores how terrorism has had a profound impact on how security is being understood and implemented, and uses a range of hitherto neglected sources of insight, such as those between political, economic, legal and ethical factors, to examine the nature and meaning of security in a rapidly changing world.

This book will be of much interest to students of Terrorism Studies, Security Studies, International Law and International Relations in general.

Alex J. Bellamy is Professor of International Relations at the University of Queensland, Australia.

Roland Bleiker is Professor of International Relations at the University of Queensland, Australia.

Sara E. Davies is Lecturer at the School of Justice, Queensland University of Technology, Australia.

Richard Devetak is Senior Lecturer in International Relations and Director of the Rotary Centre for International Studies in Peace and Conflict Resolution at the University of Queensland, Australia.

Contemporary Security Studies

NATO's Secret Armies
Operation Gladio and terrorism in Western
Europe
Daniele Ganser

**The US, NATO and Military Burden-
Sharing**
Peter Kent Forster and Stephen J. Cimbala

**Russian Governance in the Twenty-First
Century**
Geo-strategy, geopolitics and new
governance
Irina Isakova

**The Foreign Office and Finland
1938–1940**
Diplomatic sideshow
Craig Gerrard

Rethinking the Nature of War
*Isabelle Duyvesteyn and Jan Angstrom
(eds)*

**Perception and Reality in the Modern
Yugoslav Conflict**
Myth, falsehood and deceit 1991–1995
Brendan O'Shea

**The Political Economy of Peacebuilding
in Post-Dayton Bosnia**
Tim Donais

The Distracted Eagle
The rift between America and Old Europe
Peter H. Merkl

The Iraq War
European perspectives on politics, strategy,
and operations
Jan Hallenberg and Håkan Karlsson (eds)

Strategic Contest
Weapons proliferation and war in the
greater Middle East
Richard L. Russell

Propaganda, the Press and Conflict
The Gulf War and Kosovo
David R. Willcox

Missile Defence
International, regional and national
implications
Bertel Heurlin and Sten Rynning (eds)

Globalising Justice for Mass Atrocities
A revolution in accountability
Chandra Lekha Sriram

Ethnic Conflict and Terrorism
The origins and dynamics of civil wars
Joseph L. Soeters

**Globalisation and the Future of
Terrorism**
Patterns and predictions
Brynjar Lia

Nuclear Weapons and Strategy
The evolution of American nuclear policy
Stephen J. Cimbala

Nasser and the Missile Age in the Middle East
Owen L. Sirrs

War as Risk Management
Strategy and conflict in an age of globalised risks
Yee-Kuang Heng

Military Nanotechnology
Potential applications and preventive arms control
Jurgen Altmann

NATO and Weapons of Mass Destruction
Regional alliance, global threats
Eric R. Terzuolo

Europeanisation of National Security Identity
The EU and the changing security identities of the Nordic states
Pernille Rieker

International Conflict Prevention and Peace-building
Sustaining the peace in post conflict societies
T. David Mason and James D. Meernik (eds)

Controlling the Weapons of War
Politics, persuasion, and the prohibition of inhumanity
Brian Rappert

Changing Transatlantic Security Relations
Do the US, the EU and Russia form a new strategic triangle?
Jan Hallenberg and Håkan Karlsson (eds)

Theoretical Roots of US Foreign Policy
Machiavelli and American unilateralism
Thomas M. Kane

Corporate Soldiers and International Security
The rise of private military companies
Christopher Kinsey

Transforming European Militaries
Coalition operations and the technology gap
Gordon Adams and Guy Ben-Ari

Globalization and Conflict
National security in a 'new' strategic era
Robert G. Patman (ed.)

Military Forces in 21st Century Peace Operations
No job for a soldier?
James V. Arbuckle

The Political Road to War with Iraq
Bush, 9/11 and the drive to overthrow Saddam
Nick Ritchie and Paul Rogers

Bosnian Security after Dayton
New perspectives
Michael A. Innes (ed.)

Kennedy, Johnson and NATO
Britain, America and the dynamics of alliance, 1962–68
Andrew Priest

Small Arms and Security
New Emerging International Norms
Denise Garcia

The United States and Europe
Beyond the neo-conservative divide?
John Baylis and Jon Roper (eds)

Russia, NATO and Cooperative Security
Bridging the gap
Lionel Ponsard

International Law and International Relations
Bridging theory and practice
Tom Bierstecker, Peter Spiro, Chandra Lekha Sriram and Veronica Raffo (eds)

Deterring International Terrorism and Rogue States
US national security policy after 9/11
James H. Lebovic

Vietnam in Iraq
Tactics, lessons, legacies and ghosts
John Dumbrell and David Ryan (eds)

Understanding Victory and Defeat in Contemporary War
Jan Angstrom and Isabelle Duyvesteyn (eds)

Propaganda and Information Warfare in the Twenty-first Century
Altered images and deception operations
Scot Macdonald

Governance in Post-Conflict Societies
Rebuilding fragile states
Derick W. Brinkerhoff (ed.)

European Security in the Twenty-First Century
The challenge of multipolarity
Adrian Hyde-Price

Ethics, Technology and the American Way of War
Cruise missiles and US security policy
Reuben E. Brigety II

International Law and the Use of Armed Force
The UN Charter and the major powers
Joel H. Westra

Disease and Security
Natural plagues and biological weapons in East Asia
Christian Enermark

Explaining War and Peace
Case studies and necessary condition counterfactuals
Jack Levy and Gary Goertz

War, Image and Legitimacy
Viewing contemporary conflict
James Gow and Milena Michalski

Information Strategy and Warfare
A guide to theory and practice
John Arquilla and Douglas A. Borer

Countering the Proliferation of Weapons of Mass Destruction
NATO and EU options in the Mediterranean and the Middle East
Thanos P. Dokos

Security and the War on Terror
Alex J. Bellamy, Roland Bleiker, Sara E. Davies, Richard Devetak (eds)

Security and the War on Terror

Edited by
Alex J. Bellamy, Roland Bleiker,
Sara E. Davies and Richard Devetak

Taylor & Francis Group

LONDON AND NEW YORK

First published 2008
by Routledge
2 Park Square, Milton Park, Abingdon, Oxon OX14 4RN

Simultaneously published in the USA and Canada
by Routledge
270 Madison Ave, New York, NY 10016

*Routledge is an imprint of the Taylor & Francis Group, an informa
business*

© 2008 Alex J. Bellamy, Roland Bleiker, Sara E. Davies, Richard Devetak
for editorial selection; individual chapters, the contributors

Typeset in Times by
HWA Text and Data Management, Tunbridge Wells
Printed and bound in Great Britain by
TJ International Ltd, Padstow, Cornwall

British Library Cataloguing in Publication Data
A catalogue record for this book is available from the British Library

Library of Congress Cataloging-in-Publication Data
Security and the war on terror / edited by Alex J. Bellamy ... [et al.].
  p. cm.
  Includes bibliographical references.
  1. Security, International. 2. War on Terrorism, 2001–
  I. Bellamy, Alex J., 1975
JZ5588.S4295 2007
909.83'1–dc22   2007018593

ISBN10: 0–415–36844–8 (hbk)
ISBN10: 0–415–36845–6 (pbk)
ISBN10: 0–203–02809–0 (ebk)

ISBN13: 978–0–415–36844–5 (hbk)
ISBN13: 978–0–415–36845–2 (pbk)
ISBN13: 978–0–203–02809–4 (ebk)

²⁄₀₈

Contents

Contributors   ix

Introduction   1
ALEX J. BELLAMY AND ROLAND BLEIKER

PART I
Security and terrorism   7

 1 Security studies, 9/11 and the long war   9
    PAUL D. WILLIAMS

 2 Cause and effect in the war on terror   25
    ANTHONY BURKE

 3 'War on terror'/'war on women': critical feminist perspectives   42
    KATRINA LEE-KOO

PART II
Ethics, emotions and law in the war on terror   55

 4 Emotions in the war on terror   57
    EMMA HUTCHISON AND ROLAND BLEIKER

 5 International law and the state of exception   71
    SARA E. DAVIES

 6 New thinking in the just war tradition: theorizing the war on
    terror   93
    CIAN O'DRISCOLL

 7 Pre-empting terror   106
    ALEX J. BELLAMY

PART III
Fighting terror   **123**

 8 Failures, rogues and terrorists: states of exception and the
    North/South divide   125
    RICHARD DEVETAK

 9 US bioterrorism policy   142
    CHRISTIAN ENEMARK

10 Ethics and intelligence in the age of terror   156
    HUGH SMITH

11 The international campaign to counter the financing of
    terrorism   177
    J. C. SHARMAN

    Conclusion   190
    SARA E. DAVIES AND RICHARD DEVETAK

    References   199
    Index   224

Contributors

Alex J. Bellamy is Professor of International Relations at the University of Queensland, Australia. He has written, co-written or edited eight books, including *Just Wars: From Cicero to Iraq* (Polity, 2006) and (with Paul D. Williams and Stuart Griffin), *Understanding Peacekeeping* (Polity, 2004).

Roland Bleiker is Professor of International Relations at the University of Queensland, Australia. His books include *Divided Korea: Towards a Culture of Reconciliation* (University of Minnesota Press, 2005) and *Popular Dissent, Human Agency and Global Politics* (Cambridge University Press, 2000). He is currently working on aesthetics, emotions and world politics and has a forthcoming book on *Aesthetics and World Politics* (Palgrave).

Anthony Burke is Senior Lecturer of Politics and International Relations at the University of New South Wales, Australia. His most recent books are *Beyond Security, Ethics and Violence: War Against The Other* (London and New York: Routledge, 2007) and *Critical Security in the Asia-Pacific*, edited with Matt McDonald (Manchester University Press, 2007).

Sara E. Davies is Lecturer in Justice Studies at the Queensland University of Technology, Australia. Her research is in the areas of international law, refugees, and global health. Her books include, *Legitimizing Rejection? International Refugee Law in Southeast Asia* (Martinus Nijhoff, 2007) and *Global Health Issues* (Polity, forthcoming), and her articles have been published in journals such as the *International Journal of Refugee Law*.

Richard Devetak is Senior Lecturer in International Relations at the University of Queensland, Australia. He is co-author of *Theories of International Relations* (3rd edition, Palgrave, 2005), co-editor of *Globalization's Shadow: Globalization and Political Violence* (Routledge, forthcoming), and has published on contemporary theoretical debates in international relations, theories of the state, justice and globalisation, humanitarian intervention, terrorism and the war on terror, as well as foreign policy, refugees and national identity in the Australian context.

Christian Enemark is Lecturer in Security Studies at the Centre for International Security Studies, University of Sydney, Australia. He specialises in non-traditional, multidisciplinary approaches to international security. His particular interests include the security significance of health threats and the ethics of armed conflict. He is the author of *Disease and Security: Natural Plagues and Biological Weapons in East Asia* (Routledge, 2007).

Emma Hutchison is a Doctoral Candidate and Tutor in International Relations at the University of Queensland, Australia. Her research focuses on photography and trauma in world politics.

Katrina Lee-Koo is Lecturer in International Relations at the Australian National University. Her research interests include Critical Security Studies, Feminist International Politics and the Gendered Politics of War. She has published articles in the *International Feminist Journal of Politics* and *Australian Journal of Political Science*.

Cian O'Driscoll is Lecturer in International Relations at the University of Glasgow, UK. His research focuses on the Just War tradition and the ethics of contemporary war and he has published articles in the *Cambridge Review of International Affairs* and *International Relations*.

J. C. Sharman is an Associate Professor and QE2 Fellow at Griffith University, Australia, after earlier teaching at the University of Sydney, American University in Bulgaria and receiving his PhD from the University of Illinois at Urbana-Champaign. His research interests include the global financial regulation, tax havens and sovereignty, and his most recent book is *Havens in a Storm: The Struggle for Global Tax Regulation* (Cornell University Press).

Hugh Smith is Professor of International Relations at the University of New South Wales/Australian Defence Academy. He is author of many books and articles on military affairs, from conscientious objection to nuclear strategy. His most recent book is *On Clausewitz: A Study of Military and Political Ideas* (Palgrave, 2005).

Paul D. Williams is Associate Professor in International Security at the University of Warwick, UK and Visiting Associate Professor of International Affairs at the Elliott School of International Affairs, George Washington University, USA. He is the author of *British Foreign Policy under New Labour, 1997–2005* (Palgrave-Macmillan, 2005), co-author of *Understanding Peacekeeping* (Polity, 2004), and co-editor of *Africa in International Politics* (Routledge, 2004) and *Peace Operations and Global Order* (Routledge, 2005).

Introduction

Alex J. Bellamy and Roland Bleiker

The purpose of this volume is to offer a critical but practically relevant engagement with security issues that are central to dealing with the threat of terrorism. We advance four propositions: that the September 11 attacks challenged core Western beliefs about the theory and practice of security, that America and its allies responded with a strategy underpinned by old and discredited ways of pursuing security, that this strategy has failed, but that alternatives are possible. These are not radical propositions. Indeed, they are propositions broadly shared by American and British voters, as demonstrated by the 2006 American elections and the dwindling support for Prime Minister Tony Blair. The chapters that follow examine these propositions in detail. All offer, in one way or another, viable alternatives to the present culture of insecurity.

The terrorist attacks of 11 September 2001 marked a key turning point in international politics. Arguing so has, of course, become somewhat of a truism. But it is nevertheless useful and important to investigate what exactly made 9/11 such an important event. The significance of 9/11 is not located in the immense loss of life that accompanied it. Catastrophic as it is, the 3,500 casualties are dwarfed when compared to the 2 million deaths caused by the civil war in the Democratic Republic of Congo (DRC), the 250,000 civilians killed by government backed militia in Darfur, and the approximately 40,000 children who die *every day* in the developing world as a result of poverty and preventable illness. Even as a single act of barbarity, 9/11 was not especially unique or devastating – its casualty rate is less than half the number of Europeans murdered after the fall of Srebrenica in 1995. Yet, it is 9/11, not 'Srebrenica', 'Darfur' or 'Congo' that is singled out as the epoch defining moment.

One could argue that the significance of 9/11 lies in its global dimension: that the attacks on New York and Washington highlight the emergence and rapid spread of a world-wide Islamist threat. This is certainly how both the Bush administration and many security analysts have presented the issues at stake. Indeed, the epithet '*global* war on terror' suggests that Islamic terrorism is a threat to us all. But to advance such an argument is to make the very mistake that E. H. Carr (1946) identified with idealist approaches in the wake of First World War: assuming that what threatens 'us' also threatens the whole world.

The threat of terrorism is neither new nor inherently global. For the great majority of the world's people, neither terrorism nor Islamism are major threats. When UN Secretary-General Kofi Annan toured Africa in 2004 he commented that not one African leader counted terrorism among the threats confronting that region, a perception certainly borne out by the casualty figures mentioned earlier. South America and Northeast Asia too stand out as regions of the globe in which Islamic terrorism poses no significant threat. In other regions, such as in Russia's 'near abroad', the Middle East and Southeast Asia, the threat was manifest, evident and preoccupying governments and security analysts well before 9/11. Indeed, Russia, Israel, Thailand, the Philippines and Indonesia were all confronting various versions of Islamist terrorism prior to 9/11. The respective governments have been conducting their own wars on terror, but without presenting their policy objectives in global terms.

September 11 is significant, and of global importance, only because it fundamentally disrupted the sense of security that prevailed in Western states. The attacks cast doubt on the efficacy and legitimacy of both the actors responsible for providing security and the political institutions that had been established for this purpose. Individuals, living in seemingly stable and safe Western countries, all of a sudden found themselves confronted with the agonies of war and mass killing. This is why for a significant number of scholars, analysts and commentators of different political orientations, 9/11 stands out as a fundamental breach of security and, in turn, of the underlying ideas and strategies.

Terrorism today represents a different type of threat, one that cannot easily be anticipated or prevented through prevailing state-based structures of security alone. The danger stems not from another state, but from a non-state actor, and one that cannot be precisely defined and located. The surprise attack itself revealed a fundamental weakness in the state's intelligence apparatus, as did the subsequent failure to accurately identify the status of Iraq's alleged program for weapons of mass destruction. The same is the case with the inability to read the warnings that preceded the Bali bombing or to predict and prevent North Korea's nuclear test.

The attacks of 9/11 were not only catastrophic and barbaric, but also unforeseen. They were perpetuated by enemies not readily connected with America's strategic foes in Baghdad, Tehran, Pyongyang and Beijing. As it was with the end of the Cold War, leading security analysts failed catastrophically to predict or even understand the emerging threat. Box-cutters rather than conventional military equipment were the decisive instruments in turning civilian aircraft into weapons. The attack was asymmetrical insofar as it did not actually involve opposing armed forces. And the attack was not directed at a battlefield or military target: it struck at the very heart of America's economic and civilian life. As such, 9/11 violated deeply held beliefs about the proper way to fight wars. The starting point for understanding the significance of 9/11 therefore lies in the dissonance it created in relation to the way that Western states think about and pursue security.

The events of 9/11 have created a fundamental paradox in the way we think about and pursue security. But while security threats have changed significantly, our means of understanding and responding to them have remained largely unchanged. America's response to 9/11 was characterised by a return to dualistic and militaristic thinking patterns that dominated foreign policy during the Cold War. Once again the world is divided into 'good' and 'evil', forcing smaller states to take positions even if they are not affected by related threats. Once again, military means are seen as the best – if not only – way of protecting the West from an external threat. This has the unwelcome effect of representing the wars of response and the numerous other uses of force – from Afghanistan and Iraq, to Yemen and Somalia – as moral crusades, obscuring deeper understandings of the threat and evoking the atavistic logic of religious war. Such an approach may make sense in the context of the shock that followed 9/11, but it creates more difficulties than it solves. The rhetoric of 'evil madmen', one commentator stresses, 'advances neither understanding of [terrorist] horror nor, for that matter, the capacity to combat or prevent it' (Euben 2002: 4). Even senior military commanders now question the usefulness of the wars of response, admitting that 'defeating terrorism is more difficult and far-reaching than we have assumed' (Clark 2004).

There are a number of serious strategic and moral dangers associated with the prevailing realist response to 9/11, which relies primarily on military means and divides the world into 'good and evil'. First, by disregarding standards of behaviour that have taken decades if not centuries to evolve, the US risks undermining the rule governed international order and the practical efficacy of moral and legal constraints on international behaviour. As the world's sole remaining superpower, the US should have a vested interest in preserving at least some aspect of the prevailing international order. The power of constraints associated with rules derives from their incorporation into customary practice. But the restraints on war can only be effective if state leaders, military commanders and individual soldiers attempt to heed them as far as possible. Restraint evaporates when powerful actors choose to overlook them in the name of strategic necessity. The consequences can be fateful, as illustrated by several historical examples: in the fifth century BC, for instance, the Athenian decision to break the customs of war for strategic purposes led to the complete erosion of those customs to the long-term detriment of both the Athenian empire and Greek civilisation as a whole. War between the Greek city states became more violent. Military strategies aimed at undermining the enemy's social cohesion. Eventually, Greek international society seriously eroded from within to the point that it was eventually destroyed by Persian and Roman forces (Ober 1994).

The second problem with the realist response to terrorism, closely related to the first, is that rule-breaking and unjust behaviour in the name of strategic necessity will encourage adversaries to use similar tactics. This, in turn, leaves no common moral ground to evaluate the justness of delicate political actions, such as possible humanitarian interventions into the internal affairs of another state.

Using unjust means, even if it is to pursue just ends, not only erodes the moral fabric of a democratic society but also provides radical terrorist movements, whether they are based in Islamic, Christian or any other religion, with a welcome opportunity to recruit disenchanted individuals. As Paul Williams argues in his contribution to this book, the most likely way of defeating Al Qaeda is through policies designed to alienate it from its potential pools of support. Far from isolating Al Qaeda, the wars of response have encouraged a new wave of volunteers to the organisation. To put it bluntly, whatever the merits of the 2003 invasion, Iraq is today on the frontline in the war on terror because America and its allies put it there. Every time the US and its allies are seen to be acting illegitimately, they play into the hands of terrorist recruiters.

This brings us to the third objection: conducting ourselves in an unjust fashion will make it more difficult to negotiate a just end to the war and build a self-sustaining peace afterwards. As St Augustine argued in the fifth century, the principle of right intention demands that war may only be waged to serve the cause of peace, not for riches or glory. Thus, Augustine advised (2001: 214–8): 'be peaceful, therefore, in warring, so that you may vanquish those whom you war against, and bring them to the prosperity of peace'. So, as James Turner Johnson points out (1999: 158), we should conduct ourselves justly in war because that is the only way we can secure a lasting and genuine peace. Violence, even if committed in a just cause, inevitably creates wounds which come to haunt a society for decades. Historical evidence also reveals that 'terrorism' cannot be defeated by killing all the terrorists. Consider how Germany's 'unconditional surrender' in 1945 required extensive negotiation. And even at that point Germany still had two million men under arms and no shortage of tanks and equipment. Although beaten, the German army could have continued a protracted and deadly insurgency.

The final problem is that describing a variety of different violent actions as all comprising a 'war against terror' may undermine the initially just cause of punishing those responsible for 9/11 and of preventing further atrocities. The dangers are particularly evident when it comes to the type of abuses that had already troubled early international jurists, such as Vattel. Using the 'war against terrorism' to justify the invasion of Iraq, despite the lack of any clear link between the Iraqi regime and anti-American terrorism, is an example of the inherent danger of defining the war on terror too broadly. Whatever the merits and problems with America's Iraq policy, it is reasonably clear that George W. Bush's claim to Congress that this particular war comprised a further element of the fight against terrorism was flawed. There are two principal problems with this strategy of lumping many different policies together under the rubric of the 'war on terror'. On the one hand, it undermines the legitimacy of perfectly reasonable measures against Islamist terrorism. If war is only justified when it is perpetrated against wrongdoers and intended to further the cause of peace, a 'war on terrorism' becomes less legitimate if it is directed against a state that has, despite its many other wrongs, not aided and abetted terrorist attacks on the US. Thus, justifying the war in Iraq as part of the war against terrorism casts doubt upon the legitimacy of the latter. It also erodes the international support and cooperation necessary for the successful establishment of a more secure and peaceful international order. On the other hand, waging war against terrorism presents an opportunity for a variety of actors to justify acts as legitimate and necessary which would otherwise be deemed unjust. The most explicit, but far from only, example here is the suspension of individual rights, even the use of torture, in the effort to collect information that is vital for the prosecution of the war against terror. As with the more general problem of rule-breaking mentioned above, such acts not only erode the very moral base of a democratic society but also offer opponents of such a society with a welcome opportunity to rally disenchanted individuals around radical terrorist motives.

In sum: the significance of 9/11 lies in the challenge it poses to prevailing ideas and practices of security. But rather than critically evaluating and rethinking those practices, the US government and its allies chose to revive the mentality of the Cold War through the shorthand of 'us' versus 'them' and the belief, supported by no concrete evidence, that the key to removing the threat sits with the military. More than five years on it is evident that this approach has failed in its headline goal: there is much more Islamist terrorism today than five years ago. To be sure, Al Qaeda has not attacked America since 9/11. We can draw little comfort from this however, because Al Qaeda has no need to attack America itself – there are enough American targets and Al Qaeda volunteers in Iraq.

To argue for a critical investigation into prevailing practices of security is not to say that Western policies *caused* Islamist terrorism. It is merely to observe an empirical fact: that since key Western states have initiated the war on terror the number of terror attacks have increased whilst the list of allies and friends has dwindled. We are also not saying that Western governments manufactured the threat of terrorism for their own purposes. Nor even are we saying that there is no place for the military in the suppression of terrorism, indeed there are arguments for pre-emptive self-defence and robust policing of terrorist financing in this volume. What we are saying is that 9/11 constituted a challenge to the way we think about and pursue security and that the way we respond to that challenge will partly determine whether the horror of 9/11 is repeated. Prevailing policy approaches have failed to recognise that the significance of 9/11 goes far beyond a mere breach of state-based security, which is dramatic but can still be understood through existing conceptual means. The terrorist attacks also engendered a more fundamental breach in human understanding, which remains largely ignored by security experts. September 11 displays all the features that Susan Neiman (2003) identified as key elements of major socio-political turning points: moments in history when certain events defy 'human capabilities for understanding' and trigger a 'collapse of the most basic trust in the world'.

The contributors to this volume open up important interdisciplinary conversations between hitherto underexploited strategic, economic, ethical and legal approaches. Linking these fields of inquiry offers crucial and practically relevant opportunities to rethink how states can best respond to terrorist threats. In so doing, we recognise a fundamental issue related to terrorism: while major crises initially tend to reinforce old ways of thinking and behaviour patterns, they also allow societies to confront and overcome entrenched habits, thereby creating the foundations for a new, perhaps more peaceful, future. Major traumas have indeed always played a major role in redefining political communities (Edkins 2003).

Questioning the key assumptions that guide security thinking should therefore be an essential element of coming to terms with 9/11 and preventing repeats in the future. And it should entail fundamental discussions about the nature and meaning of security in a rapidly changing world – discussions that include the use of a range of hitherto neglected sources of insight, such as those between political, economic, legal and ethical factors that the present book explores.

Part I
Security and terrorism

1 Security studies, 9/11 and the long war

Paul D. Williams

What is security and how should it be studied? For some analysts, security is an essentially contested concept (Buzan 1991). Yet a majority adopt a working definition of security as the alleviation of threats to acquired values. Of course, different individuals and groups will hold different (perhaps conflicting) values, define threats in various ways, and argue about how those threats can best be alleviated. Thus while there is agreement that security is an important value, there is no agreement as to what it entails and how important it is relative to other values such as order or justice. In short, world politics contains many, often competing, security agendas (for useful overviews see Sheehan 2005; S Smith 2005; Dannreuther 2007; Fierke 2007).

That the members of international society conceive of multiple security agendas was made abundantly clear by the Report of the UN Secretary-General's High Level Panel on Threats, Challenges, and Change, *A More Secure World*. This identified six clusters of threats exercising the world's states (UN High Level Panel 2004: 2):

- Economic and social threats, including poverty, infectious disease and environmental degradation.
- Inter-State conflict.
- Internal conflict, including civil war, genocide and other large-scale atrocities.
- Nuclear, radiological, chemical and biological weapons.
- Terrorism.
- Transnational organized crime.

In terms of the number of human lives lost, the first three clusters of threats have accounted for the vast majority. And yet the members of the United Nations (UN) accord them very different levels of priority. As a result, the UN faces the impossible task of trying to devise collective security policies without collective agreement on either the priority of the threats or the most appropriate way to overcome them. The task for analysts of international security is thus to gain a clear understanding of these multiple security agendas, to figure out the interrelationships between them, and to help resolve disagreements in situations where they clash.

The task for this chapter, however, is much more limited: to analyse how the events now known simply as 9/11 have shaped the international security terrain. The short answer is that the subsequent US-led 'global war on terrorism' (GWoT) has dominated the international agenda. This has had two important, largely negative consequences. First, it has revitalized the fortunes of political realism as a philosophy for theorizing security and given the upper hand in policy debates to those who think of security as being based on the ability to exercise (usually military) power against and over one's rivals (for a damning critique of the realist mentality and agenda see Booth forthcoming). Second, it has pushed to the sidelines a wide range of other important security challenges, notably the struggles to promote human rights, environmental sustainability, and humane governance. Fundamentally, security studies after 9/11 needs to grapple with roughly the same wide range of issues that were apparent well before 9/11 but it needs to do so without succumbing to realist dogma and naïve, Manichean narratives that see world politics in simplistic terms as a struggle between the good and the evil. In spite of all the hype, 9/11 did not fundamentally alter the primary structures or dynamics of world politics. In this sense, the assault on America was not akin to a political earthquake that fundamentally altered international tectonics. Rather, it was more like a bolt of lightning that emerged from an already stormy atmosphere and illuminated the contours of a political landscape that was previously shrouded in darkness. From that point on, Western, especially US, decision-makers saw world politics in a different, more sinister light. It is this mental shift in Western threat assessments that represents 9/11's biggest impact. Its legacy will be the way in which this new mind-set shapes Western responses to the world's major security challenges for some time to come.

Understood in this sense, the GWoT shares several characteristics with a black hole. First, it is difficult to see the inner-workings of a black hole because it is so dense that even light has difficulty escaping from it. Much the same can be said about the secretive mechanisms and directives driving the GWoT. This is a war that has been fought in the shadows and behind a veil of secrecy erected in the name of national security. Second, black holes absorb an enormous amount of energy. In both human and financial terms, the GWoT has also absorbed enormous quantities of resources; the final cost of US involvement in Iraq alone is estimated to be as high as $2 trillion, with Washington currently spending about $8 billion per month (Iraq Study Group 2006: 32). More generally, since 9/11, the US government has consistently increased its military expenditure in order to fight its war on terror. By 2005 its military expenditure stood at $537 billion or 48 per cent of all global spending with no other single state accounting for more than 5 per cent (Stålenheim *et al.* 2006). This raises the crucial question of whether transferring some of this money to projects addressing non-military challenges and developing non-military solutions would not save more lives and enhance global security. Third, black holes exert a gravitational pull on anything that strays within their reach. By influencing the way in which a range of issues and challenges are approached, the GWoT has had precisely this distorting effect on international relations. Perhaps most notably, it has skewed Western aid budgets towards recipients on the frontlines of the war on terror (Woods 2005) and provided a wide range of authoritarian governments with an excuse to curtail civil liberties and dismiss domestic opponents as terrorists. In the rest of this chapter I provide an overview of how this long war emerged, how it is being fought, and how at least one part of it might be brought to an end.

The Bush doctrine and the global war on terrorism

For the US government at least, 9/11 heralded the start of its GWoT. For America's primary opponents, the clandestine al-Qa'ida network, the war against its 'far enemy' had started much earlier, as evidenced by earlier strikes against the World Trade Center (1993), the US embassies in Kenya and Tanzania (1998), and the USS *Cole* (2000).

As noted above, the main consequence of 9/11 for international relations was the change it induced in the mindset of the US government and its allies. In particular, 9/11 did three things. First, it significantly lowered the level of threat that Washington was prepared to accept without engaging in an active response. This, in turn, encouraged a more widespread preference among Western governments for pursuing policies involving (often military) action rather than restraint (see Bailes 2006: 14–17). Second, 9/11 highlighted the vulnerability of Western cities to the nightmare scenario of an al-Qa'ida cell armed with weapons of mass destruction (WMD). As President George W. Bush put it in the preface to the 2002 National Security Strategy, 'The gravest danger our Nation faces lies at the crossroads of radicalism and technology' (NSC 2002). Third, 9/11 reinforced the argument that the US and its allies were facing a new type of enemy: a globalized network of insurgents who ignored the laws of war and revelled in trying to cause as much fear and carnage as possible.

These effects led quickly to a rethinking of US grand strategy and the emergence of what became known as the Bush doctrine. This was codified in the 2002 US National Security Strategy. At its core were the three concepts of unilateralism (if necessary), pre-emption (when required) and pre-eminence (forever?). The first – the idea that the US did not need an international 'permission slip' to engage in action to protect its vital national security interests – was a familiar feature of US foreign policy. The second was more controversial. After 9/11, a right to engage in pre-emptive self-defence – a last-minute reaction to a threatening process already underway – had a strong if not uncontested basis in international law. The trouble was that especially after spring 2002, the Bush administration's notion of pre-emption began to look far more like prevention – action taken to prevent a hypothetical future scenario from occurring – which was clearly illegal in international law (see Byers 2002; Greenwood 2003). The third concept of pre-eminence, especially with regard to US military power, was unremarkable as a statement of fact: the US was clearly the world's pre-eminent actor. But as a political aspiration that the US would work to maintain this state of affairs indefinitely, employing military force as it saw fit, it was difficult to interpret this as anything other than an offensive stance. The net effect of the Bush doctrine was to signal to the rest of the world that America would not be bound by international norms, conventions and institutions that it perceived as being contrary to its best interests (Daalder and Lindsay 2003). This even included the Bush administration declining NATO's offer of military assistance to conduct Operation Enduring Freedom in Afghanistan.

The Bush doctrine was not concerned solely with the war on terrorism but it did receive pride of place as debates about other issues such as the growing power of states like China and India as well as the 'responsibility to protect' agenda were pushed out of the spotlight. The central debate revolved around whether the GWoT had the potential to become the Third World War (Freedman 2001/2) or whether as an act of securitization it could become successfully embedded as the new Cold War (Buzan 2006). Buzan concluded that this was unlikely to happen, not least because the GWoT is not representative of US grand strategy as a whole; al-Qa'ida does not pose a strategic challenge to Western states nor does it offer a viable political alternative to liberal democracy in the way that communism did; the means being used to pursue the GWoT are eroding the core things they are meant to be defending (liberal values and Western unity); and because the Bush administration has lost a good deal of its legitimacy to act as a securitization leader within international society. Finally, the strategy of presenting the invasion of Iraq as a crucial part of the GWoT has backfired inasmuch as it has convinced many people that the GWoT is doing more harm than good.

There were other reasons why the GWoT slogan was problematic. First and foremost, waging war is best done with a clear understanding of the enemy. In this case, however, the enemy was defined as 'terrorism', which effectively meant that war was being waged on a tactic. The implication that the use of terror tactics was indicative of some kind of political alliance between its proponents did not hold up to scrutiny (Barkawi 2006: 154).

Many Westerners also considered the declaration of war unwise because it elevated the status of criminal activities (the 9/11 attacks were clearly illegal under both US and international law). This, in turn, gave their perpetrators an unwarranted degree of dignity and political status. Yet while many Westerners were uncomfortable thinking of 9/11 as an act of war, al-Qa'ida had clearly seen itself as being at war with its 'far enemy' for many years. Unsurprisingly, given America's conventional military dominance it sought to exploit asymmetric methods of warfare by using the trappings of industrialized society – in this case jet airliners – as weapons of war (see Barkawi 2004). Consequently, as Freedman (2002: 45) suggested, 'after an attack on such a scale, mounted by a political entity based in a distant country, war was not a matter of choice but a strategic imperative'. It was thus arguably necessary for Western governments to engage in a war against al-Qa'ida. It did not follow, however, that it was sensible to engage in a war against terrorism in general.

A third problem was that as a label, GWoT was inaccurate. Most obviously, the US and its allies were preoccupied with ending terrorism against their own interests rather than terrorism in general. Moreover, the terrorist label was applied selectively with most governments defining terrorism as synonymous with the activities of non-state actors. States became targets in the 'war' only when they harboured and/or supported (non-state, anti-Western) terrorists. This ignored the fact that terrorism by states continues to dwarf that conducted by non-state groups. Rather predictably, therefore, the GWoT quickly attracted some unsavoury allies who saw the instrumental value in signing up to the Bush administration's discourse in order to criminalize their domestic opponents.

Another effect of declaring a 'war on terrorism' was that the objectives were often cast in terms of military victory rather than in terms of law enforcement and the successful prosecution of the perpetrators (Howard 2002). Not only did this ignore the fact that most counter-terrorism is performed by the police and intelligence services rather than the military but it also glossed over the impossibility of determining when the last act of terrorism had taken place. A war on terrorism was thus a war without end since victory could never be permanently verified.

Finally, waging war has effects at home as well as abroad. In wartime the official gloves often come off and governments find it easier to engage in activities that are proscribed in times of peace. In this case, numerous governments have been embroiled in debates about curtailing civil liberties in the name of state security and several have looked for ways to bypass the rights of those they suspect of being implicated in terrorism. In addition, the GWoT has seen a centralization of power within many governments and a willingness to shelve diplomacy before it has been exhausted in favour of more militaristic policies. It has also seen emphasis placed on capturing and killing individual terrorists rather than addressing the political conditions that encourage them to join extremist movements in the first place.

For all these reasons, the GWoT slogan was unhelpful. Arguably a more sensible and accurate descriptor would have been to declare that the US and its allies were engaged in an 'international campaign against al-Qa'ida'. Perhaps in recognition of some of these criticisms, by early 2006 it was clear that Washington had decided to shift its language: out went the GWoT and in came the notion that the US was engaged in the opening phases of a 'long war'.

Fighting the long war

By the time the Bush administration published its second Quadrennial Defense Review (QDR) in February 2006, it was clear the 'long war' analogy had become the slogan of choice. This war centred on combating al-Qa'ida and promoting liberal market democracy around the world. The QDR was presented as providing 'a roadmap for change, leading to victory' in the long war (United States Department of Defense 2006a: ix). Yet it continued Rumsfeld's project of transforming the US military in order to generate more combat capability with fewer numbers of weapons platforms and lower levels of manning. This was considered vital in the new strategic environment characterized by uncertainty and surprise, and where the US military needed 'the ability to surge quickly to trouble spots across the globe' (United States Department of Defense 2006a: v).

The QDR identified four priorities in the long war: defeating terrorist networks; defending the homeland; shaping the choices of countries at strategic crossroads; and preventing hostile states and non-state actors from acquiring or using WMD. Here, I will focus on the central international dimensions of the long war, namely, the struggle against al-Qa'ida; reconstructing Afghanistan and Iraq; and preventing the proliferation of WMD.

Defeating al-Qa'ida

As the QDR made clear, 'The enemies in this war are not traditional conventional military forces but rather dispersed, global terrorist networks that exploit Islam to advance radical political aims' (United States Department of Defense 2006a: 1). Public enemy No.1 was al-Qa'ida (The Foundation), which according to Washington operated in over 80 countries (United States Department of Defense 2006a: 21). Al-Qa'ida had been forged in the crucible of Afghanistan's wars but was first and foremost a movement that developed around Arab Sunni radicals with the primary purpose of assuming power in the Arab states, especially Saudi Arabia (Halliday 2005: 154–5). In this sense, it is important to recall that despite much of the rhetoric (from Western governments and the movements themselves) describing international terrorism as a global phenomenon, in many respects 'Islamist movements were primarily caused by, and directed at, conditions *within* their own societies' (Halliday 2005: 158). This is not to deny al-Qa'ida's evident desire to kill infidels wherever they might be found, but merely to point out the regionally specific origins and primary goals of America's principal enemy. This is important to bear in mind when searching for ways to bring the long war to an end.

In organizational terms, al-Qa'ida is distinct from most other terrorist organizations in four main respects (Cronin 2006: 32–9). First, its organizational form is fluid. Since the 9/11 attacks it has come to be thought of as representing both a global jihadist movement consisting of *ad hoc* cells linked together via the virtual sanctuary of the internet as well as a label for a broader umbrella group of independent entities that share some ideological assumptions and are willing to cooperate over certain issues. Second, al-Qa'ida's method of recruitment is distinct from its predecessors. In this respect it is more akin to a social movement than a terrorist organization, often attracting followers to join its ranks voluntarily rather than recruiting them into service. Nevertheless, as Cronin notes, exposure to al-Qa'ida's ideology alone has not been sufficient to attract recruits – as its failure to attract many members in either Sudan or Afghanistan suggests. Rather, evidence from al-Qa'ida's operatives suggests that links of friendship and kinship facilitated by a 'bridging person' have been crucial. This method of recruitment has worked particularly well in the Maghreb and Southeast Asia (Cronin 2006: 35). Third, al-Qa'ida's means of supporting its activities are novel in several respects. The relatively small amounts of money required to launch its attacks have come from diverse sources including charitable donations, petty crime and fraud. It has also extracted funds from a wide range of businesses related to the organization – at one point, Bin Laden was estimated to own around 80 companies world wide. Finally, al-Qa'ida has successfully harnessed the revolution in information technology to carry out its communication through such mechanisms as mobile phones, text messaging, instant messaging, e-mail, internet chat rooms and blogs. It has even managed to assemble its own virtual training manual; the so-called 'The Encyclopedia of Jihad'.

To combat this enemy, the US government decided to increase its Special Operations Forces by 15 per cent and its Department of Psychological Operations and Civil Affairs by 33 per cent (United States Department of Defense 2006a). It also stated that US forces would have to maintain a long-term, low-visibility presence in many areas of the world where the US does not traditionally operate (United States Department of Defense 2006a: 23). Of particular concern was the potential for so-called 'failed states' to act as safe havens for this new type of enemy. This had been a central theme of US foreign policy since 9/11. For example, in its 2002 National Security Strategy, the US government stated it was 'now threatened less by conquering states than ... by failing ones' (US 2002: 1).

Beyond the obvious concern with Afghanistan, much of the focus fell upon Africa in general and its horn in particular. As a result, the US National Security Strategy published in March 2006 acknowledged that 'our security depends upon partnering with Africans to strengthen fragile and failing states and bring ungoverned areas under the control of effective democracies' (NSC 2006a: 37). The problem with this approach is that there is not always a strong correlation between state failure and the proliferation of terrorist organizations, or indeed transnational security challenges more generally (see Patrick 2006).

Arguably the archetypal case in point is Somalia: collapsed state par excellence and the focus of much US counter-terrorism activity since 9/11. However, Somalia has not become a major safe haven for terrorist organizations in spite of the ascendance of political Islam and the lack of effective government institutions. For one thing, until the middle of 2006, Islamic extremists struggled to gain ascendancy over more moderate Islamic voices within Somalia. For example, in 2005, US intelligence gathering in Somalia produced no evidence of al-Qa'ida bases or that Al Itihad Al Islamiya was operating as one of its subsidiaries (Menkhaus 2005).

As Ken Menkhaus (2005: 39–41) has persuasively argued, there are six main reasons that explain this state of affairs. First, terrorist cells and bases are much more exposed to international counter-terrorist action in zones of state collapse where US Special Forces could violate state sovereignty regularly and with impunity. The US airstrikes in January 2007 against al-Qa'ida suspects in Somalia are a case in point. Second, areas of state collapse tend to be inhospitable and dangerous, particularly for foreigners. Consequently, since few foreigners choose to reside in such environments, foreign terror cells will find it very difficult to blend into the local population and retain the degree of secrecy necessary to conduct their activities. A third factor is the double-edged nature of the lawlessness that accompanies situations of state collapse: while lawlessness reduces the risk of apprehension by law enforcement agencies, it increases the likelihood that terror cells will suffer from more common crimes such as kidnapping, extortion or assassination. As Menkhaus (2005: 40) suggests, 'it appears that lawlessness can inhibit rather than facilitate certain types of lawless behavior'. A fourth problem is that any terrorists would be susceptible to betrayal by Somalis looking to ingratiate themselves with the US authorities. Fifth, Somalia represents an environment in which it is very difficult to stay neutral and outside the inter-clan rivalries. Relatively mundane activities such as hiring personnel or renting buildings will inevitably be seen as evidence of taking sides and once this perception has been established the external actor in question becomes a legitimate target of reprisals by rival clans. Finally, the collapse of the Somali state has left it without the usual array of 'soft' Western targets such as embassies and businesses. As a result, Somalia is more likely to be used as a transit point for materiel than to act as a more permanent base for cells. Even terrorists, it would seem, require a degree of political order to conduct their activities. The 'security paradox' identified by Menkhaus (2005: 45) is that at least in the short-term, attempts to resurrect effective state institutions in Somalia may create an environment that is more, not less, conducive to terrorist cells basing themselves in the country. It would appear that terrorist organizations prefer to operate out of weak states with corruptible personnel such as Kenya, Indonesia, Pakistan, the Philippines, and Yemen rather than collapsed states. The frontlines of the long war should be redrawn accordingly.

Reconstructing Afghanistan and Iraq

As the opening battle in the long war, the failure of Operation Enduring Freedom and the International Security Assistance Force (ISAF) to stem the deterioration of the security environment in Afghanistan should be a major cause of concern for the US and its allies. In Afghanistan, the US opted to take the lead in defeating the Taliban and al-Qa'ida forces while leaving the task of nation-building to its allies. In both cases, a light footprint approach was chosen. In the former, what has become known as 'the Afghan Model' involved the US military and intelligence agencies relying upon local proxies (in this case the Northern Alliance) to topple the Taliban and its al-Qa'ida supporters without a large commitment of US ground troops (see Andres *et al.* 2005/6; Biddle 2005/6). In the latter, a woefully small peace support operation was deployed to Kabul and its environs. Although nation-building was its ostensible aim, in reality ISAF was engaged in little more than city-building. Over time, it was incrementally extended into the rest of the country through the use of small Provincial Reconstruction Teams tasked with promoting local security sector reform and engaging in civic/humanitarian operations.

Not surprisingly, despite the holding of elections and the installation of Hamid Karzai's government, by early 2006 the news coming out of Afghanistan was seldom good. As Seth Jones (2006) observed, there were many indications that the security environment – the crucial precondition for effective nation-building – was deteriorating rapidly. First, insurgent attacks (by a combination of Taliban,

Hezb-i-Islami, and foreign jihadists mainly from Pakistan, Uzbekistan and Tajikistan) had risen dramatically between 2002 and 2005. An additional trend was that more of these attacks were being targeted against Afghan civilians and NGO personnel rather than US and ISAF troops (a similar trend was also noticeable in Iraq, see Kaldor 2006: 163). Second, local opinion polls suggested that although most Afghans considered the country to be heading in the right direction, they were deeply concerned about the security environment. Third, the international presence had failed to curb the power of warlords, despite some notable successes in ousting Herat Governor Ismail Khan and Kandahar Governor Gul Agha Shirzai. Fourth, the rising levels of opium production provided a huge source of revenue for a wide variety of non-state actors, all of which reduced the power of the central government. Finally, all efforts to build a viable criminal justice system had failed, not only because of the central government's limited control over the hinterland but also because of endemic corruption within the officials that have been appointed.

As Jones (2006: 119–23) pointed out, a winning formula for Afghanistan would need to be built on several pillars. First, the number and capability of international and Afghan troops and police needs increasing by some 80,000. Second, the outstanding insurgents and warlords need to be dealt with either by offering them incentives to participate in a genuinely national project of reconstruction or removing them by force. This task is greatly complicated by the absence of a peace agreement and Pakistan's role as a staging post for the insurgents. Finally, a successful strategy of nation-building will require large amounts of time and money, at least US$3 billion per year, roughly double what the country has received in 2006. On the issue of time, the US decision to hand control of the volatile southern provinces to NATO, and the reluctance shown by many NATO members to contribute sufficient numbers of their troops to this operation have raised fears among Afghan leaders about the depth of international commitment to the country's future. Afghanistan's major problem in this regard was that since late 2002 it was overshadowed by events in the second major battlefield: Iraq.

In relation to Iraq, between April 2002 and November 2003 the Bush administration proposed four different solutions to the problem of how to reconstruct the country (Dodge 2006). All of them revolved around different ways of encouraging Iraqis to rebuild their country in a liberal democratic mould. All of them were quickly jettisoned or failed to produce the desired results.

The first concerted plan, the *Future of Iraq Project*, was concocted by the State Department in conjunction with some 240 Iraqi exiles 11 months before the invasion. This was jettisoned even before the invasion got underway when in January 2003 Bush signed a National Security Directive which centralized responsibility for Iraq within the Pentagon. With the Pentagon running the invasion and its aftermath, the door was opened for the administration's neo-conservatives, notably Donald Rumsfeld, Paul Wolfowitz and Douglas Feith to project what Dodge called 'their own dogmatic dreams' (2006: 160). They saw Iraq as a blank slate and a laboratory for the lightweight approach to state-building favoured by Rumsfeld and his transformed US military. At its core was the idea that a new exile-led Iraqi government could be installed and successfully grafted onto the remnants of the old regime within a matter of months. The Achilles heel of this vision was the tendency of its advocates to believe their own hype and to listen only to advice from their supporters, the most problematic of which turned out to be Ahmed Chalabi and Kanan Makiya. The fall guy was retired general Jay Garner, who Washington had summoned to direct operations in Iraq but was quickly sacked when things failed to turn out as planned.

The third approach unfolded under Paul Bremmer's direction from mid-May 2003. After it had become clear that the Iraqi state had collapsed following a period of lawlessness and looting, Bremmer suggested that the US would have to engage in a longer-term project of nation building whether it liked it or not. While Bremmer's diagnosis was more accurate than the previous neo-conservative version, he presided over several crucial mistakes. The first was the decision not to form an interim Iraqi administration but to instead retain power within the Coalition Provisional Authority. This alienated the Iraqi exiles upon whom Washington had pinned many of its hopes. Second, Bremmer purged the civil service of senior Ba'ath Party members, making between 20,000 and 120,000 people unemployed at a time when restoring government services and meeting the basic needs of the local population was arguably the key issue on which the whole state-building enterprise rested. It also left Bremmer with a major headache: where to find an alternative, non-Ba'athist Iraqi elite that could run the institutions of government efficiently. Finally, the decision was taken to disband the Iraqi army. Although the Bush administration argued that the army simply disbanded itself, this decision was at odds with the recommendations of the *Future of Iraq Project* and Garner's earlier efforts. Whatever motives lay behind this decision it made redundant some 400,000 armed and trained men, many of whom had initially elected not to fight the invaders, and gave them yet another grievance against the US-led coalition. It is now clear that some of them vented their frustration by engaging in attacks against coalition troops. The occupying coalition paid a heavy price for these decisions throughout the rest of 2003.

The fourth shift in policy came with the 'November 15 agreement'. This sought to end the occupation in seven months and co-opt the former Iraqi exiles the US had brought into the country rather than support an alternative indigenous administrative and ruling elite. Like the other approaches, it proved largely unworkable.

Each of these policies suffered from problems common to all grand experiments in social engineering: they were overly abstract, pushed through too hastily, and lacked a sophisticated understanding of the society in question. In addition, Washington's attempt to pursue a light footprint approach to state-building was based on a problematic understanding of the nature of military power and its application in counter-insurgency operations. The limitations of the US approach were exemplified in the tragic case of Operation Vigilant Justice in the town of Falluja in April 2004.

As Alice Hills (2006) has argued, US military operations in Falluja highlighted the Bush administration's tendency to think of power in possessional rather than relational terms. The former sees military power as an instrument to coerce and destroy enemy targets. The latter sees power as part of a relationship between different institutions and actors that together form systems of governance. Understanding the role of military power in building such systems of governance is crucial to the success of counter-insurgency operations where the goal is to mould the conduct and identity of the social networks concerned. According to Hills, the inability of the US operations to defeat the insurgency in Falluja can be explained with reference to three interrelated factors: the culture of the White House under President Bush, which simplified complex security problems to Manichean narratives between good and evil and suggested the use of military force provided the quickest and surest route to victory; the US military's preference for muscular operations and its willingness to fix the identities of Falluja's inhabitants as unflappable, anti-American insurgents before the siege began; and the ongoing transformation of the US military which emphasized rapid-dominance war fighting, that is, its ability to impose technological solutions at a distance and without having to rely on the painstaking process of gathering human intelligence. The resulting operation left over 600 (mainly civilian) dead and yet failed to stop the insurgency, which required another much larger US military assault seven months later. In sum, 'Falluja revealed the Bush administration's inaccurate assessment of the limitations of US military power in a politicized struggle in which the primary objective is control' (Hills 2006: 636). Control was also the key word when it came to the place of WMD in the long war.

Preventing the proliferation of WMD

According to the QDR, 'The principal objective of the United States is to prevent hostile states or non-state actors from acquiring WMD' (United States Department of Defense 2006a: 33). In spite of this, the US has continued and even enhanced partnerships with states in possession of nuclear weapons but outside the Nuclear Non-Proliferation Treaty, notably India, Israel and Pakistan. Since 9/11, the Bush administration's primary counter-proliferation instruments have been an aggressive form of export control enforcement known as the Proliferation Security Initiative (PSI) and various attempts at coercive diplomacy aimed primarily at the 'axis of evil' states of Iraq, Iran and North Korea. According to the QDR, if the preventative dimension of its policies fail, the US must be prepared to engage in 'WMD elimination operations' which may involve the use of force (United States Department of Defense 2006a: 34). Indeed, officials within the Bush administration have even hinted that in the case of Iran, Israel may strike the country on Washington's behalf (Sagan 2006: 54).

The Bush administration has made two central arguments as the basis for its non-proliferation strategy (Montgomery 2005: 154–5). First, it has suggested that dense networks among second-tier proliferators such as Iran, North Korea and Libya, as well as private agents, exemplified by the A.Q. Khan network, have facilitated proliferation. As a result of this diffusion of knowledge and capabilities, global measures rather than policies tailored for individual states are needed to slow these processes. Second, it has argued that certain 'rogue states' are dead set on obtaining nuclear weapons programmes and thus have no interest in bargaining; what Scott Sagan (2006) has called 'proliferation fatalism'. North Korea's apparent explosion of a nuclear device in October 2006 and Iran's unwillingness to abide by various demands made upon it by the UN Security Council and the International Atomic Energy Agency have only enhanced this line of thinking within Washington.

As Sagan (2006) has persuasively argued, the history of counter-proliferation suggests that it succeeds when the US and other actors satisfied the concerns that drove a state to pursue nuclear weapons in the first place. In Iran's case, the motive appears to be avoiding attack, first from a hostile Iraqi regime, and since at least 2002 from the US, which signalled its desire to promote regime change and let Iran know that it was a potential target under Washington's 2002 Nuclear Posture Review. Yet since the US lacks a viable military option that could guarantee the elimination of any Iranian WMD, all that remains is for the US and its allies to give Tehran sufficient reasons to relinquish its pursuit of nuclear weapons. At a minimum, Sagan concluded, this must involve the US relinquishing its threat of forcible regime change, and perhaps engaging in the sort of framework agreement devised between the US and North Korea in 1994. The fact that this framework collapsed should not be taken as a reason to abandon all diplomatic efforts in favour of pursuing a more rigorous coercive policy. Rather, its failure should serve as a warning about what to avoid next time around.

Of course, the proliferation conundrum is more complicated when factoring in the role of non-state actors like al-Qa'ida. Nevertheless, it seems highly unlikely that such organizations could build nuclear weapons themselves. Consequently, international efforts to monitor and restrict the activities of second-tier proliferators and private networks would seem to offer the most prudent course of action.

Ending the long war

As noted above, while a war waged against the tactic of terrorism is likely to be a war without end, the international campaign against al-Qa'ida will eventually end. As Audrey Kurth Cronin (2006) has shown, previous research indicates that there are at least seven broad (and often interrelated) explanations for how non-state organizations employing terrorism decline or end:

1   Capture or killing of the leader (e.g. Shining Path, Kurdistan Workers' Party, Real Irish Republican Army).
2   Failure to transition to the next generation (e.g. Red Brigades, Weather Underground, Baader-Meinhof group).
3   Achievement of the group's aims (e.g. Irgun/Stern Gang, African National Congress).
4   Transition to a legitimate political process (e.g. Provisional Irish Republican Army, Palestine Liberation Organization).

5   Undermining of popular support (e.g. Real Irish Republican Army, Basque Homeland and Freedom, Shining Path).
6   Repression (e.g. Kurdistan Workers' Party, Shining Path, People's Will).
7   Transition from terrorism to other forms of violence, notably criminality and/ or insurgency (e.g. Abu Sayyaf, Revolutionary Armed Forces of Colombia, Khmer Rouge, Communist Party of Nepal-Maoists).

'The pressing challenge', as Cronin suggests, 'is to determine which lessons from the decline of earlier terrorist groups are relevant to al-Qaida and which are not' (2006: 39).

Given al-Qa'ida's organizational characteristics, it will clearly not end if Osama bin Laden is captured or killed, not least because he has ensured that the organization has not become a personality cult by downplaying his own importance and emphasizing the insignificance of his own fate. Nor will al-Qa'ida fail because of its inability to convince future generations of the importance of its struggle. It has already transitioned from the type of organization based in Sudan and Afghanistan in the 1990s, and it is clearly operating with a long-term strategy that sketches the outlines of a global jihad but keeps the fine print details hazy enough to allow for numerous flexible and pragmatic interpretations. In this way, it has continued to attract sufficient numbers of volunteers as well as cooperation and support from independent actors engaged in more locally focused struggles of their own, for example, in Algeria, Chechnya, the Philippines and Pakistan/ Kashmir. As a consequence, al-Qa'ida's objectives are constantly evolving and now include assuming power in the Arab states, establishing a transnational caliphate, overthrowing non-Islamic regimes, expelling or killing infidels in Muslim lands, and supporting the Palestinian struggle. This means that the organization is unlikely to achieve its aims as envisaged in strategy 3. Nor is it likely to transition into an actor content to work within a legitimate political process. Indeed, many analysts have pointed to the fact that al-Qa'ida does not appear to be an actor with whom negotiation is possible. Strategy 6, repression, also has limited utility when faced with an organization based on such virtual and disparate foundations as al-Qa'ida. Capturing or killing individual operatives, even senior figures, will do little more than temporarily disorient certain cells and provide the organization with mild public relations headaches at the broader, strategic level. At worst, a repressive strategy that accidentally kills innocent bystanders may fuel the organization's propaganda and enlarge its pool of potential recruits.

This leaves strategies 5 and 7. As Cronin points out, to some extent, al-Qa'ida is already engaged in forms of criminality, especially related to narcotics trafficking. In that sense, the struggle to erode al-Qa'ida's resources through policing and financial activities will be of critical importance given that as much as '95% of the important action in any campaign against terrorism consists of intelligence and police work' (Roberts 2005: 109). Given the ease with which goods and people can be moved through parts of the world beyond the control of governments – what the Pentagon refers to as 'ungoverned spaces' – and the way in which information technology has facilitated the transfer of remittances at the touch of a button, this will be an incredibly difficult task.

Moreover, al-Qa'ida may also have transmuted into a full-blown insurgency in certain parts of the world, most notably through the alliance negotiated between bin Laden and Abu Musah al-Zarqawi in Iraq and through its association with the Taliban in Afghanistan/Pakistan. In this sense, Iraq and Afghanistan have become the new focal points and training grounds for al-Qa'ida's vision of conducting an insurgency on a global scale (see also MacKinlay 2002). Given al-Qa'ida's intimate relationship with the Taliban it was unsurprising that it should assume insurgent form in Afghanistan. Until autumn 2003, however, it was not at all clear that al-Qa'ida would direct much of its efforts towards Iraq; its focus instead falling upon Afghanistan, Pakistan and Saudi Arabia. The fact that one of the longest running caliphates – the Abbasid Caliphate, which lasted some 500 years from 749 CE – was centred on the city of Baghdad provided further ammunition for al-Qa'ida's propaganda machine. As Paul Rogers (2006: 74) put it, for al-Qa'ida 'the foreign occupation of Iraq, the seat of the most distinguished caliphate in early Islamic history, is an unexpected but quite remarkable bonus'. By early 2006, most estimates suggested that foreign fighters in the 'al-Qa'ida brigades' accounted for between 5 and 10 per cent of total insurgents, but a higher percentage of the suicide bombers (Kaldor 2006: 161).

Since al-Qa'ida has assumed the form of an insurgency in certain parts of the world, putting an end to this struggle will require appropriate counter-insurgency techniques. As David Kilcullen (2006) has argued, these must appreciate the transnational nature of al-Qa'ida; its urbanized quality; and its reliance upon the internet and other elements of the revolution in information technology that allows it to engage in real-time cross-pollination with insurgent groups across the globe. In this sense, insurgents must be engaged in different theatres, including in urban settings which reduce the comparative advantage of Western militaries (see Hills 2004), and there must be a concerted effort to win the battle of ideas that is being fought within the world's mass media outlets. Ultimately, although many of the insurgents' strategies have modernized, people's hearts and minds remain the prize. Of primary importance in Kilcullen's analysis is the idea that counter-insurgency must displace the enemy's influence over social networks in the context concerned. In the long war's case, the 'theatre of operations' covers the entire globe. But arguably the most important social networks are those participating in the ongoing civil war within the Islamic world over how best to react to Western hegemony and the spread of liberal values. In sum, counter-insurgency is no longer about defeating a specific enemy but attempting to control an environment. This can be done in several ways but an important element of the struggle will involve the strengthening of liberal norms throughout the globe, particularly those against the killing of innocent civilians (see Freedman 2004a; Cronin 2006: 45).

The focus on strengthening liberal norms ties in with Cronin's fifth strategy, eroding the popular support enjoyed by organizations like al-Qa'ida. In its insurgent form, al-Qa'ida and its affiliates require the support of at least some segments of the local populace in the theatre of operations. However, the situation is sometimes reversed from traditional situations where insurgents needed the locals to provide them with food or hide their weapons and other resources. In both Afghanistan and Iraq, for instance, the insurgents are well equipped (often by foreign donors) and can afford to buy the support of poverty-stricken locals. Indeed, they can even subcontract desperate locals to carry out attacks for them (Kilcullen 2006: 119). Nevertheless, at a more general level al-Qa'ida's amorphous and pragmatic nature provide an opening for the US and its allies to 'emphasize the differences' within its 'agenda and to drive a wedge between the movement and its recent adherents' (Cronin 2006: 42).

The US and its allies have repeatedly suggested that the liberalization and democratization of the Islamic world represents the core of its strategy to reduce al-Qa'ida's popular support. This is clearly a long-term strategy that even the most optimistic advocates would admit will take decades if not centuries. The problem is that the evidence from both Afghanistan and Iraq suggests that the opening phases of this strategy have not unfolded as planned. Indeed, Operations Enduring Freedom and Iraqi Freedom are generally acknowledged to have expanded rather than reduced al-Qa'ida's support base. For Cronin (2006: 42–5), the West should concentrate instead on al-Qa'ida's means of funding and communication, that is, erode its ability to disseminate its message and challenge the content of those messages by every means and in every forum available. In this regard, it is important to recall that al-Qa'ida's fundamentalist version of Islam has not succeeded in gaining enough adherents to pose as a realistic political alternative to either liberal market democracy or more reformist Islamic regimes. In this sense, its message is one that appeals to those alienated by modern societies (both Western and Islamic) and who think in extremes. Reducing the numbers of people who fit this description both at home and abroad will help erode al-Qa'ida's support base. In the short-term this means taking a far more aggressive approach to exploiting the organization's blunders and massacres of civilians and providing resources to reduce the prevalence of extremist ideologies and to enhance the reputation of liberal norms and values. It should also involve emphasizing the point that ultimately the most destructive effects of these terrorist movements tend to be suffered in the societies that produce them (Roberts 2005: 108). As Roberts has concluded, ending extremist movements requires 'not the capture of every last terrorist leader, but their relegation to a status of near-irrelevance as life moves on, long-standing grievances are addressed, and peoples can see that a grim terrorist war of attrition is achieving little and damaging their own societies' (2005: 126).

Conclusion

As the US government is well aware, the long war 'is both a battle of arms and a battle of ideas … ultimately [it] will be won by enabling moderate Muslim leadership to prevail in their struggle against the violent extremists' (United States Department of Defense 2006a: 22). Unfortunately, the Bush administration has pursued policies that have made this outcome less, not more, likely. It has pursued a doctrine that has sought to articulate a different set of rules for itself than the rest of the world's states, it has declared war on a tactic that should indeed be eradicated but has pursued that war selectively and often with blunt instruments, and it has engaged in botched state-building projects that have enhanced the popularity and strength of its primary enemy. It is too early to say what the long-term implications of these policies will be. Perhaps many of their negative consequences could be alleviated by a change of guard in the White House; perhaps not. The challenge for the field of security studies is to restore some balance to the study of international security by placing terrorism not on an analytical pedestal above other challenges but in its appropriate political, economic and geographical contexts. There are many realities of insecurity in world politics and it is unwise to let one vision dominate them all.

2   Cause and effect in the war on terror

Anthony Burke

'We have been fighting you because we are free men who cannot acquiesce in injustice. We want to restore security to our *umma*. Just as you violate our security, so we violate yours ... You should remember that every action has a reaction'. With these words in October 2004 the terrorist financier and ideologue Osama Bin Laden admitted responsibility for the 9/11 attacks and explained why they were carried out. His words were contained in a longer statement – designed both as a message to the people of Europe and as an intervention in the US elections – which whilst certainly propaganda, was about as close to diplomacy as the movement now known as al Qaeda will ever come (Lawrence, 2005: 146–9). If violence can be thought of as a form of *communication* as much as coercion, Bin Laden was trying to be heard: to communicate the purpose and meaning of the attacks, to speak of causes and effects, and ultimately to produce an effect.

Yet when it comes to violence and meaning, cause and effect so often fail to meet, like pieces of wreckage scattered over the charred landscape of an airliner crash. Only a reconstructive effort of logic and analysis can establish that the blackened and twisted fragments were once integral parts of a single vehicle and trajectory. US professor of religion Bruce Lawrence argues that Bin Laden's objective was 'to isolate the Bush administration, and beyond it the American political establishment as a whole, from American popular feeling – as well as European opinion'. Yet the result, according to Democratic presidential candidate John Kerry, was to turn the tide of US opinion against him and hand Bush another term (Lawrence, 2005: 237). Under US pressure Al Jazeera broadcast only an edited five minute extract and, within the US its content was drowned out by a chorus of anger and outrage. Bush's reaction was typical: in a short statement seizing on Bin Laden's veiled threat that 'there are still motives for a repeat [of 9/11]' he said that 'Americans will not be intimidated or influenced by an enemy of our country' (BBC News Online, 2004). What was supremely ironic was that Bin Laden's threat was spurred by frustration about the meanings given to al Qaeda's campaign. Early in the statement he said:

> When disasters happen, intelligent people look for the reasons behind them, so that they can avoid them in the future. But I am amazed at you. Although

we are into the fourth year since the events of September 11, Bush is still practising his deception, misleading you about the real reason behind it.

(Lawrence, 2005: 238–9)

What is the significance of statements like this? Given our abhorrence of their author, why should we listen to them or grant them any status or credibility? There are many registers upon which we can analyse them, but this chapter proposes to consider them, and al Qaeda's campaign and ideology more broadly, in terms of their strategic importance and of their meaning for strategy. Their importance lies in their *meaning*: in the light they cast, however perversely and unwelcomely, on cause and effect in the war on terror. The chapter argues that while a 'strategic' analysis that rationally analyses the use of force and other means of policy is certainly necessary, the phenomenon of mass casualty terrorism directed against the US and its allies puts many of the fundamental tenets of strategy into question. If this is true, a 'war on terror' may simply not be possible.

Tracking and predicting relations between cause and effect in global politics is both tremendously difficult, and utterly essential. There are simply too many actors, variables and processes, each complicated by a clash and proliferation of meanings, for this to be a simple and unproblematic task. Yet traditional strategic thought either rejects this complexity or professes to be able to control and manage it: it holds to a linear causal model that sees war as 'an act of force to compel our enemy to do our will' (Clausewitz, 1976: 75). Yet in a 'war on terror' where the adversary's most potent weapons are their will and ingenuity, and beliefs and interpretations are often more important than capabilities, such a model no longer holds. By paying close attention to the writings and statements of terrorist leaders, and through a critical analysis of strategic and counter-terrorist doctrines, this chapter seeks to develop a historical model of cause and effect based on language, meaning and (mis)interpretation. In such a model, acts either of state or terrorist violence cannot be assumed to have predictable effects, and traditional modes of strategic power and geopolitical hegemony are rendered less and less sustainable because of the uncontrolled and dangerous proliferation of meanings, and subsequent acts, they produce.

In this light, this chapter takes up Christian Reus-Smit's call for constructivist analysis to grapple with the 'normative politics of transnational terrorism … [because such] organizations operate in the social space transcending state borders and … use forms of moral suasion and symbolic politics to redefine the terms of political discourse affecting state interests and actions' (Reus-Smit, 2005: 210). Taking Osama Bin Laden's writings seriously, the chapter traces a number of crucial decisions in US and Israeli policy which had causal importance for 9/11 and later atrocities. This causal importance lies in the inspiration and ideas al Qaeda took for future attacks, and in the meanings they ascribed to western policy and actions. Against this background the continuation of Israel's occupation of the West Bank and Gaza strip (including its brutal 2002 offensive and its post-withdrawal strangulation of Gaza) and its 2006 war on Lebanon, along with the containment, invasion and occupation of Iraq, are examples of the fundamental disutility of military action as a counter-terrorist strategy. Some Israelis and their western supporters may argue that force can be an effective and manageable way of controlling Palestinians and avoiding diplomatic pressure for a two-state solution; but even if this were arguably true, it has been both deeply unjust and come at an enormous cost to the security both of Israel and the West. As the retired Israeli general Shlomo Gazit remarked ironically to this author in 2004, Israel's use of force against the Palestinians had been *too* successful and hence sent 'the wrong message to the political echelon – that there is no need for a political agreement' (Gazit, 2004).

My argument is not that military action in some cases may be both justified and viable, but that a purely instrumental strategic analysis, and dominant currents of strategic thought, provide an imperfect guide to the kind of action that may be worth taking. For example, while it is arguable that a military effort to destroy al Qaeda camps and sanctuaries in Afghanistan was at least justifiable as one of many measures that could be taken to reduce the threat they posed, this is not the same as arguing that the kind of war actually waged made sense as part of a counter-terrorist strategy, or that its further causal and human consequences were acceptable, predictable and controllable. The civil war, and the terrible economic and humanitarian crisis faced by Afghanistan in 2001, further compounded the complexities raised by military intervention, which gave al Qaeda further fuel for its anti-Western propaganda and directly contributed to events such as the October 2002 Bali bombings.

Concepts: force, war, terror

The phenomenon of a networked, cell-based, religiously and ideologically motivated terrorism, not linked to territorial struggles and overwhelmingly directed against civilian targets, puts existing paradigms of strategic security into crisis. In response, we are seeing broad counter-terrorist strategies seeking to incorporate the use of force in ways that remain wedded to existing strategic paradigms whilst also seeking to overcome their limitations. However, this rarely extends to a fundamental rethinking of the strategic paradigm *as such*.

In its modern, instrumental, Clausewitzian form, strategy assumes a linear transition between violent means and political ends – ends whose scope, legitimacy and priority are defined solely by the user of violence, not by the enemy or their community. Even if this transition is not always smooth – Clausewitz cautions that battle and logistics are difficult, information is partial, and the enemy may be unpredictable – it is seen as achievable. After all, the concept Clausewitz uses to express these problems, *friction*, is a metaphor taken from natural science that refers to physical forces that impede a moving body (1976: 100–19). This idea of *force* as a purposively violent transition between means and ends is central to Clausewitzian strategy, expressed in his influential formulation that 'war is an act of force to compel our enemy to do our will':

Force, to counter opposing force, equips itself with the inventions of art and science ... Force – that is physical force, for moral force has no existence save as expressed in the state and the law – is thus the *means* of war; to impose our will on the enemy is its *object*. To secure that object we must render the enemy powerless; and that, in theory, is the true aim of warfare.

(Clausewitz, 1976: 75)

To impose our will on the enemy is the *object* of force, which can only be secured by rendering the enemy powerless. These are important formulations that are worth considering in the case of a war on terrorists and terrorist organizations, one that has the objective of securing society against their attacks. What is clear in Clausewitz's reasoning is that military violence is the chosen means for imposing one's will and exercising power, and that this is thought of immediately in Newtonian terms *as* force: as something that moves things, according to physical laws, in the face of opposing force and the friction of the effort. The concept of force, then, assumes that if the means is deployed the end will almost automatically result, and the contest is thus too often thought of in merely physical terms: a clash of quantities and firepower that ingenuity and technology can make more effective. In short, like the related notion of 'military power', the idea of force assumes the outcome it seeks, and the human is reduced to a physical effect, merely an intelligent and sometimes recalcitrant element in a machinery of violence.

These are the deterministic assumptions underpinning a model of what former NATO deputy commander General Rupert Smith argues is an outdated concept of 'industrial war', He argues that we are in a new paradigm of 'war amongst the people' in which 'there is a continuous criss-crossing between confrontation and conflict' and war 'is no longer a single massive event of military decision that delivers a conclusive political result'. The new strategic context is complex, protean and confusing: war is fought amongst civilians and all kinds of regular and irregular forces in conflict zones; it is fought via the media in living rooms around the world; its ends shift 'from the hard absolute objectives of interstate industrial war to more malleable objectives to do with the individuals and societies that are not states'; new uses are found for old weapons; loose coalitions not states fight against non-state adversaries; and the strategic end is not victory but to create the conditions for politics, aid delivery or diplomacy (R. Smith, 2005: 16, 1–17). Smith was not writing specifically of the war on terror but his general argument, derived from experience in Ireland, Bosnia and Kosovo, and through keen observation of interventions in Africa, Afghanistan and Iraq, is a telling one.

To be true, many mainstream strategists and policy makers are painfully aware of the new paradigm, even if they are resistant to the conceptual revolution that Smith and others – like Martin van Creveld (1991), Mary Kaldor (1999, 2003) and Chris Hables Gray (2005) – argue must occur. What we instead see are efforts to preserve the basic integrity of the Clausewitzian system, and to overcome operational friction and the disruptive elements of the new paradigm, with new technology and concepts. In such efforts neo-Clausewitzian doctrines of limited war and coercive diplomacy are updated with new force concepts such as asymmetric warfare, the revolution in military affairs (RMA), defence transformation, or effects-based warfare.

Limited war doctrines emerged in the 1950s in the United States as scholars grappled with the apparent dilemma of the need to wage limited war against communist aggression in a context where the existence of nuclear weapons made the dangers of escalation to total war too great. Robert Osgood described limited war as 'part of a general strategy of conflict in which adversaries would bargain with each other through the medium of graduated military responses, within the boundaries of contrived mutual restraints … in order to exert the desired effect on an adversary's will' (Osgood, 1979: 10–11). Osgood and the RAND Corporation scholar Thomas Schelling also emphasized the value of force for 'coercive diplomacy': Osgood said that 'the art of coercion short of war has never been as finely developed or deliberately applied' and Schelling portrayed limited wars and threats as 'a power to hurt' which, while 'it can usually achieve nothing directly, is potentially more versatile than a straightforward capacity for forcible accomplishment' (Osgood and Tucker, 1967: 26; Schelling *et al.* 1966: 8–9). In a 1979 book revisiting the limited war doctrine, Osgood admitted that its utility had been tarnished by the loss in Vietnam but nevertheless insisted that 'the rationale of limited-war strategy and the strategic theories derived from it … have become more widely accepted'. If there was a problem, it is that 'there has been a gap between strategic doctrine and the operational plans and capabilities for carrying it out' and that the US Army's preference for using overwhelming force and attrition may not be as effective as 'wars of maneuver and mobility' (Osgood, 1979: 11–12).

Most of the new western strategic concepts developed since then have arguably been efforts to square this circle. Of most importance has been the so-called 'revolution in military affairs', a set of ideas which emerged from the Pentagon's Office of Net Assessment and were re-badged by US Defense Secretary Rumsfeld as 'military transformation' (Office of Force Transformation, 2003). This updated the US combined forces (AirLand Battle) doctrine with innovations in satellites, computing, telecommunications, real-time video and precision weapons technology to increase the invulnerability, speed and destructive power of US and allied forces. In a recent analysis Alan Stephens and David Connery claim that: 'The concept promises an unrivalled degree of battlespace awareness … as well as the ability to apply force with discrimination, which together present a war-winning capability of the first order'. They suggest that transformation could be relevant to the kind of non-state conflicts and threats (which include 'groups such as al Qaeda and their ideological affiliates [which] are deliberately eschewing any attempt to tackle modern joint forces head on') that Rupert Smith sees as more profound disruptions of the paradigm. 'The ability to operate across the spectrum of conflict [is] essential for a modern military force', they write, and in such contexts 'many forces will attempt to use the technological advantages conferred by the information and communications technology revolution' (Stephens and Connery, 2006: 57–8). The US Defense Department suggests something similar, when it defines transformation as 'new combinations of concepts, capabilities, people and organizations that exploit our nation's advantages and protect against our asymmetric vulnerabilities to sustain our strategic position' (Office of Force Transformation, 2003: 2).

Stephens and Connery also discuss how a new concept – Effects-Based Operations (EBO) – is 'emerging as the philosophy' for transformation and promises to 'reduce the fog, friction and uncertainty that Clausewitz properly identified as being characteristics of war'. They define EBO as 'a methodology in which the desired effect/outcome of any action, regardless of its scale, should be identified before that action is initiated, and which ideally should be complemented by its associated ways (the form through which a strategy is pursued, including military power, diplomacy and economic sanctions) and means (the resources available, including people, weapons, international influence and money)' (2006: 60–1).

What is most striking about their EBO concept, which appears to be far more nuanced than current practice, is how it is framed as a direct response to the complexity of cause and effects that I am examining here:

> A critical component of [EBO] will be a constant, iterative process of comparing the effects actually caused by our actions to the effects we wish to cause, noting that almost inevitably the two will not coincide perfectly. In addition to unintended or unforeseen first-order effects for both sides, there will be second and third order effects which will have to be identified and assessed – and managed.
>
> (Stephens and Connery, 2006: 61)

With this last phrase Stephens and Connery betray a confidence in the ability of transformed military forces to cope with the complexities of using force amid unpredictability, even if they acknowledge that they can never do so perfectly and that 'managing chaos will remain the fundamental preoccupation of military leaders, even where they adopt an effects-based approach' (2006: 61). The Pentagon's report is even more bullish. Even as it admits the strategic paradox that 'today's winner is tomorrow's target' and that 'surprise is the norm', there is confidence in the ability of new concepts and technology to grapple with any problem: 'the emerging way of war will result in US forces conducting powerful effects-based operations to achieve strategic, operational and tactical objectives across the full range of military operations. Transformation is yielding new sources of power' (Office of Force Transformation, 2003: 12, 3).

The Pentagon's drive for transformation is integral to a new strategic posture and 'global war on terror' that is extraordinarily ambitious and expansive, based on a desire to strengthen and entrench US primacy, confront and defeat a range of threats including rogue states, WMD proliferators, peer competitors and 'terrorism' as such, and stimulate widespread political and geostrategic change through regime change and democracy promotion. This represents, as Jeffrey Record remarks, 'an endless and hopeless search for absolute security' (2003: 46). It also represents a hubristic and in many cases deeply unjust desire for hegemonic dominance that includes radical and destabilizing new norms about the use of force (preventive war and nuclear use) and seeks to militarize and control 'global commons' such as space (Kaufman, 2006). There is no hint of retrenchment or caution: the Office of Force Transformation in fact states that its work seeks options to help the US military implement 'an enhanced forward deterrent posture … for a new strategic environment in which U.S. interests are global and new challenges, particularly anti-access and area-denial threats, are emerging' (2003: 6).

Hence the US and its allies envisage using force in the war on terror in a range of ways and contexts: directly against terrorist sanctuaries, personnel and infrastructure, such as in Afghanistan, the Philippines, Palestine and Lebanon; against the regimes that are perceived to support, harbour or tolerate them, as with the Taliban, the Baathist government of Iraq and the Palestinian authority (and potentially Iran and Syria), using operations ranging from small assassination and special forces operations to the full force of airpower or combined forces against both military and civilian targets. Small operations include Israeli raids and bombings in the occupied territories and special forces operations in Afghanistan, and the latter the invasion of Iraq, Operation Enduring Freedom in Afghanistan, and Israeli operations in 2002 against the Palestinian authority in the West Bank (2002), against Hamas and other factions in Gaza (2006), and the war against Lebanon (2006). To conservative western and Israeli policymakers these are all seen as combined parts of the war on terror, even if they are in fact related to other objectives such as perpetuating control over the Palestinian territories or regime-change in Iraq. And while the US and British forces in particular can plausibly claim to have worthwhile policies in place to limit collateral damage, all these operations involved either considerable collateral civilian casualties and damage to civilian housing and infrastructure, or direct attacks on civilians.

Barring the more nuanced conceptualization of the effect-based operations, these tactics are all seen in instrumental terms as either the direct degradation of terrorist capabilities or as a deterrent message, a form of coercive bargaining. They express the Clausewitzian idea of force as a 'means' to 'impose our will on the enemy'. In this context it is worth returning to the claim Clausewitz makes directly after: 'to secure that object we must render the enemy powerless; and that, in theory, is the true aim of warfare' (Clausewitz, 1976: 75). The ultimate strategic question then is: can either the terrorists, or terror*ism*, be rendered powerless? Can force be the means?

Analysts like Clive Williams, Louise Richardson and Jeffrey Record have understandably questioned the idea of a war on terror*ism*, saying that 'it is not an ideology' but 'is a strategy: a form of conflict used for political purposes'; it is 'a tactic and will continue to be deployed by those seeking change' and 'a method of violence, a way of waging war' that has an 'inherent attraction to the militarily powerless' (Williams, 2006: 71; Richardson, 2006: 247; Record, 2003: 25, 8). Record still sees counter-terrorist operations against particular organizations in instrumental terms ('intelligence-based arrests and assassinations, not divisions destroyed or ships sunk, are the cutting edge of successful counter-terrorism') and sees the war against al Qaeda, as opposed to terrorism as such, to be 'a war of necessity'. But this does not mean it is simple to fight: 'the very nature, modus operandi and recruiting base of al Qaeda make it a very difficult enemy to subdue decisively through counter-terrorism operations' (Record, 2003: 22). They are right in identifying the definition of the enemy, and of terrorism, to be a major policy problem – with current versions generating an imprudent escalation of military conflict beyond what is absolutely necessary or viable. However they are perhaps too quick to dismiss the value of attacking terrorism as such. Record scoffs at the idea of waging war on a *method*, which would 'create unnecessary enemies at a time when the United States has more than enough to go around', and his answer seems to be to focus on its capabilities. Yet even this can be self-defeating: as the International Institute of Strategic Studies' 2002–3 *Strategic Survey* speculated that the war in Afghanistan 'perversely impelled an already highly decentralised and elusive transnational terrorist network to become even harder to identify and neutralise' (cited in Record, 2003: 5). Attacks in Bali, Madrid and London, among others, underpinned this assessment with a lethal truth.

From Lebanon to 9/11 and back

If the capabilities of terrorists are hard to attack with armed force, and doing so can have serious unanticipated consequences, what can be done? Obviously legal routes are promising: police and intelligence work can and has prevented a number of serious attacks, but they have sometimes failed. If, as in the London case, nascent terrorist cells are difficult to identify, wherefore counter-terrorism?

In this light, I suggest that is it exactly the *methods* of terrorism, along with the desires, grievances and motivation of terrorists, which needs to come into renewed analytical focus. The phenomenon of the 'home grown' bomber suggests that it is three important processes that we need to understand and tackle: first, the development of grievances against an undifferentiated 'West' as such; second, the movement from grievance to the use of violence; and, third, the exercise of a form of moral reasoning that can justify the murder of innocent civilians. All of these processes are carried on a wave of narrative, information and meaning, and it is at those levels they can be analysed and ameliorated. In short, what is most important in fighting terrorism is an understanding of – and ability to interrupt – the social and psychological process by which grievance is created and turned into violence.

What this means is that terrorism cannot be treated as merely a matter of capabilities or intentions, and it cannot be seen as isolated from either the actions we take to deal with it or the state of our political culture – including past and present international policy – more generally (Silke, 2005). Yet policymakers and especially neo-conservative analysts refuse to treat terrorist motivations or statements with seriousness. In an interview with PBS just after 9/11 former US Deputy Secretary of State Richard Armitage responded to a question about Islamist grievances and 'root causes' of terrorism by saying 'I suggest you don't play on his court' (PBS, 2001). Writing in *The Jerusalem Post*, Israeli Likud politician Benjamin Netanyahu praised Bush's moral clarity in stating that 'terrorism, like Nazism, must be seen as an unmitigated evil ... [we must not be] duped into believing that there is some justice behind terrorist demands and therefore these demands must be partially met' (Netanyahu, 2002). Similarly the *9/11 Commission Report*, even as it acknowledged that al Qaeda was motivated by 'grievances stressed by bin Laden and widely felt throughout the Muslim world ... including support of Israel', argued that 'it is not a position with which Americans can bargain or negotiate. With it there is not common ground – not even respect for life – on which to begin a dialogue. It can only be destroyed or utterly isolated' (National Commission, 2004: 362). The once neo-conservative intellectual Francis Fukuyama argued soon after 9/11 that the real issue was 'not American foreign policy in Palestine or towards Iraq ... the basic conflict we face is much broader, and concerns not just a small group of terrorists, but a much larger group of radical Islamists and Muslims for whom religious identity overrides all other political values'. These movements (which he describes in somewhat misleading and inflammatory terms as 'Islamofascist') reject 'the most basic principle of modernity itself, that of religious tolerance' (Fukuyama, 2002: 22, 31).

All of these writers may have had salient points to make, but what is common to all is a view that violence as such cannot be placed under critical scrutiny. This myopia we share with our enemies. Hence I would not choose, as Record does, between rendering terror*ists* and terror*ism* powerless. If we define terrorism as the large scale use of political violence against the innocent – the form in which it is currently most threatening and destabilizing – it becomes crucial to find ways to render terrorism *as* a method fundamentally illegitimate and eventually powerless. In this light, war will be the last means we should want to choose.

We are thus moving in the realm of *norms,* which by their protean nature, can be either a force for terror or hope. Bin Laden explained how they became a force for terror when he was interviewed by US ABC television in 1998. The journalist, Jon Miller, asked him if the 'fatwa' he had recently declared extended to all Americans:

American history does not distinguish between civilians and military, and not even women and children. They are ones who used the bombs against Nagasaki. Can these bombs distinguish between infants and military? ... The only way for us to fend off these assaults is to use similar means ...We do not differentiate between those dressed in military uniforms and civilians; they are all targets in this fatwa.

(Miller, 1998)

An even more chilling justification was asserted by another al Qaeda figure, Sukeiman Abu Ghaith, who claimed in an essay on the organization's website that in Iraq and Palestine the US and Israel had killed 1.2 million Muslims (sic) 'in the past decade':

According to the numbers, we are still at the beginning of the way. The Americans still have not tasted from our hands what we have tasted from theirs...We have not reached parity with them. We have the right to kill four million Americans – two million of them children – and to exile twice as many and cripple hundreds of thousands. Furthermore, it is our right to fight them with chemical and biological weapons ... America knows only the language of force.

(Bergen, 2006: 347)

These Islamist arguments for the killing of civilians – even with weapons of mass destruction – are grossly immoral and dangerous. However we must face two sobering facts: al Qaeda has been inspired to strike by Muslim and Palestinian suffering at the hands of the US and its allies, and they draw *normative legitimation* from it. However misguided or repugnant their logic, there is a cause and effect relation here that we dismiss at our peril.

What we are witness to here is the dynamic relation between semiosis, violence and chaos, a process that is the antithesis of strategy. When violence is involved both action and the simultaneous production and dissemination of meaning resists our intentions. Violence turns into meaning, and thence into further violence, in a way that thwarts any linear translation of strategic means into political ends. A simple thought exercise is helpful here. Were the 9/11 attacks the objective of US policy towards Iraq and Israel during the 1980s and 1990s? Was the possibility even contemplated?

We could similarly ask if Israeli Defence minister Ariel Sharon thought of the possibility of 9/11 when he planned and oversaw the massive 1982 invasion of Lebanon – which involved some 45,000 IDF troops, a naval blockade and massive airstrikes on infrastructure and homes, and resulted in Israeli troops occupying half of Beirut and the expulsion of the leadership and armed militias of the Palestinian Liberation Organization (PLO). The death of at least a thousand Palestinians in massacres by Christian militias allied to Israel is well known; less well known are the Israeli air strikes on civilian areas, including the destruction of residential apartment blocks, which took the lives of thousands. These attacks, however, had a striking impact on Osama bin Laden. In his October 2004 statement, he said:

The events that made a direct impression on me were during and after 1982, when America allowed the Israelis to invade Lebanon with the help of its third fleet ... It was like a crocodile devouring a child, who could do nothing but scream...As I looked at those destroyed towers in Lebanon, it occurred to me to punish the oppressor in kind by destroying towers in America ...

(Lawrence, 2005: 239)

Lebanon was crucial in other respects. The war stimulated the emergence of two determined Islamist political movements, Hezbollah (party of God) and Islamic Jihad, the first of which has become a major political force within Lebanon and fought a successful guerrilla war against Israel in the south, and the second of which has become active in Palestine (Shehadi, 2004). These organizations were believed to be responsible for terrorist bombings of the French and US embassies in Beirut, the US marine barracks, and Israeli military headquarters in Sidon (twice). They were the first Islamic suicide bombings performed by *shahid* (martyrs), attacks notable both for the religious commitment of their perpetrators and their tactical efficacy as a technique, in which human beings dressed as civilians could become devastating but cleverly disguised weapons, evading existing military and border control security measures. This technique has since taken an enormous number of lives.

Sharon launched the 1982 invasion of Lebanon in the hope of smashing the PLO and entrenching Israeli control over the occupied West bank and Gaza Strip; instead it saw Israel bogged down in a draining war in southern Lebanon, stimulated the creation of a new Palestinian leadership in the West Bank, and contributed to the emergence of the Islamist Palestinian movement Hamas. In 1987 the Palestinian civil uprising (Intifada) began in Gaza, which attracted a brutal response from the Israeli armed forces but convinced the administration of George H.W. Bush to place pressure on Israel to negotiate a two-state solution with the PLO (Shlaim, 2000: 400–24, 593). In August 1988 al Qaeda was founded, and in 1990 Saddam Hussein launched the invasion of Iraq, which stimulated the imposition of UN sanctions and basing of US troops in Saudi Arabia, an event which deeply angered bin Laden (Bergin, 2006: 78).

In 1993 Ramsi Yousef – who trained at an al Qaeda camp in Afghanistan and was the nephew of Khaled Sheikh Mohammed, the director of the 9/11 operation – bombed the World Trade Center with $20,000 worth of explosives. He told FBI interrogators that 'the reason for the bombings was because of the US military, financial and political support of Israel'. In April 1996 Israel launched a new offensive against Lebanon, Operation Grapes of Wrath – which included the apparently deliberate shelling of a UN base where civilians had sought shelter, killing 106 – and in August the same year bin Laden issued a declaration of war against the United States, citing the Qana attack, the Iraqi sanctions, and the presence of Jews in Palestine and Americans near Mecca and Medina as a *casus belli*. 'The walls of oppression and humiliation', he stated, 'cannot be demolished except in a rain of bullets'. In May 1998 bin Laden, Mohammed Atef and Egyptian Jihad leader Ayman Al Zawahiri held a press conference to announce the creation of the World Islamic Front for Jihad against Crusaders and Jews. There they publicized a February 1998 statement issued by bin Laden which included the controversial *fatwa*, 'the ruling that to kill the Americans and their allies – civilians and military – is an individual duty for every Muslim'. A CIA memorandum analysing the statement said that 'these *fatwas* are the first from these groups that explicitly justify attacks on American civilians anywhere in the world...this is the first religious ruling sanctifying such attacks' (Bergin, 2006: 144–5, 164–5, 196). The bombings of the embassies in Nairobi and Dar es Salaam, the attack on the USS *Cole* in Aden, and the 9/11 attacks followed in rapid succession.

The 9/11 attacks, which were so shocking and terrible, and which brought the threat posed by bin Laden's movement to world attention, could have potentially been a profound turning point, a great historical hinge around which US strategy and foreign policy should have been rethought. Many voices were indeed raised in favour of renewed efforts to end the Israeli occupation of Palestine and to rethink the containment of Iraq. However the Bush administration chose to rapidly militarize the conflict and prepare for war against Iraq, to declare that established norms relating to the treatment of suspects were outdated, and to give blanket support to (now Prime Minister) Ariel Sharon's government in Israel, who cleverly painted his struggle against the second Palestinian *Intifada* as part of the global war on terror and PLO leader Arafat as a second bin Laden. In 2002, under cover of the war in Afghanistan, he launched a massive military operation into Palestinian autonomous areas in a new effort to destroy the (PLO dominated) Palestinian authority, with distressing scenes of Palestinian suffering beamed around the Muslim and Arab world. It did little to prevent Palestinian suicide attacks against Israeli civilians, which were only slowed by the construction of a vast wire and concrete barrier throughout the West Bank.

Settlement growth and other forms of dispossession continued, and under cover of the Quartet-sponsored 'road map' Israeli strategy now focused on heading off international pressure to dismantle the wall and return to negotiations with the Palestinians (Burke, 2007: 71; Reinhart, 2006). In what should have been recognized as a major public relations disaster (and security threat) US endorsement of Sharon's plans for a unilateral 'disengagement' from Gaza and declaration of final borders was widely interpreted throughout the Arab world as a new 'Balfour declaration' (Howeidy, 2004). If one important index of western vulnerability to al Qaeda is measured by the level of global anger provoked by their foreign policies, by the time the US, Britain and Australia had launched the invasion of Iraq in March 2003 – again to widespread if simplistic perceptions they did so at the behest of Israel – things were a great deal worse than they were prior to September 2001. A little over a year later, in October 2004, the Australian embassy in Jakarta was bombed by the Islamist group Jemaah Islamiyah, with the bomber later telling police he did so because 'the Australian Government is the American lackey most active in supporting American policies to slaughter Muslims in Iraq' (Wroe, 2005: 1). By the time Osama bin Laden made his statement during the US election campaign, in the same month as the Jakarta attack, it seemed no one of importance was listening:

> Security is one of the pillars of human life. Free men do not underestimate the value of their own security, despite Bush's claim that we hate freedom … We have been fighting you because we are free men who cannot acquiesce in injustice. We want to restore security to our *umma*.
>
> (Lawrence, 2005: 238)

The power of the example: rethinking cause, strategy, and effect

In March 2006 US Vice-President Richard Cheney said in a media interview that the Democratic Party has a 'a pre-9/11 mind-set. They've got a tendency to look at the terrorist attacks, for example, in terms of law enforcement and only law enforcement. But it was only … the President's aggressive determination to go after these guys … that I think have protected the US from another attack' (Snow, 2006). Such braggadocio is cold comfort for the residents of Madrid, Bali, Jakarta, Sharm El Sheikh or London, but it remains an article of faith for the Bush administration and a number of strategists. This was affirmed in the US Government's 2006 revision of the *National Strategy for Combating Terrorism*, which states that 'America is at war with a transnational terrorist movement fueled by a radical ideology of hatred, oppression and murder':

> The paradigm for combating terrorism now involves the application of all elements of our national power and influence. Not only do we employ military power (sic), we use diplomatic, financial, intelligence and law enforcement activities … we have broken old orthodoxies that once confined our counter-terrorism efforts primarily to the criminal justice domain.
>
> (NSC, 2006: 1)

Despite this generally sensible list of multifaceted options, and a list of unexceptional objectives (among them to prevent attacks against the US, deny WMD to terrorists, and deny terrorists the sanctuary of rogue states) what is striking is that they are also simplistically instrumental and reactive, embodying a linear and largely mechanical (capabilities-based) model of causation. The strategy assumes that terrorists want to attack the United States and its allies, which is portrayed as a timeless ontological fact. However illegitimate, their *desire* to do so, and the process by which this desire was formed, is apparently of no moral, historical or strategic importance. This is especially ironic given the Strategy's claim that this 'has been a battle both of arms and a battle of ideas', and its obtuse complaint that 'the ongoing fight for freedom in Iraq has been twisted by terrorist propaganda as a rallying cry' (NSC, 2006: 1, 4). Instead, as the 2003 Strategy set out, the major objective is to 'compress the scope and capability of terrorist organizations' (NSC, 2003: 12–13).

Yet if the 2003 Strategy's goal is to 'diminish the underlying conditions that terrorists seek to exploit', the socio-historical process of terrorists' motivation and justification must be treated as of crucial strategic importance. Yet whereas the 2003 Strategy acknowledged that 'finding a solution to the Israeli-Palestinian conflict is a critical component of winning the war of ideas' and that 'we must use the full influence of the United States to delegitimize terrorism', the mantra in 2006 is that 'terrorism is not simply a result of hostility to US policy in Iraq', 'Israeli-Palestinian issues' or 'a response to our efforts to prevent terror attacks' (NSC, 2003: 23–4, 2006: 9).

Indeed when Israel chose to attack Lebanon again in July 2006 with a massive campaign of air strikes, killing over a thousand Lebanese, wounding thousands more and causing $4 billion in damage to homes and infrastructure, the US and British governments gave them vocal support and used their diplomatic weight to buy the Israelis time to prosecute the campaign. As if to underline the terrible sense that history was repeating itself, Qana was again bombed in an attack on an apartment building that killed 28 civilians and wounded many more. Following this attack, al Qaeda second in command Ayman al-Zawahiri issued a video statement declaring that Israel's attacks on Lebanon and Palestinians in Gaza would not be allowed to stand:

> As they attack us everywhere, we will attack them everywhere. As they have joined forces to fight us, our nation will unite to fight them ... The shells and rockets which are tearing the bodies of Muslims in Gaza and Lebanon are not purely Israeli. They are produced and financed by all the countries of the Crusader alliance ... We cannot just watch these shells as they pour wrath on our brothers in Gaza and Lebanon and sit back in submission.
>
> (BBC News Online, 27 July 2006)

The best mainstream strategists are now becoming painfully aware of the strategic price being paid for a failure to think more creatively and self-critically about western foreign policy, war-fighting and geopolitical power. During the 2006 Lebanon war Professor Anthony Cordesman, of Washington's Center for Strategic and International Studies, published an important commentary. 'Qana', he wrote, 'is more than a horrifying human tragedy; it is a brutal lesson in the changing nature of modern war ... a lesson that applies just as much to Iraq, Afghanistan, and the war on terrorism as it does to the fighting in Lebanon. The lesson is simple: limited wars must be fought in ways that give avoiding collateral damage and civilian casualties at least as much priority as destroying the enemy' (Cordesman, 2006).

Cordesman's short analysis amounts to what ought to be a major revision of limited war doctrine, one that supports the arguments I have been seeking to make here. Citing the civilian deaths and damage to infrastructure in Lebanon, Afghanistan and Iraq, he excoriated traditional strategic doctrines which 'carelessly seek immediate tactical advantage at the cost of major strategic risks and penalties'. This, he said bluntly, 'is stupid and dangerous. Creating more enemies than you kill is self defeating; making it politically and ideologically impossible to end a war and so is spreading new levels of anger and hatred to other countries and/or factions'. Victory against terrorists and insurgents 'will ultimately occur at the political and ideological level, and in the tactics of shaping the psychological, perceptual, and media dimensions of the conflict' (Cordesman, 2006). This, he concludes, is of great relevance for doctrines of defence transformation, net-centric warfare and effects-based operations:

> All of these concepts have tended to downplay the ideological and political dimensions of war, and the dangers of civilian casualties and collateral

damage. They call for impossible levels of near real-time intelligence and situational awareness even in narrow tactical terms in dealing with the enemy. Until recently, they have given far too limited priority to the ability to know the political sensitivities of the operations they are meant to conduct and civilian casualties and collateral damage, and even today the efforts to modernize and adapt them are generally crude.

(Cordesman, 2006)

Cordesman's concerns speak strongly to the practice of choosing and using military force; but what is just as important is the larger normative and geopolitical framework that is global in scope, that extends widely and unpredictably across time and space. In this space questions of meaning, legitimacy, and belief are of much greater moment than material measures of power. So how to make better meanings? How to render terrorism powerless?

What bin Laden's speeches demonstrate is *the power of the example*. While the US was exercising its geopolitical and military power over the past half-century, according to the instrumental strategic theories of the day, their actions were being observed, interpreted and then signified in a very different way – as an imperative, licence and justification to attack American civilians in a systematic campaign. What may have been seen as an exercise in rational war making, containment or coercive diplomacy was in fact also a process of making meaning that *its authors could never control*. Who would have thought that the tragedies of Hiroshima and Nagasaki, which stimulated a profoundly pacifistic disposition amongst many Japanese, would come to form part of the normative apparatus of legitimation with which an Islamist insurgency would, 40 years later, launch a campaign of terror against the West? In turn the war in Vietnam, the containment of Iraq and Israel's wars against the Arabs were interpreted to the same ends – as more in a long list of *examples* that justified a commensurate violence. It does not matter that Islamist interpretations of western actions are often selective, erroneous and self-regarding, concerned only with the safety of Muslims and scornful of the lives of other peoples and faiths. Once they are folded into an ideology of violence such interpretations become *strategic facts* that no amount of political 'spin' or argument can dislodge; they become crucial components of a strategic process that is only marginally susceptible to our influence or control.

Hence even thoughtful arguments for efforts 'to shape' the 'perceptual and media elements' of a conflict, as Cordesman suggests, may still betray too much instrumental confidence. It is always another actor and community that will 'shape' and determine the meaning of our actions, and the best we can do is to act with integrity and understand the background discourse that will guide this process of interpretation. We may rightly dislike or fear Islamist ideology, but it all too often forms such a discourse, and hence the Bush Administration's arguments for promoting democracy in the Middle-East as 'the antithesis of terrorist tyranny' will dangerously backfire (NSC, 2006). Indeed the Chatham House scholar Nadim Shehadi argues that 'talk about spreading liberalism is a spontaneous knee-jerk reaction but the real policy that is developing is that of promoting Islam' (2004).

Viewed against the background of Palestine, Iraq, Qutb's critique of western reason as 'a conscious arrogation of God's authority' (Euben, 2002: 15), and the long-standing Islamist critique of Arab elites' co-operation with western powers, 'democracy' takes on a very different meaning: as dangerously threatening to Arab and Muslim communities. Even if we accept that the motives for overthrowing Saddam Hussein were many, and that some genuine goodwill was involved, the key strategic question is what kind of *example* contemporary Iraq is.

The *example* is a particularly powerful form of meaning: the exemplar, the exemplary, the event transformed into a normative principle that can be disseminated and used until it takes up the entire space of the possible. Abu Ghraib and Camp X-ray then are not merely prisons; they are examples, and their meaning, as Richard Jackson suggests, is that we are involved not in a war against terrorism but a 'war of terrorisms' (Jackson, 2005: 183). Such a war cannot be won; terror will be its only victor, steadily taking up more and more of the space of the possible.

My view is that the best hope of delegitimating and eventually eliminating terrorism lies in attention to the power of the example. The hope lies in developing genuinely multilateral frameworks, at the level of both governments and international civil society, and in building and implementing genuinely consistent and morally defensible normative frameworks about the use of violence – of all kinds and from all sources – against innocents. What might now be the case if the United Nations' Security Council had created an international tribunal, which included Islamic judges, to try bin Laden and his accomplices for the 9/11 and similar atrocities? What might now be the case if the US had planned its war in Afghanistan more thoroughly, involved NATO and other allies as equal partners, been far more careful of the impact of military operations on civilians and the humanitarian crisis, and in turn been committed to rehabilitating its economy and ensuring long-term stability? What might now be the case if the US had treated terrorist suspects according to US law and the Geneva conventions, and rejected the practice of extraordinary rendition? What might now be the case if Israel had not conducted Operation Defensive Shield or invaded Lebanon, but instead returned to negotiations with the PLO and concluded a final agreement based on the Clinton parameters and the Palestinian position at Taba in 2001? What might now be the case if Iraq had been left untouched, and pressure for a final UN accounting of its WMD capabilities been exchanged for a lifting of sanctions? If western politicians had avoided passing legislation that undermined civil rights, and actions that could be perceived as demonizing Muslims and Arabs? True, none of this would have been simple or easy, and what remains of Hamas, Hezbollah, Islamic Jihad and al Qaeda might still be preaching hatred and seeking to stage attacks. However I venture that their organizations and their ideologies – their material *and* moral force – would be weaker than they are today, and we would all be a great deal safer. In the last resort, direct forms of action against terrorists may remain necessary, but by themselves they will fail unless we succeed in building a new global normative architecture that resonates deeply with Islamic communities.

Hence, in the search for security against terrorism the widely held view that security can be sought through force – that force is force at all – must be rethought, along with many of the fundamental Clausewitzian assumptions of strategic doctrine. But Clausewitz also cautioned that 'the first of all strategic questions' was 'the kind of war upon which [we] are embarking' (1976: 88), and if we reject the ontological presumption for violence inherent in his thought, he still has something to teach us. Think of the future terrorists, currently unknown to us *or* themselves. We could rewrite the famous Clausewitzian formula thus: in a time of terror, security is many acts of *non-force* that change the enemy's will, that may prevent them becoming an enemy at all.

3 'War on terror'/'war on women'

Critical feminist perspectives

Katrina Lee-Koo

The fight against terrorism is also a fight for the rights and the dignity of women

This claim was made by the First Lady of the United States, Laura Bush, in a radio address to the nation two months after the September 11 terrorist attacks. It was designed to 'kick off a world-wide effort to focus on the brutality against women and children by the al-Qaida terrorist network and the regime it supports in Afghanistan, the Taliban' (Bush, 2001). Fulfilling a long-held feminist ambition, the world's most powerful leaders (and their wives) turned their focus and resources to the abuses suffered by Afghan women at the hands of the brutal Taliban regime. After decades of neglect, complicity, and perhaps even tacit involvement in the terror facing Afghan women, the United States government now claimed to be taking the lead in addressing gendered oppression. While most feminists applauded the attention that this issue was now receiving, many did so with caution. And they were right to be cautious.

It has been over half a decade since Laura Bush's proclamation. Yet, in this ongoing and bloody 'War on Terror', now fought in both Afghanistan and Iraq, security still eludes women. If anything, the situation for women has dramatically worsened. Unfulfilled promises of economic, personal and political security linger in Afghanistan while increasing, deliberate, and chaotic violence rages against women in Iraq. The 'War on Terror' has distanced many women in these battle zones from any sense of basic physical security. Consequently, when examined from a critical feminist security studies perspective, the 'War on Terror' has in many ways become a 'War on Women' as multiple terrors infiltrate their lives.

Critical feminist intervention has sought to reveal and analyse these new terrors burgeoning out of the 'War on Terror' project. Overwhelmingly this research points to a security project which is driven by a western hyper-masculinity, relies upon the use of force, and attempts to enforce a singular, hegemonic notion of political security. All three of these designs disparage characteristics assigned to the feminine. Feminist analysis reveals how the 'War on Terror' project sometimes relies upon this denigration, while at other times carelessly causes and disregards it. This analysis reveals, embedded in the 'War on Terror's' design, the potential for a plethora of human security threats to women. For example, US servicewomen fighting the war in Iraq have reported some of the worst sexual harassment the

US military has seen. Since the 2003 invasion there have been over 500 filed complaints of sexual harassment in the US military (Goldenberg, 2006b) while cases of domestic violence in military families in the US have risen dramatically since the US deployment to Afghanistan (Komp, 2006). Furthermore, gendered identities are tightly patrolled and the 'War on Terror' is played out on women's bodies. In Australia and the UK, the debates surrounding Muslim women's wearing of the veil in workplaces and public spaces (BBC, 2006) see the use of women's bodies to patrol and discipline identity and belonging in this time of terror.

Elsewhere, the perceived emasculation of Afghan and Iraqi men by the presence and power of occupying Coalition troops is considered a contributing factor to the rise in domestic violence in those countries (see IRIN, 2006a and Hammer, 2003). Approximately 90 Iraqi women become widows every day (IRIN, 2006c) and women in both Iraq and Afghanistan are now more likely to become victims of honour crimes, trafficking, poverty and spontaneous violence than they were prior to the invasions of their countries (Beaumont, 2006). While this is only a snapshot, critical feminist analysis carefully traces, reveals and documents these consequences of the 'War on Terror' for women.

This chapter applies a critical feminist security studies analysis to better account for these crises facing women's lives. In doing so it peels away the layers of misrepresentation that suggest this 'War on Terror' is a 'War for Security'. Instead, it points to the terror that bedevils women's lives to argue that the current course of action will not address terrorism, in any of its forms, or bring security to people's lives in a way that encourages peace to geminate. By investigating examples from both the Afghanistan and Iraq campaigns of the 'War on Terror', this chapter suggests that a critical feminist approach offers three useful insights into the study of security and the 'War on Terror'. First, it offers a new way of theorising key decisions, issues and events by highlighting the gendered dynamics implicit in them, as well as the gendered effects of them. Here, the manipulation of the identities of the 'Afghan women' during the bombing of Afghanistan, the rescue of Pfc Jessica Lynch in Iraq, and Lynndie England's role in the Abu Ghraib scandal is revealed. These examples demonstrate the deep seated gendered assumptions that the 'War on Terror's' claim to moral justification, ethical behaviour, and an emotional/political sense of 'right', relies upon. Second, this chapter offers a hitherto unexamined range of gendered issues which are clearly embedded either as integral to, or a product of, the ongoing conflict. It looks particularly at the appalling raft of insecurities facing women in central and southern Iraq in the current phase of the 'War on Terror' campaign. In doing so, it does not claim that women are the only victims of the 'War on Terror' or that their suffering is necessarily more drastic than other members of their community. Rather, this analysis demonstrates the utility of feminist methodologies in reflecting gendered experiences and therefore constructing and revealing more honest narratives of the 'War on Terror'.

Unveiling gendered wars

The dramatic opening of the 'War on Terror' reads like an old-fashioned rescue romance drama. Smarting from an attack on its homeland, the strong and brave hero/protector seeks out those supposedly responsible and not only exacts revenge but rescues oppressed and vulnerable damsels in the process. Far from being facetious, this underlying tale of powerful masculinity and feeble femininity motivated the moral, political and ethical justification for the US attack upon Afghanistan in the wake of the September 11 tragedies. In doing so it relied upon a widespread acceptance of what feminists refer to as the 'protection myth'. The 'protection myth' simply identifies uncivilised 'bad' men torturing or threatening vulnerable and powerless women who require rescuing by enlightened and heroic 'good' men. Stiehm (1982) articulates this as being a triangular relationship between the protected/victim, the threat/villain, and the protector/hero. However, despite its simplicity, the 'protection myth' only functions if each party conforms to their gendered roles. For the protector, his gendered identity reveals a parallel masculinity in operation. On the one side his masculinity is embodied in the aggressive and militaristic characteristics required to launch war, but attending that is also a chivalrous and gallant attitude towards the vulnerable feminine (Young 2003: 224). On the other hand, the threat/villain identity embodies masculinity's dark side: uncivilised, barbarous and cruel, while the victim/protected remains helpless and often voiceless. The 'protection myth' is a powerful narrative that has a long association with wars and colonial and frontier projects. It directs and disciplines gendered identities in ways that serve the state project. Men who refuse to defend women's honours in war are labelled cowards and unpatriotic; women who refuse to accept help or support their men are considered similarly treacherous or ignorant of their own good.

It was within this framework of a 'protection myth' that the US drew much of its moral and political justification for launching the 'War on Terror'. The US drew upon the very real barbarism exacted upon Afghan women by the Taliban regime to assuage any doubt that the enemy they were facing was indeed 'evil', or that the US wanted more than revenge. In order to establish an emotional and moral grounding for this campaign, Afghan women were cast into the role of the feminine victim in need of rescue. Promoted by war leaders and the media, the plight of Afghan women became one of the main international news stories after September 11. Coverage of Afghan women in print and broadcast media across the US increased dramatically in the weeks after September 11 (Stabile and Kumar, 2005: 772). Images of Afghan women in burqas were splashed across front pages and in the period between September 11, 2001 and January 1, 2002 US mainstream newspapers published six times as many articles on the plight of Afghan women than they had in the previous 18 months (Stabile and Kumar, 2005: 772). Behind their burqas these women remained largely silent but were nonetheless the dividing line between the 'evil' Taliban and 'good' Coalition forces. Furthermore, suggestion of the women's overwhelming gratitude for their liberation was a focal point of the 'success' of Operation Enduring Freedom.

For instance, as US ground troops forced their way into Afghanistan *USA Today* described a scene where 'six (Afghan women) shed the enveloping burqas that the Taliban forces all women to wear, threw them on the fire and lit the way for their rescuers' (quoted in Stabile and Kumar, 2005: 773).

While the role of Afghan women was more visual than vocal, the wives of both the US and UK's leaders provided the moral, feminine legitimacy to the bombing campaign. In what were unique interventions into politics by both Laura Bush and Cherie Blair, each made a major address to their respective nations on the issue of women's rights in Afghanistan. Bush's address from her family's Texas ranch on 17 November 2001 was the first time that a First Lady had given the weekly radio presidential address. She used her on-air time to describe the oppression of the 'Taliban and its terrorist allies' and claimed that 'civilized people throughout the world are speaking out in horror – not only because our hearts break for the women and children in Afghanistan, but also because in Afghanistan we see the world the terrorists would like to impose on the rest of us' (Bush, 2001). Two days after Mrs Bush's speech, Cherie Blair, along with women Cabinet ministers, made a similar plea on behalf of Afghan women. Mrs Blair claimed that 'the women in Afghanistan are as entitled as the women in any country are to have the same hopes and aspirations for ourselves and for our daughters – a good education and career outside the home if they want one, the right to healthcare and, of course, most importantly, a right for their voices to be heard' (BBC, 2001). References by Bush to 'civilised people' and Blair to the universalising of women's rights alludes to both an orientalism as well as a universalism of liberal feminist views on women's rights. Furthermore, the use of the 'wives' to speak of 'women's issues' suggests a maternal or feminine knowledge which legitimises only women to speak with authority and empathy of these issues as if they weren't human rights concerns. In this sense, it neatly demarcates the gendered roles and responsibilities of the issue. In her address Laura Bush spoke as a mother, a wife and a woman from her home in Texas while her husband directed a military campaign from his office in Washington. For Laura Bush, the abuse in Afghanistan was not a political or a politicised issue but one of morality and common humanity. After all, what civilised person would stand idly by while innocent and defenceless women were tortured?

Reminiscent of the 'white feathers campaign' of the First World War where British women goaded young men to join the Army, Laura Bush linked the 'War on Terror' and the violence against women in a way that suggested that to *not* support the war was tantamount to complicity and cowardice. As a strong and powerful feminine (but not feminist) character, Laura Bush played an important role in legitimating the protection scenario and disciplining gendered identities. She was aptly suited to her role as feminine mother of the nation sending her sons to war in a just cause. Less prominent, however, were those whose behaviour did not conform to the dominant narrative. For example, the US and UK media and political establishments had a short-lived alliance with RAWA (Revolutionary Association of the Women of Afghanistan). RAWA, a women's rights NGO founded in 1977, used the opportunity provided by the media interest to expose the treatment of women in Afghanistan. In return, their stories and resources were used by the war leaders to demonstrate the demonic nature of the enemy. However this became politically inconvenient for the war leaders as RAWA behaved less as vulnerable and grateful damsels in distress and more as active, self-determining feminists. With a long tradition of political activism, RAWA independently stepped out of the feminised private realm and into public sphere politics unchaperoned by a male protector. When it became clear that RAWA's emancipatory ambitions diverged from those of liberal feminists in the US and, particularly, when they opposed the US-led bombing of their homeland (Pettman, 2004: 90) the alliance came to an abrupt end. On the fifth anniversary of the US bombing of Afghanistan, RAWA member Zoya (2006) proclaimed: 'No doubt the war on terror toppled the misogynist and barbaric regime of Taliban. But it did not remove Islamic fundamentalism, which is the root cause of misery for all Afghan people; it just replaced one fundamentalist regime with another'. Such conclusions, contrary to those of the architects of the 'War on Terror', meant that RAWA lost its legitimacy and alliance with the US war leaders.

During the Iraq campaign, the political manipulation of gendered identities as a means of encouraging an emotional and moral response to the war was best seen during the dramatic rescue of US Private Jessica Lynch by US Navy Seals and Army Rangers in April 2003. The rescue of Jessica Lynch 'was one of the most extensively covered events [by media in the US] of the 2003 US-led invasion of Iraq' (Kumar, 2004: 297). Lynch was a 19 year old woman from West Virginia who had been deployed to Iraq as a supply clerk with the US Army. During a transport mission in Nassiriya her convoy had taken a wrong turn and was ambushed by Iraqi soldiers. A gun battle ensued in which 11 US soldiers were killed. Lynch was taken by Iraqi soldiers to a nearby hospital where she was held for eight days and given medical attention before her comrades, in spectacular fashion, burst through the doors of the civilian medical facility and whisked Lynch to nearby transport. The rescue was filmed and edited into a five minute tape which was released to media networks. When Lynch returned to the US she arrived home to a mass of media and public interest who lauded her heroism and bravery in the face of the enemy. She was the subject of a mass of print and broadcast media. The documentary *Saving Private Lynch* and the drama *Saving Jessica Lynch* were both aired in November 2003. This coincided with Veterans' Day in the US and the publication of her book *I am a Soldier, Too* written by journalist Rick Bragg. She was interviewed in the US by Diane Sawyer, Katy Couric and David Letterman, and was the feature story in many news magazines. Yet, while this simple narrative remains largely uncontested, the rest of her story has been a complex matrix of competing interests and intrigues most of which have been motivated and mobilised in pursuit of a particular political vision about the war, and the roles of gendered identities within it.

Read in its simplest terms, the rescue of Lynch was a rare, yet spectacular, good news story from a war zone that was degenerating for the United States. The narrative of brave, heroic and self-sacrificing hyper-masculine identities who stormed in to save a weaker, captive, distressed feminine identity from a brutal and calculating enemy provided a number of simple moral metaphors for which the US, as a nation, could once more feel good about the war. In each of these metaphors Lynch plays the identities which have been feminised by September 11. She plays the feminine nation of the United States, aggressively and violently attacked and violated on September 11: a simple, kind-hearted, home-grown all-American girl. She loves her family and is from a small, close-knit community where she once won Miss Congeniality in a beauty pageant. References to her homeland, her femininity and her vulnerability all play into the broader representations of the US nation and its innocence. For Takacs (2005: 302), 'this exclusive yet reassuring image of national identity conforms to the Bush administration's own conception of the homeland as a vulnerable community in need of militarised protection'. In this case the military protection of the feminine nation is provided by the masculine state. Yet, in Iraq, Lynch provided a clear juxtaposition of American identity against that of the alien Iraqi Other. Against the backdrop of the Iraq desert, Lynch was both familiar and modern. Her blue eyes and blonde hair, her Army fatigues and big smile dramatically contrasts those of war weary Iraqi women who are largely covered up, denied many liberal rights, and lack the familiarity that Lynch inspires. Here Lynch embodies freedom, equality and modern entitlements, the very qualities which the US proposed to defend in the 'War on Terror'.

This representation of Lynch, as soldier (yet feminine), and hero (yet in need of rescue) served a number of agendas within the US. On the one hand, the Lynch drama reveals the US to be a liberal, and indeed liberal feminist state. Initial reports, which later proved to be false, that Lynch 'fought fiercely and shot several enemy soldiers … firing her weapons until she ran out of ammunition' (Schmidt and Leob, 2003) during the dramatic gun battle in Iraq reminded the nation of its liberal equality in allowing women to be heroes. On the other hand, while the 'fact' that Lynch is a hero is unquestioned, 'her heroism is tempered by sexist notions of women's bravery' (Kumar, 2004: 301). After all, at the end of the day, she was still in need of masculine protectors. Either way, the narrative served as a sound and rational justification for the need for a hyper-masculine foreign policy, one which acts chivalrously and with aggressive determination, but is nonetheless in service of the moral good. While it superficially raised feminist issues relating to the role of women in fighting the 'War on Terror', the manipulation of Lynch as a gendered identity was ultimately undertaken in the service of a patriarchal foreign policy designed to use gender to generate 'good spin' on a war going badly. It encouraged an emotional, rather than strategic, response to a situation by manipulating the perceived vulnerability of femininity in international politics. This femininity was literally embodied in Jessica Lynch but metaphorically graphed onto the nation of the United States and to an extent, the nation of a feminised Iraq, brutally raped by Saddam Hussein and rescued by American soldiers. The public acceptance of the multiple metaphors of Lynch's rescue relied upon, and needed to be unsuspicious of, deep-seated gendered politics manipulated by the Pentagon and the Bush Administration. These gendered politics promoted and privileged a powerful and hegemonic hyper-masculinity and reinforced its obligation to do whatever it takes to protect the weak, the powerless and the vulnerable: in other words, the feminine. In Jessica Lynch's own words, 'they used me as a way to symbolize all this stuff' (quoted in Kumar 2004: 308).

The use of gendered identities becomes more complex when we include those of another young woman who, like Jessica Lynch, hailed from West Virginia and became an emotional, gendered symbol of the 'War on Terror'. Lynndie England represented Jessica Lynch's antithesis: England was not attractive, bright, bubbly, pure or adored by the nation. Yet, like Jessica Lynch, she prompted an emotional reaction to the 'War on Terror' and fuelled a particular public understanding of its role as a security project. Lynndie England was one of the seven reservists (three of whom were women) who were initially charged with prisoner abuses at the US run Abu Ghraib prison in Iraq. Images of England and her colleagues torturing and sexually abusing Iraqi prisoners became infamous around the world. Most recognisable of these photographs was one depicting England, only 20 years old when the photograph was taken, holding a naked Iraqi prisoner on a dog's leash. While the raft of photographs included a number of England's colleagues, with 13 eventually charged in relation to the abuses, it was England who became the poster-girl of Abu Ghraib.

Like Lynch, the representations of England's femininity are both complex and, at times, carefully choreographed. Her gendered identity, within the context of Abu Ghraib, enabled her to be both powerful (though not in a feminist sense) and powerless. Her power derived from her ability, as a woman, to exact torture upon Iraqi prisoners. Her use of torture upon Iraqi prisoners elevated her to a position of masculine power while simultaneously serving to further feminise her victims. In addition to this, England's position as American, part of an occupying force, in command of the prisoners, and being white all encouraged a masculine image of England. In the context of the Abu Ghraib prison these were all powerful identity markers in comparison with being Iraqi, brown-skinned, Muslim and captive. Juxtaposed to England, the Iraqi captives were stripped of their masculinity, and thereby their power. This also accounts for the sexualised nature of the violence. Now infamous pictures of naked men being forced to lie on top of each other, to masturbate in a line, to wear women's underwear, and simulate homosexual acts can all be read as a manipulation of power dynamics designed to feminise the captives and masculinise the captors in a powerless/powerful dynamic. With her short hair and tomboy appearance England was assimilated into this role with comparative ease. The same could not be said, however, of her colleague Sabrina Harman, also convicted in the Abu Ghraib scandal, whose her blond hair and blue eyes made her seem, perhaps, uncomfortably like Jessica Lynch.

However, England's relative position of power, obscene though it was, should not be read as a successful project of women's empowerment. Lynndie England may have had the power to 'hold the leash' but she was still, as a woman, in an extremely vulnerable position. Perhaps she 'chose' to engage in torture but she did so within a military culture whose foundation lies in a commitment to hegemonic masculinity. While England admits thinking that the prisoner abuse was 'weird' (quoted in McKelvey, 2005), she claims that she was ordered to be involved. This was heightened by her personal involvement with Charles Graner, 15 years her senior, with whom she later had a child. Graner, when he first sent the photograph of England holding the prisoner's leash to his family annotated the photo with 'Look what I made Lynndie do' (quoted in McKelvey, 2005). A more sympathetic reading of England's femininity, then, sees her beholden to Graner, and to the military. Colonel Janis Karprinski, who was in charge of the Abu Ghraib facility, suggested that England saw a protector in Graner and was powerless against his whims and the orders from above (McKelvey, 2005). One commentator notes 'England was a small-town girl, not even of legal drinking age, when she found herself halfway around the world, in an amoral place, surrounded by violence and infatuated with a volatile, manipulative man' (McKelvey, 2005). Yet, the fact that Charles Graner, who had a history of violence against women, orchestrated much of the prisoner abuse did not offend the nation as much as the possibility that a young woman should have stepped so far out of her traditional gender role.

Attempts by the Bush Administration to explain away England and her colleague's actions as those of a few 'bad apples' (Carter, 2004) also saw her complex gender identity used against her. Her masculine actions (and even appearance) were particularly deplorable to mainstream America. Yet there was the sense that because England's behaviour was so abnormal to her gender, then her actions could be explained away as being an isolated aberration rather than a systemic problem within the military culture. Consequently, the Abu-Ghraib scandal could be dealt with by scapegoating an unprotected, junior ranked woman. In doing so, however, it does not address the possibility of systemic problems within the military's culture that may have enabled the torture in the first place. Furthermore, it reinforces, rather than critically examines, the deployment of gender in this 'War on Terror'. Currently serving a three-year sentence, England's military attorney has advised her before she appears before the parole board to grow her hair long, in order to look more feminine (McKelvey, 2005).

'War on terror'/'war on women'

From American servicewomen to civilian women, the subordination of the feminine remains a constant feature of the 'War on Terror'. In particular, the invasion of Iraq in March 2003, designed to lift the Iraqi people from 'insecurity and tyranny' (White House, 2003) has caused widespread insecurity for Iraqi women. Of course women have not been alone in their suffering, nor do they suffer necessarily to a greater extent than other members of the community. Feminist research however, has been important in highlighting specific violences against women, and analysing the specifically gendered impacts arising from the broader humanitarian tragedy currently engulfing Iraq. With international preoccupation focusing upon the broader, public issues of terrorism, state integrity, governance, sustainability of the occupation, and the general humanitarian crisis, often little attention is given to the effects of the war on women.

Claims that the 'War on Terror' is a 'War for Security' resonates little across Iraq. Institutional and effective security is not uniformly or consistently available to individuals, communities or the state itself. Personal or physical security,

security in the form of access to clean water, healthcare, electricity or stable employment is similarly not widespread (Lasky, 2006: 2). Within this environment of general chaos, women are finding their personal security particularly targeted. While the experiences of women across Iraq vary, and can depend upon class and geographic region, women in southern and central Iraq are finding their lives particularly threatened in the post-invasion period. The increase of kidnapping, rapes and murder of women has been documented by a number of human rights organisations and NGOs working in the conflict zone (see, for example, Amnesty International, 2005). Women have been targeted by individual Coalition troops and contractors (Goldenberg, 2006a; Harding 2004a and b), the Iraqi police, local criminal gangs and religious extremists (Beaumont, 2006). They are targeted for a number of reasons: to send a political message to their male 'protectors'; to intimidate and discipline women's beshaviour and activities; for criminal and illegal profit; and as a violent opportunity arising from the state's lawlessness. A number of women professionals and activists have been targeted for assassination by religious militia groups who are trying to redesign the rights and opportunities available to women through violent intimidation (Shumway, 2005). For example, in 2005 the body of well-known pharmacist and women's rights activist Zeena al-Qushtaini was discovered on a Baghdad highway ten days after her abduction. She had two bullet holes close to her eyes, had been dressed by her captors in the Islamic *abaya*, which she rarely wore, and had attached to it a message that read: 'She was a collaborator against Islam' (quoted in Shumway, 2005). She is one of dozens of women targeted because of their visible public profile.

The assassination of professionals constitutes only a small number of women who have been murdered or 'disappeared' in the new Iraq. The 'Organisation for Women's Freedom in Iraq' has estimated that more than 2,000 Iraqi women have disappeared since the fall of Saddam (Bennett, 2006) while 'Women's Freedom' has estimated nearly 3,500 (IRIN, 2006d). Many of these women have been stolen (or sold) into sexual slavery. Despite the new constitution explicitly prohibiting the trafficking of women and children (under Article 35), the chaos engulfing Iraq has made it easy for traffickers to force women out of Iraq and into prostitution industries and sexual slavery in Yemen, Syria, Jordan, and the Gulf countries (US State Department, 2005: 232). In a June 2005 report on trafficking the US State Department claimed that the extent of the problem in Iraq is 'difficult to appropriately gauge' but quoted evidence suggesting that 'in Syria and Yemen, there are thousands of Iraqi women working in prostitution in the two countries under conditions that constitute severe forms of trafficking in persons' (US State Department, 2005: 232). Taking advantage of women's vulnerability and families' desperateness, traffickers have lied, coerced and forced their way into a booming market where women and young girls are the commodity. Research indicates that women are abducted by organised criminal groups, sold by family members or tricked into believing that they will be working abroad for real wages (IRINd, 2006d). Attempts to stem the tide of trafficking by Iraqi police have been minimal. The State Department reports that efforts to train police on issues regarding trafficking have been 'substituted with additional security training in order to address ongoing insurgent activities' (US State Department, 2005: 233).

The rise of Islamic fundamentalism that has become evident in post-invasion Iraq has had mixed responses and mixed effects on the lives of Iraqi women. In central and southern Iraq particularly, radical clerics, conservative Shi'a political parties, and paramilitary forces have regained power after years of having their influence curtailed by Saddam's regime. Consequently, Lasky (2006: 8) points out, 'radical religious groups can more openly harass women who defy their interpretations of Shari'a'. This has seen a social patrolling and disciplining of women's dress, behaviour and activities. Anecdotal evidence collected by NGOs and researchers suggest that women, particularly in urban areas, have been 'terrorised' into wearing the *hijab* (veil) or *abaya* (full length Islamic dress). Young women at colleges and universities have particularly been victims of attack and harassment designed to intimidate them to conform to radical interpretations of Islamic behaviour (Abdela, 2005). As already discussed, women participating in public issues and affairs have been subject to verbal threats and intimidations, acid attacks and assassination. Similarly, men and women advocating women's rights have been subject to attacks. Reports suggest that 38 lawyers have been murdered and hundreds attacked for defending cases seen by radicals as contrary to Islam (IRIN, 2006b). The Iraqi Lawyers Association have indicated that lawyers advocating on behalf of women in cases of child custody, inheritance and honour crimes are particularly vulnerable to attack (IRIN, 2006b). In July 2006 a well-known lawyer, Salah Abdel-Kader, who handled cases of honour killings and custody issues, was shot dead in his Baghdad office. A note near his body stated 'This is the price to pay for those who do not follow Islamic laws and defend what is dreadful and dirty' (see IRIN, 2006b).

Lawyers have been particularly vocal in their criticisms of the new Iraqi constitution which will potentially see women stripped of their rights. Prior to the October 2005 unveiling of the constitution, US President George Bush told the American people in August that 'the fact that Iraq will have a democratic constitution that honors women's rights, the rights of minorities, is going to be an important change in the broader Middle East' (Bush, 2005). Yet, for many Iraqi women, the ironic 'fact' is that women's rights had better guarantee and consistency of access under Saddam's dictatorship (Hunt and Posa, 2004: 42). While the new constitution 'aims to achieve a percentage of women's representation not less than one-quarter of the Council of Representatives members' (Article 47), it does not necessarily translate into a clear women's rights agenda. While the quota was successfully achieved in the transitional National Assembly elected in January 2005, nearly half of the women elected are members of a conservative Shi'a coalition and have not vocally deviated from the party's conservative line (Lasky, 2006: 14). This supports suggestion that the parliament has been stacked by clerics 'with women who had few qualifications or political ambitions of their own but who would blindly support their agenda' (Philp, 2005). Most vocal of the women parliamentarians is Dr Jenan Al-Ubaedey who has spoken out in favour of polygamy and wife beating claiming that 'If you say to a man he cannot use force against a woman, you are asking the impossible ... So we say a husband can beat his wife, but he cannot leave a mark' (quoted in Philp, 2005).

Similarly, the interpretation of the constitution could also undermine efforts to protect women's rights. While the new constitution ensures that 'Iraqis are equal before the law without discrimination based on gender, ...' (Article 14) it also establishes under Article 2 that 'Islam is the official religion of the State and it is a fundamental source of legislation' and 'no law that contradicts the established provisions of Islam may be established'. As has been evident in a number of countries using Shari'a principles, the 'established provisions of Islam' are open to interpretation (see Lasky, 2006: 13). Interpretation of the constitution is undertaken by the Supreme Court, but the members of the Supreme Court will be determined by the Parliament. Lasky (2006: 13) points out that if conservative groups control the Parliament then conservative rulings will follow. Evidence of this has been the power of conservative Islamists to block the appointment of a female judge in Nijaf. This 'compromise' 'of sacrificing Iraqi women's political participation to pacify vocal minorities is hardly anomalous' (Hunt and Posa, 2004, 40). This trend suggests that negotiations over governance and legislation will see the loss of women's rights as the compromise between radical and moderate factions. Yet for the most part it still remains to be seen how this new constitution and its implementation will affect women with regard to issues such as inheritance, child custody, divorce, and justice for honour crimes and gendered violence. However early indications suggest that Iraq, which had previously been lauded as having some of the most progressive family and personal laws in the Middle East, will take a step backwards.

In short, the 'War on Terror' has brought terror to the lives of Iraqi women. Recognition of this highlights a deep, surging, and intricately interwoven counternarrative of the 'War on Terror' which sees it *not* as a 'War for Security' but rather as a 'War *of* terror *on* Women'. While careful not to romanticise women's lives under Saddam, the current chaos, uncertainty and tragedy in their lives engrains a basic physical and emotional insecurity that had been recently unknown in Iraq. Subsumed by the grand narratives of democracy, freedom and liberty, their tragedies, as demanding as those who perished in the twin towers, remain largely unheard. This is not historically peculiar. Throughout history, periods of dramatic political upheaval, which laud opportunities for 'progressive change', have simultaneously seen women's rights and feminist agendas overwhelmed or compromised by apparently more pressing ambitions (see Bleiker, 2000). Lost in the clamour of international politics, many of these crises only become visible under a critical feminist lens which draws upon methodological, ontological and epistemological techniques specifically designed to focus on women's lives. The result is research, analysis and knowledge that gives voice to the silent and legitimacy to the vulnerable.

This chapter has sought to add to this research by using a critical feminist approach to examine the claim that the 'War on Terror' is a 'War for Security'. It has done so first by analysing the political manipulation of gender and gendered identities. In doing so it has demonstrated how this manipulation has provided an important foundation for the creation of knowledge about the 'War on Terror' project. A critical analysis of the gendered uses and representations of women such as Laura Bush, Cherie Blair, Jessica Lynch and the collective 'women of Afghanistan' revealed a specific manipulation of their gendered identities toward a particular end: a moral justification and reinforcement for the 'War on Terror' in the Afghanistan and Iraq campaigns. Meanwhile, the un-ladylike behaviour of Lynndie England could be dismissed as an aberration of her gender in the same breath as the immoral acts of Abu Ghraib could be dismissed as an aberration of the nation of the United States. Yet in both cases, public acceptance of a certain understanding of gender was vital: the feminine, be it either distressed or malicious is, in the grand scheme of things, vulnerable and powerless.

It is this understanding that has encouraged a healthy ignorance, and even a quiet expectation, of the hidden violence experienced by women in the 'War on Terror'. It also goes some way to explaining how a war can be launched with the claim of fighting for 'the rights and dignity of women' (Bush 2001) yet remain so derelict in demonstrating any sustained concern for women's basic security needs. The rhetorical regard for women as enumerated by the architects of this 'War on Terror' is devoid of any genuine feminist ambition. The second part of this chapter addressed the extent to which this has been the case by focusing specifically on the ongoing crisis in Iraq. In doing so it revealed how the injection of a feminist analysis uncovers a very different 'War on Terror' to the one often portrayed by the war's leaders. Instead, it reveals a conflict which, on both sides, uses women's identities and abuses women's bodies in pursuit of its own goals. Critical feminist intervention seeks to highlight, analyse, and combat this culture which has already become so ingrained in the 'War on Terror'. And while feminists continue to amass insights into, and micro-narratives of, women's experiences, there is, emerging in Coalition nations, a broader public support for the critical feminist argument that a war for security is an oxymoron (Weeks, 2007).

Part II

Ethics, emotions and law in the war on terror

4 Emotions in the war on terror

Emma Hutchison and Roland Bleiker

Terrorist attacks are deeply traumatic. They disrupt the normal course of life and leave a profoundly emotional impact, often generating fear, anger and resentment. Dealing with the legacy of such traumas is a major political challenge. Yet this challenge is often exacerbated by prevailing ways of confronting the threat of terrorism. In most instances, political elites deal with the legacy of pain and death by re-imposing order. Emotions, such as fear, are manipulated to justify particular policy approaches. A case in point here is the situation following the terrorist attacks of 11 September 2001 (9/11), when the US government and its allies employed a strong rhetoric of evil to gain broad support for their 'war on terror', most notably for their invasions of Afghanistan and Iraq. Such an appropriation of emotions builds a sense of identity and political community that rests on a stark separation between a safe inside and a threatening outside. Dealt with in this way, the threat and continuing trauma of terrorism can come to inscribe and perpetuate exclusive and often violent ways of configuring community. Rather than solving the problems at stake, ensuing political attitudes generate new antagonisms which, in turn, increase rather than reduce the spectre of terrorism.

A thorough understanding of the powerful but often neglected role of emotions is essential to move from conflict-prone patterns towards the possibility of establishing a culture of healing and reconciliation. Rather than understanding security as simply the management of fear, anger and resentment, one must examine how emotions are linked to notions of identity, belonging and community.

We argue that confronting the threat of terrorism more effectively requires paying much closer attention to this process. To be more precise, our argument is two-fold. First we outline in detail why and how prevailing antagonistic and militaristic ways of dealing with terrorism risk producing violent and destructive forms of community. The second part of our argument considers alternative ways of working through the threat and legacy of terrorism. We point out that an understanding of how emotions permeate political policies and actions provides inroads into how cycles of violence may be fundamentally reconfigured. Emotions such as compassion and empathy could be actively cultivated in an effort to construct more inclusive, non-violent and rehabilitative configurations of community.

On some level the main point we want to make – that restoring security after a terrorist attack requires a conscious political engagement with emotions such as empathy and compassion, rather than merely fear and anger – is commonsensical. Of course, the spectre of violence can be reduced if political elites on all sides advocate their objectives through compassion, rather than hatred. However, the issue is not as self-evident and straight-forward as it seems. Although the role of emotions has been debated extensively among philosophers, sociologists, anthropologists and psychologists, few if any of these insights have entered the study of security and international relations. Emotions are largely assumed to be personal and irrational reactions, and thus of little relevance to conceptualizing political issues. Those few approaches that do look at emotions, such as psychological explanations of foreign policy decision making, tend to see them as mere 'deviations from rationality', as factors that could explain misperceptions (Mercer 2005: 97). As a result, emotions are seldom seen as politically relevant in themselves, even while political events – and terrorism in particular – are so evidently emotional. Indeed, responses to fear have become rationalized to the point that we can no longer recognize, let alone deal with, the emotions that lie at the origin of the events in question.

A few scholars have already begun to recognize linkages between emotions and security. In a recent *Foreign Affairs* article Dominique Moïsi (2007) comments that 'the clash of emotions' – rising fear in the 'West' and a deep-seated sense of humiliation in the 'Arab' and 'Muslim' world – has created a world order of distinct complexity, if not perpetual anxiety, uncertainty and instability (on this theme, see also Saurette 2006; Danchev 2006). Moïsi explains that emotions play a crucial role in determining the dynamics of the international system; they help to shape institutionalized political processes and decisions, and ultimately whether conflict or peace will prevail. John Mercer (1996, 2005), Neta Crawford (2000), William Connolly (2002) and Andrew Ross (2005, 2006) also suggest that much can be learnt from recognizing how emotions ubiquitously filter through the social structures that underpin political behaviour and policies, ranging anywhere from voting to the waging of war. We build upon these and other contributions, whose main common theme is that emotions help to constitute the social and political world. Emotions influence perceptions and beliefs, mobilize agency and constitute the forms of community that shape political interactions.

Once emotions are taken seriously the very notion of a 'war on terror' becomes problematic, for it undermines the security it seeks to create. Military means alone can never provide comprehensive security. Even the world's most mighty military power was not able to prevent the attacks of 9/11, which were carried out with simple means. The situation is no different with the wars of response that have been fought since 9/11. Daily suicide attacks have been the norm in Iraq under the occupation of the US and allied troops. Terrorism must be fought with a range of different means and strategies, not merely those offered by coercive force. Besides obvious alternatives, such as policing, intelligence and diplomacy, attention needs to be directed towards how belligerent forms of community come to be in the first place. To stress this point is not to deny that military means are necessary to provide security and, at times, to promote justice and human rights. Nor is it to absolve the perpetrators of 9/11 of responsibility or to neglect the need to hold them accountable for their actions. Nor does our plea to take emotions seriously underestimate the danger of radical terrorist movements, whether couched in religious or secular terms. There will always be extremist individuals who engage in acts of terrorism. One can minimize, but never exclude this danger. But the ensuing challenges must be approached with a mindset that learns from past mistakes and is willing to actively seek out new strategies for understanding and dealing with terrorism. Understanding the role of emotions is an essential element in this ongoing process.

Manipulating terror: communities of fear and anger

A terrorist attack, be it experienced as a direct witness or observed from a safe distance, is often so shocking that our understanding of how the world works is severely disrupted. The comfort and stability of normal habits and expectations are stripped away. No longer can life be envisaged as a smooth trajectory from here to there. Bonds between personhood and community are broken, and the social context we ordinarily place ourselves in feels betrayed. Those who survive traumatic experiences may well have preserved their physical lives, but the meaning ascribed to being becomes altered, often in revelatory and irreconcilable ways.

Terrorist attacks are thus not processed in the same way as other political events. Their sudden and often unpredictable nature prompts feelings of disbelief and terror. Cathy Caruth (1995: 153) describes trauma as 'the confrontation with an event that, in its unexpectedness and horror, cannot be placed within the schemes of prior knowledge'. The practical implications of this insight becomes clearer when considering the aftermath of the terrorist attacks on New York and Washington. A common, immediate response to the events was one of overwhelming shock: a feeling that something like this is too unreal to be true. The attack shattered our understanding of normality; it interrupted the daily flow of events and confronted us with our inability to represent something that, in essence, cannot be represented, something that is beyond our imagination (Bourke 2005: 357–91; Edkins 2002: 243–4; 2003: 2–9, 57–60, 111–14; Humphrey 2002: 11–25; Zylinska 2004: 231–3). The terrifying visual presentation of death and suffering superseded our understanding of what could conceivably happen.

The terror and trauma reaped by terrorist attacks not only uproots deeply entrenched political patterns and expectations. They also mark the beginning of a new political era. Emotions play a central role in this process too.

Emotions help construct a sense of identity and solidarity that can emerge despite – or, rather, as a direct response to – the feelings of pain, solitude and fragmentation that are generated by the trauma. Traumatic events can pull people together, giving them a sense of common purpose. Injury and death – or what some commentators call a 'culture of pain' – can therefore become instrumental to the constitution of community and the sense of collective identity that emerges in the wake of trauma (see Morris 1993). The ensuing dynamics decisively shape the political patterns ahead. They play a crucial role in determining whether conflict or peace will prevail in the long run. This is why it is important to gain a better understanding of the emotional factors that are involved in setting up these patterns in the first place.

The disruptive, chaotic and emotional situation that follows terrorist attacks constitutes a unique political opportunity to construct new forms of identity and community – forms that are less likely to lead to violence and new conflict. In reality, though, such opportunities are far too often lost. In most cases, the experience of dislocation wrought by traumatic events is swiftly countered with political projects that seek to mobilize the unleashed emotional energy for projects of mastery and control (Humphrey 2000: 13). Certain forms of emotions – hatred, fear and anger – become central tools for political manipulation while others, such as compassion and wonder, become marginalized. The consequences are often fatal, leading to new sources of hate which in turn spiral into new forms of conflict.

Of central importance here are manipulations of the politics of fear (Ahmed 2004: 62–81; Brown 1995: 68–73; Butler 2004: 19–49). By removing feelings of security, representations of terrorism manifest immense uncertainty, anxiety and alarm. This is not simply the case for those who have survived or witnessed trauma first-hand, but also applies to society more generally (Lisle 2004: 8; Edkins 2004: 248–9, 253–6). In the aftermath of terrorist attacks the notion of fear saturates the journalistic and political discourses available for public consumption (Hoskins 2006: 453–7) This was, for instance, the case with 9/11, with the Bali Bombing of 2002 and the terrorist attack on London in July 2005. It is through the ensuing public discourses that fear can be passed down, constructing not only perceptions of an ongoing threat but also drawing clear boundaries between zones that are safe and those that are not. Fear, then, comes to generate a culture of anxiety and resentment, pitting people against whatever or whoever is perceived to threaten them. Individuals are being mobilized around what seems the only natural response to terrorism: war.

The events of 9/11 highlight how politicians frequently manipulate feelings of fear and anger that are associated with trauma. Look at the policy responses to 9/11, particularly in the United States. Washington's foreign policy became immediately centred around this major event. Couched in a rhetoric of 'good' versus 'evil', the US reaction to 9/11 re-established the sense of order and certitude that had existed during the Cold War: an inside/outside world in which, according to the words of president George W. Bush, 'you are either with us or against us'. But this very rhetoric of evil removed the phenomena of terrorism into the realm of irrationality. Evil is an emotional term of condemnation for things that can neither be fully comprehended nor addressed, except through militaristic forms of dissuasion and retaliation (Klusmeyer and Suhrke 2002: 27, 29, 35, 37; Euben 2002: 4). The presentation of 'evil' as irrational and incomprehensible provides an ideal opportunity to engage in political manipulations.

In the absence of rational or even knowable phenomena, and without under-standing the complex interplay of emotional factors, the notion of a war on terror could be justified and legitimized with relative ease. The ensuing policy positions have then become very difficult to challenge. This is the case even in the face of highly convincing conceptual or even empirical critique, such as the fact the war in Iraq was presented as essential in the fight against global terrorism, even though it was waged against a government that had no known links to the perpetrators of 9/11. Add to this that the war was directly legitimized by the immanent need of a pre-emptive attack designed to destroy dangerous weapons of mass destruction which, as it later turned out, never existed. But even in the absence of legitimacy the respective policy discourses could not be seriously challenged, for all critique was dismissed as unpatriotic subversion (Butler 2004: 1–18; Der Derian 2003: 20–2, 27). No matter how authoritarian the Iraqi regime may have been, and no matter how much its removal may have been desirable, one can view the US legitimization of the war in the same terms that were used by Al Gore (Gore 2004: 779) to characterize terrorism itself, as 'the ultimate misuse of fear for political ends' (see also Booth and Dunne 2002; Chan 2005).

Half a decade after 9/11 the spectre of terrorism remains as threatening and elusive as ever. The wars of response in Afghanistan and Iraq have not brought peace but have instead generated new forms of hatred and political violence. No end to the spiralling cycle of violence is in sight. Fault lines of conflict have instead been set for decades. They have been drawn around arbitrary and highly stereotypical perceptions of what and who might constitute a threat. A case in point here is the much discussed clash of civilizations, which assigns essential attributes to diverse cultural traditions, and then juxtaposes them in an inherently conflict-prone manner. Although dating back to Samuel Huntington's (1996) search for identity and community in the wake of the collapsing Cold War structure, the (il)logic of the clash of civilization applies well to the situation following 9/11. And the (il)logic is the very same that dominated realist strategies during the Cold War: that feelings of identity, belonging and community can only be constituted in reference to an external threat, which has to be warded off at any cost. The only difference is that civilizations replaced states as the main actors, and that foreign cultures, evil rogues and terrorists now took the place of communist subversion and the evil Soviet empire. In either case, though, the roots of the conflict remain unaddressed. All this is not to deny that threats did and do exist. Rather, it is to point out that prevailing ways of dealing with them have not healed the wounds opened up by traumatic events but, instead, have set the stage for new tensions and conflicts.

The long-term consequences of such political manipulations are far-reaching. Numerous problematic scenarios emerge when emotions such as fear, anger and hatred form the basis for new forms of political identities and communities. The most worrying of these is that a political community constituted by feelings of anger and fear of the outside will inevitably be dragged into new forms of conflict. The stakes are particularly high in the current context of a war against terrorism. Political elites have constituted a world where to be secure means to be cordoning off a safe inside – a sovereign state protected by military means – from a threatening outside. Without unravelling the impact of the various emotions associated with terrorism and political trauma, the issues that cause conflict in the first place remain concealed and therefore unaddressed. Healing the wounds of trauma becomes a matter of retribution and revenge, rather than a project begetting a mutually considered peace and emotional catharsis.

Emotions are more than individual and irrational impulses

A more productive way of dealing with terrorism starts with investigating its emotional aspects. Attention needs to be given to the role emotions play in constructing identity and community. As the previous section discussed, emotions can play a key role in mobilizing the collective agency needed to both commit acts of atrocity and to retaliate through prolonged periods of military force. To understand the significance of these factors we now take a brief detour and embark on a conceptualization of emotions, so that we can then return to the events of 9/11 with a more appropriate appreciation of the linkages between emotion and the current 'war on terror'.

Prevalent scholarly approaches to politics, security and international relations pay little or no attention to emotions. They are generally considered subjective and irrational reactions of an individual being, and are thus seen to involve neither thought nor knowledge that could be relevant for public and political deliberations. Complicating a scholarly understanding of emotions further is the absence of methodological means to examine their role and impact. Indeed, the type of rationalistic and organizational models that prevail in most policy analysis of security issues conceive of emotions as rather ephemeral phenomena, unable to be quantified, or otherwise evaluated, even in qualitative terms. Investigating their political relevance would seem to result in research that is speculative or tenuous at best. Such views are part of a deeply entrenched western philosophical tradition that has sought to decouple emotion and rationality (Elster 1999; Calhoun 2001). Emotions have come to be seen as the opposite of reason. Historically perceived to encapsulate women's 'dangerous desires', emotions were thought to be feelings or bodily sensations that overtook us, distorting thought and the ability to make 'rational' and ethical judgement (Jeleniewski Seidler 1998: 193–210). 'Justice' must be free of passion, it was believed, because emotions impel people to perform irrational acts of violence and harm (Homes 1995; Jamieson 1992).

Although largely neglected by security experts and international relations scholars in general, emotions have been of central concern in psychology, anthropology, sociology, philosophy and feminist theory. Many of these scholars disagree with each other. They wage passionate debates about the manner in which emotions should be understood and appreciated.[1] But there are still some common themes, which we would like to identify briefly here in an attempt to map out the role that emotions can play in cultivating a more adequate approach to security in the wake of a terrorist attack. Two key aspects of this literature stand out. First is the recognition that emotions are more than mere personal reactions. They play an important social and political role, particularly in the process of constituting identity and community attachments. The second involves an investigation into the extent to which emotions are not just irrational reactions, but also forms of insight and judgement.

A first key challenge consists in recognizing and exploring the socio-political nature and role of emotions. Rather than simply considering emotions as biologically grounded, as it was once thought, emotions are phenomena shaped by socio-cultural interactions. Ways we feel emerge from and are constitutive of the social and institutional processes that bind society together. This presents an understanding of emotion as derived from a social context rather than internal psychological conditions alone. Particular experiences evoke particular emotions, but they are shaped through patterns of communication and language, and more broadly, through the socialization into particular historically grounded ways of being (Nussbaum 2001: 107–9, 175–81; Shilling 1997: 197–8). In this way, as Ian Burkitt (1991: 2) suggests, 'Feelings say more about the type of social relations in which we live ... than anything about our essential nature as human beings'. Even though emotions surface from a person's instantaneous evaluation of circumstance, they can, at the same time, reflect socio-culturally embedded ways of understanding and being in the world (Hochschild 1998).

Important here is the notion that feelings are an active component of identity and community.[2] Emotions influence attitudes, behaviours and actions (Marcus 2000: 225–7). They help us to make sense of our self, and to situate us in relation to others and the world that surrounds us. By framing forms of personal and social understanding, emotions are inclinations that lend individuals to locate their identity within a wider collective. As Sara Ahmed suggests, emotions are an intimate part of the attachments that bind individuals to particular objects and to others; they shade the relational ties that can come to constitute identity and belonging (2004: 28). Feelings of both pleasure and pain are implicated here. Just as an experience that brings pleasure can create a certain kind of attachment to whatever brings joy, a painful encounter may create a similar attachment, arguably a fearful or anxiety-filled one, to the object or person that inflicted the pain. Thomas Scheff stresses that claims for identity and recognition are intrinsically emotional. Indeed, as Scheff contends, 'the urge to belong, and the intense emotions of shame and pride associated with it, may be the most powerful and divisive forces in the human world'. Feelings of affection, love, and loyalty, he claims, can act as the adhesive that bind community in the face of a common threat or fear (Scheff 1994: 277, 279–80).

The second key point is that emotions are more than just irrational impulses. A substantial body of literature now rejects the traditional dichotomy of rational/irrational and dismisses the connotations this duality ordinarily imposes on the cultural sociology of emotion (Nussbaum 1995a: 53–78). Like other aspects of culture, emotions can be seen as an element of all social interaction. Emotions accompany so-called 'rational' actions as much as 'irrational' ones, positive experiences as much as negative. Robert Solomon and Martha Nussbaum are two authors who stress that emotions are important forms of knowledge and evaluative thought (Nussbaum 2001: 1–22; Solomon 2003: Solomon 1993). Both fiercely defend the proposition that emotions can tell us certain things, providing insights and pointers that could be of use in our attempts to address social and political challenges. 'Emotions are not irrational pushes and pulls', Nussbaum argues, 'They are ways of viewing the world. They reside at the core of one's being, the part of it that makes sense of the world' (Nussbaum 1995b: 374). Thus, for Nussbaum and Solomon the strength of emotions lie in that they are, at minimum, perceptions. An emotion is a cognitive activity reflective of a 'kind of knowing'; emotions are a 'piece of understanding' (Nussbaum 1990: 45).

Understood in this way emotions either involve, or indeed are, judgements. Emotions are always about something, or are directed at something for specific reasons. They can be seen as elements of appraisal. Anger implies that something thought to be bad or wrong has happened; fear can be attributed to the feeling that something untoward may happen; and similarly, joy and happiness imply something good. They are formed through interaction and involvement (or a lack of) with the social world, and are at least partly emblematic of the way individuals and collectives apprehend or perceive the world (Sartre 2002).

This so-called cognitive approach to emotions, epitomized by the work of Solomon and Nussbaum, has always been juxtaposed to more biologically based assumptions about emotions. Such positions, influenced by William James but going back to ancient Greek philosophy, assume that emotions are not primarily thoughts, judgements and beliefs, but bodily sensations. We refrain from entering these debates in detail here, in part because they lie outside the scope of this chapter, in part because several international relations scholars, such as Crawford (2000: 126–8), Marcus (2000: 231–2), Mercer (2005: 93–4), Ross (2005; 2006) and Connolly(2002), have now drawn attention to the issues at stake. The latter two authors have, in addition, outlined the relevance of recent insights on affects from the neurosciences and attempts to apply them to the study of political phenomena. They also stress the need to go beyond locating specific 'feelings', such as anger, resentment or shame. A view that considered emotions as 'affective energies' or 'motives', they suggest, may be a more holistic way of conceptualizing political issues (Ross 2006: 212).

Reconstructing political community in the wake of terror

Although scholars in the sociology of emotions disagree on numerous fronts, they all acknowledge, in one way or another, that emotions are more than the irrational and private reactions they were once thought to be. Emotions are more than feelings of vulnerability that emerge in response to events that lie outside of control, such as terrorist attacks. But if emotions do indeed play a significant role in constituting identities and political communities, then they can and must be seen as playing a central element in how conflicts are generated, viewed and solved.

We now provide a few broad suggestions about how emotions could be understood and employed more constructively. A brief essay can, of course, not provide an exhaustive account of the role that emotions play in security policy. Nor can it come up with concrete, practical steps towards countering terrorism. Doing so is primarily the task of politicians, security experts and diplomats. It also requires assessing the unique circumstances that surround individual acts of terrorism. But viable policy advice requires a prior engagement with the complex issues at stake. This is why we focus on a preceding step that is just as important: identifying and exploring the type of emotional and political mindsets with which existing conflicts can be understood and managed more successfully.

We concentrate on one particular but important aspect in the relationship between terrorism, emotions and security policy: how an alternative, more positive sense of identity and community can be constructed following the traumatic experiences of a terrorist attack. At its broadest, the strategy for restoring security and promoting a culture of healing that we propose involves sensitivity towards the emotional and psychological trauma that follow acts of terrorism. We highlight two key aspects.

First, we stress that there are no compelling reasons why fear must necessarily lead to political manifestations that promote and justify more violence and war. The emotions associated with terrorism, such as sadness, anger or anxiety, do not automatically necessitate a retaliatory response. Recognizing the profoundly emotional nature of terrorism can provide an opportunity to rethink prevailing ways of dealing with events that seem to evoke a sense of social and political damage. Rather than constructing community and formulating policy around fear alone, the strategy we propose suggests that feelings of vulnerability can be considered in a politically enabling way. Indeed, the sense of contingency that ensues after trauma – the sense of insecurity – can be thought as creating a space for political change.

Second, a more thorough and active engagement with emotions such as compassion and empathy is key to moving towards a culture focused on understanding, acceptance and the genuine effort to ameliorate divisive socio-cultural and political relations. As commonsensical as this point may seem, seldom does it explicitly feature in conventional modelling of security issues or policy. But if scholars and politicians have a better understanding of emotions, then they would also be able to employ them more effectively in attempts to promote healing and reconciliation in the aftermath of trauma.

Deciding how to respond to terrorism thus entails not only questions of strategy, but also issues related to ethics and responsibility. Political leaders and the public at large must actively contemplate and debate how individuals and societies live on after a terrorist attack: how they could reconcile the pain that they endured or may continue to suffer. To minimize the danger of re-emerging patterns of violence the act of remembering must thus remain open for critical reflection. The ensuing process would involve leaders in politics and the media becoming more aware of the implications involved in the proliferation of fear and suspicion. But essential as well would be an attempt to draw more actively from the experiences and understandings of ordinary people. It is in this light that Phillip Darby (2006: 460) argues for 'locating a politics of security within society, rather than above it'.

Breaking cycles of violence entails establishing a sense of political community that views difference not as a threat to identity, but as an inevitable and perhaps even enriching aspect of life. The work of Emmanuel Levinas (1996: 166; 1987; 1969) offers some crucial signposts here, for his notion of ethics resolves around articulating a relationship to difference that displays understanding of, and respect for, the other's identity performances, even if they are inherently incommensurable. Several international relations scholars, such as David Campbell (1994; 198: iix; 2005), Michael Shapiro (1997) and William Connolly (1995), have started to employ such understandings of ethics to the realm of political conflict, thus viewing questions of ethics and justice primarily as 'the relationship to the other'. The point of such attitudes to the political is not to deny or erase difference, be they related to religion, ethnicity, ideology or language. The key, rather is to recognize that the most serious cause of violence today stems not from interactions with difference, but, as Connolly (1995: xxi–ii) convincingly argues, from doctrines and movements that suppress it by trying to reinstate a unified faith in one form of identification.

In an ideal scenario, such respect for difference should go beyond tolerance, for tolerance assumes a basic standard against which anything else is to be judged. Accepting alterity, by contrast, requires abandoning this privileged standpoint, perhaps even at those moments when one is deeply convinced of the superiority of one's own moral position. Some even argue that an engagement with alterity is most crucial precisely at those moments when the other's position poses a fundamental danger to one's own values (Euben 1999: 16). Scholars who engage questions of reconciliation have long sought to understand how it might be possible to nullify cycles of violence and create prosperous and respectful engagements between adversaries. The key issues involve, as Andrew Schaap (2005: 10) puts it, the challenge of 'how to transform a relation of enmity into one of friendship'. Considered in these terms, reconciliation is not about 'settling accounts' but about breaking with the violence of the past and initiating political arrangements that will secure ethical reflection.

Instead of institutionalizing and commemorating traumatic events and their memory in ways that perpetuate existing prejudices and exclusions, trauma and violence need to be reconfigured as something to be learnt from, something that can prompt the inspiration that is needed to conceptualize the political in less disparaging and more inclusive ways. An approach to security that sees emotions as both part of the social fabric and as forms of knowledge and judgement would consist of articulating identity and notions of community in less destructive ways, and in rendering these articulations politically acceptable. A political process of healing would place fear and anger in context, thus drawing more actively upon feelings of compassion and empathy in order to articulate and realize a more respectful relationship between identity and difference. Placing emphasis on processes of healing and reconciliation is not to minimize the danger of terrorist threats or to absolve terrorist of responsibility. It is, rather, a resourceful attempt to come up with policy approaches that can overcome, rather than perpetuate, the stereotypical understandings of identity and difference that often drive conflict in the first place.

Conclusion

Our attempt to map out an emotionally attuned way of dealing with terrorist treats has been both broad and preliminary. Much more is, of course, needed to translate such general suggestions into concrete and viable policy recommendations. But before such a task can begin we must have a much clearer understanding of how emotions operate in the context of international security. Drawing attention to the need for such an understanding has been the main ambition of this chapter.

A more appropriate approach to security begins by recognizing that terrorist attacks, such as 9/11, trigger a range of powerful and often seemingly contradictory emotions: fear of death and suffering, awe at the sheer magnitude of a traumatic event; anger at whoever or whatever caused the tragedy; relief for having survived; hatred towards those deemed responsible, compassion for those who died or are in pain. The protagonist of Jonathan Safran Foyer's fictional attempt to deal with the impact of 9/11 puts it better than any 'real' analysis could: 'right now I am feeling sadness, happiness, anger, love, guilt, joy, shame, and a little bit of humor ... My insides don't match up with my outsides' (2005: 163, 201).

Experts on terrorism and international security are not adequately equipped to understand the complex emotional dimensions of terrorist threats. Emotions are, by and large, still seen as purely private and irrational phenomena – and thus of little relevance to political analysis and public deliberations about security issues. But excluding the role of emotions from scholarly inquiries and political analysis is paradoxical, for traumatic events, such as terrorist attacks, are highly emotional phenomena. The motives and means of terrorists are usually presented in emotional terms, as 'fanatical', 'irrational' or simply 'evil'. Reactions to terrorist attacks are equally emotional. They involve dealing with the memory of death, suffering and trauma, leading to emotional calls for political action, often involving feelings of retribution that go far beyond the mere need to provide security. Political leaders do not shy away from drawing upon emotional appeals, such as nationalist rhetoric, to win support for their positions. And yet, the actual policy analyses of terrorist threats are advanced in a highly detached and rationalized manner. This has been the case during much of the Cold War and continues today (Cohn 1987; Scarry 1985). Consider, as one example among many, a recent media release by the Australian Law Reform Commission, which aims at generating public debate on the effectiveness and need for sedition laws. Its main objective is to come up with constructive policy advice by taking 'some of the emotion out of the debate' (Australian Government 2006).

The neglect of emotion in policy analysis and international relations scholarship has lead to a situation where emotions can easily be manipulated by political elites, even if this is achieved unconsciously. But this phenomena is neither surprising nor new. Numerous modern philosophers have long drawn attention to the key role that fear plays in projects of political renewal. Politicians have, indeed, always used fear to manipulate the population in the manner that served their particular interests. Thomas Hobbes even went a step further. Fear, he believed, not only leaves strong marks on public debates and policy making. It can also serve as an important source for collective political and moral foundations (Robin 2004: 4, 16, 34). Numerous scholars – before and after 9/11 – have stressed how the fear created by terror can create moral certainty and lead otherwise diverse and disagreeing constituencies to swift, universal agreements on basic principles and actions. As a result, though, the foundations of our morals are articulated mostly in negative ways, based on fear and closure, rather than on a willingness to openly discuss difficult issues and ground political positions in a positive affirmation of basic values and principles (Robin 2004: 145–6; Shklar 1984: 5, 9).

The political manipulation of fear has fostered approaches to security that fail to draw upon the possibilities of both individual and social healing. Emotions tend to be seen as something to either struggle against or work through. The result is a very narrow understanding of how security and peace are being constituted – one that fails to conceptualize emotions a source of political imagination, inspiration, caring and hope.

Applying emotional insight to the traumatic events of 9/11 would entail a fundamental rethinking of prevailing approaches to politics and security. Rather than dealing with the trauma and its breach of security primarily in militaristic terms, a process of healing would seek to use the positive opportunities opened up by the disruptive event. Identity and community would then not be constituted in the context of a discourse of good versus evil, of inside versus outside, but in a manner that highlights the need to overcome the very antagonistic oppositions and conflicts that such distinctions generate. Instead of wars of retaliation, which are unlikely to solve any of the issues at stake, a more productive approach would, for instance, consist of establishing more cross-cultural respect and new forms of collaboration, which can build empathy and trust among parties once engaged in conflict. Societies may thus be able to work through trauma in politically transformative, rather than merely restorative ways. Instead of inscribing dichotomous or even righteous forms of defining identity, this alternative would generate more accepting and empathetic configurations of community.

Processes of healing in the wake of trauma do, of course, inevitably take time. Entrenched identities cannot be uprooted over night, nor can the antagonistic political attitudes and practices that are intertwined with these identities. Reconciliation is a long term project. But traumatic events, precisely because they disrupt existing patterns of identity and community, offer unique opportunities to initiate such a long term process of healing. However, to do so scholars and political elites must have a better understanding of the emotional aspects involved in this process. Crucial here are collective efforts to draw upon the whole range of emotions, not only fear, anger and hatred, but also empathy and compassion. Rendering the latter more politically acceptable could make a crucial difference, particularly at future moments of acute political crisis, when levels of understanding, acceptance and trust can play a decisive role in determining whether conflict or peace will prevail.

Acknowledgements

This paper has emerged out of a project that was first presented at a workshop on 'Reconciliation, Politics and the Emotions' at the Monash Prato Centre, 26–28 June 2006. Thanks to the two workshop conveners, Michael Ure and Mervyn Frost. For their support and critical feedback the authors warmly thank all workshop participants. Emma would also like to acknowledge the support of the University of Queensland Graduate School Research Travel Award. Roland's work on this project was generously supported by a fellowship from the Centre for Research in the Arts, Social Sciences and Humanities at Cambridge University.

Notes

1 See, for instance, Lila Abu-Lughod and Catherine A. Lutz (eds), *Language and the Politics of Emotion* (Cambridge: Cambridge University Press, 1990); Claire Armon-Jones, *Varieties of Affect* (New York: Harvester Wheatsheaf, 1991); Jack M. Barbalet (ed.) *Emotions and Sociology* (Oxford: Blackwell, 2002); Jack M. Barbalet, *Emotion, Social Theory and Social Structure: A Macrosociological Approach* (Cambridge: Cambridge University Press, 2001); Gillian Bendelow and Simon J. Williams (eds) *Emotions and Social Life: Critical Themes and Contemporary Issues* (London: Routlege, 1998); Jon Elster, *Alchemies of the Mind: Rationality and the Emotions* (Cambridge: Cambridge University Press, 1999); Peter Goldie, *The Emotions: A Philosophical Exploration* (Oxford: Clarendon Press, 2002); Rom Harré, *The Social Construction of Emotions* (Oxford: Blackwell, 1986); Alison M. Jaggar, 'Love and Knowledge: Emotion in Feminist Epistemology', in Susan R. Bordo and Alison M. Jaggar (eds), *Gender/Body/Knowledge: Feminist Reconstructions of Being and Knowing* (New Brunswick, NJ: Rutgers University Press, 1989), pp. 145–71; Martha C. Nussbaum, *Upheavals of Thought: The Intelligence of Emotions* (Cambridge: Cambridge University Press, 2001); Stephen Leighton (ed.), *Philosophy and the Emotions* (Peterborough: Broadview Press, 2003); Chris Shilling, 'Emotions, Embodiment and the Sensation of Society', *Sociological Review*, vol. 45, no. 2, 1997, pp. 195–219; Robert C. Solomon, *Not Passions Slave: Emotions and Choice* (Oxford: Oxford University, 2003); Simon J. Williams, *Emotions and Social Theory: Corporeal Reflections on the (Ir)Rational* (London: Sage, 1991).

2 See, in particular, Ahmed, *The Cultural Politics of Emotion*; Lauren Berlant, 'The Subject of True Feeling: Pain, Privacy, Politics' in Jodi Dean (ed.), *Cultural Studies and Political Theory* (Ithaca, NY: Cornell University Press, 2000), pp. 42–312; Mabel Berezin, 'Emotions and Political Identity: Mobilizing Affection for the Polity', in James Jasper, Jeff Goodwin, Francesca Polletta (eds), *Passionate Politics: Emotion and Social Movements* (Chicago, IL: University of Chicago Press), pp. 83–98; and Mabel Berezin, 'Secure States: Towards a Political Sociology of Emotion', in Jack Barbalet (ed.), *Emotions and Sociology* (Oxford: Blackwell, 2002), pp. 33–52; Karin M. Fierke, 'Whereof We Can Speak, Thereof We Must Not Be Silent: Trauma, Political Solipsism and War', *Review of International Studies*, Vol. 30, 2004, pp. 471–91; Kate Nash, 'Cosmopolitan Political Community: Why Does It Feel So Right?', *Constellations: An International Journal of Critical and Democratic Theory*, Vol. 10,

No. 4, 2003, pp. 506–18; Thomas J. Scheff, *Bloody Revenge: Emotions, Nationalism and War* (Boulder, CO: Westview Press, 1994, and Thomas J. Scheff, 'Emotions and Identity: A Theory of Ethnic Nationalism', in Craig Calhoun (ed.), *Social Theory and the Politics of Identity* (Oxford: Blackwell, 1994), pp. 277–303.

5 International law and the state of exception

Sara E. Davies[1]

The US and its allies invaded Afghanistan on 7 October 2001 citing their inherent right to self-defence as enshrined in Article 51 of the UN Charter and supported by Resolutions 1368 (2001) and 1373 (2001).[2] In November 2001, President Bush signed a Military Order creating a framework for military commissions that could try those being detained within Afghanistan and on the borders of Pakistan for 'reasons related to the conflict' (Duffy 2005: 379; Leitzau 2005: 49). In January 2002, hundreds of people – estimates ranged from 550 to 698 detainees – had been detained and forcibly removed from Afghanistan to the US Naval Base in Guantanamo Bay (Duffy 2005: 379; Steyn 2004: 7).[3]

The conditions under which these individuals have been held has elicited concern and strong criticism.[4] Concerns over the detainees' welfare, the lack of transparent judicial proceedings and an apparent recalcitrance by the US administration to adhere to due process and the rule of law, has provoked condemnation of the US administration. For instance, in an address for the British Institute of International and Comparative Law, Lord Steyn stated that:

> At present we are not meant to know what is happening at Guantanamo Bay. But history will not be neutered. What takes place there today in the name of the United States will assuredly, in due course, be judged at the bar of informed international opinion.
>
> (Steyn 2004: 8)

The International Committee of the Red Cross (ICRC) has reported that those held in Guantanamo Bay have been 'subjected to unusually long periods of interrogation' (ICRC 2005). The interrogation techniques have included many forms of abuse and human rights violations sometimes conducted with the assistance of defence medical personnel (Clark 2006: 571). The US Department of Defense (DOD) has stated that Guantanamo is the 'only DOD strategic interrogation center and will remain useful as long as the war on terrorism is underway and new enemy combatants are captured and sent there' (United States Department of Defense 2006c: 4). Out of the 422 detainees presently being held, ten have been charged (United States Department of Defense 2006b: 1). Many still remain in solitary confinement, and are subject to regular coercive 'interrogation techniques' (Clark 2006). With the exception of these ten individuals charged (first charges were laid against four detainees in 2004), none of the remaining detainees have been charged or are able to test the legality of their detention (Steyn 2004: 10).

There have been a number of legal challenges lodged on behalf of the four originally charged for violating the laws of war (United States Department of Defense 2006b). The US Supreme Court has, thus far in 2004 and 2006, made four important judgments on the charges made against these individuals, their detention and the nature of the military commissions:

- Each individual in Guantanamo Bay has the right to challenge their detention on US soil (the right to habeas corpus).[5]
- Each detainee has the right to legal counsel and to appear before the Commission.
- The procedures of the Military Commissions set up to hear the cases of the four individuals tried for various offences must be consistent with the Uniform Code of Military Justice (UCMJ) and cannot be authorized by the President alone – the Commissions must be approved by Congress.
- The detainees have the right to claim Prisoner of War (POW) status under Common Article 3 of the Geneva Conventions.

However, in spite of these findings the detention of these individuals continues. While a number of states such as the United Kingdom has secured the release of all their citizens (all of whom were later released with no charges); other states such as Afghanistan and Pakistan have remained unable to secure the release of their detained citizens upon request or gain knowledge of the precise number of citizens detained, with the exception of circumstances where the US has let them go due to them being 'of no further use or value' to the United States Department of Defense (United States Department of Defense 2006a).

This chapter seeks to understand the legal status of the detainees at Guantanamo Bay and what their status tells us about the relationship between law and politics. In particular, this chapter will explore whether Guantanamo Bay represents a 'legal black hole', an exception to the rule of law, or a situation where the application of existing law has simply not been strong enough. This chapter will unfold in three parts. The first section will provide a brief account of how Guantanamo Bay has been commonly understood in legal terms. Establishing the legal understandings of Guantanamo Bay provides us with three possible explanations for Guantanamo Bay's legal character. All of these explanations are concerned with understanding whether Guantanamo Bay is an *exceptional* response to the threat posed by terrorism or an illegal response which requires the swift administration of law and international political pressure to bring about its end.

The second part of this chapter will then explore the case of David Hicks, the only Australian citizen to remain in confinement at Guantanamo Bay since his arrest in Afghanistan in December 2001 and detention in Guantanamo Bay since January 2002.[7] David Hicks is one of the four detainees originally charged and called to appear before the Military Commission. His case is of particular note due to the refusal of the Australian government to seek his release or even demand that the guidelines for treatment of prisoners, as set out in international humanitarian law, be applied (*Sydney Morning Herald* 2006). The focus on Hicks' case provides an illustration of the conditions that detainees face in Guantanamo Bay and will provide an effective case study for evaluating the applicability of the three legal understandings that seek to explain the legal character of Guantanamo Bay.

Finally, this chapter will address whether any of the three approaches shed light on why the detainees remain in continued detention. I make three arguments in this final section. I argue first, that there is little evidence that Guantanamo Bay is a 'legal black hole'. The US administration has not been able to isolate it from judicial reach. As evidenced by the US Supreme Court findings, there is a great amount of law that is applicable to the detainees in Guantanamo Bay. Second, Guantanamo Bay is not an exception to the US rule of law. There are limits to the derogations that the US executive can call upon to excuse itself from providing the detainees with access to due process. Again, the Supreme Court findings have been immensely significant in demonstrating that the US President will be held to account for acting under 'emergency powers', and furthermore that his powers, even under these circumstances are finite. The court also found that the US government cannot derogate from international law, arguing that the Geneva Conventions still apply even in war as complicated as the 'War on Terror'. My third argument is that legal instrumentalists have thus far appeared to be most persuasive in explaining Guantanamo Bay. However, the actions taken by the US administration since the findings of the Supreme Court does not mean that we should take comfort from this finding.

Guantanamo Bay

The existence of a territory where prisoners can be forcibly moved and then held for an undetermined amount of time without charge seems unfathomable in the twenty-first century. The progress made in the treatment of prisoners under international humanitarian law, such as the Third and Fourth Geneva Conventions which concerns the treatment of combatants and civilians (respectively) in times of war[6] appears to have been eroded by one act of a US President. In early 2002, President Bush's administration outlined why those captured and associated with al Qaeda would be (and could be) labelled as 'unlawful combatants' (Lietzau 2005). This status was, ostensibly, to remove any protections that could be afforded to them under the Third or Fourth Geneva Convention. Lietzau argues that President Bush did this because he correctly engaged with the 'the body of law applicable in armed conflict – the law of war' and that the Geneva Conventions only regulated those 'entitled to participate in hostilities' (Lietzau 2005: 45).

This use of legal means to legitimize the treatment of Guantanamo Bay detainees, while at the same time attempting to deny them legal remedy to challenge these means, has aroused many concerns. For example, despite the fact that Guantanamo Bay detainees' status as terrorists has not yet been proven in a court or tribunal, the US administration constantly refers to them as 'terrorists' and 'evil people' (The Age 2004).[8] The primary concern is how can the treatment of detainees in Guantanamo Bay be explained when the state responsible is meant to have one of the most sophisticated separation of powers model of government, which guarantees judicial independence from the legislative and executive branches of government (Slaughter 2005)? In addition, how does a country that bears a domestic rights protection bill which has inspired other states seeking to strengthen their own standing as a liberal democratic society (Koh 2005), get away with such human rights abuses?

Three appreciations of Guantanamo Bay

Attempts to understand the US administration's justification of, as well as the continued detention of prisoners in Guantanamo Bay has resulted in three predominant explanations: first, legal state of exception; second, political state of exception and third, the legalist challenge. I will introduce each approach in order to offer three ways of thinking about the case of David Hicks. In doing so, I seek to understand which approach, if any, best explains the actions of the United States administration and the consequences that may stem from the continued existence of Guantanamo Bay.

Legal state of exception

The choice of Guantanamo Bay (GB) as a facility to hold people deemed to be beyond the 'pale of law' certainly seems to support the first explanation, which holds GB to be a legal state of exception. GB is located in Cuba, but GB's territory falls under the sovereignty of the United States even though up until the US Supreme Court decision in 2004, it was excised from the reach of US judicial law (Fisher 2005: 246–7). GB was first used as an exceptional holding ground when Haitian refugees were detained in GB during the early to mid-1990s. While, no doubt, the detention of refugees was an attempt to deter others thinking of making the dangerous trip into US waters for refuge, it was also an attempt to physically isolate these individuals from the bureaucratic and legal structures of the liberal democratic state (Kaplan 2005: 840–1). GB is an attempt to make individuals physically, emotionally and legally isolated from the liberal democratic trappings that would be available in the US. There are no human rights groups nearby. The media can only access the grounds with permission. It is difficult for legal counsel to gain access and the conditions in these camps are bleak (Mori 2006). Essentially, this is a zone where the US Bill of Rights *seems* to have not reached.

The use of GB for detaining 'enemy combatants' transported from the deserts of Afghanistan and borders of Pakistan reveals two important things. First, that these people are powerless – decisions over their lives are in the hands of the US government. Second, it sustains the perception that these people have committed heinous crimes that make them far too threatening to be allowed access to the legal procedures that US citizens enjoy. The detention and treatment of GB detainees is a demonstration of the power of the US government, the threat that it perceives the state to be under and the steps that the Executive is willing to take against those who they believe threaten it. The position of the US to many thus reflects the state of exception (SOE) that Carl Schmitt wrote of in the 1960s when he argued that liberal states, like any other powerful institution, will see to deny liberty if they feel that their own survival is threatened.

Carl Schmitt, a supporter of the Nazi Party in Germany during World War II, wrote the *Nomos of the Earth* and *The Partisan* after the defeat of Nazism and in the wake of the Cold War. Both volumes argue that the liberal democratic state is not the ultimate universal provider of freedom and liberty as its advocates would argue (Scheuerman 1994; Gross 2000). Schmitt argues that liberal states were no different from totalitarian states if threatened. In such cases, liberal states abandon their 'pre-established general norms' that cover all possible situations in the face of a 'sudden, urgent, usually unforeseen events or situations that require immediate action, often without time for prior reflection and consideration' (Gross 2000: 1827). The state of emergency is denied by liberalism as a norm in 'ordinary state of affairs', but in the face of an emergency the very basis of freedom which underpins liberalism is abandoned (Gross 2000: 1828). Therefore, the 'norm' that appeared to exist prior to the exception was actually not reality. Exception, argues Schmitt, is the reality for it is at this moment that we truly know the scope of the state's powers according to law and of individuals' powerlessness. As Schmitt argues in *Political Theology*, 'the rule proves nothing; the exception proves everything: it confirms not only the rule but also its existence, which derives only from the exception' (Schmitt 1985).

In relation to GB, Schmitt's argument exemplifies how the liberal state is able to create legal exceptions to its legal norms (Scheuerman 2006). Al Qaeda, for example, fights for a cause which is not state connected or affiliated to 'normal' inter-state politics. So then, how does a liberal state make sense of an actor that fights to fulfil fundamentalist religious dogma? It doesn't. Essentially, the West has been able to create a legal system where it can justify extreme acts of violence against those who do not 'fit' the Western state system (Scheuerman 2006). For example, Scheuerman argues that the Geneva Convention calls for legal combatants to bear their weapons openly and wear uniforms to signify that they are part of a combatant force: yet, he asks, what power do these symbols really have when guerrilla fighting is being conducted in Fallujah or when insignia are invisible in the dead of the night (2006: 117). According to Schmitt, liberal states have created these types of rules so as to create legal vacuums which allow them to treat enemies with extreme violence that can be justified by reference to a legal state of exception.

Scheuerman (2006) and other supporters of Schmitt's work argue, essentially, that liberal governments create legal black holes to in order to develop power beyond the discretionary norm of a liberal society (Aron 1986; Tushnet 2005). The Bush administration argues that international laws don't apply to the terrorists found in Afghanistan, and that there are no laws that adequately deal with the potential gravity of their actions. The state of emergency compels the need for administrative action in the face of a 'legal vacuum'. A legal vacuum was caused by the refusal of the US administration to treat al Qaeda combatants as being on the same footing, or level, as their own combatants. As Scheuerman argues:

> For the Bush Administration, as for Schmitt, the weaknesses of the existing legal regime for terrorism are not simply a lamentable reminder of the limits of statutory law, or reason for reforming international law in order to make it better suited to the challenges of terrorism. It interprets the existing legal lacunae instead as evidence for the necessity of a fundamentally *norm-less* realm of decision making in which the executive possesses full discretionary authority.
>
> (Scheuerman 2006: 118)

As a result, the US administration's argument that there are no laws to deal with terrorists becomes a justification for dealing with them as the administration sees fit (Gross 2006). The executive has created a justification for the legal vacuum. The state of exception becomes legal through the executive's invocation of it. This act has led, others argue, to further consequences post 9/11. Steven Lukes for example, argues that the use of torture on detainees had led to a point where liberal democracy in the US and UK 'may not these days be in such good shape as … thought' (2005: 15). Lukes argues that the readiness in which executive branches of government agree to torture now may be permissible in circumstances we never thought possible before (2005). The brutality of 9/11 and the bombings in London in July 2005, justify the exceptional acts that liberal states such as the US and UK must take to survive (Lukes 2005).

Paul Hoffman, Chair of the International Executive Committee of Amnesty International, argues that though he disputes it, the 'war on terrorism' has been waged with the evocation that the rule of law is unable to effectively respond to the threat (hence the need to allow for new interpretations and new laws) (2004). David Luban (2005) argues that the liberal state has to label terrorism as an unlawful act of war, and thus place it beyond a typical criminal act. Labelling terrorism as just a criminal act doesn't allow the government, for example, to shoot the terrorists; rather, it forces them to provide the terrorists with due process (which makes burden of proof potentially problematic). In war, there are a range of acts that become legitimate if you treat terrorists as enemies against the state. To begin with, burden of proof is weaker in war – no need for proof beyond reasonable doubt when a soldier faces someone that they suppose is an enemy soldier. Legitimate targets are those who might harm, rather than have harmed (Luban 2005) and ultimately, detainees lack the usual rights of criminal suspects (presumption of innocence is just one example). Luban argues that GB is thus the perfect example of a hybrid war-law model that the US administration has created to fill in the void where neither war law nor criminal law is adequate to deal with the war on terror (2005: 221). Essentially, these arguments seek to demonstrate how GB correlates with Schmitt's argument that the liberal state will construct exceptions that have no legal remedy, i.e. the 'unlawful combatants' in Guantanamo Bay, in order for the state to retain ultimate authority. Schmitt argues that the norm is emergency, not order; while liberalism putatively rests on the opposite being true (Gross 2000: 1854). As a consequence, when liberalism is unable to deal with the exceptional it has to find a way to incorporate the suspension of the rule of law into law to survive.

Political state of exception

Giorgio Agamben's recent work, *The State of Exception*, also directly refers to the situation in GB. However, Agamben challenges or 'rewrites' (Minca 2005: 406) Schmitt's depiction of the state of exception (SOE), arguing that Schmitt creates a legal vacuum which paradoxically allows for the *legal justification* of violence. Agamben questions this legal vacuum and argues that Schmitt's depiction is no more than a justification for violence (2005). While Agamben doesn't doubt the existence of the exception, he believes that its existence is based on much more than excusing the violent deprivation of liberty. Rather, the key is to understand the political decisions that led to its invocation:

> In truth, the state of exception is neither external nor internal to the judicial order … The suspension of the norm does not mean its abolition, and the zone of anomie that it establishes is not (or at least claims not to be) unrelated to the juridical order. Hence, the interest of those theories that, like Schmitt's, complicates the topographical opposition into a more complex topological relation, in which the very limit of the juridical order is at issue. In any case, to understand the problem of the state of exception, one must first correctly determine its localization (or illocalization). As we will see, the conflict over the state of exception presents itself essentially as a dispute over its proper locus.
>
> (Agamben 2005: 23–4)

Agamben argues that the SOE can be a legal justification for political action because of the codification of derogation in domestic law and international law.[9] All states, when threatened with an emergency that could threaten their existence, are allowed to temporarily derogate from their ratification of international human rights treaties and domestic constitution (Humphreys 2006: 678). As a result, states can lawfully transgress human rights. The consequence of derogation, Agamben argues, is that defining when the nation is under a state of emergency becomes a 'subjective judgment' (2005: 30). Thus even though the declaration of SOE is a lawful suspension of the rule of law, it has required a political justification for determining its necessity.

Under this model of derogation, Agamben argues, the SOE has moved from its original 'state of siege' emphasis where it was only acceptable to claim emergencies in times of war to now being an acceptable declaration for democratic states when they need to 'cope with social disorder and economic crises' (Humphreys 2006: 679). Agamben shows how through the nineteenth and twentieth centuries, the

SOE has been used by the US and European states to justify extensive government powers during times of political crisis (such as economic depressions, union strikes and Lincoln's abolition of slavery) (2005). Essentially, the SOE takes on a political meaning – where the state's continued existence becomes dependent on the executive having greater powers to manage the crisis.

Agamben argues that what is crucial about SOEs is that the executive does not seek to incorporate the suspension of the law *into* law, as Schmitt argues. Rather, the SOE is sought by the executive in order to create a 'space without law' where the conduct of violence cannot be declared as lawful, but nor can it be declared as unlawful (Minca 2005). Thus Agamben is at pains to show that the SOE is not a lawful act, nor does it seek to inhabit the judicial realm: it is a zone of anomie, where the executive does not wish its actions to be subjected to the law (Agamben 2005).

The executive can enable a zone of anomie, for a time where law does not apply, because of the existence of derogation. Derogation from individual rights have been justified by democratic states through domestic and international law providing an 'escape clause' in times of 'emergencies' (Agamben 2005). States can thus legitimately declare a zone of anomie – a zone where state will not be held accountable to the rule of law – if they believe that it is a political necessity. Thus the social contract between a liberal democratic state and its citizens will be abandoned in the face of external threats that threaten the very existence of the state.

Therefore, to Agamben, Guantanamo Bay is a zone of anomie. Unlike Schmitt, Agamben does not see Guantanamo as the product of a legal vacuum that has been crafted by the executive to legitimate its actions. Rather, more frighteningly, GB represents the complete suspension of the rule of law. GB cannot be legislated into existence because there is no legislation or laws that legitimate its existence – as the Supreme Court demonstrates when it rejects the US administration's arguments. However, in spite of the judicial rejection of the GB detentions, the facility continues to exist. The continued existence of Guantanamo Bay *in spite* of the US Supreme Court findings does indicate, disturbingly, that GB is a zone created with the intent of being outside the law, where the law cannot capture and overturn the anomie.

The result, according to Agamben, is that the state of exception is a political act where, in this case, it can be justified as a necessity to preserve the rule of law and security of the society. Guantanamo Bay has become a state of necessity for the protection of American citizens, as President Bush argued when the US Supreme Court overruled the charges against the four charged in Guantanamo Bay in June 2006: 'I am not going to jeopardize the safety of American people. People have got to understand that. These people were picked up off a battlefield, and I will protect the people' (Miles 2006: 1). When statements like these are made, arguments against the necessity for this type of action only have a greater hurdle to jump. The historical right of democratic governments to use derogation in times of emergency is a subjective judgment (Agamben 2005: 30), but it nonetheless creates a political environment where arguments against the right to derogate, to challenge its necessity, have higher hurdles to jump. This is the zone of anomie that Agamben argues is Guantanamo Bay.

Legalist challenge

The legalists have paid a lot of attention to the arguments presented by Agamben and his supporters as well as the Schmittian explanations for GB's legal status. However the legalists, as their name suggests, desperately seek to bring the law back in as a challenge to both Agamben and Schmitt. They reject the argument that a 'legal black hole' exists in the case of GB and also dispute that a suspended rule of law hangs over GB (Johns 2005; Marks 2006). Rather this group draws on a combination of legal positivist rules and naturalist legal principles to argue that GB does fall within the realm of law. Principally, the legalists argue that the continued existence of GB is not due to the absence of legal norms telling us whether GB is lawful or unlawful or a derogation from the laws that exist; rather, it is because there is a political lack of will to enforce the laws as they should be enforced (Duffy 2005; Marks 2006; Johns 2005; Stewart 2006; Fletcher 2006).

The problem that the legalists have been unable to answer is that if their legal arguments cannot force the closure of Guantanamo, or at least guarantee treatment of detainees according to international humanitarian law (IHL), will it indicate a shift of legal precedent where such establishments may become legal? This could result in a situation even worse than the state of exception that Agamben or Schmitt followers envision: it could become a legal, non-exceptional, justified addition to legal and political processes across the world (Steyn 2004).

There is a large cohort of legalists that have challenged the idea that GB is an exception to the rule of law or represents a legal black hole, so I will not be able to cover all of their writings. However, a select number including Fleur Johns (2005), Elizabeth Dahlstrom (2003), Susan Marks (2006), Paul Hoffman (2004), Helen Duffy (2005), and James G. Stewart (2006) have argued, very persuasively, that we need to 'rethink Guantanamo' (Stewart 2006).

Their arguments are threefold. First, they hold that the lack of reference to international law and/or refusal to acknowledge the clarity of international humanitarian law on the matters of POWs, detention, court tribunals and torture is not an 'interpretative challenge'. The legalists argue that there is a 60 year tradition of interpreting, refining and using the laws of war to create a set of rules or principles (depending on whether you are a positivist or naturalist in your interpretation of international law) that guide states on how they should act. Indulging, they argue, in descriptions of GB as a zone of anomie or 'black hole' enables the US administration to essentially get away with illegal practices that the international community, the US included, would not abide from another state (Johns 2005; Stewart 2006).

Second, the legalists argue that the right to derogation, which Agamben speaks of, is indeed a legitimate part of international and domestic law, recognized by a number of conventions that states have ratified, including the ICCPR. However, what the legalists do not agree with is the argument that derogation has an unspecified time frame where it is up to the administration to decide when the threat is over (i.e. Greenwood 2002). This interpretation of derogation has, most notably, been neglected by the US Supreme Court in June 2006 and a number of academic interpretations of the Geneva Conventions (Fletcher 2006; Stewart 2006). Other legalists present the argument differently, stating that if the US wished to use the state of emergency argument there are legal avenues that they could take to do this while still remaining within the rule of law. Under Article 4 of the ICCPR there is a clause that allows the temporary suspension of certain rights 'in time of public emergency' (Dahlstrom 2003: 670), as Agamben earlier mentions. However, Article 4 (3) does not allow derogation from the rights to life, religion, freedom from torture, slavery and the prohibition against *ex post facto* laws, even in times of emergency. Dahlstrom does point out that Article 9 – the right to be free from arbitrary detention – is not on this list of rights and therefore if the US is seeking a temporary derogation they would be well within their legal rights to notify the UN Secretary General of their temporary suspension (2003: 670). Susan Marks (2006) argues that this refusal to follow legal convention is the result of the US administration seeking to use, as exemplified by John Yoo and Jay Bybee, another set of legal arguments that can justify their actions. Yoo and Bybee wrote the infamous 'torture memos', which took an 'aggressive approach to the war on terrorism in general and to the detention and interrogation of terrorism suspects in particular' (Wippman 2005: 22). This, argues Marks, is not the product of a legal black hole or a legal anomie, but a legal construct that international law and domestic law allows to be constituted (2006: 347).

Third, if legalists are able to create a whole set of arguments stating why GB is an illegal, inhumane breach of human rights, international humanitarian law and thus US's own domestic law (Johns 2005, Hoffman 2004 and Duffy 2005), why has GB continued to exist for five years with, all things considered, little condemnation by allied (or non allied) states (Steyn 2004)? This is the third concern of the legalists: if there are a clear set of international laws stipulating the unlawfulness and inhumanity of GB, but little attempts by states to insist the US adhere to them, is this the beginning of a new legal precedent? A division then occurs here, where the legal naturalists argue that the traditional of politics 'interfering' with law obscures how it *really* should be interpreted and adhered to (Roberts 2004; Duffy 2005; Johns 2005; Hoffman 2004); while the positivists start to look at the precedent that these interpretations of the Geneva Conventions, for example, will have on international law with little concern beyond the instrumental implications (Greenwood 2002; Dworkin 2004; Dahlstrom 2004). Greenwood (2002), for instance, argues that the US interpretation of international law is permitted because of how international law is framed and therefore as long as they remain within the bounds of customary law and a plausible legal argument, we are simply witnessing how international law develops in response to events.

So where do we go from here? Is the legalist challenge simply to bring the US back from the legal black hole or zone of anomie, or is it to understand how political choices made in the name of law account for GB's continued existence? We are left with three very different explanations for GB's political and legal status. Meanwhile, individual lives are being left in limbo behind the concrete walls of GB. I will now look at the story of David Hicks to see if we can get any closer to understanding these different explanations.

David Hicks: exception or norm?

David Matthew Hicks is an Australian citizen who has been detained at Guantanamo Bay since January 2002. David Hicks was detained by the Northern Alliance and then handed over to US custody in Afghanistan in December 2001. Hicks is allegedly a member of al Qaeda and is suspected of assisting the Taliban in the early stages of the US allied invasion into Afghanistan (Yoch Jr 2006). Hicks is one of the few detainees to be charged by the US administration on the following: first, conspiracy to commit murder, attack civilians and civilian objects and terrorism; second, attempted murder of allied soldiers; and third aiding the enemy (Martyn 2005; The Age 2004). Hicks has been charged under the Military Order that President Bush signed on 13 November 2001, and the jurisdiction of the Military Tribunal that charged him with these three offences was based on President's orders on 3 July 2003 (United States Department of Defense 2006c).

David Hicks joined the Kosovo Liberation Army (KLA) in May 1999 after, it seems, he was rejected by the Australian Defense Forces (ADF) (United States Department of Defense 2004: 1). While with the KLA, it is alleged that Hicks engaged in basic military training and fought on behalf of the Albanian Muslims. Upon his return to Australia Hicks converted to Islam and by November 1999, he had travelled to Pakistan to join Lashkar e Tayyiba (LET) or 'Army of the Righteous', which is now listed as a terrorist organization by the US (United States Department of Defense 2004: 1). Within a few months of training, Hicks with a letter of introduction from LET, went to the Afghanistan border. It is alleged that upon his arrival, Hicks attended al Qaeda terrorist training camps. His entry into Afghanistan was in January 2001 and on 9 December 2001, Hicks was arrested by the Northern Alliance and then transferred to the US custody (United States Department of Defense 2004: 2).

After a short detention in Afghanistan, Hicks was one of the first prisoners to be moved from Afghanistan to Guantanamo, he arrived at the US Naval Base on 11 January 2002 (Hovell 2005). President Bush then labelled those arrested and held in Guantanamo Bay as 'unlawful combatants' under a directive issued on 7 February 2002 (Hovell 2005). Hicks' family, meanwhile, registered his possible arrest with the Centre for Constitutional Rights and lodged a habeas petition on his behalf in federal court in Washington DC along with the families of Shafiz Rasul and Asif Iqbal from Britain (Miami Herald 2005). Eventually, the first petition filed – *Rasul v. Bush* – would be heard by the Supreme Court. Before the hearing though, Rasul and Iqbal were returned to Britain and then set free by UK authorities on 9 March 2004. On 28 June 2004, the Supreme Court found in Rasul's favour, ruling 6-3 that Guantanamo detainees can challenge their imprisonment in federal courts (Miami Herald 2005). However, on 10 June 2004, the US administration brought charges against David Hicks for prosecution before a US military commission. The military commission was the first to be used in the US since the 1940s during World War II (Martyn 2005). The commission was set up under a Presidential Order, which did not have any '*explicit* basis in legislation or other Congressional authorization' (Martyn 2005). The commission would only try non-US citizens 'who are current or former members of al Qaeda or any person that has aided or conspired to commit acts of international terrorism against the US or its interests' (Martyn 2005). This original commission had three senior military officers presiding, only one with legal experience. Standard rules for evidence applicable in US and Australian courts did not apply to this commission and only a majority vote was needed for a verdict to be reached (Martyn 2005).

Hicks' first charge was conspiracy on the grounds of contacting al Qaeda operatives 'known and unknown' that have engaged in terrorist attacks (United States Department of Defense 2004: 3). Hicks is alleged to have trained as a member of al Qaeda in a number of military camps. The charge details that Hicks, on a brief visit to Pakistan in September 2001, returned to Afghanistan after seeing the images of the World Trade Center Towers collapse on television. Upon his return, Hicks was assigned to Qandahar Airport where he and others guarded a Taliban tank – this was at the same time that the Allied forces began invasion in late October 2001 (United States Department of Defense 2004: 4–5). Within a month, Hicks had been arrested by the Northern Alliance, on his way to Konduz, Afghanistan.

For these actions, Hicks has been charged by the US Administration for conspiracy which they define as 'attacking civilians; attacking civilian objects; murder by an unprivileged belligerent; destruction of property by an unprivileged belligerent; and terrorism' (United States Department of Defense 2004: 3). It is alleged that because Hicks knowingly participated in al Qaeda's insurgency that he should be charged for being a conspirator, though no evidence has been presented that Hicks personally committed any of the crimes defined as constituting conspiracy (those listed above).

Hicks' second charge is 'attempted murder by an unprivileged belligerent' (United States Department of Defense 2004: 5). Under this charge Hicks, as a member of al Qaeda who was in Afghanistan

> between on or about September 11, 2001 and December 1, 2001 as a perpetrator, co-conspirator, member of an enterprise of persons who shared a common criminal purpose, an aider or abettor, or some combination thereof, attempted to murder diverse persons by directing small arms fire, explosives, and other means intended to kill American, British, Canadian, Australian, Afghan and other Coalition forces, while he [Hicks] did not enjoy combatant immunity and such conduct taking place in the context of and associated with armed conflict.
>
> (United States Department of Defense 2004: 5)

Hicks' final charge is 'aiding the enemy'. The content of this charge is that due to his presence in Afghanistan 'between on or about January 1, 2001 and

December 1, 2001, intentionally aided the enemy, to wit: al Qaida and the Taliban' (United States Department of Defense 2004: 5) and participated in armed conflict. Hicks' military appointed lawyer, Major Michael Dan Mori and his civilian legal team have both strongly denied the lawfulness of these charges and expressed concern about the overt political tone dominating their client's treatment (Wilkinson and Pearlmann 2004). Major Mori has repeatedly raised the fact that states such as Britain, Yemen and France have secured their citizens' release from Guantanamo Bay, while Hicks remained in detention for two years without charge and then the grounds on which he was charged, they allege, are spurious. In a hearing before the US District Court of the District of Columbia, Hicks' legal team argued that:

> At no time did Hicks engage in any criminal or terrorist conduct. Nor did he kill, injure, fire upon, or direct fire upon, any U.S. or Coalition Forces, or the Northern Alliance forces initially responsible for his seizure. Nor did he attempt any such conduct. He did not at any time commit any criminal violations, or any violations of the law of war. Nor did he ever enter into any agreement with anyone to do so.
>
> (Martyn 2005)

Despite pleas from Hicks' defence counsel, his family and all of the Australian States and Territories Attorney-Generals, the Commonwealth government repeatedly refused to seek the return of Hicks to Australia. The Australian government's recalcitrance is believed to be based on the fact that Hicks cannot be charged with any offence in Australia (McNally 2004; Coorey 2006). This would result in Hicks' immediate release and the Australian government does not wish to let an individual associated with al Qaeda not face charges (*Sydney Morning Herald* 2006). The reason for the belief that Hicks cannot be charged are as follows. First, Hicks was literally on the other side of Afghanistan when the allied troops invaded. Therefore, the second charge against Hicks: 'attempted murder of allied soldiers' is physically impossible. Hicks only ever encountered the Northern Alliance during the period of allied invasion, which led to his arrest before being turned over to the US troops in early December 2001 (Mori 2006).

Hicks is also charged with conspiracy on the grounds of contacting al Qaeda operatives 'known and unknown' that have engaged in terrorist attacks. As will be discussed in the *Hamdan v. Rumsfeld* case, the US Supreme Court found that under the laws of war (which is what these individuals must be tried under), there is no legal precedent for including conspiracy (Fletcher 2006). Therefore, the charge of conspiracy has been deemed by the Supreme Court as being unlawful and there is no reason to suspect that a similar finding wouldn't be made in Australian courts (Rothwell 2006).

Finally, the armed belligerent charge is extremely contentious. The 2006 Supreme Court ruling (Supreme Court of the United States (2006): hereafter 548 US 2006) found that combatants such as Hicks are entitled to a trial based on the laws of the country that they are detained in and furthermore, that their status as combatants should also be evaluated. Common Article 3 of the Geneva Convention recognizes conflicts may apply in cases where the enemy is not a signatory to the Geneva Convention and that in these circumstances, those arrested still should be treated under the general provisions of the Convention (Rothwell 2006). In essence, this also removes the validity of the 'armed belligerent charge' because, technically, there cannot be a law *against* being a soldier; or in times of war, firing your rifle when another combatant is firing theirs at you (Mori 2006).

The likelihood that Hicks could not be charged with any crime is politically unpalatable to the Australian government. This has resulted in their efforts being limited to ensuring that Hicks has a 'speedy trial' and that he does not face the death penalty (Hibbitts 2006; O'Malley 2006). Unsurprisingly, Hicks has pleaded 'not guilty' to all three charges and his legal counsel has repeatedly expressed strong reservations about the charges, the military commissions and the treatment of Hicks in detention (McNally 2004; *Sydney Morning Herald* 2006; Martyn 2005; Hibbitts 2006; Mori 2006). However, the Australian government and the US administration have criticized his legal counsel for advising their client to enter this plea, arguing that this will only create 'unnecessary delays' (Downer 2005a). For example, Major Mori has sought stays on his client's behalf while fellow detainees such as *Rasul v. Bush* (US Supreme Court 2004) and Hamdan (US Supreme Court 2006) tested the validity of the charges, their status as unlawful combatants and the Military Commission itself. Despite criticism from the Australian government, Major Mori's actions were supported by US District Judge, Colleen Kollar-Kotelly. Judge Kollar-Kotelly ruled on 14 November 2005 that until the *Hamdan v. Rumsfeld* case is decided on, the military commission trying Hicks must not resume (Miami Herald 2005). This, argues Hicks' defence counsel, reveals how important these cases are and the necessity for their legal validity to be established before Hicks is personally submitted to these proceedings (Mori 2006).

The result of *Hamdan v. Rumsfeld*, decided on 29 June 2006 was crucial for David Hicks. The Supreme Court found (5-3) that Salim Ahmed Hamden, a 35-year-old citizen of Yemen and one of the four charged with war crimes, could not be subjected to the 'executive power' (Fletcher 2006: 443) of the United States administration. Hamdan was Bin Laden's personal driver for five years up to 9/11. Upon his arrest he was sent to Guantanamo Bay and deemed eligible for trial by military commission a year later. Another year after this, Hamdan was charged with 'conspiracy ... offenses triable by military commission' (548 US 2006: 1).

The three findings made in the Hamdan case by the Supreme Court was a crucial outcome for Hicks. First, the Supreme Court found that there were significant procedural defects in the composition of the Military Tribunal itself that *violated international law* (Fletcher 2006: 444). The military commission, argued the Supreme Court, was not 'expressly authorized by any congressional act' (548 US 2006: 3). There is no legal precedent, the court argued, for the President to 'invoke military commissions whenever he deems them necessary' (548 US 2006: 3). The President must comply with the law of war and thus require congressional authorization – which he did not obtain prior to setting up the tribunal.

In its composition, the military tribunal was also found to breach the United States Uniform Military Code of Justice (UMCJ) and the 1949 Geneva Conventions (548 US 2006: 4). The commission's procedures allow the accused and his counsel to be excluded from learning of, or obtaining, evidence presented during the proceedings by the prosecution. Essentially, all evidence gathered against an individual could be 'closed'. The court ruled that the present commissions would result in the 'denial of a full and fair trial' (548 US 2006: 4). In referring to the rules stated under UMCJ (particularly Article 36), the court argued that the present composition of the commission meant that Hamden's commission trial (and thus Hicks') was 'illegal' (548 US 2006: 5). The court further argued that if the commission's procedures continued it would also 'violate the Geneva Conventions' (548 US 2006: 6).

This is the second crucial finding made by the US Supreme Court – that the Geneva Conventions *do* apply to the detainees held in Guantanamo Bay. The US government had repeatedly attempted to deny that the Geneva Conventions applied in this case because (a) they are not judicially enforceable and (b) Hamdan was not entitled to their protection as an enemy combatant (548 US 2006: 6). Both arguments, the Supreme Court found, were not persuasive. First, the Geneva Conventions are 'indisputably part of the law of war' and under domestic law, compliance with the Conventions is a condition under UCMJ Article 21 (548 US 2006: 7). On the second point raised by the US government, the court agreed that al Qaeda is not a signatory to the Conventions and that it could be argued that the US conflict with al Qaeda was 'distinct from the war with signatory Afghanistan' (548 US 2006: 6). However, this was not the matter that needed to be determined by the court (548 US 2006: 6). The US Supreme Court argued instead that one provision of the Geneva Conventions applies regardless of whether the conflict is between signatories or not. This provision is Common Article 3, which is included in all four Conventions and 'affords some minimal protection, falling short of full protection under the Conventions, to individuals associated with neither a signatory nor even a non-signatory who are involved in a conflict "in the territory of" a signatory' (548 US 2006: 6–7). Article 3 also calls for a 'regularly constituted court', which is understood to mean a military court established 'in accordance with the laws and procedures already in force in a country' (548 US 2006: 7). In the US, military courts are established by congressional statute and thus the President's military commissions not only breached domestic law, but also the Geneva Conventions (548 US 2006: 7).

In addressing the conspiracy charge, the court argued that such a charge precluded the military commissions, which were set up only to prosecute laws of war. Conspiracy is a common law charge and thus it cannot be considered a violation under the law of war (Fletcher 2006). The crime does not appear in the Geneva Conventions or The Hague Conventions and the court noted that it was 'pointedly rejected' as a violation in the International Military Tribunal at Nuremburg (548 US 2006: 8). Essentially, the crime of conspiracy emphasizes 'police intervention before criminal plans develop into harmful activity' (Fletcher 2006: 446). There is no such possibility under international law for sovereigns to be able to function in this manner and therefore the conspiracy charge cannot apply to combatants captured during war. The Supreme Court upheld the argument presented on the behalf of Hamdan and found that conspiracy is 'not triable by law-of-war military commission' (548 US 2006: 7). In particular, the crime of 9/11 cannot be associated with the charges laid against Hamdan or others detained in Guantanamo Bay – only their engagement in the theatre of war and offences committed during the war could be heard by the military commission (548 US 2006: 7).

Finally, the Supreme Court found that individuals could not be held indefinitely in a detention facility such as Guantanamo Bay. The Constitution 'permits indefinite detention only in narrow circumstances and based upon rigorous procedural safeguards – precisely the opposite of the CSRT's [Combatant Status Review Tribunal] sweeping definition of "enemy combatant" and woefully inadequate fact-finding process' (548 US 2006: 4–5).[10] This finding was after the Supreme Court had already found (6-3) in *Rasul v. Bush* in 2004 that Guantanamo Bay detainees had the right to challenge their captivity and plead as combatants under the Geneva Conventions (Miami Herald 2005).

After the US Supreme Court findings in late June 2006, the US President sought to pass a Military Commission Act (MCA) through Congress which would meet the Supreme Court's demand for military commissions to be set up under a congressional statute (Miles 2006).[11] However, the contents of this Act have also proven controversial (AIA 2006). The Act awards the commission with the right to determine combatant status; to charge individuals associated with terrorist organizations or conspiracy; any evidence obtained by the prosecution does not need to be handed over to the defence; and the composition of those presiding over the commissioner can be determined at the President and Secretary of Defense's discretion (Rothwell 2006; AIA 2006; Pantesco 2006). Essentially, the Act attempts to legislate what the US Supreme Court argued was not in accordance with existing rule of law. The key test, as the Hamdan and Hicks lawyers are already preparing to argue, is whether instituting these acts as law will still breach the scope of Presidential and Congressional authority according to UMCJ and the Geneva Conventions.

Where to from here?

The preceding discussion reveals three key points in relation to GB's legal status and continued existence. First, each of the charges laid against the four detainees originally charged have, under the *Hamdan v. Rumsfeld* findings, been ruled as unlawful. In addition, the proceedings under which these charges were laid and the Presidential authority for the commissions were all declared to be unlawful according to US rule of law, the UMCJ and the Geneva Conventions. The US Supreme Court findings thus challenge the argument of advocates of Carl Schmitt that Guantanamo Bay represents a 'legal black hole'. The Schmitt argument relies upon the two key claims: first, that the judicial branch of government will adopt and even promote legally dubious practices in order to appease the executive; and second, that the 'legal black hole' that evolves from such practices will be seen as justified when measured against the threat. What the last five years of Guantanamo Bay has demonstrated is that the highest judicial branch of government, the US Supreme Court, has not sought to ratify the US President or his executive powers as being beyond legal reproach. Rather, the US Supreme Court in its June 2006 findings on *Hamdan v. Rusmfeld*, disagreed with the US President's justification for the lack of uniform procedures in the handling of Hamdan's trial compared with other court-martials. Justice Stevens, who delivered the opinion of the court, stated:

> [T]he 'practicability' determination that the President has made is insufficient to justify variances from the procedures governing courts-martial ... The absence of any showing of impracticability is particularly disturbing when considered in light of the clear and admitted failure to apply one of the most fundamental protections afforded not just by the Manual for Courts-Martial but also by the UCMJ itself.
>
> (548 US 2006: 5)

This finding was in addition to the same court's finding two years before, where it found that all detainees in Guantanamo Bay had the right to petition for *habeas corpus* in federal courts. Essentially, the court denied that the President had powers in *any circumstances* to remove an essential right such as *habeas corpus* from particular persons (Dworkin 2004: 5).

In the case of Hicks, whose charges were dropped in the wake of *Hamdan v. Rumsfeld*, we see that his conditions of detention are not beyond applicable law. There are a clear set of rights and legal processes that Hicks has been denied; and this indicates not a failure of the law *per se*, but the failure of politics as intimated by Antonio Agamben. However, even this argument needs to be reconsidered in light of the important role that *international* law has played in sustaining the case that the continued detention of these individuals in Guantanamo Bay is unlawful.

Antonio Agamben has argued that the right of derogation permits liberal states to depart from the rule of law when survival of the state is threatened. The permission for states to claim 'exceptional' circumstances which enables a 'hold' on the application of the rule of law and international law (particularly in the area of human rights) leads to *necessitas legem non habet* (necessity has no law) (Agamben 2005: 24). The necessity is the event or occurrence that threatens the existence of the state and this necessity, Agamben argues, allows states to legitimately declare a zone of anomie. Anomie is an area where, in instances of political necessity, the state will not be held accountable to the rule of law. Agamben has likened the zone of anomie, as shown above, to Guantanamo Bay. However, derogation from the law by a state requires that the judiciary accepts this derogation and that existing international laws applicable to the treatment and detention of individuals can be derogated. However, as we see in the case of

Guantanamo Bay, the derogation argument has been refuted by the US Supreme Court.

The Supreme Court is uniquely positioned in that it holds the US government accountable to the rule of law and thus the court's acquiescence on the derogation argument is crucial for lending legitimacy to the government's actions (Fisher 2005; Slaughter 2005). However, the US Supreme Court has found that while the US government's claim that the individuals held in GB may constitute a serious threat to the state and that the US President is entitled to claim a 'state of war' against Al Qaeda, this makes the application of the Geneva Conventions all the more important in the case of Guantanamo Bay.

First, the reference and use of international law, i.e. Geneva Conventions, by the US Supreme Court needs to be noted. There has been a long supported view that the US Supreme Court has a history of reluctantly applying international law to domestic cases because, previous court judges have argued, the supremacy of domestic law is vindicated by democratic processes (Steyn 2004; Slaughter 2005). However, there has been an increasing move by members of the court to refer to and utilize international law jurisprudence (Slaughter 2005). The cases that the US Supreme Court has presided over in the matter of Guantanamo Bay have been landmark cases. This is not just because the court has sought to apply international law in the case of foreigners being detained; but also in the cases of American citizens that have been detained in GB (Dworkin 2004). Unlike Agamben's argument, the US Supreme Court found that derogation to certain laws does not have unlimited application. The US Supreme Court found, in support of many legalist advocates, that the Geneva Conventions did apply. The court rejected the government's allegations that the Conventions were not judicially enforceable, or that Hamdan was not entitled to their protections (548 US 2006: 6). The court found that the Geneva Conventions were in fact judicially enforceable because the Geneva Conventions are 'indisputably part of the law of war' (548 US 2006: 6) and also part of the domestic UCMJ; and in neither case was derogation allowed at the level that the President was requesting.

Second, the court also rejected the government's argument that the Geneva Conventions did not apply to Hamdan because, like Hicks, he was a member of al Qaeda (which is not a signatory to the Convention) and that the conflict itself was distinct from those defined in the Conventions (548 US 2006: 6). While the court avoided arguing whether al Qaeda and the conflict itself fell under the Geneva Convention; what it found was even more important when considering the derogation argument. Justice Stevens stated that:

> [T]he Court need not decide the merits of this argument [above] because there is at least one provision of the Geneva Conventions that applies here even if the relevant conflict is not between signatories. Common Article 3, which appears in all four Conventions, provides that, in a 'conflict not of an international character occurring in the territory of one of the High Contracting Parties [i.e., signatories], each Party to the conflict shall be bound to apply, as a minimum', certain provisions protecting '[p]ersons

... placed hors de combat by ... detention', including a prohibition on 'the passing of sentences ...without previous judgment ... by a regularly constituted court affording all the judicial guarantees ... recognized as indispensable by civilized peoples'.

(548 US 2006: 6)

Thus the Supreme Court argued that any reason *not* to apply Common Article 3 to Hamdan, Hicks and others in Guantanamo Bay would be *erroneous* (548 US 2006: 6). This is because Common Article 3 is precisely about providing minimum protection for those cases where the derogation argument may attempted. This understanding by the US Supreme Court of Common Article 3 and its applicability to the detainees in Guantanamo Bay is crucial because it reveals that international law is not an instrument that states can place outside their judicial system in times of emergency. As Justice Stevens states: '[E]ven assuming that Hamdan is a dangerous individual who would cause great harm or death to innocent civilians given the opportunity, the Executive nevertheless must comply with the prevailing rule of law in undertaking to try him and subject him to criminal punishment' (548 US 2006: 6). When considering Agamben's argument, the importance of this statement cannot be overstated. Essentially, the judiciary is not only holding the President to account for the processes by which he declared the detentions in GB lawful, they are also refuting the state of emergency claim that the President is using to justify the detention practices. The Supreme Court has essentially said that (a) no derogation from domestic law or international law, which frames law of war and court martial proceedings, is allowed and (b) no emergency is great enough for the Executive branch of government to claim zone of anomie – a zone where the rule of law does not apply.

However, even though we can see that the legal black hole and zone of anomie descriptions of Guantanamo Bay are not entirely accurate, we need to be cautious in agreeing with the legalist case. The legalists assume that if only the law was properly applied the situation in Guantanamo Bay would change or even end. Yet what has really changed through these court findings? We can point to positive developments such as the law being 'restored' to Guantanamo Bay through the detainees having a Supreme Court declared right to challenge their imprisonment and denial of access to domestic courts. The judicial branch has not been subsumed by the emergency itself, in that they have referred to the invalidity of the US President's actions in spite of the emergency and the need to still uphold international laws such as the Geneva Conventions. While these are important developments, approximately 430 individuals still remain in Guantanamo Bay. David Hicks still remains in solitary confinement, despite cooperating with authorities, and isn't permitted regular access to legal counsel or consular officials (Hibbitts 2006; Rothwell 2006).

While the legalists are able to argue that the US government has not successfully constructed Guantanamo Bay as a legal black hole or zone of anomie, do we need to see the government change its actions before we can take comfort from the court's findings? The detainees in Guantanamo Bay still remain in limbo despite the court ruling that their status, legal access and court proceedings need to be changed according to the UCMJ and Geneva Conventions. The reaction of the US government has been simply to remove the processes further away from the realm of the court by legislating the illegalities away (Miles 2006; Garamone 2006). This is best exemplified by the US administration's success in having both houses of Congress pass the MCA – Military Commissions Act – on 16 September 2006. The MCA seeks to strip the US courts of jurisdiction to consider habeas corpus appeals from any foreign national held in US custody; defines any individual held in US custody as an enemy combatant; while section 948(b) prohibits detainees from invoking their rights under the Geneva Conventions; and the prosecution is allowed to bring evidence to the court that was obtained under torture, with the defence counsel denied access to any information deemed as 'classified' (AIA 2006: 2; Mori 2006).

The government has essentially sought to continue their detention by creating laws that will inevitably face federal court challenges in another five or so years (Fletcher 2006: 446). The response of the US government to the Supreme Court findings has thus led to two significant outcomes. The first is that while the victory for international law has been a 'win' in the short term, it could establish a longer term loss. What is the point of referring to the Geneva Conventions in landmark decisions if the Executive continues to refuse its applicability? Do the efforts by the US government, now passed by Congress, to remove the right of these individuals to access the Geneva Conventions reflect a win for the Supreme Court's findings? These political acts do bear some consideration for Schmitt's argument – that the political will to power consumes everything, even the rule of law, when a state feels threatened.

The second concern with the current state of ambiguity is the political grounds on which David Hicks and other detainees in GB are held. The justifications are overwhelmingly political. David Hicks and his fellow detainees are now subject to MCA of 2006, which 'will help secure this country, and it sends a clear message: This nation is patient and decent and fair, and will never back down from the threats to our freedom' (White House 2006a). Ergo, even if Hicks' imprisonment is not legal, it still feels right for many US citizens and Australians.[12] As demonstrated by the fact that the only request Australia's Prime Minister and Commonwealth Attorney General have made is that Hicks trial resume as soon as possible (O'Malley 2006; Pantesco 2006; ABC 2006). That the findings of the Supreme Court have not led to Australia's demands for Hicks' release is evidence of the political necessity that Hicks continued detention has become. It is at this point that Agamben's warnings come into play: necessity has no law. Hicks is a threat that must be contained.

State leaders now refer to doing what is right, rather than what is lawful. Releasing David Hicks would be a 'victory' for the terrorists (White House 2006a). Releasing Hicks would do nothing for democracy, but threaten its very foundations (White House 2006a). These types of statements cast a shadow on the legalists' adherence to law. It reminds us that there is no opposition between law and politics (Koskenniemi 2005: 613).

So where to from here? We have learnt thus far, that GB cannot be completely explained by the Schmittian legal state of exception or Agamben political state of exception. The legalist interpretation of GB has been supported by the US Supreme Court rulings. But we cannot take comfort from this fact. The legalist faith that just implementing the law will provide the answer has fallen short of producing the expected outcome because, as this chapter has shown: law is politics. Therefore, even though the legalist explanation has come closest to explaining GB's existence to date – it has not led to a significant change of conditions for those in Guantanamo Bay. The US administration has, since the court ruling, sought through Congress to legislate away the illegalities that the Supreme Court found. The legal status of David Hicks and other detainees in Guantanamo Bay has fallen now into a new state of limbo. This period will be most crucial for testing core liberal values and thus this time, the stakes for legalists will be much higher than for the advocates of Schmitt or Agamben.

Notes

1 Since this chapter was written, David Hicks pleaded guilty to the lesser charge of providing material support to terrorism and received a short sentence which he is serving in Australia. He will be released on 31 December 2007.
2 There is debate about the claim that Resolutions 1368 and 1373 supported the US invasion into Afghanistan. Compare Greenwood (2002) against Megret (2002).
3 The US Department of Defense reported in a document dated 4 March 2005, that Joint Task Force Guantanamo Bay held 550 'enemy combatants' in custody (US DOD 2005a: 1). In a defence news report dated 17 October 2006, it was reported that 440 detainees remained in custody at Guantanamo Bay (Garamone 2006: 1). A report on 16 October 2006 announced that 'approximately 340 detainees have departed Guantanamo'; and a further 435 detainees remained in custody in Guantanamo (US DOD 2006a: 1). This report also states that approximately 110 detainees are eligible for transfer; with their departure pending on an agreement between the US and other nations. On 17 December 2006, 18 detainees were returned to Afghanistan. This brings the total remaining in Guantanamo Bay to either to 417 or 422 detainees, depending on the October figures.
4 Peter A. Clark (2006) details the level of concern raised about the health and psychological well being of detainees, citing the documentation of abuses against them. Helen Duffy also details the international responses as being extremely strong in their condemnation of Guantanamo Bay. She refers to statements from the ICRC, the UN High Commissioner for Human Rights and the Working Group on Arbitrary Detention; as well as the UK Parliament lodging an amicus brief with the US Supreme Court (Duffy 2005: 434–7).
5 The US administration originally tried to argue that Guantanamo Bay was beyond US Sovereign Territory for judicial hearings, see *Rasul v. Bush* 2004.
6 The second Australian, Mandoob Habib was arrested on the borders of Pakistan in the same time period and held at Guantanamo Bay until his release in January 2005. Mr Habib was released without explanation after two years and nine months spent in detention (*Sydney Morning Herald* 2005).
7 There has been great debate about whether the 'War on Terror' constitutes an actual war under international law. The detainees held in Guantanamo Bay were captured while the US was at war with Afghanistan. The question that follows from this is whether the continued holding of the detainees is justified now that Afghanistan has

been returned to domestic authority; nor is there any knowledge as to when the 'War on Terror' will end or if it is defined as a War that justifies continued detention of prisoners under the Geneva Conventions. (Greenwood 2002; Dworkin 2005; Wippman 2005; McAlea 2004; Stewart 2006).

8 President Bush said in response that to the Supreme Court ruling on *Hamdan v. Rumsfeld* that it 'won't cause killers to be put out on the street' (Miles 2006: 1). Lieutenant Colonel Judge Advocate Michael Newton, assigned to the US Military Academy at West Point, has argued that those who are in US custody are terrorists and the 'concept of 'unlawful combatants' is merely a rhetorical description. It does not imply that terrorists are entitled to any of the rights accorded to 'combatants' under the law of war (Newton 2005: 86).

9 This is contested by many, and I return to it later in the chapter.

10 CSRT was set up to investigate and charge the four Guantanamo Bay detainees. The *Rasul v. Bush* finding led to the Pentagon creating the CSRT, where a panel of military officers reviewed each detainee's enemy combatant status. The CSRT was declared unlawful by the Supreme Court in 2006 (Hafetz 2006: 2).

11 The MCA was passed by Congress on 16 September 2006 and passed into force on 17 October 2006.

12 However, it must be noted that there has been support for Hicks within Australia. Australia's state and territory governments signed the Freemantle Declaration in October 2006, which calls for David Hicks to be returned home. On 7 December 2006, four Commonwealth Parliamentarians filed a case calling for Hicks' return to Australia (ABC 2006). Rallies for David Hicks were held in a number of cities around Australia on 9 December 2006 (ABC 2006). The Hicks legal team has also lodged papers with the Federal Court in December 2006, calling for the Government to ask the US Administration for the release of Hicks because of a Commonwealth Constitutional duty to protect him (Coorey 2006).

6 New thinking in the just war tradition

Theorizing the war on terror

Cian O'Driscoll

The present age, defined by the war on terror, has been characterized by President Bush as a time of 'chaos and constant alarm' (Bush 2003b). It might also be described as a time of flux or change. Indeed, some commentators have suggested that the current period reflects a great degree of 'uncertainty' and 'disequilibrium' (Clark 2005: 224–80; Hurrell 2002). In the aftermath of 11 September 2001, they argue, a whole series of truths, conventions, and practices, previously taken for granted, have been called into question. This is certainly evident with respect to the just war tradition. The right of states to wage war in certain circumstances has been subject to concerted scrutiny as theorists and interested observers have examined whether received doctrine should be retained unaltered, scrapped, or modified to fit today's security environment. This chapter will argue that there is, at present, a move afoot within the just war tradition towards re-casting the idea of the just war along more morally expansive lines which extol the imperatives of justice, responsibility, judgement, and struggle-against-evil. This is more in tune with classical articulations of the *jus ad bellum* than with the legalist approach to war dominant in the twentieth century. This chapter further contends that this move is echoed in the public rhetoric of state leaders today and is potentially very consequential: at the same time as it fosters a broader right to war, this expansion sets the possibility of restraint in war, the *jus in bello*, on a precarious footing. This is surely something to be guarded against lest we allow war to resume the semblance of 'monstrous barbarity' and riotous fury that Grotius warned against in his 1625 masterpiece, *The Rights of War and Peace* (2005: 106).

Theorizing the war on terror: the current state of the art

Contemporary just war literature certainly supports a rather broad-based, expansive approach to the *jus ad bellum*. This tendency is reflected, for example, in recent landmark works by Jean Bethke Elshtain (2004), James Turner Johnson (2005), and Oliver O'Donovan (2003) – three of today's most prominent and influential just war theorists.[1] All three are concerned to re-visit and re-examine the state of the just war question in light of the on-going war on terror. Their offerings provide, perhaps, the best indication of any new developments taking place within the contemporary just war tradition. It is to an analysis of these works that I turn now, with a view to highlighting the trends and developments that they suggest.

Jean Bethke Elshtain's *Just War Against Terror*, first published in 2003 (and re-published in 2004), aroused a storm of controversy upon its launch.[2] Many of Elshtain's peers in the academy were critical of her apparent acquiescence to the demands of US power, branding her an apologist for the Bush administration. While there is certainly much to consider when it comes to Elshtain's vociferous support for the war on terror, this chapter is concerned instead with the vision of the just war tradition that she presents in this book. The first thing to say in this respect is that Elshtain sets her stall out in Augustinian terms. Indeed, her approach to the just war tradition is heavily influenced by the fourth-century writings of St Augustine, Bishop of Hippo. It is his elaboration of the notion of *Tranquillitas Ordinas* (equivalent to the modern notion of a limited civic peace) and the burden of order that provides the tradition's point of departure, and most visible landmark, according to Elshtain (1992: 323–4).

> When citizens evoke justice [in relation to war], they tap into the complex Western tradition called 'just war'. The origins of this tradition are usually traced from St Augustine's fourth-century masterwork, *The City of God*. In that massive text, Augustine grapples with how best to think about force and coercion in light of the fact that the Christian saviour was heralded as the Prince of Peace by angels proclaiming 'peace on earth and goodwill' to all peoples.
>
> (2004: 50)

Augustine's political theology, then, provides the point of departure for Elshtain's treatment of the just war tradition.

According to Elshtain, Augustine's thoughts on these matters provide the genesis of the just war tradition, framing subsequent centuries of theorizing on the justice of war in the quotidien world. It identifies the human condition with the problematic of the proper relationship between force, order, justice, and peace, and suggests the *Tranquillitas Ordinas*, rather than utopian idealism, as the proper standard for human conduct. Order of a limited and partial nature is posited as the condition for civic life, and governments are charged with the responsibility for its preservation (2004: 49). Thus Elshtain claims: 'The presupposition of just war thinking is that war can sometimes be an instrument of justice; that war can help to put right a massive injustice or restore a right order where there is disorder, including those disorders that ... call themselves "peace"' (2004: 50). The primary responsibility of government, then, is the same today as it was in the days of Rome: it is to provide for basic security and ordinary civic peace – or, in Elshtain's words, derived from Augustine, to uphold the *Tranquillitas Ordinas*. This leads to a recognition of four possible just causes for war: punishment, re-claiming something wrongly taken, defence-against-aggression, and the protection of the innocent.

In a revealing move Elshtain also delves into the theological origins of Augustine's just war thought by drawing on the Pauline refrain that the prince is the minister of God in support of her claim that the act of governing is a godly vocation. In Elshtain's words, the duty of government is a 'solemn responsibility for which there is a divine warrant' (Elshtain at The Pew Forum 2002). This charge may sometimes extend even to the punishment of wrongdoers by means of armed force: 'St. Paul claims that earthly dominion has been established to serve God and to benefit all human beings. It is the rightful authority of earthly kings and kingdoms to punish wrongdoers' (2004: 52). Indeed, so far as Elshtain is concerned, the Pauline refrain, and the Christian tradition of which it is a part, informs us that 'government is instituted by God'. This does not mean that 'every government and every government official is godly, but rather that he or she is charged with a solemn responsibility for which there is a divine warrant' (Elshtain 2002: 64). In line with this, the just war tradition 'offers a way to exercise that responsibility'.

James Turner Johnson's *The War to Oust Saddam Hussein*, published in 2005, is hardly less forthright in tone (2005). Writing as a self-styled 'liberal hawk', Johnson sets out to re-state the just war tradition in order that it might aid us in posing the correct questions as we struggle to make sense of the rights and wrongs of the war on terror (Johnson 2006: 135). Johnson is concerned that the just war tradition as we know it today is an impoverished imitation of its proper form. Corrupted by an over-wheening strain of pacifism and a (deviant) proclivity to emphasize consequentialist over deontological reasoning, the just war tradition today resembles something approximating the *jus contra bellum*, as described by Paul Ramsey. Put simply, it assumes as its starting point a 'presumption against war' and conveys a thoroughgoing scepticism regarding the utility (and therefore morality) of force in general (2005: 26–32). It is Johnson's aim to correct what he sees as this perversion of the just war tradition, and to provide a template for future just war analysis that is more faithful to the tradition as he understands it.

Johnson is especially keen to dispel the idea that there is a presumption against war at the core of the just war tradition. He is, he writes, highly 'critical of the concept that the just war idea begins with a presumption against war ... and that the function of the just war criteria is to override this general negative presumption. To think of the just war idea this way makes it over into something very different from what it properly is' (2005: 34). Indeed, in place of an unfounded presumption against war, Johnson suggests that a 'presumption against injustice', lies at the heart of just war reasoning (Johnson 1999: 38). A faithful reading of the tradition, he contends, is cognizant of the limits of the existing order and always mindful of the injustices it conceals. It accepts that it is sometimes necessary and proper to employ force against the status quo so that a more just order may be achieved. Viewed in this way, war is not perceived as an intrinsically immoral exercise, or even just the ugliest of things; instead it is an instrument of justice. In Johnson's words:

It takes its moral character from who uses it, from the reasons used to justify
it, and from the intention with which it is used. (…) Just war tradition has to
do with defining the possible good use of force, not finding exceptional cases
when it is possible to use something inherently evil (force) for the purpose
of good.

(Johnson 2005: 36)

This instrumental understanding of the use of force produces a broader reading
of the right to war; it supposes an interventionist ethic in place of a *jus contra
bellum*. Rather than starting with the presumption that the use of force is itself
morally problematic, this concept of the just war is centred upon the responsible
use of force directed against wrongdoing and injustice. The just war tradition
properly understood, Johnson concludes, is all about 'the use of the authority
and force of the rightly ordered political community (…) to *prevent, punish, and
rectify injustice*' (Johnson 1996: 30).

Johnson shares with Elshtain, then, an appreciation that force may be employed
as a 'servant of justice' (Elshtain 2004: 57). However, he devotes more time than
Elshtain to discussing the matter of restraint in war – that is, the preserve of *jus
in bello*. In particular, he re-asserts the imperatives of non-combatant immunity
and proportionality in the conduct of war, but perceives the American way of war
(driven by the so-called revolution in military affairs) as working in synchrony
with these moral requirements.

Oliver O'Donovan's latest book, *The Just War Revisited,* purports to re-examine
the just war tradition in the wake of the tragedy of 11 September 2001. Building
upon a neo-scholastic foundation, he attempts to re-cast the idea of the just war
as a 'praxis of judgment', essentially an updating of the Pauline idea that the
prince must act as the minister of God to execute His wrath upon the evildoers
(O'Donovan 2003: 13). In this regard, he is on the same page as Elshtain. He
states that any account of the just war must flow from the central proposal that
armed conflict is to be 're-conceived as an extra-ordinary extension of ordinary
acts of judgment' (16). War, on this view, is an extension into the international
sphere of governmental responsibility for the maintenance of law and order. As
such it ought to reflect the very same processes and principles that are enacted
on a daily basis in courtrooms and magistrate's offices across the land. Such
an account suggests, first, that conflict can be 'brought within the scope of the
authority on which government may normally call, and, second, that it can be
undertaken in such a manner as to establish justice' (16). Of course, this is a
rather expansive conception of the just war. It betrays a 'natural law rather than a
positive law orientation', and proposes that states might have responsibility for,
and jurisdiction over, other communities (23–8). The practical result of this is that
O'Donovan's conception of the just war, like that of Elshtain and also Johnson,
is amenable to such practices as penal (or punitive) war, as well as humanitarian
and so-called constabulary uses of force. In this respect, the First Gulf War (1991)
stands as the paradigmatic just war: it marks an occasion where war served as
a means of enacting justice and the will of the society of states by overturning

an act of international wrongdoing (125). The 2003 invasion of Iraq rested on more dubious grounds according to O'Donovan, largely due to the fact that it was justified as an anticipatory war which denigrated the judicial aspect of war.

Bush and Blair's just war against terror

A common concern with order and responsibility unifies Elshtain, Johnson, and O'Donovan. Elshtain writes of the 'burden of American power' in Augustinian terms which stress the prerogatives of just government; Johnson treats the problematic of how force might be employed in the service of proper authority; and O'Donovan places great weight on the praxis of judgement and the enforcement of right in the international arena. Each of these preoccupations fails to correspond to the legal stipulations of the UN Charter, the Covenant of the League of Nations, or the legalistic approach to war more generally; instead they reflect an overriding concern with what Johnson terms 'vindicative justice'.

Vindicative justice, as Johnson describes it, is related to the responsibility of state leaders and governments to exercise authority in the service of order and justice. It denotes that the government is the repository of three primary duties: to maintain order within a given community by defending against internal wrongdoing and external attack; to restore justice by punishing those responsible for wrongdoing; and to re-establish the conditions for future civic order.[3] The government is thereby charged with the object of, in Augustine's words (also cited by Thomas Aquinas and Francisco de Vitoria), 'securing the peace by coercing the wicked and helping the good' (Johnson 1999: 49; Augustine 1998: 933–7; Augustine 2001: 214–8; Aquinas 2002: 241; Vitoria 1991: 83).

It is this preoccupation with the governmental responsibility for order that is the defining mark of the contemporary just war tradition, as it is represented by Elshtain, Johnson, and O'Donovan.[4] Indeed, a broader survey of the just war literature reveals that this pre-occupation is actually quite prevalent within contemporary just war discourse.[5] More significantly, however, this willingness to countenance the possibility of a more expansive right to war on the basis of vindicative justice is not just confined to the academy; it appears to have fed into public debate, most notably in the rhetoric of state leaders as they speak about war.

An emphasis on vindicative justice is evident in the public rhetoric of certain state leaders, most notably President George W. Bush and Prime Minister Tony Blair, in the context of the war on terror. In the years following 11 September 2001, Bush and Blair have displayed a marked tendency to address the issue of war and peace in a morally charged manner. Consider the Old Testament style sloganeering – 'whether we bring our enemies to justice, or bring justice to our enemies, justice will be done' – that Bush indulges in when discussing the war on terror (Bush 2001). Statements such as this are rich with allusions to what might otherwise be considered archaic notions of justice which stress the virtues of retribution, and call to mind the biblical injunction of an eye for an eye and a tooth for a tooth. Indeed, Bush regularly refers to the war on terror in sweeping, moralistic overtones that make recourse to the rhetoric of good and evil and even divine providence.[6] Typical here is his 2002 West Point address which committed America to leading a worldwide fight against evil. 'We are in a conflict between good and evil, and America will call evil by its name. By confronting evil and lawless regimes, we do not create a problem, we reveal a problem. And we will lead the world in opposing it' (Bush 2002). Similarly, in an interview with Bob Woodward, Bush even went so far as to suggest that he considers himself to be an instrument of the 'Lord's will' on Earth, and prays daily for the strength to be 'as good a messenger of His will as possible' (Woodward 2004: 279).

Similar references to good and evil also appear in Blair's public statements. For instance, just hours after the terrorist attacks of 11 September 2001, Blair condemned the culprits of this outrage and committed that he would 'not rest until this evil is driven from our world' (Blair 2001). Following the London bombings of July 2005, Blair again reverted to the language of good and evil, describing the war on terror as a 'global struggle' against an 'evil ideology' (Blair 2005). This style of rhetoric is, however, nothing new for Blair. As early as 1993, he contributed a foreword to a collection of essays on Christianity and Socialism edited by Christopher Bryant wherein he presented the challenge of politics as a call to stand in judgement against all that is wrong and bad in this world (1993: 12). Blair, then, is a leader who favours Christian values in the public sphere (Rentoul 2001: 351–7; Stephens 2004: 32).

Notably, the invasion of Iraq was also justified as part of this struggle to eradicate evil from this world. Indeed, Bush and Blair offered a variety of justifications for the invasion of Iraq. They variously presented the invasion of Iraq as a pre-emptive war to eliminate Iraqi weapons of mass destruction (WMD), a punitive war to hold Iraq to account for its violation of the writ of the UN Security Council, a humanitarian war designed to bring human rights and democracy to the people of Iraq, and part of a greater struggle to rid the world of evil.[7] In each case, the invasion was represented as a means to securing the peace by coercing the wicked and helping the good. The imperative of vindicative justice was, it seems, prominently in the foreground of Bush and Blair's rhetoric with respect to both the invasion of Iraq and the broader War on Terror.

The 'defensive matrix': end of a century?

This broad-based approach to *the jus ad* bellum evident in the writings of Elshtain, Johnson, and O'Donovan, as well as the public rhetoric of Bush and Blair, stands in stark contrast to the narrow and legalistic form the right to war assumed for the best part of the twentieth century. It is this sharp break, and what it suggests, that I intend to explore in the final section of this chapter. Presently, however, a few words on twentieth-century just war thought are required in order to provide the background for this discussion.

The consensus view in the twentieth century was that only defence-against-aggression (urgent and necessary) justifies the recourse to war. Following the 'mechanized slaughter' of the First World War, and the belated acknowledgement that industrial age warfare threatened death and destruction on a previously unimaginable scale, peace societies sprung up all over Europe and America questing for a ban on war of all forms (Ignatieff 1997: 112; Howard 1978). This was partially realized by the Covenant of the League of Nations (1919) and the Kellogg-Briand Pact (1928) which led the way in criminalizing the non-defensive use of force (Karoubi 2004: 102–3). This position was further endorsed in the aftermath of the Second World War as the advent of nuclear weapons magnified the risks of modern war. The drafters of the UN Charter were mindful of this, and they reaffirmed the ban on all recourse to non-defensive war. According to William V. O'Brien, the UN Charter confirms the blanket ban on the use of force as an instrument of foreign policy, and stipulates that the self-defence is the sole just cause for war in the modern era (1981: 22–3). The drafting of the Charter, then, copper-fastened the idea that there was only one proper ground for war, defence, and that all other recourse to war would be equated with aggression. Johnson would later label this position the 'aggressor-defender' model of *jus ad bellum* while O'Donovan refers to it as a defensive matrix.

This position was re-asserted once more during the course of the Nuremberg and Tokyo Criminal Tribunals as the surviving leaders of Germany and Japan were tried for their roles in planning, preparing and waging an aggressive war (Falk 1963: 74). Indeed, it passed over into state practice and political theory as the twentieth century progressed. With respect to state practice, national leaders confirmed it every time they sought to present their wars as acts of self-defence and the actions of any hostile third party as instances of criminal aggression. Where political theory is concerned, the association of the just war with the defensive use of force gathered pace within the community of just war scholars. Writing in 1960, for example, Robert Tucker argued that 'The just war is war fought either in self-defence or in collective defence against an armed attack. Conversely, the unjust war […] is the war initiated in circumstances other than those of self- or collective defence against armed aggression' (1960: 11). Michael Walzer lent further credence to this viewpoint in his classic 1977 work, *Just and Unjust Wars*, when he declared that 'nothing but aggression can justify war'. Defence-against-aggression, he offers, is the 'single and only just cause' for war in the twentieth century and the basis of the 'legalist paradigm' – his term for the twentieth century *jus ad bellum* (1992: 62). Walzer, of course, connected this position to the twentieth-century commonplace that the *jus ad bellum* and *jus in bello* must be treated as 'logically independent' categories which share no relation to one another (21–7). A state's justification for war, he contends, should not impact upon the *jus in bello* restraints owing to its soldiers on the battlefield. In other words, the strictures of the *jus in bello* apply 'equally and indifferently' to all soldiers, regardless of whether they are fighting for a just cause or not (124).

Ostensibly there is little connection between twentieth-century just war thought, as I have just laid it out, and the visions of the just war presented by Elshtain, Johnson, and O'Donovan, and indeed Bush and Blair, in the context of the War on Terror. In fact, Johnson and O'Donovan both seek to distance themselves quite explicitly from the mainstream of twentieth-century just war thought. Johnson, for example, is critical of the idea that defence-against-aggression provides the only just cause for war, branding this a 'reductionist' doctrine (1981: 328; 1975: 268). He proposes that the *jus ad bellum* should, ideally, be cast in broader terms than the legalistic strictures of defence and aggression (1981: 328). Historically speaking, he suggests, the *jus ad bellum* does not speak solely to the stipulations of the UN Charter but relates to overarching questions of justice and good government. O'Donovan pursues a similar argument. He is adamant that the emphasis on defence-against-aggression in twentieth-century just war thought is misplaced and damaging. It produces, he submits, a vacuous reading of justice and war which pits states against one another in a survival contest rather than encouraging them to cooperate for the common good in a spirit of public international responsibility (O'Donovan 2003: 55). Elshtain's argument follows a different path, but also expresses a degree of disillusionment with the legalistic tenor of twentieth-century just war thought. She looks beyond the formalities of the UN Charter, and indeed the basic norms of state sovereignty and non-intervention, in order to reconcile the just war tradition to what she recognizes as the requirements and opportunities afforded by American hegemony and the nascent human rights regime. With respect to Bush and Blair, they have both tended to frame the War on Terror in moralistic terms which stress the imperatives of judgement and responsibility over the narrower optics of defence-against-aggression.

Viewed collectively, then, the recent writings of Elshtain, Johnson, and O'Donovan – the toast of contemporary just war tradition – as well as the speeches of Bush and Blair, do not seem to correspond in any robust manner with twentieth-century just war thought. Yet this does not mean that they stand apart from the just war tradition altogether. Indeed, they seem to share certain points of convergence with a more classical conception of the just war, one that we might associate with a series of medieval and early modern thinkers from Augustine to Grotius. The next section will explore these points of intersection.

Vindicative justice: echoes of the classical just war tradition

The main point of confluence relates to vindicative justice, which I mentioned earlier in connection to Johnson. Of course, the notion of vindicative justice is not Johnson's invention; it possesses a significant lineage within the medieval just war tradition. We might find, then, some parallels to developments in the contemporary just war tradition within that particular strand of medieval just war thought from which the idea of vindicative justice is drawn. This leads to an interesting opportunity: by examining this medieval strand of just war thought we might gain a deeper understanding of the recent tendency to hark to the idea of vindicative justice, as signalled by the recent writings of Elshtain, Johnson, and O'Donovan.

While Johnson extracts the idea of vindicative justice from the writings of Aquinas, Vitoria, and Francisco Suárez, it has much deeper roots than this, and is ultimately derived from St Paul's proclamation (Romans 13:4) that the prince (or state leader) is the minister of God to execute His wrath upon the evildoer.

This conception of authority empowers the prince to use the sword to establish (or re-establish) a just and peaceful political order. It is in this spirit that Aquinas remarks that it pertains to the prince to use the sword of war in order that we may have true peace: 'Those who wage war justly aim at peace, and so they are not opposed to peace, except to the evil peace' (Aquinas 2002: 241; Suárez 1944a: 802). The just war, on this view, is a war fought on princely authority with the object of vindicating proper relations between communities where they have been disrupted by some instance of wrongdoing. As Suárez writes, 'that war is justified which is taken under legitimate and public authority, with the intention of holding an enemy to his duty and of reducing to its due order that which was disorderly' (1944a: 819).

It was Augustine who first related the prince's right to war to the duties of good government and judgement. In a much quoted letter, Augustine addresses Macedonius to the effect that the question of justice and war is at heart a matter of judgement and must be considered in these terms. 'The might of the emperor' and 'the soldier's weapons' are essentially an extension of the judicial office into the international realm, he advises, and may be used in order to 'put a check on the bad so that the good may live peacefully' among them (Augustine 2001: 80).

This thematic line also runs right through the writings of Vitoria and Suárez. Vitoria, for instance, is explicit in comparing the role of the warring prince to that of the domestic judge. 'The prince who wages a just war', he writes, 'becomes ipso facto the judge of the enemy, and may punish them judicially and sentence them according to the offence' (Vitoria 1991: 288). James Brown Scott writes that this comparison is central to Vitoria's thinking on the rights of war. Vitoria's doctrine, Scott argues, is properly understood as a judicial system for international society where the princes are posited as judges responsible for prosecuting any violation of natural rights on the writ of the law of nations. 'Hence it is that Vitoria's prince may redress rights and punish wrongs just as may a judge of civil or criminal jurisdiction … On an international scale, the prince is the executor of the judgement which he has rendered' (Brown Scott 1934: 211). If anything, Suárez amplified this idea that princely authority functions as a means of judgement. The power of declaring war, Suárez states, is a 'power of jurisdiction'.

> Wherefore just as the sovereign may punish his own subjects when they offend others, so may he avenge himself on another prince or state which by reason of some offence becomes subject to him; and this vengeance cannot be sought at the hands of another judge, because the prince of whom we are speaking has no superior in temporal affairs; therefore, if that offender is not prepared to give satisfaction, he may be compelled to do so by war.
>
> (Suárez 1944a: 806)

There is also an element of continuity between this position and Hugo Griotius' argument that any state may undertake to punish a delinquent state on behalf of international society on the basis that by violating the natural order the delinquent state has rendered itself inferior to all other parties, and is therefore subject to their justice.[8] The core of this argument is the view that the prince may preside in judgement over the wrongdoing of others, and it is on this basis that he may lead his community or kingdom to war.

This thematic line clearly resonates quite strongly in the contemporary just war literature represented here by Elshtain, Johnson, and O'Donovan, and also in Bush and Blair's rhetoric regarding the war on terror. O'Donovan's 'praxis of judgment', Johnson's concern with proper authority, Elshtain's insistence that power and responsibility must go hand in hand, and Bush and Blair's determination to present the war as an instance of international law-enforcement stand as testimony to the prevalence of this trope within the contemporary just war tradition. In their efforts to map out a course, for both the moralist and the world at large, through the war on terror, these theorists and state-leaders have 'tapped into' that strand of medieval just war thought which emphasizes the imperative for the prince to act as the agent (and executor) of order in the quotidian world (Elshtain 2004: 50). In doing so, they present a vision of the *jus ad bellum* which is at odds with twentieth-century thought regarding the right to war. Where in the twentieth century the recourse to force was scrutinized against a legalist matrix, bracketed by the tightly circumscribed concepts of aggression and defence, today it seems more likely to be examined as a 'juridical' exercise in responsibility. War is thus represented as an instrument of international order and a means of enforcing the right rather than, as in the twentieth century, a challenge to peace and security.[9] This opens the way towards a revised and more open approach to the right to war. All indications, then, point towards the emergence of a broader conception of the *jus ad bellum*, cast in terms of governmental responsibility and judgement, in the context of the contemporary security environment.

Conclusion

In conclusion, this chapter has argued that the contemporary just war tradition reflects a shift away from the legalistic approach to the *jus ad bellum*, which was prevalent for the best part of the twentieth century. In its stead, the contemporary just war tradition indicates a pre-occupation with the problematic of war as a practice of responsible government, and in this respect resonates with the Pauline-inflected strand of medieval just war tradition which stresses the judicial/punitive function of war. This, however, is not merely a matter of academic interest; it has serious implications for the manner by which wars are waged in the present age and, consequently, the shape of international society in the years to come. Most obviously, it suggests a shift towards a broader, more expansive conception of the *jus ad bellum*, one which is more amenable to an interventionist ethic and suggestive of the inception of an 'age of liberal wars' (Freedman 2005).

Where war is viewed as a practice of responsible government or judgement, the conviction that self-defence constitutes the only possible just cause for war is displaced, resulting in a more permissive licence for the use of force in international affairs. This development is evident in state practice today. President Bush and Prime Minister Blair, for example, have tended to address the issue of war and justice in a more morally charged manner in recent years. This is apparent even just from the names originally assigned to the respective military operations in Afghanistan and Iraq: 'Infinite Justice' and 'Iraqi Freedom'. Rather than referring to a restrictive right to war equated solely with defence-against-aggression, they have utilized a much further reaching set of concepts which pertain to the imperatives of punishment, justice, humanitarianism, and good and evil.

This style of rhetoric marks a sea change from the days of the twentieth century when state leaders often went to great lengths in their efforts to represent each and every use of force they engaged in as a defensive action, in conformity with article 2(4) of the UN Charter.[10] Of course, some leaders such as President Ronald Reagan did occasionally (and very famously) invoke the language of good and evil, but it was generally distinct from any justifications for the use of force. Indeed, Reagan followed the twentieth-century model rather faithfully by attempting to stretch the bounds of self-defence to justify American acts of war – such as the 1986 bombing of Libya – that did not obviously fall within this bracket (Byers 2003: 179). Thus, where in the twentieth century only defence-against-aggression provided a secure grounds for war, there is some momentum today behind the idea that war may be waged for a number of purposes; most prominently to forestall future threats from emerging, to manage international peace and security, to enforce the writ of the UN, to intervene in countries where the government is repressing its own people, and to spread the principles of good government. In this respect, one might like to say that new thinking in the just war tradition is stretching the boundaries of what is acceptable.

This is immensely important. By setting out the *jus ad bellum* justifications for war in such emotive, charged terms, the likelihood of the war being conducted in a restrained manner is minimized. Put simply, where war is justified in such a sweeping, all-encompassing manner, the imperative of restraint is diminished. The modern *jus in bello*, based as it upon rights and protocols, necessarily appears shallow when confronted with the language of divine justice, responsibility, and struggle-against-evil. As the Bob Dylan song goes, 'you don't count the dead with God on your side'. This is a shortcoming that more classical approaches to the *jus in bello* avoided as they were typically cast in the same expansive terms as the *jus ad bellum* – and were stronger for it. It is only when the symmetry between the *jus ad bellum* and the *jus in bello* is lost, as it arguably has been in the context of the war on terror, that trouble ensues. The refusal on behalf of the US to treat captured enemy combatants as prisoners of war who fall under the protection of the Geneva Conventions, the practice of prisoner abuse and torture in detainment facilities such as Abu Ghraib and Camp X-Ray, and the use of prohibited weapons such as white phosphorous in Fallujah present themselves for consideration in this regard (Marqusee 2005; Monbiot 2005). These deviations from the standard norms of the *jus in bello* are, however – and this is my point – quite intelligible when placed in the context of a global war on terror that has been justified as the 'highest calling of history' (Bush 2003a).

It is precisely this slide into licentiousness that must be guarded against with the utmost vigilance lest we allow for a resumption of the unfettered barbarity that once prompted Grotius to write *The Rights of War and Peace*. Grotius's response to the horror that faced his generation was simple. He reminded his readers that wars may be undertaken as a judicial act, but 'to render Wars just, they are to be waged with no less Care and Integrity, than judicial proceedings are usually carried on' (2005, 102). This is a lesson which I would contend is worth re-iterating today. The tragedy is that this lesson is unlikely to be respected when the *jus ad bellum* justifications for war are offered in such strong and morally charged terms.

Acknowledgements

I would like to thank Lisa Denney, Columba Peoples, Darren Brunk, and Nick Vaughan-Williams for their helpful comments. I would also like to acknowledge my debt to Toni Erskine and Ian Clark for their support and guidance over the past few years. Finally, I am grateful to the editors of this volume for the invitation to participate in this project.

Notes

1   One would also include Michael Walzer as one of the foremost contemporary just war theorists. However, he has not produced any book-length treatment of just war thought since the advent of the war on terror. *Arguing About War* is, of course, a compendium of essays written between 1977 and 2004; it is not a concentrated re-examination of the just war tradition in the context of the War on Terror. See: Walzer 2004.

2   For example, see Rengger 2004 and Burke 2005b. This topic will be the subject of a panel discussion at ISA 2007, entitled 'Jean Bethke Elshtain's Just War Against Terror: The Response from the Academy', and a special section of *International Relations* (forthcoming: 2007).

3   Interestingly, Johnson's treatment of vindicative justice is modelled on Thomas Aquinas's response to the question 'Is War always a Sin?' See: Aquinas 2002: 241.

4   It is not, of course, the only defining feature of recent just war thought – a willingness to present war as a force for good in the world is another – but it is perhaps the most prevalent one.

5   The recent writings of scholars such as Fernando Tesón (2005), Whitley Kaufman (2005), Allen Buchanan and Robert Keohane (2004), Anne-Marie Slaughter and Lee Feinstein (2004), Anthony F. Lang Jr (2004), Neta Crawford (2003a; 2003b), Anthony Burke (2004; 2005), George R. Lucas Jr (2003), and Christian Reus-Smit (2005) have all explored the possibility that a broader right to war is emerging in international society. They have treated, in no particular order, the matters of anticipatory war, punitive war, wars of democratization, the constabulary use of force, and an extended right to humanitarian war. Not all of these scholars support these ventures, but the fact that they examine them within the frame of the just war tradition is significant in its own right.

6   Bush spoke about evil on 319 separate occasions, between the moment he took office and June 2003 (Singer 2003: 2). With respect to Bush's predilection to refer to divine providence, the clearest example is his address to a Joint Session of Congress and the American People on 20 September 2001: 'Freedom and fear, justice and cruelty, have always been at war, and we know that God is not neutral between them. Fellow citizens, we'll meet violence with patient justice – assured of the rightness of our cause, and confident of the victories to come. In all that lies before us, may God

grant us wisdom, and may he watch over the USA' (Bush 2001). For more on Bush's invocation of Christian tropes, see Lafeber 2002.

7 The question of anticipation is taken up in the next chapter by Alex J. Bellamy. Specifically, Bellamy examines the vexed matter of pre-emption in the context of the war on terror. I have dealt with the representation of the war on terror as a punitive war and struggle against evil elsewhere. See: O'Driscoll 2006.

8 Though of course Grotius had his disagreements with how Vitoria and Suárez addressed this matter. See Grotius' treatment of punishment in Book II, Chapter 20 of: Grotius 2005. For more on Vitoria and Suarez, see: Hamilton 1963.

9 We might think of the distinction set out by Hedley Bull between different historical conceptions of the use of force in international politics: 'The rules and institutions which international society has evolved reflect the tension between the perception of war as a threat to international society which must be contained and the perception of it as an instrumentality which international society can exploit to achieve its purpose' (Bull 1977: 188).

10 For example, consider India's tortuous justification for its intervention in East Pakistan (Bangladesh) in 1971. India claimed that it deployed forces in East Pakistan in response to 'refugee aggression', rather than pursuing a more straightforward humanitarian justification for their actions (Wheeler 2000: 62).

7 Pre-empting terror

Alex J. Bellamy

The right to use force in self-defence has been described as a 'fundamental principle' of international law and is also the bedrock of the natural law tradition's just causes for war (Schwarzenberger 1955: 195). Traditionally, Just War scholars have admitted that the right to self-defence comprises a right to respond with force to both actual and imminent attacks. The ambiguous place of pre-emptive self-defence in Article 51 of the UN Charter gave rise to a debate between 'restrictionists' who call for a literal interpretation of the Charter (thus ruling out the use of force prior to an armed attack) and 'counter-restrictionists' who argue that the UN Charter does not override a state's inherent right of pre-emptive self-defence. Since 9/11, these debates have become more pointed. Many scholars and policy-makers began to insist that the ability of terrorists and 'rogue states' to inflict mass casualties at short notice required a less restrictive way of thinking about self-defence. The so-called 'Bush doctrine' (National Security Council (NSC) 2002), described by one leading writer as the new American 'grand strategy' (Ikenberry 2004: 44), claimed a right for the US to act pre-emptively against terrorists, states harbouring terrorists and other 'rogue' regimes. According to at least two commentators, it amounts to claiming an 'unlimited' right of self-defence (Myjer and White 2002: 5).

This chapter takes up the challenge to re-examine the right of self-defence in the wake of 9/11. It accepts the view that self-defence needs to be rethought to take account of the fact that massive threats may emerge more rapidly and quietly than before. Though appealing for its simplicity, a restrictionist view that there is and should be no right of pre-emptive self-defence against terrorists and those harbouring them is flawed on at least two counts. First, a 'right' of self-defence that does not permit states to use force to pre-empt attacks is not much of a right. As Abraham Sofaer (1986: 53) put it, if the restrictionists were correct, it would mean that 'international law would serve to insulate the perpetrators of international violence for any control or punishment for their crimes'. Second, in the contemporary context, denying the global hyperpower the right to pre-empt attacks is only likely to encourage that power to reject the normative restraints on recourse to force. On the other hand, however, there are at least two good reasons for avoiding an entirely permissive order. First, a permissive rule of self-defence could encourage states to abuse that right. In the modern era, almost every war has been justified in terms of self-defence by both sides (see Mullerson 1991). Second, a permissive right of pre-emption would blur the distinction between aggression and defence.

This chapter aims to develop a new way of thinking about pre-emptive self-defence to take account of the threat of terrorism. The first section outlines the traditional view on self-defence found in the Just War tradition and positive international law. It shows that both permit a limited right of pre-emption where such acts are justified by necessity, the temporal imminence of the threat and proportionality. These ideas were articulated between 1837 and 1842 during a dispute between the US and UK over the sinking of the *Caroline*. The *Caroline* case remains a good guide to the limits of pre-emptive self-defence, not because it was singularly important in its own right but because it reflected, and still reflects, the position of both Just War thinking and positive international law. The second section details recent American attempts to redesign the right of self-defence. It identifies three broad schools of thought. The first, sometimes referred to as 'new liberals', holds that a liberal state's duty to protect the fundamental right to life of its citizens should override its duty to respect the sovereign inviolability of others in cases where the two principles collide. The second, which I label 'new realists', insists that the legal and moral rules limiting the right to self-defence have been broken so often since 1945 that they simply no longer apply. Both these approaches, I will argue, are flawed in important respects. The third approach, one signalled by the United States' 2002 *National Security Strategy* (hereafter referred to as the *Strategy*), holds that whilst traditional concepts of self-defence should remain largely intact, the concepts of 'imminence' and 'necessity' require reformulation. I will adopt this approach and attempt to articulate a concept of pre-emptive self-defence that permits application against terrorists and those that harbour them whilst guarding against the perils of creating a too permissive regime.

Although the essence of my approach is similar to that articulated in the *Strategy*, it is important to note three important differences. First, the *Strategy* does not elaborate a new concept of 'imminence', a cornerstone of the approach taken here. Second, whilst the *Strategy* talks about a limited right of pre-emption, in practice and in its rhetoric the Bush administration has adopted a strategy of *prevention*. In contrast to pre-emption, prevention attempts to remove a potential threat before it has emerged, something expressly ruled out here (Freedman 2004a: 83–4). Third, unlike the *Strategy*, my approach insists that the threat be demonstrable. It is not enough for a state to simply convince itself that it confronts a threat in order for it to claim a right to pre-empt: it also has to persuade as many others as possible. The basic idea here is that the greater the number of states and other actors that validate a decision to act pre-emptively, the greater the level of legitimacy the action should be accorded (see Franck 2002: 185), particularly when that validation is a product of free and open dialogue.

Self-defence and the legitimacy of war

The just war tradition

The Just War tradition's justification of killing in certain circumstances is based on an extrapolation of the individual's right to use violence to defend herself from attack (Walzer 1977: 127; Anscombe 1961; Fullinwinder 1975). Each of the tradition's variants recognised self-defence as the primary just cause for war. For many writers, sovereigns had not only a right but also a *duty* to defend their communities. As Vattel (1916: 246) put it, 'self-defence against an unjust attack is not only a right which every nation has, but it is a duty, and one of the most sacred duties'. Both Suárez (1944a: 4) and Wolff (1934: 804) supported this view. This obligation derived from the sovereign's responsibility to protect his or her subjects.

There was a similar level of consensus about pre-emption. On the whole, writers tended to permit a limited right of pre-emption in the face of an imminent threat but expressly rejected the morality of preventive war, viewing it as tantamount to aggression. Grotius listed as the first 'just cause' of war 'an injury not yet done which menaces body or goods'. In cases where one is 'menaced by present force with danger of life not otherwise evitable, war is lawful, even to the slaying of the aggressor ... as a matter of self-protection' (1913: 172). This right, however, was limited by necessity: 'the right of self-defence exists only when necessary: where the danger can be avoided, delay is proper to allow recourse to other remedies' (p. 210). The danger, Grotius argued, must be 'immediate and imminent in point of time' (p. 549). Lest there be any doubt about the limits of this right, Grotius went on to specifically reject the legality of preventive war as an 'intolerable doctrine' (pp. 224–5). Importantly, for our purposes, Grotius supplemented his argument by noting that 'advantage does not confer the same right as necessity ... For in order that self-defence may be lawful, it must be necessary, and it is not necessary unless we are certain, not only regarding the power of our neighbour but also regarding his intention' (p. 549).

Likewise, Samuel Pufendorf agreed that a man may kill an aggressor once 'the aggressor, showing clearly his desire to take my life, and equipped with the capacity and the weapons for his purpose' and 'has gotten into the position where he can in fact hurt me' (1994: 264). Like Grotius, Pufendorf also sought to limit the right, insisting that force could only be used in the absence of viable alternatives (such as escape). Emmerich de Vattel was a little more permissive than the others insisting that:

> When once a state has given proofs of injustice, rapacity, pride, ambition, or an imperious thirst of rule, she becomes an object of suspicion to her neighbours, whose duty it is to stand on their guard against her ... [O]n occasions where it is impossible or too dangerous to wait for an absolute certainty, we may justly act on a reasonable presumption.
>
> (1916: 308)

However, he insisted that if there were reasonable doubts about these proofs, states should take care 'not to act upon vague and doubtful suspicions lest it should run the risk of becoming itself the aggressor' (p. 130). Although Vattel accepted the idea that a state may pre-emptively attack another without knowing for certain that the other is close to attacking it, he expressly forbade preventive war. The fact that a state increases its power was not enough grounds for war, Vattel argued, because 'we must have good grounds to think ourselves threatened ... before we can have recourse to arms' (p. 308).

Positive international law

These views found their way into positive international law. The 1928 Kellogg-Briand pact, whose signatories renounced the use of force in their international relations, nevertheless reserved a state's right to use force in self-defence. That right, it was widely conceded, included the right to pre-emption. According to Frank Kellogg, the US Secretary of State who co-wrote the pact, the right of self-defence was 'inherent in every sovereign state and is implicit in every treaty. Every nation is free at all times and regardless of treaty provisions to defend its territory from attack or invasion and it alone is competent to decide whether circumstances require recourse to war in self-defence' (Kellogg 1928: 142).

Article 51 of the UN Charter also grants states an inherent right of self-defence, though the status of pre-emption is a little murkier in relation to Charter law. It declares that:

> Nothing in the present Charter shall impair the inherent right of individual or collective self-defence if an armed attack occurs against a member of the United Nations, until the Security Council has taken measures necessary to maintain international peace and security. Measures taken by members in the exercise of this right shall be immediately reported to the Security Council and shall not in any way affect the authority and responsibility of the Security Council under the present Charter to take at any time such action as it deems necessary in order to maintain or restore international peace and security.

It is worth noting that in the French version of this article, the phrase 'inherent right' is rendered *droit naturale* (natural right) (Dinstein 1988: 169).

Interpretations of Article 51 have tended to fall into one of two camps, what I label 'restrictionist' and 'counter-restrictionist'. Two issues in particular have separated them: what constitutes an 'armed attack' and do states have a right to act pre-emptively? Restrictionists argue for a narrow interpretation of the Charter on both counts (e.g. Combacau 1986; Delbrück 2002). The question of what constitutes an armed attack was first raised in 1948 when the USSR intervened in Czechoslovakia to overthrow the government because it expressed a wish to participate in the Marshall Plan. Despite Czechoslovak pleas to the contrary, the Security Council did not see this intervention as an 'armed attack'. Likewise, in the same year, whilst the UN sent monitors to observe alleged border incursions by

Yugoslav communists into Greece it stopped short of identifying an armed attack. These experiences led restrictionists to claim that an 'armed attack' was limited to cases of actual invasion and not limited incursions. This view was supported by the ICJ in its judgment in the *US v. Nicaragua* case (1986). Whilst finding that the sending of armed bands into another state may constitute an armed attack, the Court insisted that it was 'necessary to distinguish the most grave forms of the use of force (those constituting an armed attack) from other less grave forms'.[1] Restrictionists therefore argue that an armed attack should be understood as limited to those instances involving the direct use of conventional military force. In cases of sabotage or state-sponsored terrorism, the victim state does not enjoy a right to use force against the host state in self-defence (Brownlie 1963: 275–80).

Restrictionists also insist that Article 51 expressly rules out pre-emptive self-defence, arguing that states have a right to use force in self-defence only *after* an armed attack has occurred. Hans Kelsen (1948: 792) concluded that Article 51 only applied 'in case of an armed attack' and that the right could not be exercised to protect states against the violation of any of their other rights. In the *Nicaragua v. US* case, the ICJ supported this interpretation, ruling that, 'for one state to use force against another ... is regarded as lawful, by way of exception, only when the wrongful act provoking the response was an armed attack ... In the view of the Court, under international law in force today – whether customary international law or that of the United Nations system – states do not have a right of 'collective' armed response to acts which do not constitute an "armed attack".[2] Restrictionists argue, not implausibly, that if these limits to the exercise of self-defence were loosened, states would be encouraged to abuse the right to self-defence and the distinction between aggression and defence would be eroded (see Cassesse 1986: 515–16).

Although there is evidence that the Charter's drafters intended Article 51 to provide only a limited right of self-defence, the idea that a state should wait to be attacked before taking measures to defend its citizens has been widely criticised by counter-restrictionists. Sir Humphrey Waldock insisted that 'it would be a travesty of the purposes of the Charter to compel a defending state to allow its assailant to deliver the first, and perhaps fatal blow ... to read Article 51 literally is to protect the aggressor's right to the first strike' (in Roberts 1999: 483 and 513). Myers McDougal (1963: 599) insists that there is no evidence in the Charter's *traveaux preparatoire* that the drafters intended to place new limits on states' pre-Charter right to self-defence. As a result, most scholars insist that Article 51 does not override the customary rights and responsibilities of states identified earlier. Simma (2002: 51), for instance, argued that Article 51 merely outlined one situation in which the inherent right of self-defence might be used.

Counter-restrictionists argue that the definition of an 'armed attack' should be understood more broadly and that Article 51 does not erode a state's right to pre-emptive self-defence. On the first issue, counter-restrictionists insist that if the phrase 'armed attack' means what it says, it must therefore mean all 'armed attacks' regardless of their scale (Kunz 1947: 848). Once again, in the *Nicaragua vs. US* case the ICJ put forward a restrictionist view, arguing that the provision of arms, logistics and other support to terrorists did not constitute an 'armed attack'. Most scholars and many states disagreed with this view. For them, state support for terrorism does constitute an armed attack so long as the level of violence reaches (or threatens to reach) what the General Assembly's 'Definition of Aggression' labelled 'sufficient gravity' (e.g. Cassim *et al.* 1975; Blum 1976).

Counter-restrictionists also argue that Article 51 does not diminish a state's inherent right to pre-emptive self-defence. There are at least two justifications for this view. First, it is implied in the Charter's language. Article 51 explicitly endorses a state's *inherent* right to self-defence; its *natural* right in the French version. That inherent right clearly included a right to pre-emptive self-defence. Moreover, if Article 51 is read as permitting the use of force against breaches of Article 2(4), then this also permits pre-emption because Article 2(4) prohibits both the 'threat' and 'use' of force (Bowett 1958: 191–2).

The second justification for a broader reading of Article 51 is customary practice. Since 1945, states have tended to judge instances of pre-emptive self-defence on the merits of each case. On some occasions, where the threat is demonstrably imminent, international society has shown itself willing to tolerate pre-emption. The paradigmatic case of this was the world's reaction to Israel's 1967 pre-emptive attack on Egypt. In that case, although some states condemned Israel, many others accepted that an invasion was imminent and whilst desisting from commending Israel also chose not to condemn it (Gray 2000: 112–13). More recently, *Operation Enduring Freedom* in Afghanistan also provides a compelling case in that the overwhelming majority of states supported the US right to overthrow the Taliban regime in Afghanistan in order to prevent further Al-Qaeda attacks. In other cases, however, states criticised as precipitate the use of force for ostensibly pre-emptive purposes. For example, when Israel launched an air strike against the Osirak nuclear reactor in Iraq in 1981, it was 'strongly condemned' by the UN Security Council even though counter-restrictionist lawyers supported Israel's case (e.g. McCormack 1996: 297–302). States found that the reactor did not pose an imminent threat and that Israel had resorted to force as a first not last resort. What this demonstrates is that states and scholars are prepared to make judgements about the legitimacy of pre-emptive force on a case-by-case basis, lending support to the counter-restrictionist claim that there is a theoretical right of pre-emption.

It seems clear from this that – restrictionist concerns notwithstanding – the right of self-defence permits the pre-emptive use of force in some cases but forbids 'preventive' attacks. The questions now are first, in what situations is the pre-emptive use of force justifiable? And second, where do we draw the line between pre-emption and prevention? We can begin to answer these questions by considering the exchange of diplomatic notes between the UK and US concerning the sinking of the *Caroline* in 1837. Although relatively insignificant as a case in its own right, the *Caroline* case is important as a basis for understanding when the right of pre-emptive self-defence can be invoked for three reasons. First, the fact that the wording of the right to pre-emption in US Secretary of State, Daniel Webster's communication with the British was accepted without question by both sides and has not been challenged by states since suggest that it is an accurate reflection of international society's consensus on this matter (e.g. Alexandrov 1996: 20). Second, the case provides an example of applying the broad right to pre-emption to a specific case. Third, Webster's formula, outlined in the *Caroline* case, has been frequently cited in legal cases since (see Travalio and Altenberg 2003: 114). For example, it was cited in the Nuremberg trials to reject German claims that the invasion of Norway constituted a legitimate act of self-defence.

In 1837, the UK and US were in a state of peace. However, there was an armed insurrection (the 'Mackenzie rebellion') against British rule in Canada. The rebels began using an American owned ship, the *Caroline*, to carry supplies from the American side of the Niagara River. On 29 December 1837, Canadian troops loyal to Britain boarded the ship, killed several Americans, set the ship alight and allowed it to drift over the Niagara Falls. At the time of the attack the *Caroline* was docked on the US side of the border not in its usual port on the Canadian side of the border. The US protested against the attack, claiming that it violated its sovereignty, but the British insisted that they were exercising their right to self-defence.

The debate began with a note from US Secretary of State John Forsyth to the British Minister in Washington on 5 January 1938.[3] Forsyth demanded a full explanation from the British and labelled the attack an 'extraordinary outrage'. The British minister responded by blaming the Americans for failing to prevent the use of its territory by the Canadian rebels and justifying the attack as 'a necessity of self-defence and self-preservation' against a 'piratical' vessel (Stevens 2004: 24–5). On further investigation in London, the British government concluded that as the *Caroline* was aiding and abetting the rebels it was a legitimate target regardless of which side of the border it was docked. Not surprisingly, the US rejected this argument disputing both the labelling of the *Caroline* as 'piratical' and Britain's claim to a right of 'hot pursuit' across the border. Instead, it argued that the level of threat that could justify hot pursuit must be 'imminent, and extreme, and involving impending destruction' (Stevens 2004: 35).

The debate was reinvigorated in late 1840 when a former British soldier was arrested in New York and charged with arson and murder in relation to the *Caroline.* The US government invited the British government to apologise for the incident and pay compensation in return for the dismissal of charges against the soldier. The British Minister agreed immediately and despatched a note to the US government apologising. In an 1842 reply to the British, the American Secretary of State, Daniel Webster explained that for the claim of self-defence to be justifiable, Britain was required to 'show a necessity of self-defence, instant, overwhelming, leaving no choice of means, and no moment for deliberation'.[4] The action taken must also involve 'nothing unreasonable or excessive; since the act, justified by the necessity of self-defence, must be limited by that necessity and kept clearly within it'.[5] In order to invoke a right of pre-emptive self-defence, therefore, a state has to demonstrate the imminence of an attack, the necessity of pre-emption and the proportionality of its intended response. Interestingly, Webster argued that the principles of necessity and proportionality were the most important and went into some detail in explaining what necessity entailed:

> It must be demonstrated that it [Britain] did nothing unreasonable or excessive; since the act justified by the necessity of self-defence, must be limited by that necessity, and kept clearly within it. It must be shown that admonition or remonstrances to the persons on board the 'Caroline' was impracticable or would have been unavailing; it must be shown that daylight could not be waited for; that there could be no discrimination, between the innocent and the guilty; that it would not have been enough to seize and detain the vessel; but that it was a necessity, present and inevitable.
>
> (Webster 1983 [1842]: 67–8)

The *Caroline* case helps to overcome the political problem caused by Article 51's insistence that a right of self-defence can only be claimed *after* an armed attack has taken place. However, in light of Article 51, state practice since 1945, and the ICJ's position, the three cornerstones of the Webster formula – imminence, necessity and proportionality – at best constitute a limited right of pre-emptive self-defence. There are therefore good grounds for arguing that contemporary positive international law permits a limited right of pre-emption that extends beyond Article 51 but is nevertheless covered by customary international law owing to the *Caroline* case and state practice since.

Between them, Just War thinking and positive international law grant states a limited right of pre-emptive self-defence in cases that satisfy the usual *jus ad bellum* criteria (all recourse to force must satisfy those criteria) plus the criteria of imminence (the attack must be demonstrably imminent) and necessity (the use of force must be the only reasonable measure available). According to this view, acts that do not satisfy all of these criteria are illegal and unjust. Jurists worry, with good reason, that expanding the right beyond that of the *Caroline* formula would significantly increase the likelihood of abuse by states and make it harder for observers to evaluate the legitimacy of a state's claims. For instance, if we remove the obligation for a state to demonstrate that an attack is imminent, it becomes impossible to judge whether or not the claim to be acting in self-defence is valid or not.

The problem, however, comes in defining what 'imminence' means if the threat comes from terrorists and rogue states that have the ability launch instant mass casualty attacks on urban centres. As George W. Bush put it, in the post-September 11 context 'we have every reason to assume the worst, and we have an urgent duty to prevent the worst from happening … [we] cannot wait for the final proof – the smoking gun – that could come in the form of a mushroom cloud' (Bush 2002a). It is for this reason that three revisionist schools of thought have come to the fore: 'new liberals' who call for a re-ordering in the relationship between states' rights and individuals' rights in international law; 'new realists' who argue that international law and ethics do not, and should not, constrain a state from using force to defend itself; and those who adopt a position similar to the *Strategy* that the traditional doctrine of self-defence continues to hold up but that the concepts of 'imminence' and 'necessity' need to be rethought to take account of the new threats.

Revisionist arguments

The idea that the concept of self-defence requires rethinking in the wake of September 11 is widely accepted. In light of what we now know about how far terrorists are prepared to go, there are at least four good reasons to rethink pre-emptive self-defence. It is important to stress that these four reasons provide a case for rethinking pre-emption to respond to the threat of international *terrorism*. They do not constitute a case for rethinking pre-emption in relation to *conventional* threats from states. By *conventional* threat I mean both threats of conventional war and the conventional use of WMD for deterrence and self-defence by states.

First, on prudential grounds, there is a good argument that prevention is better than cure. In hindsight, Clinton's decision not to take firmer action against Osama bin Laden between 1996 and 1998 was a bad misjudgement (see Clarke 2004: 101–204). By this logic, the norm of pre-emptive self-defence must be refashioned to place fewer costs on political leaders who wish to take earlier action against would-be terrorists. Second, whereas conventional wars are preceded by clear warnings, most obviously troop mobilisations and deployments, such clear indicators do not usually precede mass casualty terrorist attacks. It is virtually impossible for a liberal democracy to guard against terrorism at all times and in all places. There is widespread agreement, therefore, that the best way to reduce the threat of terrorism is to take the offensive and adopt a proactive strategy (e.g. Betts 2002; David 2003). Third, the potential for mass casualty terrorism renders a reactive strategy imprudent at best. If one accepts Vattel's insistence that self-defence is the sacred duty of states, a reactive strategy in the face of such a threat may even be immoral. Finally, although deterrence still has an important role to play in world politics – particularly in relation to so-called 'rogue states' – its ability to constrain the type of terrorism witnessed on September 11 in the short-term is limited. The challenge to rethink the concept of pre-emptive self-defence has been taken up by at least three groups.

'New liberals'

'New liberals' argue that the world can be refashioned through law (and force) into a stable and orderly society that guarantees the rights of individuals. They insist that liberal states are more likely to resolve their disputes peacefully and through legal mechanisms (Slaughter 1995: 503). As such, they are committed to spreading democracy, protecting democracies that are under attack from anti-democratic forces, and creating more robust forms of enforcement to strengthen international law. Some, such as Fernando Tesón (1998: 62–3), insist that liberal states may use war against illiberal states as a means of realising this ambition, whilst others argue that the process of liberalisation should be slower and predominantly non-violent (Slaughter 2000: 240). Such debates aside, the 'new liberals' agree that international law should be changed to make the world safer for liberal democracies.

The starting point for the 'new liberal' call to reform pre-emptive self-defence is recognition that international law is a vital tool for regulating the behaviour of states and individuals but that it must be refashioned to meet the challenges of the post-September 11 era (Slaughter 2003). Feinstein and Slaughter (2004) therefore suggested a new principle to guide action: 'the duty to prevent'. The new principle, they argue, is warranted by the fact that 'we live in a world of old rules and new threats' (p. 138). Although the Security Council is the most appropriate forum for dealing with these new threats, they argue that the burden of proof needs to be shifted from the suspicious states to nations suspected of WMD proliferation and collusion with terrorists. In such cases, waiting for pre-emption in the traditional sense 'is usually impractical because suspected facilities are often difficult to spot or hit' (p. 147). They continue, 'this is not to suggest that the use of [pre-emptive] force should be discounted as ineffective but that the most effective action is preventive' (p. 147). Preventive action may involve the use of force, and that use of force may even be unilateral so long as the intervener attempts multilateral avenues (the UN, regional organisations) first (pp. 148–9).

There are a number of problems with this proposal. First, it conflates the threat of terrorism with that of WMD proliferation by states. Whilst there are good grounds for rethinking pre-emptive self-defence in response to terrorism, there is no evidence to suggest that by itself WMD proliferation by states poses a new and unusual threat. WMD programmes and states' intentions can be monitored and when a state has the ability and intention to launch a WMD attack, the traditional doctrine of self-defence permits pre-emptive action. Second, the right of prevention it seeks to create would blur the distinction between aggression and defence. The targets of such actions, and other significant portions of global society, would undoubtedly see such 'preventive' wars as acts of aggression. Moreover, in a case where a state chooses to follow Feinstein and Slaughter's path to legitimation (try the UN first, then a regional organisation and if that fails launch a unilateral attack), the failure to secure multilateral agreement would surely indicate that the rest of the world does not share the concerned states' threat perception. As we noted earlier, to use a 'threat' as a justification for war, it is imperative that the threat is demonstrable. Third, a doctrine of prevention often leads to empire when potential future threats are removed and the obligations of governance fall on those who have effected 'regime change' (Snyder 2003). Fourth, given the widespread consensus that preventive war is both immoral and illegal, recourse to prevention risks undermining the rule of law that the 'new liberals' insist is imperative in the struggle against tyranny.

'New realists'

A second school of thought, the 'new realists', insists that international law on self-defence is simply irrelevant and that states, particularly the US, should be guided by their own interests in deciding whether or not to use pre-emptive or preventive force. According to two Republican hawks, the US should not bind itself to either positive law or commonly agreed ethical rules by restricting its pre-emptive strikes to cases where there is demonstrable imminent threat. Instead, 'where intelligence is uncertain, prudent leaders will inevitably minimize risks by erring on the side of the worst plausible assumption. And rightly so' (Frum and Perle 2004: 27). This assertion of America's right to decide for itself when and where it will act pre-emptively is based on a three-pronged critique of the rules governing self-defence.

The first prong is a denunciation of Article 51 of the UN Charter. 'New realists' argue that the Article 51 regime is redundant because it does not permit the use of force against those who aid and abet terrorists; it rules out forcible 'regime change' in states that provide safe havens for terrorists; and does not permit a right of pre-emptive or preventive self-defence (Glennon 2002). The second angle of attack is a rejection of the Security Council's relevance and its ability to protect states from attack. 'New realists' point to the Security Council's 'paralysis' during the Cold War and its 'failure' to sanction military force in Kosovo (1999) or Iraq (2003) as proof of its inability to protect international peace and security (Glennon 2003; Yoo 2004: 740). The third line of argument is to insist that the UN Charter's rules regulating the use of force have been broken so many times that the rules themselves are invalid. As Glennon (2002: 540) put it in an oft-quoted passage, 'between 1945 and 1999, two-thirds of the members of the United Nations – 126 out of 189 – fought 291 interstate conflicts in which over 22 million people were killed'. The 'upshot' of all this, Glennon concludes, is that the Charter's use of force regime has 'all but collapsed' and that the Just War alternatives are little more than 'archaic notions of universal truth' (2003: 19). As a result, the traditional view of self-defence outlined in the first part of this chapter should not act as a guide to responsible state behaviour. Instead, the US should make its own decisions about how best to defend itself and the US administration need only justify itself to the American public.

'New realism' is problematic for a number of reasons. First, the claim that the UN Charter's rules on the use of force are defunct is not credible. Rule-breaking only has the effect of altering the law if the rule-breakers justify their actions by articulating a new principle and other states validate that justification. In the cases of NATO's intervention in Kosovo and the US-led invasion of Iraq did states did not consistently claim a new right (in the Kosovo case, only Belgium and the UK levelled legal defences of their actions; in the case of Iraq the legal justification insisted that the invasion was authorised by the Security Council) and there is certainly no indication that other states recognised a change in the law (Byers 2003a). Second, Glennon's claim that the Security Council is irrelevant and ineffectual is not supported by the Iraq case. The Council was the hub of the debate about using force against Iraq. Third, 'new realism' fails the reciprocity test and offers a self-fulfilling prophecy instead. It is highly unlikely that any US government would tolerate others having the freedom of manoeuvre that the 'new realists' claim for the US. Moreover, if other states were to behave in the way they prescribe, that would almost certainly bring about the collapse of the legal and moral constraints on recourse to force. Finally, the 'new realists' ignore the warnings of earlier realists such as E.H. Carr and Hans Morgenthau by erroneously equating US interests with universal good and suggesting that what is good for the US must be good for the whole world.

The national security strategy

In its 2002 *Strategy*, the US government offered a third avenue for rethinking pre-emptive self-defence. It is predicated on the view, put forward by former Defence Secretary Donald Rumsfeld (2001) that, 'the problem with terrorism is that there is no way to defend against the terrorists at every place and every time against every conceivable technique. Therefore, the only way to deal with the terrorist network is to take the battle to them'. The *Strategy* insisted that:

> [G]iven the goals of rogue states and terrorists, the United States can no longer solely rely on a reactive posture as we have in the past. The inability to deter a potential attacker, the immediacy of today's threat, and the magnitude of potential harm that could be caused by our adversaries' choice of weapons, do not permit that option. We cannot let our enemies strike first. (p. 15)

Unlike the 'new liberals' and 'new realists', the *Strategy* advocated neither a radical reformulation of the law nor rule-breaking behaviour. Instead, it situated the new doctrine firmly within customary international law and argued for the revision of one of the three elements of Webster's test outlined during the *Caroline* affair: imminence. Thus, it insisted that, 'for centuries, international law recognized that nations need not suffer an attack before they can lawfully take action to defend themselves' (p. 15). However, it argued that the concept of 'imminent threat' required reform to permit action 'even if uncertainty remains as to the time and place of the enemy's attack. To forestall or prevent such hostile acts by our adversaries, the United States will, if necessary, act pre-emptively' (p. 15). Such an approach was justified because the US could not wait until a terrorist threat was 'fully-formed' (see Byers 2003a: 11).

The *Strategy* has been widely criticised for stretching the concept of 'armed attack' to such an extent that it loses any legal meaning and for being deliberately misleading in labelling what is in essence a strategy of *prevention* as pre-emption (Johnstone 2004: 832). The problem though is not so much what the *Strategy* itself says but with the Bush administration's rhetoric and actions. Indeed, a few states including Russia and India responded favourably to the document (Byers 2004: 541). There is an important disjuncture between the *Strategy* and US rhetoric (see Byers 2005: 72–83). Recall that the *Strategy* only permits doubt about the time and place of the attack. According to this document, the enemy target must still be shown to have both the *intent* and *means* to attack. In practice, Bush's rhetoric has been much less nuanced. In a speech to the German parliament in May 2002, Bush argued that the US would be prepared to use force against 'rogues', whether or not those rogues had displayed a specific intent to attack the US or its allies and *before* they acquired the means of doing so (in Halper and Clarke 2004: 140). A month later, he told a West Point graduation ceremony that 'we must take the battle to the enemy and confront the worst threats before they emerge' telling the graduates to prepare for 'pre-emptive action' (Bush 2002a). Thus, in its public statements, the US administration certainly implied that it supports a right of preventive war, not the more limited right of expanded pre-emption claimed in the *Strategy*. According to the rhetoric, a potential target need possess neither an intention nor the means of attacking the US and its allies.

Furthermore, the Bush administration's efforts to justify the 2003 invasion of Iraq as an act of pre-emptive self-defence has helped to solidify the view that the US has actually adopted a strategy of prevention. However, the US administration was clearly divided on the issue. When asked whether Iraq was an example of the *Strategy* in practice, Secretary of State Colin Powell emphatically replied 'no, no, no' (Weisman 2003: B1). Instead, Powell preferred to argue that the war was justifiable because it was authorised by UN Security Council resolutions. However, Vice-President Dick Cheney, consistently justified the war in terms of the need to *prevent* Iraq acquiring WMD and since the war Bush himself has fallen back on the argument that 'America is safer' as a result of it (see Daalder and Lindsay 2003: 127).

Thus, although the *Strategy* itself offers a reasonable starting point for rethinking the concept of pre-emptive self-defence, it is important to bear in mind that in both its rhetoric and practice the Bush administration has deviated considerably from it and has equated prevention with pre-emption.

A new right of pre-emption?

How, then, should pre-emptive self-defence be reconceptualised to meet the threat of terrorism? There are two important caveats to begin with. First, as with every type of war, those engaging in pre-emptive self-defence must satisfy the *jus ad bellum* criteria. What is offered here is a framework for assessing whether claims of pre-emptive self-defence count as a 'just cause' in particular circumstances. If the other criteria are not satisfied, especially proportionality of ends, the resort to force cannot be justified. Second, the expanded concept of pre-emptive self-defence offered here only applies to the threat of terrorism (be that from states or non-state actors). If the nature of the threat is conventional, the *Caroline* criteria continue to apply.

As I noted earlier, the two central concepts of pre-emptive self-defence are 'imminence' and 'necessity'. According to the *Strategy*, it is only the concept of 'imminence' that needs rethinking. Traditionally, both the Just War tradition and positive international law have defined 'imminence' in temporal terms. A threat is imminent only immediately before the hammer is about to fall. An attack is imminent when the enemy has displayed an intention to attack, has armed itself, has deployed its forces into an offensive formation and is about to strike. The problem, of course, is that if the planned attack is a mass casualty terrorist attack, it is usually too late to respond at this point. This is an unreasonable expectation. We cannot overlook the fact that the existence of such a tight definition of imminence derived from the *Caroline* case may be due, at least in part, to the fact that the two parties to the dispute were liberal states with reasonably good relations (Sofaer 2003: 219). In cases where mutual mistrust is considerably higher, and doubt and mistrust is seldom higher than when confronting terrorism, a wider concept of imminence ought to be conceded to provide states with realistic means of preventing terror attacks against their citizens.

The need for a more flexible concept of imminence has been recognised by the ICJ. In 1997, the Court ruled that:

> 'Imminence' is synonymous with 'immediacy' or 'proximity' and goes far beyond the concept of 'possibility' ... the 'extremely grave and imminent peril' must 'have been a threat to the interest at the time'. That does not exclude, in the view of the Court, that a 'peril' appearing in the long term might be held to be 'imminent' as soon as it is established, at the relevant point in time, that the realization of that peril, however far off it might be, is not thereby any less certain and inevitable.[6]

In other words, the ICJ recognised that an imminent threat could be temporally distant yet nevertheless imminent depending on the likelihood of realisation and the gravity of the peril. In situations where a state can demonstrate that an actor has the intention and means to launch terrorist attacks against it or its allies, it is reasonable to suggest that the 'imminence' test is satisfied. The *demonstrability* of the intent and the means is critical. It is not enough for a government to convince itself of the threat. It must present reliable and accurate evidence both to its own citizens, other states and global civil society. Others will evaluate the evidence to decide whether, on a case-by-case basis, the pre-emptive attack was legitimate by reference to the demonstrable gravity of the threat, the known intentions of the potential terrorists and their ability to satisfy those intentions. The more actors that validate the action, the more legitimate it can be considered. In some cases it is not always appropriate for a state to reveal what it knows *before* it launches a pre-emptive attack, because doing so risks informing the terrorists of what it knows and losing the opportunity to strike them, but the burden of proof falls squarely on those that use pre-emptive force to demonstrate its case either before or immediately afterwards.

The second criterion that must be satisfied is necessity. According to Webster, necessity required that the threat be 'instant, overwhelming, leaving no choice of means and no moment for deliberation'. State practice itself has recognised that this sets the bar too high. Neither Israel's 1967 attack on Egypt nor the 2001 invasion of Afghanistan by the US and its allies would satisfy these criteria because of the possibility of deliberation. Nevertheless, international society legitimated both instances to a greater or lesser extent. Writing in 1961, McDougal and Feliciano (1961: 231) offered a more appropriate understanding of necessity. For them, the necessity criterion is satisfied when the degree of imminence is 'so high as to preclude effective resort by the intended victim to non-violent modalities of response' a view supported by Bowett (1958: 53) who insisted that the necessity requirement was fulfilled when there were no reasonable alternative means of protection. Pre-emptive self-defence is warranted when the use of force is the only reasonable way in which the threat can be averted. It does not require that all other means be exhausted first, but we are entitled to ask whether those that use pre-emptive force had reasonable alternatives. For instance, in most though not all instances of pre-emptive attacks against terrorists we might expect the state using force to explore options with the state whose territory it is using force in beforehand. At very least, we would expect a government using pre-emptive force in this way to be able to demonstrate that it seriously considered other, non-violent, options and for it to explain its reasons for not choosing these other courses of action.

This leaves the thorny question of whether it is only the intended victim that enjoys a right to act pre-emptively? I suggested that it was not necessary to know with certainty either the target or time of the intended terrorist attack. This approach therefore permits states that are not the intended target to use force pre-emptively if the twin conditions of imminence and necessity, as well as the other *jus ad bellum* conditions, are satisfied. This expansion of the right can be justified on three grounds. First, such acts could be interpreted as collective self-defence, which is expressly permitted by the UN Charter. Unless the actual intended target is a suicidal state, we can safely presume that it would welcome a pre-emptive strike by a third party that removed an impending threat. Second, terrorism can be viewed as a universal crime with a global jurisdiction. As such, states have a moral right to pre-empt terrorism globally. Finally, mass casualty terrorism represents such an affront to natural law that it grants states a moral right to use force to pre-empt it everywhere.

Although this expanded concept of pre-emption helps to meet the strategic challenge posed by terrorism, it creates three potential problems that positive law attempted to overcome by setting such a high threshold. The first is the problem of abuse. Making the concept of pre-emptive self-defence more flexible blurs important moral distinctions and creates avenues for political leaders to justify aggressive wars in terms of pre-emption. Henry Kissinger (*Financial Times*, 27 September 2002), for example, observed in relation to the *Strategy* that 'it cannot be either in American national interests or the world's interest to develop principles that grant every nation an unfettered right of pre-emption against its own definition of threats to its security'. The principal barrier to abuse is accountability. Governments are obliged to demonstrate their case to their own citizens, other states and global civil society.

The second problem is that by adding further ambiguity to the application of the right of pre-emptive self-defence this revised doctrine places greater emphasis on the factual elements of each case (see Byers 2003a: 182). Assessments of factual evidence are never free of values and politics and the emphasis on facts gives the powerful an opportunity to sway others by bringing financial, military and political pressure to bear. As Byers argues, this means that 'it is more likely that the criterion of imminence would be regarded satisfied when the United States wished to act militarily than when others wished to do the same' (p. 182). It is certainly the case that weak states, and states that are out of favour in the West, would have a much more difficult time persuading the most powerful members of international society of their cause than the US and its allies. That is not to say that the US claims will always be generally accepted, as the Iraq case demonstrates. Moreover, as with the ethics of war in general, the powerful have much more room for manoeuvre than the weak. Rule breaking always imposes costs, but the powerful are better able to bear those costs than the weak, at least in the short-term.

The third problem is that a more permissive doctrine of self-defence may significantly increase the potential for error (Crawford 2003a: 35). In a more permissive normative context states may be encouraged to use force precipitately based on flawed intelligence or misperceptions about threat. There are no sure ways of eliminating this problem. It stands to reason that the earlier a state acts to pre-empt a perceived threat the more likely the chances for error and misperception, and vice-versa: a state that waits longer will be more certain of its case but risks waiting too long. The problem can be moderated but not resolved by the requirement of *demonstrability*. The more perspectives that are brought to bear on a particular problem, the less likely the chances of error and misperception. A government is required to be sure of its case when it acts pre-emptively and it must demonstrate that it has taken every reasonable step to verify its evidence. If a state fails to demonstrate due care, it acts unjustly.

It is therefore important to limit this expanded right to pre-emptive self-defence. This expanded right is limited to cases where the anticipated threat is terrorist. There are no good grounds for reforming the traditional concept of self-defence in response to perceived conventional threats from so-called 'rogue states'. To claim the expanded right, a state must satisfy the *jus ad bellum* criterion plus the revised requirements of imminence and necessity outlined above. On top of all that, a state claiming this right must make itself accountable by presenting its case for others to evaluate either before or immediately after the pre-emptive attack and it must be able to demonstrate that it has shown due care in order to reduce the likelihood of error or misperception.

The expanded right of pre-emption poses only two tests: imminence and necessity. To satisfy the first test, those invoking the expanded right must demonstrate that a group or state has both the intention and means to conduct terrorist attacks against it or its allies. However, unlike the traditional concept, under the expanded concept it is not necessary to know with certainty precisely when or where the terrorists will strike. To satisfy the second, it must demonstrate that the use of force is necessary: that is, it is the only way that the threat can be addressed.

Acknowledgements

This chapter draws its argument and some of its text from (Bellamy 2006). Thanks to Richard Devetak, Roland Bleiker, Nick Wheeler, Paul D. Williams and especially Sara E. Davies for helpful comments and suggestions on earlier drafts.

Notes

1   *Case Concerning Military and Paramilitary Activities in and against Nicaragua* (Merits) [1986], ICJ Report, p. 103.
2   *Case Concerning Military and Paramilitary Activities in and against Nicaragua* (Merits) [1986], ICJ Report, p. 14.
3   The following discussion draws on (Stevens 2004).
4   *The Caroline.* Letter from Mr Webster to Mr Fox (24 April 1841), *British and Foreign State Papers*, 1129, 1138.
5   *The Caroline.* Letter from Mr Webster to Mr Fox (24 April 1841), *British and Foreign State Papers*, 1129, 1138.
6   *Case concerning the Gabcikovo–Nagymaros Project (Hungary vs. Slovakia)*, 1997.

Part III
Fighting terror

8 Failures, rogues and terrorists

States of exception and the North/South divide

Richard Devetak

The foreign policy and security discourses of the North have increasingly come to focus on two types of states: failed and rogue states. Failed states signify the descent into lawless violence, a kind of post-sovereign nightmare within the territorial boundaries of an erstwhile state. Rogue states, by contrast, denote the wilful defiance by a sovereign state of international law's rules and norms. While the former type of state calls for international assistance, the latter demands punishment. Failed and rogue states thus represent two different problems and two different responses. But for all the differences exhibited by the two types of state, there are some significant commonalities in the way the North views these states, largely because they are identified with the South. This chapter seeks to elaborate some of the distinctive features that characterize how the North views the South.

I begin by offering a sketch of changes introduced by the Cold War's close. In particular, I want to show how the North began to see the South essentially as a *distant problem*. Let me dwell on that emphasised noun and accompanying adjective for just a moment. A 'problem' because the South came to represent enduring social, economic and political crises: from chronic famine and massive refugee flows to 'new wars' and 'complex emergencies'. If the North represented a model of social, economic and political development, the South came to embody the continuing lack of all the North's virtues and achievements. 'Distant' in the sense that the North felt safely removed from the violence associated with the South, spatially and temporally. I will elaborate this point below. Next, I will briefly comment on how the September 11 terrorist attacks called for a rethinking of this conception of the North–South relationship. To put it bluntly, no longer a distant problem, the South became the North's problem. I'm even tempted to say a problem 'internal' to the North.

The remainder of the chapter will elaborate some of the political rationalities and practices that govern the North's conception and interaction with the South. This will revolve primarily around the North's dealings with rogue and failed states. I shall use some ideas from Italian philosopher, Giorgio Agamben, to explain how the North's security practices have increasingly revolved around states of exception which cast the South into a kind of 'no-man's land' beyond the protection of the international legal order. In essence, I argue, the North has come to see the South as a direct and immediate source of threats to its own well-being, though without acknowledging its complicity in the South's problems or acknowledging how it too has come to exhibit some of the traits it condemns in rogues and failures. In particular, the North has come to associate the South with terrorism, of both state and non-state varieties. I think that is the reason why the North no longer sees the South as a distant problem, but a pressing and adjacent one, requiring either forcible intervention (in the case of rogues) or governance assistance (in the case of failures).

Changes in strategic cartography: from the end of the Cold War to September 11

The end of the Cold War and the September 11 terrorist attacks are obvious markers in the transformation of the international security agenda as conceived by states of the North. I think we need to understand the post-Cold War changes before grafting the post-September 11 changes onto them. In this section I will provide a brief overview of these changes with the intention of outlining the conditions that govern how the North views the South. The North's image of the South is politically important because it shapes how the North interacts with and acts towards the South. It also helps reinforce the idea that the planet can be neatly divided between distinct zones of war and peace.

To outline the shifting contours of international security I will draw attention to the changing strategic cartographies that reshape how the North views the South. While political upheavals and events may widen or narrow the physical or geographical distance between North and South, the North's perception of its civilizational distance ahead of the South remains unchanged. The point will be to show that the changing cartography modifies the North's strategic vision, changing the way it perceives and responds to threats, but all the while retaining enduring assumptions about its civilizational superiority.

Widening the North–South gap: after the Cold War's collapse

An exhaustive description of the post-Cold War security agenda is out of the question here. But we can briefly point to several key factors that characterized post-Cold War geopolitics. First, the strategic rivalry that defined the Cold War came to an end. Between the breaching of the Berlin Wall in late 1989 and the collapse of the Soviet Union in 1991, the US was deprived of its enemy, thereby dissolving the bipolar system. Second, the 'Third World', as the South was previously known, declined in strategic significance as great powers disengaged (Van Evera 1990). Capitals in the North could dispense with containment in the South now that the Soviet Union was dead. Third, perceptions grew of the USA's hegemony and invulnerability. Fourth, in the developed world of the North, while geopolitics never disappeared, it certainly appeared according to many liberals to diminish in importance *vis-à-vis* 'geo-economics'. Fifth, in the underdeveloped world of the South the phenomena of 'complex emergencies' and 'new wars' multiplied.

In this context, and with the implosion of the East-West conflict, commentators and scholars increasingly came to view the world split between a pacified core and a conflict-riddled periphery. James Goldgeier and Michael McFaul (1992), for example, tell a 'tale of two worlds'. In one world the major powers converge around an agreed set of norms, by contrast, in the other, no such consensus exists or is foreseeable and violent conflict is prevalent.

Differences between states in the core (or North) and periphery (or South) were said to revolve around the goals and the behaviour of states. Goldgeier and McFaul (1992) asserted that core states would not need to remain 'essentially war making machines', to use Robert Gilpin's words. They could put wealth ahead of power in pursuit of the national interest. By contrast, peripheral states would persist in their preference for power over wealth. To put it differently, geopolitics would retain its primacy over geo-economics. In the core, realist theory was said to have lost its power as an explanation because Northern states were thought to have moved beyond war. In the periphery, by contrast, where the security dilemma was still central, realism was said to be as powerful as ever because wars continued unabated.

By the late 1990s, however, even the continuing violence in the periphery was thought to be beyond realism's account. Mary Kaldor (1999) made a strong case for seeing the violence in the periphery as novel and a departure from the violent conflicts associated with the Cold War. She identified several characteristics of the 'new wars' which, again, I simply list. First, conflicts seemed to be bereft of the decisive battle between state military forces that Clausewitz envisaged. Second, and again allegedly outside Clausewitz's imaginary, war declarations and peace treaties were said to be absent. Third, many of these conflicts seemed to involve the deliberate targeting of civilians. Practices of ethnic cleansing and genocide were common across wars in the Balkans and Africa. Fourth, the rise of non-state violent actors such as mercenaries, warlords and terrorists, seemed to augur the waning of the state's monopoly over the instruments of violence. Fifth, these 'new wars' often produced humanitarian catastrophes that, conveyed via global news media, shocked the consciences of humankind. Sixth, the cruelty and inhumanity in these 'new wars' sparked calls for humanitarian intervention.[1]

The purpose of Kaldor's argument was to mark a temporal break between the Cold War and post-Cold War period on the basis of the transformation of organized violence. Interestingly, this 'new wars' discourse may be seen to reinforce the sense of distance between North and South. Even humanitarian intervention could be interpreted as a means by which the North reaffirmed the gap between itself and the South. Dispatching troops to far away places would help confirm the image of an orderly, civilized North pacifying a chronically underdeveloped and violent South.

There are three points I wish to make about the post-Cold War discourses. First, that as Anne McClintock (1995: 40) observes in her analysis of nineteenth-century imperialism, 'Geographical difference across *space* is figured as a historical difference across *time*'. The zones of war/chaos are figured as 'anachronistic spaces', zones which are 'perpetually out of time in modernity, marooned and historically abandoned' (McClintock 1995: 41). In Fukuyama's Hegelian terms, they remain 'mired in history', as opposed to the West/North which has reached history's end. The point is, spatial distance is converted into temporal progress. Second, the North perceives itself as essentially a spectator watching tragedies unfold in the South's zones of chaos. Though it occasionally participates in the South's politics, it does so through selective humanitarian intervention only, thus preserving its sense of distance, and of course its sense of moral and military superiority. Third, the 'tale of two worlds' narrative allowed the North to reproduce a dual pattern of international order whose historical purpose, as Edward Keene (2002) brilliantly demonstrates, was simultaneously to promote co-existence and toleration among legal equals in Europe, and to promote civilization in the extra-European world by introducing or imposing European norms and institutions.

All of this has helped to create a sense of distance between the North and South – both physical and civilizational. The North assumed itself to be secure against the South's problems, safe from the dangers of its anachronism. The strategic and economic imperatives of the North were thought to be unconnected to political dynamics in the South. The South's problems, often viewed as chronic – think for example of enduring 'Afro-pessimism' – were relegated to the bottom of the security agenda. The North's civilizational ascendancy was thought to reinforce its physical separation, making its prosperity and security safe from the South's privation and insecurity.

Collapsing the North–South gap: after September 11

The September 11 terrorist attacks however caused a dramatic upheaval of this assumption. The world's strongest military and economic power was struck in its greatest city, New York, and in its capital, Washington. The US was, it turned out, more vulnerable than at first thought. Most importantly for my purposes here, the strategic cartography was profoundly re-ordered. In words taken from 'The Failed States Index', 'Failed states have made a remarkable odyssey from the periphery to the very center of global politics' (Foreign Policy and Fund for Peace 2005: 57). The distance between North and South has narrowed considerably since that day in September 2001; the US, and the North more generally, became mired in history, wounded by the South's violent anachronism.

This collapsing of distance is crucial in understanding why the 'failed states' and 'rogue states' discourses have become so central to defence and foreign policy discussions today in the North. As Michael Ignatieff (2003: 21) remarks, 'Terror has collapsed distance, and with this collapse has come a sharpened focus in imperial capitals on the necessity of bringing order to the barbarian zones'. If previously the North was content to neglect the South, the rise of global terrorism seems to have provoked a rethink. Globalization makes it possible for political violence to overcome distance, impacting in locations far removed from the origin (see Devetak and Hughes forthcoming). In the words of USAID's *Fragile States Strategy* (2005: 1), 'the events of September 11, 2001, profoundly demonstrated the global reach of state failure and focused attention on their drivers and products

– weak governance, poverty, and violent conflict'. And it is not just aid agencies making this argument. The White House in its 2002 and 2006 National Security Strategy papers emphasizes the dangerous spillover effects generated by failing or failed states. 'Regional conflicts do not stay isolated for long and often spread or devolve into humanitarian tragedy or anarchy', the 2006 NSS reports. This is why it asserts that 'even if the United States does not have an direct stake in a particular conflict, [its] interests are likely to be affected over time' (NSC 2006: 14).

While the North could rest content with occasional and selective humanitarian interventions into the South during the 1990s, western capitals, especially in Washington, London and Canberra, came to the conclusion after September 11 that their own security could no longer be abstracted from the South. Under conditions of globalization geographical distance presented less of an obstacle to those intent on harming westerners, western interests or western cities. The North was no longer an external observer or spectator of events in the South – instead, it became a participant. We might say that the North was drawn into the South's orbit, perhaps even became part of the South insofar as problems associated with the South now penetrate the North. But, as we shall see, this is a reality that the North seeks to resist vigorously. Its response to September 11 has been to try and restore as much distance between itself and the South as possible through two particular strategies that I outline below. For the moment, however, I simply wish to identify one of the key functions performed by this cartography, which is to spatialize the sources of violence and, in particular, terrorism. The flipside of this spatialization of violence is the identification of civilization with the North. It is for precisely this point that President Bush (2001 speech) repeatedly equates the 'war on terror' with 'a war to save civilization'.

Many post-Cold War analyses of international relations, as we have noted, divided the world into zones of peace and war, a division that was intended to coincide with the distinction between liberal and non-liberal states. Liberal states resided in the North, whilst the South's zones of chaos are coterminous for the most part with non-liberal states. Liberal theorists such as Anne-Marie Slaughter (1995) believe that liberal theories actually demand discrimination between states based on their liberal democratic credentials. 'The most distinctive aspect of Liberal international relations theory', she says, 'is that it permits, indeed mandates, a distinction between types of states, based on their domestic political structure and ideology' (1995: 504).

The zones of chaos comprise at least two types of states: failed and rogue. In the following section I want to focus on the ways that liberal and neo-conservative discourses of international relations tend to identify the sources of terrorism with failed and rogue states in such a way that the North's preferred strategic cartography and the moral assumptions it entails remain fundamentally unaltered. As we shall see, the 'failed states' and 'rogue states' discourses are intended to reinforce distinctions between the 'civilized' and the 'barbaric'. However, the intentions are ultimately outflanked by the contradictions between ideals and reality. The North's credentials as the repository of civilization, liberalism and even democracy are arguably undermined by the foreign policy strategies it adopts.

States of exception: from Schmitt to Agamben

In this section I want to introduce some of Giorgio Agamben's key ideas in *Homo Sacer* (1998) and *State of Exception* (2005). I cannot do justice to the historical richness and theoretical complexity of his arguments here, but I do want to sketch some of the ways his thought may be turned to an analysis of rogue and failed states. In short, I suggest that Agamben's writings can help us see how the North's 'war on terror' has established spaces of exception where the North can subjectively apply law and violence to states it deems rogue or failing.

To understand Agamben's argument, however, we must first revisit Carl Schmitt's argument about sovereignty and the political. For Schmitt, sovereignty and the political are inseparable; neither can be understood independently of the other. Schmitt (1996: 26), it should be recalled, believed that the essence of politics lies in the fundamental distinction between friend and enemy. It defines the political, Schmitt thought, in the same way that right and wrong define law, and beautiful and ugly define aesthetics. The 'intense and extreme antagonism' (Schmitt 1996: 29) that interposes itself between groups, making violent confrontation an ever-present possibility between friend and enemy, makes politics what it is, to Schmitt's mind.

Schmitt (1985: 5) argued that 'Sovereign is he who decides on the exception'.[2] Sovereignty denotes the power and authority to make ultimate political decisions and to declare a state of exception, that is, suspend the normal workings of the constitution. A few words on the exception are worthwhile here. A state of exception refers to situations in which a government responds to a crisis or emergency by temporarily suspending the normal legal order. Most constitutions provide governments with the power to declare a state of exception so as to defeat a threat faced by the state. The purpose of this authority, as Ferejohn and Pasquino (2004: 210) explain, is to preserve the state and its constitutional or legal order. Such a suspension is meant to be exceptional and provisional; that is, it is only meant to be invoked when the state faces an existential threat, and normalcy is meant to be restored as soon as the threat disappears. Agamben (2005: 1) believes states of exception to be paradoxical in that they are 'juridical measures that cannot be understood in legal terms'; that is to say, they are the result of a *political* decision to suspend the normal legal order.

The purpose behind suspending the law is, as counter-intuitively as it may sound, to conserve the state in the face of a crisis or threat so severe that it imperils the state's continued existence. 'What characterizes an exception', says Schmitt (1985: 12), 'is principally unlimited authority, which means the suspension of the entire existing order'. Political theorist, Clinton Rossiter (1949), made a similar case from mid-twentieth century USA. In fact, he defended what he calls 'constitutional dictatorship' as the most effective and legitimate, albeit temporary, response to a case of existential peril. Returning to the German jurist, Schmitt's thought operates around a distinction between the norm and the exception. In normal situations the state's legal order can function on the basis of norms. But in times of emergency, exceptional measures are required; measures that may be outside the powers normally granted to the sovereign by the constitution.[3] The sovereign suspends the law in the exception because the normal application of the law is inadequate; because, as Schmitt (1985: 13) says, '[t]here exists no norm that is applicable to chaos'. To Schmitt's way of thinking, that would be like trying to regulate the 'unregulatable'. It would be futile at best, dangerous at worst, because it would put the state's existence at risk. That is why he counterposes his view to Kant's liberal constitutionalism which, he thinks, tries to regulate the exception (Schmitt 1985: 14), and in so doing fails to meet the threat.

Agamben makes two main departures from Schmitt. First, he argues, contra Schmitt, that the key distinction in Western political metaphysics is not between friend and enemy, but between 'bare life' and political life. Indeed, Agamben (1998: 7) avers, the originary exclusion of bare life is what constitutes the political. Aristotle and the classical Greek thinkers distinguished between *zoē* and *bios*, natural and political life. Natural life, for the Greeks, was outside or excluded from the *polis*. The politically qualified life was opposed to and elevated above the simple biological fact of living. The political life (*bios politikos*) concerned, or presupposed, speech as the pre-eminent instrument of power, the capacity to communicate, to engage in open dialogue, to negotiate, to respect rules and to disagree without resort to violence.[4] It involved relations among equals, and it was aimed at achieving the good life. In Arendt's (1958: 26) words, 'To be political … meant that everything was decided through words and persuasion and not through force and violence'. Bare life, on the other hand, was about survival, mere existence, bodily and species reproduction. It generally involved relations of domination; between a man and his wife, a parent and child, a master and slave. In bare life, where necessity governs, force and violence are justified 'because they are the only means to master necessity' (Arendt 1958: 31).

Though the Greeks sought to maintain the separation of bare or 'natural' life and political life, Agamben follows both Hannah Arendt (1958) and Michel Foucault (1978) in noting the way 'natural life' has intruded upon political life. In fact, whereas Arendt and Foucault tend to see this as a largely modern development, Agamben sees it as extending back to the ancient Greeks themselves. Additionally, Agamben (1998: 7–8) wants to emphasize that the exclusion of bare life is also an inclusion, or in his words, 'an inclusive exclusion'. Bare life remains included in politics insofar as it takes the form of the state of exception. Agamben's purpose is to highlight the unavoidable intersection or 'zone of indistinction' between bare life and political life. That is why he retains Foucault's term, 'biopower'. But if Foucault thought biopower defined a mode of government that succeeds sovereignty, Agamben insists that sovereignty has always rested on a form of biopower; that bare life has always been politicized. In other words, sovereign power is always already biopower, and is always already producing bare life and its defining but ambivalent figure, the outcast *homo sacer* (sacred or accursed man). *Homo sacer* was a figure of Roman antiquity who could be killed but not sacrificed (Agamben 1998: 83), the Latin *sacer* meaning sacred or damned. Banned from the political community and confined to bare life, *homo sacer* is less than a full political being; that is why his killing qualifies as neither murder nor sacrifice. He is 'the one with respect to whom all men act as sovereigns' (Agamben 1998: 84).[5]

Second, Agamben adapts and further develops Schmitt's thinking about the exception by linking it to bare life and the production of *homines sacri*. The state of exception thus has a biopolitical significance that Agamben wishes to elaborate. He argues that the state of exception 'binds and, at the same time, abandons the living being to law' (Agamben 2005: 1). *Homo sacer* is abandoned or excluded insofar as he is denied a political voice and legal equality, but included insofar as he is punishable by the law. Hence Agamben's (1985: 17–18) insistence that the exception is '*a kind* of exclusion [my emphasis]'. It is only a qualified exclusion because what it excludes is still, in important ways, included in the law, subject to the force of law. At any rate, *homines sacri* will always be subject to the sovereign power's monopoly to decide the exception, and will always live under the threat of its force. That is why Agamben employs the notion of 'zones of indistinction', because it 'is literally not possible to say whether the one who has been banned is outside or inside the juridical order' (Agamben 1985: 28–9).

I want to suggest that the post-Cold War and post-September 11 discourses reproduce 'zones of indistinction', spaces of exception where life and politics, law and violence pass incessantly into one another. In these international spaces of exception, rogue and failed states are neither clearly outside nor clearly inside the law. The rogue state is like the *wargus* or 'wolf-man', German and Scandanavian antiquity's name for the bandit or outlaw that Agamben (1998: 104–6) describes and links to Hobbes's state of nature. The failed state is like the *homo sacer*, less than a complete political being, concerned with 'mere' survival. Both are posited as variations of *homo sacer* and located in or cast out (*ex-capere*) into a space of exception by sovereign power.[6] They are therefore always vulnerable to a decision to enforce the law, even though they have been banished to the exterior of international society.

Failures, rogues and terrorists

In this final section of the chapter I want to suggest that Agamben's analysis may be usefully applied to the study of the North's view of the South. Both rogue states and failed states, we shall see, are situated *outside* politics by the North, they are both marked as 'bare life'. Rogue states lack political language; failed states reduce politics to bare life. Each instance evokes a different response from the North. In the case of rogue states, a more Schmittean response is developed – one that suspends the rule of law and operates in a state of exception. Rogue states are deemed incorrigible; incapable of being civilized, they must therefore be eliminated. They are 'hopeless cases' to use Barry Hindess's (2001) terms from another context. In the case of failed states, the North applies biopolitical governmental practices developed around health, wealth, poverty, security, migration and structures of governance – in short, 'good governance'. These states are, in contrast to rogues, redeemable. They are what Hindess (2001) would call 'subjects of improvement', capable of being civilized as long as they are subjected to the North's disciplinary measures designed to foster life. Both rogue and failed states are rendered external to the political realm, outside international society.

Rogue states as/and terrorists

In this section I want to outline the way that rogue states are cast outside international society only to be subjected to the law's force. Rogue states are deemed to exist outside the political because they stand accused of rejecting international society's rules and norms. They represent a threat not just to regional or global security, and not just to their own citizens, but to international law. They are serial law-breakers, dangerous recidivists, 'hopeless cases' incapable of being reformed. Nevertheless, they are still subject to the punishing force of law.

This was President Bush's (2002c) point in his infamous State of the Union address where he invoked the 'axis of evil'. Rogue states were condemned for sponsoring terrorism and/or committing terrorist acts against their own citizens. Iraq under Saddam Hussein was, of course, the rogue state *par excellence*. In the words of the USA's Department of Defense's (DOD) *National Defense Strategy* (United States Department of Defense 2005: 2), Saddam was 'a tyrant who used WMD, supported terrorists, terrorized his population, and threatened his neighbors'. Even the Clinton administration saw Saddam's Iraq as cast out into a space of exception. Assistant Secretary of State Martin Indyk said, 'Iraq, under Saddam Hussein, remains dangerous, unreconstructed, defiant, and isolated'. It would 'never be able to be rehabilitated or reintegrated into the community of nations' while Saddam was ruler (quoted in Kagan 2003: 44).

I do not intend to get into detailed discussion of what makes a state a rogue, suffice to say that consensus on the criteria remains elusive. Rather, I simply want to highlight the political function of the adjective 'rogue'; a word which can function as either an attribute or a substantive. Jacques Derrida remarks that the adjective 'rogue' can sometimes be applied to a subject who is occasionally, rather than substantively, a rogue (Derrida 2005: 79). We might then speak of someone acting the rogue, or we may even refer to someone as a 'loveable rogue'.[7] 'Rogueness' here is an aspect of the subject's identity, though it does not determine or define it; it is one among many attributes.

On the other hand, 'rogueness' may be a quality that defines a subject's identity through and through. To name someone or something rogue here is to make an accusation or denunciation, and thence prepare the way for, and justify, some kind of sanction. A rogue state will need to be 'punished, contained, rendered harmless, reduced to a harmless state, if need be by the force of law [*droit*] and the right [*droit*] of force' (Derrida 2005: 79). This is, of course, precisely the manner in which 'rogue state' has come to be used in contemporary international relations. It leads to the conclusion, to 'the armed conclusion', as Derrida says, 'to use force to confront them, in the name of a presumed right and the reason of the strongest' (Derrida 2005: 80).

It has the effect of not just characterizing the other state as substantively rogue, but suggesting, if only by implication, that the denouncing state is substantively *not* rogue. Roland Bleiker (2003: 732) makes a similar point, showing how the concept of rogue state draws upon a Manichean distinction between good and evil. Moreover, 'the rhetoric of evil moves the concept of rogue states into the realm of irrationality. "Evil" is in essence a term of condemnation for a phenomenon that can neither be fully comprehended nor addressed other than through militaristic forms of dissuasion and retaliation' (Bleiker 2003: 732). The implication is that reason is beyond the rogues' capabilities. Rogues cannot be persuaded by reasoned argument, and they will not be reasonable. That is why they are seen as incorrigible, 'hopeless cases', who must be dealt with differently from all others.

Responding to rogues: from speech to the language of force

In this section I suggest that the North's response to rogue states follows a Schmittean understanding of politics. Abandoning the ancient Greek and democratic pre-eminence given to speech and equality, the North, led by the US, has arrogated to itself the position of sovereign power, free to decide unilaterally the use of force.

Rogue states, it is commonly said, understand only one thing, the use of force. On 4 February, 1999, just prior to the Rambouillet meeting on Kosovo, US Secretary of State Madelaine Albright said: 'we learned in Bosnia, and we have seen in Kosovo, that President Milosevic understands only the language of force. Nothing less than strong engagement from NATO will focus the attention of both sides; and nothing less than firm American leadership will ensure decisive action'.[8] Assigning rogue status to another state thus opens the path to the use of force. In this way, states such as Serbia under Milosevic or Iraq under Saddam are said to differ from liberal democracies, which value civility, dialogue, and the peaceful resolution of conflict. Liberal democratic states can therefore legitimately suspend their commitment to liberal democratic principles and the rule of law because rogue states signal an exception.

Interestingly, but perhaps not surprisingly, the same view about the language of force finds expression in Osama bin Laden. A month after September 11, in a filmed interview given on 20 October, 2001, he says: 'Bush and Blair ... don't understand any language but the language of force. Every time they kill us, we kill them, so the balance of terror can be achieved'.[9]

Such assertions as these uttered by Albright and bin Laden rest on a notion that force is a kind of language. Diplomacy, language, communication, though apparently favoured by liberal democracies, are thought to be useless in dealing with rogues. Their stubborn refusal to understand their interlocutor means that negotiations will always break down. Patient diplomacy and conventional communication will never succeed in negotiations with rogue states, as President Bush (2004) has emphasised. Where missives fail however, missiles work. Unlike words, which always carry the potential for misunderstanding, weapons are thought to be devoid of ambiguity; they cannot be misinterpreted, not even by rogue states.

The view of language expressed by the assertion that rogue states 'only understand the use of force', is that force is itself actually a language too. It communicates. In fact, it communicates effectively, especially to rogue states who are inveterately unable or unwilling to engage in dialogue. In a sense, force is a pure language of communication, according to this viewpoint. While weapons may sometimes miss their intended target, as we know, their meaning is thought never to be in doubt, unlike words. This point of view 'leaves no room for equivocation, confusion, misunderstanding; no room for any others at all, for any back and forth, for exchange, for the delays and relays of a dialogue or a conversation' (Keenan 2004).

Indeed, this view of force as language reflects what American realist Stephen Van Evera (2006: 32) calls 'the Bush administration's macho approach to foreign policy'. This macho foreign policy presumes that 'reasoning with others is ... pointless' since they are 'immoral cowards who understand only the threat of force'; and that '[p]ublic diplomacy is for wimps' (ibid.). As Stefan Halper and Jonathan Clarke (2004: 13) point out in their comprehensive analysis of neoconservatism's influence over the Bush administration's foreign and defence policies, neo-conservatives are suspicious of confidence-building, dialogue and consensus. Indeed, they are even suspicious of stability and normalcy (ibid.). Their attraction to nationalism, war culture, and use of maximum force (George 2005: 181) naturally makes them averse to international rules and institutions that may restrain them (Ikenberry 2004: 9; see also Kagan 2003: 27–40). This is entirely consistent with a Schmittean conception of politics. To use force is, to use the title of Tom Keenan's fascinating paper, 'to speak in a language that needs no translation', an act of pure communicative force unburdened by the impurities of diplomatic dialogue, negotiation and compromise – that is to say, unburdened by the stuff of politics from Aristotle to Arendt.

Adopting this viewpoint has the effect, quite deliberately, of avoiding and indeed censuring dialogue and negotiation. Rogue states, because they are evil and because they misunderstand or distort normal communication are cast into the space of exception. Outside the law, they can only be communicated with by force. However, as Bleiker shows, a residual belief in the capacity of rogue states to understand normal communication persists. Though Bush sees North Korea firmly lined on the 'axis of evil', he does not preclude the possibility of engaging it in dialogue. 'Indeed, the assumption is that threats will induce dialogue' (Bleiker 2003: 732). Once the threat of force has communicated the point to the rogue, the rogue will thenceforth be able and willing to negotiate with the US. This marks a slight twist on the original supposition that rogue states only understand the language of force: after the deployment of force, *après coup*, normal communication can be resumed and they can return to the fold. Indeed, it is not quite right that rogue states reside entirely outside the law, for they are still punishable under the force of law asserted by the North.

All of this simply functions to reinforce the strategic cartographies I elaborated earlier. The barbarians and animals (recall Hobbes's *homo hominibus lupus* – man is a wolf to other men), those beyond the North's frontiers, mired in history and the zone of chaos, do not speak *our* language. They speak only the language of force, not our native (liberal democratic) tongue; but, as the US has made clear, even the North is capable of speaking the language of force when necessity demands. This 'bilingualism' bespeaks an ambivalence in the North's identity – it is capable of being both rogue and, when necessity demands, non-rogue. For all the differences that exist between, say, the US and Iraq, rogueness will not provide a stable or reliable criterion for distinguishing them.

Failed states as incubators of terrorism

In this section I want to show how failed states too have become closely aligned with the terrorist threat. In short, they have come to be viewed as 'incubators' or 'breeding grounds' of terrorism. This is a point made by leading scholars such as Stephen Krasner, Robert Rotberg and Stephen Van Evera as well as politicians from George W. Bush to John Howard. Once again, an 'inclusive exclusion' casts failed states out of international society whilst simultaneously including them as reformable subjects, capable of re-entering international society on condition of restoring the political through 'good governance'.

Rotberg, one of the leading scholars on the subject, defines failed states as 'incapable of projecting power and asserting authority within their borders, leaving their territories governmentally empty' (2002: 128). Various economic and political factors lead to state failure, but I shall not discuss them here. I merely want to point to the consequences. As violent conflict and lawlessness escalate, human insecurity deepens; a kind of Hobbesian *bellum omnium contra omnes* develops, or at least a war of some against some. As Rotberg explains, the humanitarian disasters generated by failed states, including large-scale human rights violations, human displacement, and continuing violence, have created critical difficulties for international society. But the critical difficulties are not simply reducible to humanitarian disaster. 'In the wake of September 11, the threat of terrorism has given the problem of failed nation-states an immediacy and importance that transcends its previous humanitarian dimension' (Rotberg 2002: 127).

Failed states have become critical features of the new strategic imperatives governing the North. 'In less interconnected eras, state weakness could be isolated and kept distant. Failure had fewer implications for peace and security. Now, these states pose dangers not only to themselves and their neighbors but also to peoples around the globe' (Rotberg 2002: 127). But the key proposition is this: 'Failed states have come to be feared as "breeding grounds of instability, mass migration, and murder" (in the words of Stephen Walt), as well as reservoirs and exporters of terror' (Rotberg 2002: 128).

Krasner and Pascual rehearse the same argument. Echoing Rotberg's claim about the changed strategic environment, Krasner and Pascual (2005: 153) say, 'In today's increasingly interconnected world, weak and failed states pose an acute risk to US and global security'. They also believe that, 'When chaos prevails, terrorism, narcotics trade, weapons proliferation, and other forms of organized crime can flourish' (Krasner and Pascual 2005: 153). Afghanistan, they say, was a prime example of a failed state generating a terrorist problem for the US. 'Left in dire straits, subject to predation, and denied access to basic services, people become susceptible to the exhortations of demagogues and hatemongers' (Krasner and Pascual 2005: 153).

In a withering attack on the Bush administration's handling of the 'war on terror', Van Evera (2006) makes the same argument, arguing that failed states pose a much greater threat to the US than authoritarian but otherwise stable states like Iraq or Syria. 'Al-Qaeda and other terror groups grow and thrive in failed states, using them as havens in which they can establish secure bases to mass-produce trained, motivated killers', he claims (Van Evera 2006: 34). Despite US success in deposing the Taliban, ungoverned zones have emerged in the southern and eastern parts of Afghanistan and northwestern parts of Pakistan that have allowed al-Qaeda to re-establish a foothold from which they can train operatives and prepare attacks. In Van Evera's (2006: 34) words, this 'terrorist cauldron' demonstrates the dangers of allowing failed states to develop unhindered, and illustrates 'that state failure can be dangerously contagious', spreading relatively freely across sovereign borders.

Such arguments are not confined to academia. George W. Bush in his Preface to the *National Security Strategy of the United States of America* (NSC 2002) observed: 'The events of September 11, 2001, taught us that weak states, like Afghanistan, can pose as great a danger to our national interests as strong states. Poverty does not make poor people into terrorists and murderers. Yet, poverty, weak institutions, and corruption can make weak states vulnerable to terrorist networks and drug cartels within their borders'.[10] The NSC (2002) bluntly declares, 'America is now threatened less by conquering states than we are by failing ones'.

The same argument is employed by the DOD and US Agency for International Development (USAID). 'The absence of effective governance in many parts of the world creates sanctuary for terrorists, criminals, and insurgents. Many states are unable, and in some cases unwilling, to exercise effective control over their territory or frontiers, thus leaving areas open to hostile exploitation' (United States Department of Defense 2005: 3). 'Weak states tend to be the vector for these destabilizing forces, manifesting the dark side of globalization, and pose a very difficult kind of national security challenge' (USAID 2005: v).[11]

The Australian government has adopted a very similar set of assumptions regarding the threat failed states pose to national and international security. Prime minister John Howard (2005) declared that September 11 'told us in no uncertain terms that weak and failing states can act as breeding grounds for disorder, chaos and misery – and, ultimately, security threats. The erosion of state capacity is related to almost every class of threat we now face – from terrorism to transnational crime, civil wars to infectious disease'. Alexander Downer, Australia's foreign minister, says the threats Australia faces today 'are generated by much more than disputes between nation states and are not readily confined by state borders. Transnational terrorism, threats posed by the proliferation of weapons of mass destruction, increased intra-state conflict and the weakening of states by poor governance demonstrate this' (2005: 7). Elsewhere he explained that two key challenges confront the world today: global poverty and global insecurity. The latter comprises, according to Downer (2004), three elements: 'the murderous fanaticism of international terrorism, the nightmarish potential of the proliferation of weapons of mass destruction, [and] the incubators of future threats in failed states'. 'We cannot afford to ignore those societies that have ceased to function through a failure of political order, economic growth or social cohesion. Terrorism has underlined the threat to international security posed by weak and failed states'.

I do not want to dwell on the validity of these claims here, so much as reflect on their political uses. Suffice to say, however, that several scholars and analysts have cast doubts on the idea that failed states offer the right environment for terrorists. Ken Ross (2003), Beth Greener-Barcham and Manuhuia Barcham (2006), Ken Menkhaus (2004) and Stewart Patrick (2006) and have all expressed reservations about the premise that failed states breed terrorism. Commenting on the Pacific Islands, Ross (2003: 694) observes that this type of argument simply reprises Cold War concerns that weak states in the region would make them vulnerable to communism. 'It is a seriously misjudged perspective', he says, 'for these [Pacific Island] states lack the necessary oxygen for would-be terrorists, for whom the concept "terror is theatre" is all important. This region lacks the facilities'. Greener-Barcham and Barcham (2006: 74) express the same doubts about the 'failed states-terrorism connection' in the South Pacific, arguing that 'the possibilities for terrorist activity are arguably lessened in the Pacific as it is characterized by a lack of land borders and soft targets, and by small-scale closely knit and predominantly rural societies where everybody knows everyone else's business. Menkhaus (2004: 71) offers a similar assessment: 'In fact, transnational criminals and terrorists have found zones of complete state collapse like Somalia to be relatively inhospitable territory out of which to operate'. And so too does Patrick (2006: 33–6). The connection between these states and terrorism is far more tenuous. As he explains, 'not all weak and failed states are afflicted by terrorism', nor is the terrorism that may arise there necessarily transnational (ibid.: 35). These analysts dispute the contention that failing or failed states are hotbeds of terrorism. In fact, if terrorists are to find any states congenial to their cause, preparations and operations, it is more likely to be functional or semi-functional states like Pakistan.

There is, however, one erstwhile rogue state that seems to have become much more important to global terrorism, Iraq. Though US-led invasion of Iraq was intended to eliminate Iraq's links with terrorism, it seems instead to have created them where none previously existed. It is now a weak or failing state where lawlessness has escalated and terrorism is rife. In this respect, Iraq has been transformed by the 'coalition of the willing' from a rogue state to a genuine failing state. In any case, it is still cast out into a space of exception.

Responding to failed states: good governance

I suggest, in this section, that the North's preferred response to failed states differs from its response to rogues. While it still treats the South as residing in a space of exception, it foregoes the use of force, favouring the imposition of a complex mix of political and economic measures to promote not just human security but state security.

In July 2004 the US Department of State established the Office of the Coordinator for Reconstruction and Stabilization (S/CRS) to respond to threats 'failing and post-conflict societies' pose to their own citizens, neighbouring populations and to the US. Its mission is to 'lead, coordinate and institutionalize US government civilian capacity to prevent or prepare for post-conflict situations, and to help stabilize and reconstruct societies in transition from conflict or civil strife, so they can reach a sustainable path towards peace, democracy and a market economy'.[12] The S/CRS will work to ensure that US governmental agencies, NGOs and foreign governments coordinate their responses to the complex emergencies thrown up by failing or failed states. This was subsequently supplemented by the Presidential Directive on US Efforts for Reconstruction and Stabilization whose purpose is to empower the Secretary of State in working together 'with other countries and organizations, to anticipate state failure, avoid it whenever possible, and respond quickly and effectively when necessary and appropriate to promote peace, security, development, democratic practices, market economies, and the rule of law'.[13]

These ideas are not exactly new; aid and development have always been susceptible to security and foreign policy interests, but the precise instruments and the mode of operation have changed. Global liberal governance has been subsumed by a *biopolitics* which finds its organizing principles in the administration and production of life, rather than in threatening death/violence. It operates on populations and seeks to promote conditions intended to secure liberty and security by investing life through and through. Biopolitics thus becomes a means of strategically ordering the periphery, of bringing order to the zones of chaos.

Mark Duffield and Nicholas Waddell (2006: 3) argue that human security represents the fusion of security and development. Most importantly, in the present context development is increasingly understood *through* security imperatives. Insofar as development is granted importance in the post-9/11 context, it is always mediated through security frames. 'Among other things, development criteria are being reprioritized towards the rebuilding of toppled states and, in order to stem terrorist recruitment, towards addressing popular disaffection in strategically defined areas' (Duffield and Waddell 2006: 3).

Mark Duffield's idea of 'the securitization of development' seems useful here. By this phrase, Duffield (2001: 312) means that the security concerns of the core states have merged with the socio-economic concerns of aid agencies. 'If poverty and institutional malaise in the borderlands encourage conflict and undermine international stability, then the promotion of development with its intention of eliminating these problems simultaneously operates as a *security strategy*' (Duffield 2001: 312). This approach is evident in the growing amount of aid the US has committed to development. The US aid budget has tripled since 2002, having risen from \$12.9 billion to \$33.2 billion. The bulk of this aid flows to strategically important countries in the Middle East such as Israel, Egypt, Jordan, and Iraq, as well as countries in or on the edge of the zones of chaos: Afghanistan, Pakistan, and Uzbekistan (Woods 2005: 397). Interestingly though, only about \$2 billion of this aid has come through the standard appropriations process, most instead comes through supplemental appropriations (ibid.). But the US has explicitly recognized the link between development and security in many of the documents examined here, including the NSS of 2002 and 2006. It cannot be stated more clearly than this: 'Helping the world's poor is a strategic priority and a moral imperative' (NSC 2006: 31).

Humanitarian aid agencies are thus being integrated into strategies designed to bring order to the so-called 'zones of chaos'. Aid has become a 'technology of security', according to Duffield (2002: 154), as networks joining governments, NGOs, and UN agencies have been established to deliver development and humanitarian assistance where states fail. These networks are part of a broader framework of emerging global governance that sees the sources of economic failure, social instability, and ethnic conflict largely in the absence of a functioning market economy and democratically governed polity. The development malaise thus requires remedial treatment in the form of 'good governance'. This is an argument advanced by scholars such as Krasner as well as governments like Australia, for whom 'good governance is now the largest sectoral focus of Australia's aid program' (Department of Foreign Affairs and Trade 2002: Overview).

Conclusion

The argument presented here is that the North has tended to see the South as comprised of failed states and rogue states, both of which are identified as sources of terrorism. The association of the South with terrorism is prepared through a strategic cartography whereby a boundary is firmly inscribed between North and South, one which by and large assigns civilization to the North and barbarism to the South. More specifically, the South is associated with spaces of exception, where threats emanate from the very nature of the states – states conceived as *homines sacri*. Rogues and failures occupy the 'zone of indistinction' insofar as they are neither fully inside nor fully outside international society. They are outside to the extent that they do not conform to legitimate state behaviour, yet they are inside insofar as the North asserts the right to punish these states according to international society's rules.

Although the distance between North and South has undergone change as a consequence of the Cold War's end and the terrorist attacks of September 11, one thing has remained unchanged. The North continues to spatialize the sources of terrorist violence in such a manner that its origins appear to be exclusive to the spaces of exception inhabited by the South. This helps shore up a deeper assumption held by the North – that it remains the sole source of good governance and civilization, and that it alone is authorized to declare the exception.

Notes

1 For thoughtful critical engagements with the 'new wars' thesis see: Bellamy (2002), Berdal (2003) and Newman (2004). See Devetak (forthcoming) for my own account of the 'new wars'.
2 We might note the ambiguity of this formulation. It remains unclear whether the sovereign attains this status on account of being able to decide the exception, or whether the sovereign is able to decide the exception on account of being sovereign.
3 Rossiter (1949: 399) makes the same point specifically about constitutional democracies: 'the complex system of government of the democratic, constitutional state is essentially designed to function under normal, peaceful conditions, and is often unequal to the exigencies of a great national crisis'. Still, Rossiter (1949: 410) diverges from Schmitt in believing that it is possible to codify the limits of presidential power during a state of exception.
4 See Vernant (1982: 49–50) on the importance of speech (*lexis*) to ancient Greece. Arendt (1958: Chapters 4–5) adds action (*praxis*) as the other vital aspect of political life.
5 See Butler (2004: Chapter 3) for a powerful exploration of Guantanamo detainees are produced as *homo sacer* under the US program of 'infinite detention'.
6 Agamben (1998: 18) tells us that exception's etymological root is *taken outside* (*ex-capere*), and not simply excluded.
7 I am indebted to Gavin Mount for reminding me of the 'loveable rogue'.
8 This quote can be found in Linda Kozarin, 'Albright Says Kosovo Matters to United States', American Forces Information Service, News Articles, US Department of Defense, available at http://www.defenselink.mil/news/Feb1999/n0208199_9902084. html.
9 See #66 in the dossier put together by the British government, *Responsibility for the Terrorist Atrocities in the United States, 11 September 2001 – An Updated Account*, available at http://www.number-10.gov.uk/output/page3682.asp.
10 The point is repeated in the NSS 2006: 33.
11 James Kelly (US Assistant Secretary of State for East Asia and Pacific Affairs) warned, on 24 August 2004, that South Pacific island states could be 'soft targets' for terrorists. Although he knew of no evidence suggesting that Jemaah Islamiyya was active in the Pacific, he advised that 'we must be constantly alert' because they 'are not far in time or space from the Pacific' (Port Vila Presse 2004).
12 See the S/CRS's website: http://www.state.gov/s/crs/c12936.htm. See also the 20 Oct 2004 speech by Ambassador Carlos Pascual, Coordinator for Reconstruction and Stabilization, on 'Strengthening US Reconstruction and Stabilization capabilities' at http://www.state.gov/s/crs/rls/rm/37430.htm.
13 See the Presidential Directive at http://www.whitehouse.gov/news/releases/2005/12/2 0051214.html.

9 US bioterrorism policy

Christian Enemark

On 18 September 2001, two letters laced with *B anthracis* bacteria, addressed to *NBC Nightly News* and the *New York Post*, were postmarked from Trenton, New Jersey. On 3 October, photo editor Robert Stevens was diagnosed with pulmonary anthrax and placed on a respirator. Two days later, he became the first anthrax death in the United States in 25 years. On 9 October, two more anthrax-laced letters, addressed to US Senate Majority Leader Tom Daschle and Senator Patrick Leahy, were again postmarked from Trenton. In the weeks that followed, a total of five Americans died of anthrax and 17 more were infected. Although this set of events and the attacks of 11 September 2001 on the Pentagon and World Trade Center were almost certainly of separate origin, in combination they generated intense fears in the United States of a future biological attack causing mass casualties. The US government had been aware of the increasing potential for biotechnology to be misused long before the anthrax envelope attacks, and the Clinton administration had begun bolstering US biodefence capabilities in the late 1990s. In the 'post-9/11' atmosphere, however, annual federal government spending on biodefence programmes has increased enormously – from US$434 million in FY2001 to US$5.2 billion in FY2007. For the years FY2002–FY2007, the average amount spent on biodefence annually was around US$5.3 billion (Lam *et al.*, 2006: 114).

US biodefence was once exclusively the domain of military agencies and was aimed at protecting battlefield troops against state-run biological weapons (BW) programmes. Today, it is engaged in and promoted by a variety of government agencies contemplating acts of 'bioterrorism' by non-state actors, and it is aimed principally at protecting the American civilian population by pharmaceutical and other means. However, current US policy arguably imposes opportunity costs as regards public health and basic scientific research, and it has the potential to generate national and international security risks. To explore this proposition, it is useful to examine three issues: first, whether and to what extent pharmaceutical defences can counter the threat of BW; second, the implications for public health of prioritising research on pathogens thought to be of BW concern; and third, the international legal status and security significance of BW threat assessment projects carried out by national biodefence programmes. The United States is singled out for critical analysis not because its policy on bioterrorism is necessarily the most problematic, but rather because it is the most conspicuous. It is possible that many of the challenges highlighted in this chapter are relevant also in countries which are less open and to which fewer scholars have turned their attention.

Pharmaceutical defence

In a conflict situation, troops can be protected against BW by well-designed protective gear and reliable detection and diagnostic equipment. Protecting civilians is different; however grave the threat of biological attacks, protective suits are not about to be distributed to every American citizen. For the purposes of protecting the US population, the 'battlefield' during a deliberately-caused (or naturally-occurring) infectious disease outbreak would be the human body itself. Biodefence is therefore primarily about researching, developing, producing and administering pharmaceutical treatments, and vaccines in particular. The idea is that, by limiting the efficacy of biological agents, prophylactic and therapeutic drugs would reduce the attractiveness of the BW option to would-be aggressors and thereby offer some means of deterrence (and defence if deterrence fails).

Technological innovation in the area of pharmaceutical protection is the centrepiece of biodefence under the administration of President George W. Bush. Project Bioshield allocates around US$6 billion over 10 years to create a market for private companies to develop and sell to the US government the necessary vaccines and drugs to treat Americans in the event of a BW attack. Accompanying legislation is designed to expedite bureaucratic processes to do with drug research, such as hiring personnel and securing facilities and supplies. It also allows the Food and Drug Administration (FDA) to make experimental treatments available in emergencies (Quirk, 2004: 540). In the absence of this extraordinary government intervention, it is almost certain that market forces would not have led to the current significant increases in vaccine research and development. For companies which are interested in infectious disease treatments, it takes an estimated US$300 million to US$1 billion to bring a single vaccine to market (Hoyt and Brooks, 2004: 135). An indication of the decline in interest is that in 1967 there were 26 companies licensed by the FDA to manufacture vaccines, compared to just 12 in 2002 (D'Esopo and Nuzzo, 2004: 134). At present, the commercial incentives are greater to produce drugs to treat ongoing, non-infectious health problems such as cancer and heart disease, rather than those related to uncertain BW threats.

The assumption behind a technology-driven policy like Project Bioshield, and biodefence in general, is that it would in fact be possible to protect populations against an adversary bent on using biological agents. In the United States, this assumption is coupled with a strong belief that scientific research into vaccines and antimicrobial drugs can defeat every known BW agent and the genetic permutations of each, and perhaps achieve defences applicable to entire categories of diseases (Guillemin, 2005: 199). However, even dramatic technological advances cannot surmount the inherent asymmetry between offence and defence. With regard to deliberately-caused infectious disease threats, it is problematic for at least four reasons to rely on pharmaceutical protection, and on vaccines especially.

First, BW vaccines would only be useful in the highly unlikely event that the identity of the biological agent was known with certainty in advance of its use, and protecting civilians against a surprise attack is virtually impossible due to the wide variety of biological agents that could be used. At a congressional committee hearing in June 2005, Deputy Assistant Defense Secretary Dale Klein acknowledged that '[i]t's very difficult for us to come up with specific antidotes, pills and vaccines for everything the terrorists might throw at us'. (Fiorill, 2005). Moreover, the diversity of potential BW agents available expands greatly when one contemplates genetic engineering methods being used to create pathogens capable of evading existing drug treatments. For example, at around the time the US government was stockpiling 300 million doses of vaccine to defend against a smallpox attack, an Australian experiment with the mousepox virus showed how the smallpox vaccine could likely be circumvented (Chyba and Greninger, 2004: 153, Jackson *et al.*, 2001).

Second, it takes considerable time to research, develop and manufacture appropriate drug treatments. In a letter to the editors of *Biosecurity and Bioterrorism*, Ken Alibek and Charles Bailey claimed that achievements in the development of BW are up to 30 years ahead of the possible defences against them. It took Soviet scientists 3–4 years to engineer a drug-resistant or more virulent pathogen, whereas it takes 10–15 years to develop a vaccine and have it approved by the FDA (Alibek and Bailey, 2004: 132). The US Department of Defense Chemical and Biological Defense Program (CBDP) does not expect to have licensed new therapeutics for exposure to plague, anthrax and smallpox until 2008–2011. In an attempt to overcome this limitation, the CBDP is also working towards broad-spectrum treatments; a 'multiple pathogen–single countermeasure' approach. However, such therapies are not expected to be licensed until 2012–2021 (CBDP, 2005: 52).

Third, to be effective, a vaccine would have to be widely administered well in advance of the attack – the latency period between vaccination and the human immune response may be as long as several weeks. As Alibek and Bailey have argued, if a BW attack has already taken place it would generally be too late to vaccinate against the disease (Alibek and Bailey, 2004: 132). Moreover, few people are likely to volunteer for advance vaccination if they do not believe that a particular BW threat is sufficiently real or serious. For example, in December 2002 the US government announced an unprecedented campaign advocating 'pre-event' mass vaccinations against smallpox (a disease which no longer exists in nature) to be carried out in two phases – 500,000 military personnel and 500,000 health workers in phase one, and up to 10 million emergency response personnel in phase two. Ultimately, fewer than 8 per cent of targeted health professionals participated, and the Centers for Disease Control and Prevention (CDC) reported 145 serious adverse events associated with smallpox vaccinations among civilians, including at least three deaths (Cohen *et al.*, 2004: 1668).

Fourth, even if the agent used in a biological attack was known in advance, the efficacy of a vaccine-based defence might not. Ethical prohibitions on human testing of vaccines against infectious diseases that pose no *current* public health threat might mean their adverse health effects are inadequately understood. In addition, an immunization strategy might fail because: first, the vaccine is not offered to or accepted by everyone exposed to the BW agent; second, individuals exposed might have underlying conditions, such as immune deficiency, that prevent immunization from being fully effective; and/or third, the dose of biological agent to which an individual is exposed during a BW attack might be large enough to overcome the protection offered by immunization (Sidel, 2002: 78).

Nevertheless, despite the shortcomings of pharmaceutical protection, pathogen research and drug development still have an important part to play in mitigating BW risks. A 2004 report by the British Medical Association (BMA) argued that

> though it is clearly impossible to cover all possible biological weaponry attacks that might occur as the revolution in modern biology progresses, there is every reason to make sensible preparation for dealing with relatively containable attacks using known agents.
>
> (BMA, 2004: 69)

Beyond the development of vaccines against specific agents, there is hope that advances in biotechnology might soon allow for the rapid development of vaccines against *any* agent. Such technology could be applied against both naturally-occurring and deliberately-caused disease threats – for example, a newly-emerged strain of human influenza or a novel BW agent. In addition, there is a case for shifting research priorities away from vaccines and towards new emergency prophylaxes and therapies for treating people in the late stages of infection (Alibek and Bailey, 2004: 133).

To conclude, it appears that pharmaceutical protection could work in some BW situations against some pathogenic micro-organisms. As such, it would be a mistake to abandon research and development in this area on the grounds that medical treatments would never be available against all possible BW threats. However, to the extent that pharmaceutical protection is worth pursuing, pathogen research conducted for the purpose of countering bioterrorism must be commissioned and conducted in a way that poses as few risks as possible to public health and safety, and to national and international security. These risks are discussed in the remaining sections on biodefence research priorities and the security significance of defensive BW programmes.

Opportunity costs and security risks

In 2003 the journal *Nature* reported that US government scientists had developed a single-shot vaccine that protects monkeys from Ebola virus and which could eventually be used to protect humans (Sullivan *et al.*, 2003). In another experiment, scientists at the US Army Medical Research Institute for Infectious Diseases (USAMRIID) gave an experimental drug to monkeys that had been deliberately infected with Ebola. The disease is usually 100 per cent fatal in monkeys, but the drug caused one-third of the monkeys to survive

(Geisbert *et al.*, 2003). US government sponsorship of Ebola research is part of a broader policy (driven by security concerns) of promoting research on pathogens which, while dangerous, are not of ongoing importance for American public health. For example, on 9 May 2005 the National Institute for Allergy and Infectious Diseases (NIAID) announced its first grants under Project Bioshield – approximately US$27 million was allocated to 10 institutions to develop new therapeutics and vaccines against anthrax, botulinum toxin, Ebola, pneumonic plague, smallpox and tularaemia (NIH, 2005). Although such grants bring the potential for greater scientific understanding of these diseases, prioritising research in the field of potential BW agents also generates opportunity costs and security risks for the United States.

On 30 September 2003, Boston University and the University of Texas were each awarded US government grants of US$120 million to build a Biosafety Level 4 (BSL-4) maximum containment laboratory. In announcing the awards, Health and Human Services Secretary Tommy Thompson described them as 'a major step towards being able to provide Americans with effective therapies, vaccines and diagnostics for diseases caused by agents of bioterror as well as for naturally occurring emerging infections such as SARS and West Nile virus' (NIH, 2003). Once built, the new laboratories will be capable of supporting research into emerging infectious disease agents, but there is little doubt that they will focus overwhelmingly on BW threats. The CDC presently designates 82 disease-causing micro-organisms as 'select agents' that could be used maliciously against humans, animals and plants. These are divided into three categories (A, B and C) based on assessments of ease of dissemination or transmission, mortality and public health impact, ability to cause panic and social disruption, and special requirements for public health preparedness. The list of Category A select agents (which are thought to pose the greatest BW danger) includes, for example, the micro-organisms that cause smallpox, anthrax and plague in humans (CDC, 2005).

It is a matter for debate within the United States whether the new money allocated to address potential BW threats agents is ultimately to the betterment of US public health. On the one hand, it is highly doubtful that the extra billions of dollars would have gone into infectious disease research anyway. According to NIAID director Anthony Fauci, biodefence research spending to jumpstart the invention of new vaccines, antibiotics and technologies for early diagnosis of disease has come on top of existing health budgets (Enserink and Kaiser, 2005: 1396). On the other hand, the prioritisation of research on select agents over basic research on model micro-organisms like *E coli* bacteria may well be hindering more valuable scientific breakthroughs. It is more difficult to work with select agents, not just because researchers are far less familiar with them, but also because they need to be handled in high-containment laboratories subject to strict safety and security measures.

In early 2005, 750 of the 1,143 scientists then in receipt of funding from the US National Institutes of Health (NIH) wrote an open letter to the agency's head, Elias Zerhouni. They alleged that the NIH emphasis on biodefence research since 2002 had diverted researchers away from potential breakthroughs in basic research, and that research on select agents was crowding out research on micro-organisms that already pose a significant disease threat. The scientists claimed to be on the verge of making major breakthroughs in basic research on bacteria, which could then be transferred to more obscure pathogens such as select agents. They described as a misdirection of NIH priorities the 'diversion of research funds from projects of high public-health importance to projects of high biodefence but low public-health importance' and called on the NIH to create a new funding category for basic microbial science (Letter, 2005). In reply to this letter, an editorial in the *Washington Post* disagreed with the scientists' judgement on public health:

> Security officials have stated repeatedly their belief that al Qaeda and others continue to search for more lethal bioweapons. Surely that makes biodefense projects of 'high public-health importance'. That this is not more widely understood means that there is still too little contact between the scientific community and national security and intelligence agencies.
>
> (Editorial, 2005)

The latter view presently has the ascendancy in the United States because of heightened domestic concerns about 'terrorism' and a prevailing official assumption that non-state use of BW is a mass-casualty threat. The danger, however, is that concentrating on select agent research may, in the longer term, diminish US capacity to resist infectious disease threats of deliberate or natural origin. Federal regulations require any laboratory that possesses one or more select agents to enforce and adhere to specific security measures. These include: facility registration and designation of a responsible official; risk assessments for individuals with access to listed agents; biosecurity plans; agent transfer rules; safety and security training and inspections; notification after theft, loss, or release of a listed agent; and record maintenance (Gaudioso and Salerno, 2004). Moreover, the Public Health Security and Bioterrorism Preparedness Act 2002 requires authorities at research and medical facilities to report work with select agents, and to submit the names of employees with a legitimate need for access to pathogens to the Health and Human Services Secretary and the Attorney General. These names are checked against criminal, immigration, and national security databases for possible 'restricted person' status (US Code, Title 18, Chapter 10, section 175b(b)(2)).

Although such precautions appear sensible and worthwhile, an important lesson from the US experience is that biosecurity regulation must strike a balance between maximising security benefits while doing the least amount of harm to legitimate research. The biotechnology sector is simultaneously a potential locus of disease-based security threats and a crucial ally for governments seeking to resist such threats. The sector performs basic research on pathogenic micro-organisms, produces vaccines and other drugs, and instructs health professionals on how to use them. Too much biosecurity regulation might cripple commercial and academic enterprise in the biological sciences and thereby diminish the ability of the public health system – particularly its diagnostic and patient care elements

– to respond to an infectious disease outbreak. Many US scientists have decided to discontinue or not pursue research on regulated agents, rather than bear the associated financial and administrative burdens. Scientists at Stanford University, for example, destroyed or transferred collections of *F tularensis* (tularaemia) and *Y pestis* (plague) because they believed the burdens of the select agent regulations outweighed the scientific need to maintain stocks on campus (Gaudioso and Salerno, 2004).

In addition to generating opportunity costs in terms of public health, research priorities for US biodefence increase the risk of infectious disease outbreaks inside the United States itself. More laboratories for investigating pathogens and potential therapies might reduce the vulnerability of Americans to disease threats of deliberate or natural origin, but they also pose risks to health, safety and security. At present there are four fully-operational BSL-4 laboratories in the United States engaged in biodefence research: at the CDC in Atlanta, Georgia; at USAMRIID in Frederick, Maryland; at the Southwest Foundation for Biomedical Research in San Antonio, Texas; and at the NIH at Bethesda, Maryland. NIAID has allocated funds to construct two National Biocontainment Laboratories, which will contain BSL-4 facilities designed for studying the most dangerous pathogens, and it plans to build two BSL-4 laboratories for its own purposes. The US Army and Department of Homeland Security also plan to construct additional high-containment laboratories (Nelson, 2004).

Supporters of this expansion argue that the anthrax attacks of 2001 exposed a shortage of the specialised, high-containment laboratory space needed to conduct research on micro-organisms that could be used as weapons, as well as on potential vaccines and therapies. However, a major concern is that the expansion of laboratory research is taking place too quickly, with insufficient trained staff to operate all the new laboratories, and without adequate safeguards. Plans to expand the number of high-containment laboratories inside the United States have already generated widespread community consternation that this could result in more laboratory-acquired infections and accidental releases of pathogens into the environment (James, 2004; Kaiser, 2004). A study by the Sunshine Project found that 97 per cent of principal investigators who received NIAID grants from 2001 to 2005 to study six pathogens (anthrax, brucellosis, glanders, plague, melioidosis, or tularaemia) were newcomers to such research. Critics argue that giving work to these so-called 'bug jockeys' increases the risks of accidental pathogen release (Schwellenbach, 2005).

There are also inherent security risks associated with having large numbers of scientists engaged in pathogen research, notwithstanding the US government's stated policy that the increase in such work is intended for defensive purposes. More than 11,000 individuals and over 300 laboratories in the United States have reportedly received government approval to conduct experiments involving select agents. The number of NIH grants for projects involving anthrax rose from 28 in 2000 to 253 in 2003. And in 2000, 25 projects mentioned 'bioterrorism' and related words, compared to 665 in 2003 (Shane, 2004). With so many people and places involved in biodefence, there is an increased chance that pathogens might be deliberately misused by a scientist. In 2004 the National Academy of Sciences called for greater security measures because it regarded biodefence research as 'precisely the sort of research likely to pose the most severe dual use dilemmas' (NAS, 2004: 3). With an increasing number of Americans being granted access to dangerous pathogens and instruction on how to handle them, the danger is that the United States could be inadvertently creating its own training ground for would-be perpetrators of biological attacks.

In most discussion of 'biosecurity', the emphasis tends to be on diversion threats posed by outsiders – that is, non-laboratory workers with malign intent who might break into a research facility. This is consistent with the political rhetoric prevalent since 11 September 2001 of 'WMD falling into the hands of terrorists'. It is important, however, not to overlook the threat from insiders – trusted members of staff with access to pathogens and who are familiar with laboratory security procedures and equipment. A rhetorical tag for such a threat might be 'people with WMD deciding to become terrorists'. It is highly likely, for example, that an expert insider with laboratory experience was the perpetrator of the most sophisticated BW attack in history. Analyses of the anthrax spores used in the envelope attacks of 2001 revealed that they were examples of the Ames strain of *B anthracis* – a highly virulent strain originally developed in powder form by USAMRIID for testing biological defence systems (Read *et al.*, 2002). The anthrax used in the envelope attacks was also reportedly 'weapons-grade' – exceptionally free of bacterial residue, of uniform particle size, treated with silica to reduce particle clumping, and dispersed easily. Its high concentration (one trillion spores per gram) and purity gave rise to suggestions that the attacks had links to a sophisticated government biodefence programme (Matsumoto, 2003).

Federal Bureau of Investigation (FBI) psychological profilers settled on 'a disaffected American loner' as the most likely perpetrator of the attacks (Gugliotta, 2002). And because so much of the evidence pointed to a plot hatched and executed within the United States, law enforcement officials concentrated on biodefence specialists; in particular on scientists familiar with weaponising pathogens. The FBI investigation focused on US Army scientists at Fort Detrick – the very ones responsible for protecting the United States from biological attack. In the course of the investigation (dubbed 'Amerithrax'), US Attorney General John Ashcroft labelled Steven Hatfill a 'person of interest'. Hatfill came under suspicion partly because he formerly worked as a medical researcher at USAMRIID (Miller, 2003). Although Hatfill has not been convicted of or charged with involvement in the 2001 anthrax attacks, his designation by the FBI as a 'person of interest' supports the proposition that personnel inside a biodefence facility are a potentially serious avenue for pathogen diversion.

Beyond generating research opportunity costs and national security risks, particular US biodefence priorities also pose risks to international security. The following section concentrates on pathogen research carried out for 'threat assessment' purposes; its status under international law, and its implications for BW proliferation.

International law and security

Most biodefence projects are purely defensive and clearly benign in nature – for example, biological detection systems, filtration and protection systems, decontaminants, training for first responders, provision of medical facilities, interagency communication and coordination, and epidemiological surveillance systems. Such technologies bring the direct, practical benefit of reducing (and possibly avoiding) the human damage that would result from the use of BW. Of particular concern, however, are biodefence projects conducted for 'threat assessment' purposes. Under the 1972 Biological Weapons Convention (BWC), a grey area between prohibited offensive activity and permitted defensive activity is the exploration of the potential of pathogens to be used as weapons in order to develop appropriate countermeasures. Although US biodefence policy is almost certainly peaceful in its intent, some forms of threat assessment nevertheless risk breaching international law and stimulating 'defensive' BW proliferation in other countries. The main challenge for the United States is to pursue biodefence in a way that does not endanger the international norms and laws against deliberate disease – any lowering of the moral and legal threshold would make biological attacks more likely.

At the Los Alamos National Laboratory in New Mexico, US scientists have built elaborate computer models of cities and then simulated the fallout from a hypothetical 'terrorist' attack. Findings from simulations of a smallpox release in a major city have been useful, for example, by contributing to the debate in the United States over whether targeted vaccinations or mass vaccination of the entire country is preferable. In July 2005 a scientist on the smallpox simulation project, James Smith, told the *Washington Post* '[w]e're trying to be the best terrorists we can be. Sometimes we finish and we're like, "We're glad we're not terrorists."' If ever the simulations got into the wrong hands, Smith said, '[i]t would be a terrorist recipe for doing something terrible' (Cha, 2005). Computer modelling of a smallpox event does not contravene international law, although the Los Alamos example illustrates how information obtained in the interests of defence could be used for offensive purposes.

Research and development projects on BW threat assessment involve experimenting with the offensive applications of pathogens so as to determine appropriate countermeasures – a practice known as 'red teaming'. In order to develop defences against a putative BW agent, it is necessary to understand: the underlying mechanisms for pathogenicity, including infectivity and virulence; the way in which a micro-organism evades the human immune system or acquires resistance to antibiotics; and the ways in which the agent may be dispersed, and its infectivity by each route. However, an understanding of these factors is also exactly what would be required for the development of BW.

Article I of the BWC prohibits development, production and stockpiling of BW, but it is silent on the question of research. In accordance with National Security Decision Memorandum 35, issued by National Security Advisor Henry Kissinger on 25 November 1969, the United States interprets its responsibilities under the

BWC as permitting 'research into those offensive aspects of bacteriological/ biological agents necessary to determine what defensive measures are required'. (Kissinger, 1969). The memorandum did not specify what types of research were justified for defensive purposes. On 23 December 1975 National Security Advisor Brent Scowcroft issued a second memorandum authorising 'vulnerability studies' as permissible under the BWC, but there was no express authority for the creation of novel pathogens or weaponisation techniques for threat assessment purposes (Anonymous, 2002). In May 1989, however, in testimony before the US Senate Committee on Government Affairs, USAMRIID commander David Huxsoll stated that research to produce more virulent biological agents, to stabilise agents, and on dissemination methods, was prohibited by the BWC (Leitenberg, 2003: 242).

Such comments by a U.S military officer today would not reflect the apparent attitude of his or her government regarding what constitutes defensive work. At present, a number of US government agencies are undertaking or plan to undertake research in exactly the areas cited by Huxsoll. Most prominent among these is the National Biodefense Analysis and Countermeasures Center (NBACC). Due to be completed in 2008, it is intended to provide the United States with high-containment laboratory space for biological threat characterisation and bioforensic research. NBACC will form part of the National Interagency Biodefense Campus at Fort Detrick, Maryland, alongside existing USAMRIID facilities. Its programmes will investigate the infectious properties of biological agents, the effectiveness of countermeasures, decontamination procedures, and forensic analysis. Part of NBACC is the Biological Threat Characterization Center, which will conduct laboratory experiments aimed at assessing current and 'future' biological threats. The centre will also assess vulnerabilities, conduct risk assessments, and determine potential impacts in order to guide the development of countermeasures such as detectors, vaccines, drugs, and decontamination technologies (DHS, 2005). The CIA has reportedly assigned to NBACC at least one member of the 'Z-Division', a group jointly operated with Lawrence Livermore National Laboratory that specialises in analysing and duplicating weapons systems of potential adversaries (Warrick, 2006).

Many of the activities to be undertaken by NBACC could readily be interpreted by outsiders as the development of BW under the guise of threat assessment. In particular, weaponisation projects and the construction of novel pathogens arguably constitute breaches of the BWC. In a February 2004 presentation, George Korch, Deputy Director of NBACC, revealed that one of the centre's research units intended to pursue a range of topics including 'aerosol dynamics', 'novel packaging', 'novel delivery of threat', 'genetic engineering', and 'red teaming'. At one point in his presentation, Korch summarised the threat assessment task areas as: 'Acquire, Grow, Modify, Store, Stabilize, Package, Disperse' (Korch, 2004). Such language is identical to that which would describe the functions of an offensive BW programme.

A 1998 report by the US Under Secretary of Defense for Acquisition and Technology stated: 'Stabilization and dispersion are [BW] proliferation concerns because these technologies increase the efficacy of biological agents' (Anonymous,

1998: II-3-7). And in light of the planned NBACC activities described by Korch, a 2005 State Department report which assessed that 'China maintains some elements of an offensive BW capability in violation of its BWC obligations' appeared to reflect an American double standard when it warned that:

> From 1993 to the present, [Chinese] military scientists have published in open literature the results of studies of aerosol stability of bacteria, models of infectious virus aerosols, and detection of aerosolized viruses using polymerase chain reaction technology. Such advanced biotechnology techniques could be applicable to the development of offensive BW agents and weapons.
>
> (Anonymous, 2005)

By comparison, the 2006 Report to Congress by the CBDP revealed that facilities at the US Army Edgewood Chemical Biological Center include: 'Aerosol simulation chambers and the Aerodynamic Research Laboratory, comprising approximately 11,000 ft² of experimental aerodynamic facilities that include four wind tunnels for component and materials tests'. In addition, the US Army Dugway Proving Ground has a Life Sciences Test Facility with multiple live biological agent test chambers with aerosolisation capability, and an Ambient Breeze Tunnel for biological simulant system tests (CBDP, 2006: 69–70). Such facilities could likewise be 'applicable to the development of offensive BW agents and weapons'.

In November 2002 a group of non-government organisations drafted recommendations for a code of conduct for biodefence programmes and distributed them to national delegations attending the Fifth BWC Review Conference in Geneva. Of particular relevance to BW threat assessment projects, the draft code included the following statements:

> The Convention's stated goal is to preclude the use of biological weapons under any circumstances; therefore it is not permissible, even for defensive purposes, to construct delivery mechanisms designed for (i.e., having a design that is appropriate for) hostile use, whether or not hostile use is intended at the time of construction.
>
> Aerosolization or other dissemination of active biological agents should be performed only in fully-contained bench-scale environments and only for the purposes of detection, prophylaxis or medical treatment.
>
> (FAS, 2002)

In the area of scientific endeavour to counter bioterrorism, a key challenge for the United States is to pursue defences in a way that does not endanger the norm against deliberate disease, as embodied in the BWC. On 4 September 2001 the *New York Times* revealed the existence of three classified US biodefence projects. From 1997 to 2000 Project Clear Vision involved building and testing a Soviet-model bomblet for dispersing bacteria. In 1999–2000 Project Bacchus investigated whether a would-be 'terrorist' using commercially available materials and equipment could assemble an anthrax production facility undetected by the US and foreign governments. And in early 2001 Project Jefferson involved the reproduction of a vaccine-resistant strain of anthrax bacteria (Miller *et al.*, 2001).

If similar projects had been carried out inside a designated 'rogue state', it is highly likely that they would have been viewed by the United States and other Western countries as violations of the BWC. For this reason, the latter cannot afford to be complacent about non-Western perceptions of ostensibly defensive BW activities. As the BMA acknowledged in 2004, 'some countries may not view the West as benign in general and some biotechnology work being carried out in the West as necessarily above suspicion' (BMA, 2004: 112). It is also worth noting the possibility that the former Soviet Union maintained its BW programme after signing the BWC in 1972 because it believed the United States intended to do likewise, notwithstanding President Richard Nixon's 1969 renunciation of biological warfare. In his 1999 memoir *Biohazard*, Soviet defector Ken Alibek reflected:

> We didn't believe a word of Nixon's announcement. Even though the massive US biological munitions stockpile was ordered to be destroyed, and some twenty-two hundred researchers and technicians lost their jobs, we thought the Americans were only wrapping a thicker cloak around their activities.
> (Alibek, 1999: 234)

The difficulty of determining BWC compliance lies in the extent to which it comes down to perceptions of a given state's intent. And because intent is difficult to gauge reliably, states naturally err on the side of caution by focusing on the capabilities of potential adversaries. Allaying BW suspicions therefore requires as much transparency as possible regarding such capabilities as is consistent with national security. The importance of transparency was recognised in 1986 at the Second BWC Review Conference when member states agreed to specific confidence-building measures (CBMs). These were extended and elaborated at the Third BWC Review Conference in 1991. The CBMs include:

- exchange of data on research centres and high-containment laboratories;
- exchange of data on and descriptions of national biological defence programmes and associated facilities;
- declarations on vaccine production facilities;
- exchange of information on unusual infectious disease outbreaks;
- encouragement of publication of experiment results and promotion of use of knowledge;
- active promotion of scientific contacts through international conferences, symposia, seminars and other forums for exchange; and
- declaration of legislation, regulations and other BWC implementation measures.
  (BWC, 1991)

A world leader on transparency is Canada's Biological and Chemical Defence Review Committee which oversees relevant research, development and training activities undertaken by the Department of National Defence to ensure that they are defensive in nature. The Committee publishes its annual reports on its website (BCDRC, 2005).

Beyond the legal issue of BWC compliance, transparency is also important for strategic reasons. Since the end of the Cold War, and beginning with the Clinton administration, the United States has shifted its focus away from the problem of state-run BW programmes and towards concerns about biological attacks perpetrated by non-state actors. However, the dynamics of proliferation by states are still important today. For at least three reasons, the very existence of the US biodefence programme might induce other countries to imitate it – BW proliferation in a defensive guise.

First, in the eyes of a suspicious adversary, the development of pharmaceutical defences might constitute an attempt to acquire protection for a nation's own military forces against a biological agent that the nation intends to use in a BW 'first strike'. Prior to the 1991 Gulf War, for example, one of the reported reasons why the US military became concerned about the use of *B anthracis* was the discovery that Iraqi soldiers captured in a covert pre-war operation had immunity against anthrax (Broad, 1998). Second, any close association between defensive BW work and existing military programmes can create nervousness in an outside observer. For example, the conduct of classified biodefence research at the Lawrence Livermore and Los Alamos National Laboratories might cause other countries to be concerned about possible US offensive intent because these facilities have historically been used for nuclear weapons development (Kelley and Coghlan, 2003). And third, the risk of BW proliferation is exacerbated by US threat assessment projects. In particular, rival nations might be concerned that American exploration of novel BW threats could generate scientific breakthroughs that put them at a strategic disadvantage (Tucker, 2004: 14). The result could be a BW arms race.

Conclusion

Since the anthrax envelope attacks of 2001, US policy on countering bioterrorism has seen billions of extra dollars invested in biodefence. Pharmaceutical countermeasures, a major pillar of this policy, are unlikely to offer protection against the vast range of pathogens that could be used in a biological attack. Nevertheless, the possibility that broad-spectrum treatments could be developed means pathogen research is an important pursuit. For the United States, the challenge is to protect its citizens from BW threats in a way that does not generate disproportionate risks and opportunity costs. Other, ongoing threats to human health compete with agents of BW concern for government research funding, so US policy needs to avoid being counterproductive from a public health standpoint. And although the planned expansion of laboratory capacity could yield a net increase in research on infectious diseases, this raises concerns over safety and the security risk that individual scientists might divert or misuse pathogenic micro-organisms. From an international security perspective, US defensive work on pathogenic agents needs to be conducted in a manner more sensitive to how that work may be perceived by others. There is a particular danger that current and planned US projects on BW threat assessment could be seen as breaches, actual or potential, of the BWC. Absent appropriate transparency measures, the development of offensive capabilities for defensive purposes poses a serious security risk of undermining the international norm against BW. This in turn would exacerbate and accelerate the problem of BW proliferation. It would be tragically ironic if US measures for countering bioterrorism served to increase the level of threat.

10 Ethics and intelligence in the age of terror

Hugh Smith

Intelligence is the business of collecting information, analysing it and providing assessments to government for policy-making in relation to national security. Most studies of intelligence focus on topics such as operations, changing technology, and the kind of threats agencies must deal with. Few discuss ethical aspects in any depth (Jones: 1989).[1] But intelligence by its nature pushes the bounds of legality and propriety, and perhaps routinely oversteps them. This chapter looks at ethical issues surrounding the gathering of information. The moral dilemmas faced by those who analyse information and advise governments deserve separate treatment (Pillar 2006).

Gathering information by governments must be seen in its context of international politics where national security, perhaps national survival, is at stake. Very different views exist about whether morality or law can exist at all among sovereign states, and about the character of such law and morality if they do exist. Here we briefly examine arguments that bear on the collection of intelligence. The rest of the chapter looks at information gathering before 9/11 and at how the 'war on terror' has affected this process. Key factors include: the nature of the contemporary struggle against terrorism, the importance of the interrogation of individuals, the circumstances which make ethical behaviour in this arena difficult, and the challenge of developing effective rules.

Ethics is concerned with both general ideas and practical action. Many rules, laws, principles, conventions and so on relate to intelligence in general, some of which have legal form. Here the principal focus is not on the legal debate but on the moral rules that may (or may not) underlie black letter law. Law, said US Chief Justice Earl Warren, floats on a sea of ethics. But ethics is also concerned with individual behaviour in concrete situations. How far can interrogators go, for example, in seeking to gain information from prisoners? It is no accident that both general and specific issues of this kind have come to the fore in public debate since 9/11.

Ethical objections

For some 'ethical espionage' is an oxymoron on a par with 'military intelligence'. In 1929 US Secretary of State Henry L. Stimson closed a code-breaking unit, known as the Black Chamber, as soon as he learnt of its existence, later saying of this decision: 'Gentlemen do not read each other's mail'. For him spying and code-breaking were inherently dishonourable at a personal level. Stimson, in short, saw ethical behaviour as more important than short-term advantage to his country. By 1940, when he was Secretary of War, he had changed his views and advocated the use of code-breaking to counter Japan's growing power – too late, critics argue, to prevent Pearl Harbor (Shulsky 1993: 187–8).

A more philosophical critique of the intelligence business is that it is unethical since it inevitably entails deception and lying. Thus for Immanuel Kant these activities are wrong since they diminish another person's capacity to act morally by positively deceiving him or at least by depriving him of full information. They also make mutual confidence among states impossible since they are practices that cannot be universalised i.e. followed by everyone. Kant condemned in particular the instigation and use of 'treachery' in dealing with other states.

The democratic objection to intelligence focuses on problems of accountability (Lustgarten and Leigh 1994). In order to be effective many activities of intelligence agencies must occur covertly and remain hidden from the public, even from elected legislators. Neither armed forces nor the police are given such latitude. Their activities take place largely in the public view, often in the presence of national and international media, and are subject to extensive legal regulation and legislative review. Nor is the judiciary well-placed to act as a check on intelligence agencies since relevant cases only rarely find their way to court. If intelligence agencies are to be kept accountable, prime responsibility must fall on the executive government.

It is also problematic from the ethical point of view that obtaining information often takes place in situations inherently liable to lead to abuse as a consequence of great disparities of power. Information, it has been argued, is more easily gained from the weak, the vulnerable and the innocent (Godfrey 1978: 629). Holding a person prisoner, above all, seems to create a natural temptation to use violence to extract information. Lord Acton's warning – 'power corrupts, absolute power corrupts absolutely' – applies not just in the political arena but also in the interrogation room.

Ethical justifications

The most common justification for intelligence gathering is that it contributes to the security of the state. Like war, it is a continuation of policy by other means and can be defended in the same way that Machiavelli justified war in *The Prince*: 'that war is just that which is necessary'. Whatever it takes to secure the state and its citizens is justified regardless of who gets hurt in the process, innocent or otherwise, and of the means employed. The end justifies any (necessary) means.

Machiavelli accepted the existence of morality among individuals but distinguished between political and personal obligations. A prince is not like an ordinary citizen since he has an overriding duty to protect his state. He must therefore overcome personal ethical qualms about what he has to do. A prince must 'learn to be bad' in order to protect his state. Actions can be justified for national security even though they may leave the ruler (or the intelligence agent) with a sense of having 'dirty hands' (Walzer 1973). This goes with the job.

Hobbes sees no place at all for ethical qualms in international politics. Since there is no sovereign authority among states, there can be no law and no morality. *Leviathan* describes this as a 'state of nature' in which sovereigns have 'their eyes fixed on one another; that is, their forts, garrisons and guns upon the frontiers of their kingdoms; and continual spies upon their neighbours; which is a posture of war'. Preparing for war and spying on neighbours are not so much justified as simply part of the struggle for survival.

Though Hobbes' ethical nihilism and Machiavelli's ethical relativism are common philosophies, states have in practice sought to identify certain moral and legal principles that are widely enough shared to guide their behaviour in some measure. The clash of military forces, in particular, is governed by the law of armed conflict which sets out rules of conduct that have found widespread, though far from total, observance. Where intelligence activities are concerned, however, moral and legal principles are much thinner on the ground.

Some black-letter rules nonetheless exist. The 1984 Convention Against Torture, for example, expressly prohibits such methods for collecting information. Other 'rules' tend to be unwritten, informal and unclear. Thus in wartime, enemy spies do not qualify as prisoners of war if captured and may be subject to the death penalty, but in practice are often treated with some leniency. During the Cold War the US and USSR on occasion exchanged captured spies. Reciprocity and the view that spies are simply doing their job help explain this pattern. As Geoffrey Best observes: '[t]he spy remains in his curious legal limbo; whether his work is honourable or dishonourable, none can tell' (Best 1994: 291).

Intelligence before the 'war on terror'

Prior to 9/11 the security of states was seen to depend primarily on the balance of military strength among rivals so that intelligence collection focused on such matters as the size and nature of military arsenals, new weapons technology, and military plans and deployments. Specific states could be identified as potential enemies and intelligence efforts targeted accordingly. In this context the moral questions central to intelligence gathering could be summed up as: 'who is fair game?' and 'what methods of collection are justifiable?'

Who is fair game?

Who can justifiably be targeted in the gathering of information? This question is important because it suggests that the business of intelligence collection might be confined to the players 'on the field' rather than involving innocent or unwitting spectators. The same moral principle of discrimination in the law of armed conflict seeks to limit killing as far as possible to military forces. Where the military generally focus on more specific threats, however, intelligence for national security has always sought to identify long-term and short-term threats of many different kinds. This requires information from numerous sources about a great range of future developments. Targets will be more diverse and difficult to identify than those in military operations, and there is in principle almost no limit to the people who may be targeted in the quest for information.

States and organisations

In the first instance, targets can be considered in terms of states and organisations as opposed to individuals. Enemy states easily qualify since they threaten our security. In time of war, hot or cold, we need information about them and can assume they are spying on us. In peacetime 'enemies' may be more difficult to identify since there is often a competitive rivalry even among allies. Britain, for example, bugged the French embassy in London from 1960 to 1963 in order to monitor France's position on negotiations over the Common Market, a policy, which R.V. Jones believed, should be abandoned on moral grounds (Jones 1989: 35–6). Can, say, Australia assume that none of its close allies spy on it? Should it refrain from spying against its allies? Is this a betrayal of trust or does a basic commonality of interests make espionage in this context more acceptable because it is less harmful?

Gaining useful information from neutral states is problematic on different grounds. Respect for neutrality may carry some weight though fear of antagonising neutrals, if caught out, is perhaps a greater factor. Spying on international organisations such as the United Nations raises other questions. In 2004, for example, a former British cabinet minister, Clare Short, expressed outrage that the UK should engage in spying on the UN Secretary General in the lead up to the Iraq war (BBC News Online 2004). As an organisation designed to promote peace, the UN can claim a certain immunity from such practices – in the same way that the Red Cross enjoys protected status. Nor does reciprocity apply since the UN does not spy on its members, if only because it is incapable of doing so.

Different issues arise when information gathering is directed against transnational terrorist groups. The difficulty is that such organisations usually operate across several countries and the governments concerned often cannot or will not take effective action against them. Regardless of the general rule of non-intervention in internal affairs, it may be legitimate self-defence for a state under threat to gather information about terrorist groups or even take military action in another state if violent attack is imminent.

Individuals

Individuals as targets of information gathering vary in ethical terms according to one principal criterion, namely the degree of their involvement in security matters (Pfaff and Tiel 2004). Most legitimate are those agents of another state, military and civilian, who have information relevant to another state's security. Such people in fact may be identified by the state they work for through the granting of security clearances; in the same way military uniforms identify legitimate targets in time of war. Of course, it is not always apparent who has clearances so that many people may have to be checked to determine their status.

More problematic as targets are individuals who are not part of a security establishment but who have knowledge that is essential to another state's security. Doctors may know about diseases relevant to biological warfare, engineers about nuclear power generation relevant to nuclear weapons production. 'Dual-use technology' means dual-status citizens. In some cases these individuals may not know of their potential vulnerability in security terms and their own government may have an obligation to inform them accordingly.

Using the family or friends of particular individuals to secure information is most difficult to justify. Such individuals may be involved purely by chance of birth, marriage or friendship. Indeed, they may have no idea that they are likely targets, kept in the dark by the target himself for security reasons. Ethical considerations might suggest they should be off limits – like civilians in war – though their value as sources of information make this unlikely in practice.

What methods of collection are justifiable?

Intelligence agencies have always employed a wide range of methods to collect information. As will be seen, these vary along several dimensions of relevance to ethical judgement:

(a) the extent of intrusion into the privacy of others;
(b) the degree of harm inflicted or threatened;
(c) the nature of any deception involved;
(d) the moral harm incurred by the agent (because of the nature of the acts he or she performs);
(e) the extent to which a target renders himself open to exploitation; and arguably
(f) the extent to which all states employ certain methods and expect to have them used against themselves (reciprocity).

The first two amount to what R.V. Jones calls a principle of 'minimum trespass' on the rights of individuals (Jones 1995: 5). It equates to the military doctrine of using only the minimum force necessary to achieve a (legitimate) objective. The second two focus on actors who are involved either actively or as bystanders – what moral harm do they suffer? The final pair deal with the target and his state – to what extent are they active and equal participants in the struggle? Different methods of collection in a debatable order of harmfulness can be assessed against these criteria.

Open sources

Open sources, notably the World Wide Web, provide most information for intelligence agencies – some estimates put it at 90 per cent. This does not create dilemmas except those of judging the reliability and significance of such data. It does raise the question whether open sources should be used in preference to more covert or harmful means of gathering information. The latter methods, however, may be valuable in confirming or disproving open source information.

Observation

As Yogi Berra said: 'You can observe a lot just by watchin''. Simple observation of others by legal means does no significant or immediate harm though it may entail a minor invasion of privacy. Much electronic eavesdropping is no more than listening to transmissions in the ether. Most states engage in such activities and expect others to do so. Targets may or may not be aware that it is occurring.

During the Cold War mutual observation by satellites became acceptable as both superpowers relied on so-called 'national technical means of verification' to verify the other's compliance with arms control agreements. These methods, it has been suggested, did 'only minimal damage to the ethical standards of the operators and processors' (Godfrey 1978: 637). But if satellites are acceptable, spy-planes in another nation's airspace are not – witness the international crises that followed the downing of an American U-2 aircraft over the Soviet Union in 1960 and of a Korean Airlines 747 suspected of spying on Soviet defences in 1983.

Deception

Deception entails the use of cover or disguise to obtain information, for example, pretending to be a journalist, trade official, representative of an NGO or an agent of a different country. Long-term 'sleepers' or 'moles' disguise themselves as ordinary citizens or workers. Such deception in itself does not seriously hurt individuals but has great potential to harm the target nation. These forms of deception resemble *ruses de guerre* such as camouflage and ambush that are permitted in warfare. Many states engage in them and all states expect them to happen.

Some deceptions, however, unfairly harm organisations that are falsely represented. The impartial reputation of the Red Cross is at risk, for example, if an individual purports to be one of its officials in order to secure information. The notion of perfidy in the law of armed conflict similarly prohibits abuse of Red Cross symbols. Other organisations falling into this protected category include the UN and perhaps certain other international bodies.

Invasion of privacy

This takes such forms as theft of documents, breaking and entering, interception of communications and computer hacking. Electronic eavesdropping may involve secretly placing bugs in government buildings or private premises. Efforts are usually made to act covertly so that the target does not know an invasion of privacy has taken place, or to disguise actions as something else, e.g. as burglary for private gain.

Such methods are likely to be illegal under an agent's national laws, under the target's national laws and possibly under international law (which, for example, protects diplomatic immunity). While minimum harm is done to the target, especially if unsuspecting, great harm may be done to his nation's security. Those in the game, of course, expect such activity and take active steps to prevent it and nullify the consequences.

Persuasion

Persuasion seeks information from a person by convincing him of the justice of one's cause. Defectors in the Cold War mostly acted out of genuine conviction – for or against communism. Attempts to win over such people can be seen as a natural part of political struggle. This is usually quite lawful on the part of the recruiter, but those recruited generally find themselves in breach of their nation's laws. A clever, if morally questionable, ruse is 'false-flag recruitment' of agents who are deceived as to which country they will be working for (Perry 1995: 96)

Those who betray their country out of genuine belief or idealism (even if naïve) nonetheless attract a certain moral aura. The West naturally praised those who abandoned Soviet Russia. But even those who went over to communism were sometimes seen as in a way admirable in taking great personal risks for the sake of an ideal. If those who betray their own government are caught, however, they are treated as less deserving of protection than foreign nationals caught spying for their government. Treason is regarded as a heinous crime almost everywhere and often carries the death penalty, even if capital punishment is otherwise unused.

Entrapment

Entrapment relies on offers of money, sex, drugs, status or some personal benefit in return for providing information on a one-off or continuing basis. Unlike persuasion on ideological grounds it exploits the target's baser motives. After the Cold War, it may be noted, money rather than ideology became the dominant motivation of nationals won over to spy against their country (Taylor and Snow 1997: 102–3).

Initial requests for information may be minor in order to induce a target to compromise himself. Once money or a bribe of some sort has changed hands, the target is 'on the hook' because of the threat, spoken or unspoken, to reveal their treachery. Alternatively, a target may already have something to hide – illegal or immoral behaviour – that invites blackmail. It is often difficult to ignore threats of exposure though some individuals have sufficient moral courage to report the situation to their organisation.

Coercion

Here violence is used or threatened against an individual – or perhaps members of his family – in order to secure information (the case of those held in captivity is considered later). Threats may be explicit or implicit and will usually be illegal (even if the threat is not carried out). Clearly, those threatened experience strong psychological pressure to cooperate. If a threat is carried out, physical harm also enters the picture – with the threat of more to come.

There are obvious moral and legal objections to making and carrying out threats of harm. The principal argument for the legitimacy of such actions is that targets may be security agents working for their government (and may carry out similar actions against their targets). Such people, it can be argued, are as much open to coercion as soldiers in uniform are open to being killed by opposing forces. It is also the case that they and their agency will be taking defensive and perhaps offensive counter-measures. Not all targets, of course, fall into this category.

Intelligence gathering post-9/11

The traditional security focus on military capabilities and intentions has not disappeared since 9/11 though it has been displaced in some measure by wider concerns such as environmental, economic and health security and greatly overshadowed by the demands of the 'war on terror'. The attacks of 9/11 and the Western response to them have meant significant changes in the type of threat perceived and in the responses to them. During the Cold War the 'intelligence-to-force ratio' was relatively low – what mattered most was military capability – but the 'war on terror' has demanded a high 'intelligence-to-force ratio' (Reveron 2000: 455). What counts now is accurate intelligence about the personnel, plans and activities of terrorist groups, rather than the weapons they have (with the exception of weapons of mass destruction).

Several characteristics of intelligence gathering in the 'war on terror' can be identified, all of which point towards greater difficulty in creating or observing any limits on targets or on methods of collection. First, threats originate not just from enemy armies and arsenals, but from any group of people anywhere in the world. The US, above all, sees terrorism as global and transnational, rather than as national and local. Once anyone, including a country's own nationals, is a potential terrorist, the range of people from whom and about whom information can be sought is unlimited.

Second, critical information is no longer focused primarily on the major weapons held by an opponent, but on an enormous range of weapons and tactics that a terrorist might use – from Kalashnikovs to kidnapping, from home-made explosives to stolen computer codes, from ground-to-air missiles to hijacked aircraft. Where nuclear espionage was the epitome of Cold War rivalry, a huge variety of possible threats now attracts the interest of security organisations. To the extent that terrorists might seek WMD, this at least provides a focus for information gathering.

Third, the means of collecting intelligence have become much more complex. In the Cold War, satellites, seismographs and listening devices provided the great powers (and still do) with much of the information they needed about each other's nuclear and conventional capabilities. In the 'war on terror' there are no easy methods. For one thing, information is not easily collected by technical means. Vast amounts of data can be sucked up from emails, mobile phones, financial transfers and the like, but identifying specific terrorist activities among billions of transactions requires immense effort and complex assessments. What is needed now above all is that most challenging form of information gathering – human intelligence.

Finally, the importance of individuals as sources of information is greater than before 9/11. Nuclear spies and defectors certainly played a useful role during the Cold War but the 'war on terror' has put a premium on securing information from captured individuals who might provide actionable intelligence that could prevent attacks or reduce terrorist capabilities. As President Bush himself put it in September 2006: 'In this war, the most important source of information on where the terrorists are hiding and what they are planning is the terrorists themselves' (White House 2006a).

The 'war on terror' is part of a broad political struggle between contending ideas but it manifests itself through actions at the individual level. While conventional war takes the form of battles and campaigns, the key engagements in the clash between terrorists and their opponents are rather different. On the one hand is the terrorist attack itself – often conducted by individuals or a small group and usually involving the asymmetrical use of force against unarmed civilians. On the other is the similarly asymmetrical pursuit, capture (or killing) and interrogation of suspected terrorists. Though referring specifically to torture, Karen Greenberg observes that this form of engagement has 'enabled the act of war to be personal again' and has restored, 'albeit ironically and perversely, the human side of warfare' (Greenberg 2006: 5). In both types of engagement the scope for abuse of human rights is prominent (inherent in the case of terrorist attack, while the interrogator may well seek to strike terror in the heart of his antagonist). In short, one of the key battlegrounds in the 'war on terror' is the interrogation of detainees.

Pressures to expand the means of collecting information

The term 'war on terror' invokes the historical precedent that executive governments are granted extraordinary powers in time of war or national emergency. But it is also presented by President Bush and his Administration as a 'new type of war' in which the enemy is believed utterly determined to attack – to the point of suicide. A religious element on both sides adds to the perceived intensity of the struggle. States must therefore be prepared to use 'every resource' for the 'destruction and defeat of the global terrorist network' (Bowker 2006: 183–4). As a CIA official put it to a Congressional committee, '[a]fter 9/11 the gloves came off' (Cofer Black in Ayres 2005: 33).

The search for security against terrorism has led to increased constraints on civil liberties and to greater freedom for security organisations to engage in activities such as assassination, covert operations, the detention of suspects and their interrogation. In this context developing rules faces two particular difficulties.

First is minimal public knowledge about intelligence collection. There are legitimate reasons for security agencies to operate clandestinely, not least the desire to protect individuals as well as methods and sources of information. Governments, indeed, may be justified in deliberately misleading others in this regard, including their own nationals (and arguably their own legislatures). It may be advantageous, for example, to keep out of the public domain the very fact that a suspect has been detained. Again, a government may state that information leading to the capture of a terrorist resulted from a confession by an existing captive when in reality it derived from infiltration of a terrorist organisation by an agent (Bowden 2003: 5). Deceiving opponents may involve deceiving friends.

A second factor undermining restraint is the inherent uncertainty and complexity in judgements about the value of information gained. In defending harsh methods of interrogation, for example, governments are prone to inflate the value of information they have obtained (Danchev 2007: 98). Claims after the event that the information allowed an atrocity to be prevented are always hypothetical and often unprovable. (The information provided about plans may have been incorrect or, if true, other means of prevention might have been found.) The scope for exaggeration and misinformation in attempting to justify extreme measures is clear.

Neither war nor crime

A central problem of finding rules in the 'war on terror' is that it does not sit easily either in the category of war or in the category of crime. The established laws and practices of war and of policing seem inadequate or inappropriate, not least where interrogation is concerned. The dilemma is clearly illustrated in the case of the detainees at Guantanamo Bay where the US finds itself pursuing three partly contradictory goals. It seeks to detain them (like prisoners of war) for as long as they may return to fight in a particular war, to convict at least some of them as criminals, and to subject them to rigorous interrogation as part of the 'war on terror'.

With regard to prisoners of war the law of armed conflict strictly limits the information they must supply to their captors and prohibits mistreatment, but detention may continue until the end of the war concerned. The law also provides that those who break the rules lose the protections due to lawful combatants. While they must not be treated contrary to international law, combatants who are deemed not to be 'lawful' must by and large take their chances with whichever state captures them. This gap in the law, some argue, is deliberate, intended to dissuade belligerents from straying outside the rules (Ayres 2005: 43–4). Observance of the law of armed conflict is aided in part by the pressure of reciprocity – abuse by one side may provoke retaliation by the other – and in part by the relatively limited value of the information most captured soldiers are likely to have.

In the 'war on terror', however, the information to be gained from captives promises to be highly useful while strict adherence to the rules of war in questioning captives is unlikely to secure the information desired, especially if prisoners know they will not be subject to mistreatment. The threat of terrorism, moreover, may continue indefinitely, creating a reluctance ever to release captured suspects. Nor is treating captured terrorists according to the law of armed conflict likely to encourage terrorist organisations to treat their captives any more decently. The kidnapping, torture and murder of captives is essentially part of the asymmetric warfare used by terrorists that they cannot abandon (Yoo 2006: 35). Reciprocity simply does not work.

Dealing with suspected terrorists through a criminal process also has major drawbacks. Though terrorists plan and commit criminal acts, police forces have very different approaches compared with security agencies. First, police serve the judicial system which demands respect for the rights of anyone under arrest e.g. remaining silent, presence of a lawyer, contact with family, and limits to the period of detention without charge. Failure to observe proper procedures can mean failure to convict. Security agencies, by contrast, serve the executive government, enjoying greater freedom to act in matters of security and operating largely outside the public gaze, or indeed that of the judiciary or the legislature. Many methods employed by security agencies clearly do not meet the standards of evidence required by courts, a difference that can cause significant problems in the sharing of information between police and security agencies.

Second, police generally focus on crimes already committed, seeking information that will prove an individual has committed a crime to the satisfaction of a court of law where the burden of proof is on the prosecution. Though naturally concerned also to prevent future crime, most of their activity is reactive to past crime. Security agencies, by contrast, are directly focused on future threats and search actively for possible conspiracies. For them merely suspicious behaviour may constitute actionable intelligence.

Third, the consequences of failure are different. If police do not secure adequate evidence to convict a person who has committed a crime, an injustice occurs. The victim feels aggrieved, the criminal may re-offend and public confidence in the police is undermined. While these consequences are unfortunate, society may not see them as dire. The widely accepted principle that it is better for ten guilty people to go free than for one innocent person to be convicted suggests that failure to punish a crime is by no means totally unacceptable. In practical terms, moreover, the victim is no worse off while the lucky criminal may end up in prison because of other offences or may simply not re-offend.

An intelligence failure, on the other hand, can mean a major loss of life (in contrast to most non-terrorist murders) and a highly visible atrocity likely to engender widespread public fears (such as occurs with only a few more notorious crimes). The public are manifestly worse off than if a past crime goes unpunished.

Political reactions are also likely to be vigorous and agencies blamed, fairly or unfairly, for apparent incompetence or negligence.

Intelligence collection in the war on terror

The question of how to treat detainees who are believed to pose a security risk and to possess information that may prevent future terrorist attacks is thus a complex one with no ready rules available. As a result dealing with captured terrorists takes place in a kind of ethical and legal limbo that lacks clear guidelines. The use of Guantanamo Bay, which is beyond the reach of American law as far as detainees are concerned, is symbolic as well as convenient. This indeterminacy is also evident in the language sometimes used to refer to captives, namely 'persons under US control' – the aim being to create a 'bureaucratic blank spot where prisoners could reside temporarily without entering any official database' (Mackey 2004: 250).

The great disparity of physical power, moreover, allows the captor to treat a prisoner as he chooses. This asymmetric relationship can be used not only to hurt and intimidate the prisoner but also to send a message to anyone else who might become a captive (Holmes 2006: 130). But the interrogator is not without handicaps. He may well have no clear idea of what information the captive has, or whether he has any at all. Nor can he be sure whether the victim has yielded all the information that may be useful, or confident that the information secured is accurate.

For their part, those held physically captive are not entirely without assets. One may be their psychological strength, perhaps reinforced by a strong ideological or religious belief. Training to resist interrogation may also be useful. Another asset is the possession of information that can be withheld (Paskins 1976: 141). Once this is given up, however, the captive has lost his best asset and perhaps his sense of self-worth as well.

Though seemingly one-sided, interrogation is a thus a complex clash of individual wills. Everything from scrupulous observance of the prisoner's rights to sustained torture up to the point of death can be and has been tried. Are any moral principles to be found in this murky area? A range of approaches will be considered in approximate order of justifiability though it is clear that all save the first raise profound moral uncertainties.

Kid gloves

This approach seeks information without the use of threats, coercion, humiliation and the like, though questioning may be incisive, probing and discomforting. Strict rules may be spelt out in national codes, especially those adopted by military forces. The moral basis for such an approach is that it maximises respect for human rights, encourages trust in official institutions and protects interrogators from demeaning practices. It may even pay immediate dividends. Mackey recounts how one prisoner in Afghanistan decided after lengthy but restrained interrogation to assist the US on the grounds that if 'this was the worst the Americans were going to do' he would change sides (Mackey 2004: 426).

Even within strict guidelines for interrogation, however, prisoners are inevitably under some pressure. They may not know the length of their confinement; they may be anxious about family and friends; they may fear mistreatment in the future despite assurances to the contrary. Another grey area is the manipulation of privileges: all prisoners may be treated according to minimum standards but those who cooperate may come to expect preferential treatment. Can interrogators play on these concerns without overstepping the mark?

Surgical gloves

This approach works on the mind of the prisoner but amounts to rather more than probing for information. It entails working on the thought processes of the captive, whether creating psychological discomfort at some level by such means as humiliation, accusations of homosexuality or promoting anxieties about families or friends, and/or by creating a (false) sense of security through, say, flattering the ego or pretending to cultivate a friendship. Cultural or religious values can also be manipulated to create psychological pressure, e.g. sexual flaunting in front of prisoners and abuse of the Koran.

Some methods do involve very limited force against the person but it is employed not to produce pain but rather a psychological effect. Examples include gentle poking, putting dog collars on prisoners, shaving their hair or making males wear a bra. Other practices, if limited in time and extent, can be used chiefly for psychological effect, including solitary confinement, blindfolding, hooding, loud noise and denial of sleep. Related methods involve calculated deceptions such as posing as agents of another country, exploiting forged documents or pretending that other prisoners have given information (Mackey 2004: 88–9, 97).

Similar, too, is the use of drugs to extract information, a process that entails minor physical hurt but which is principally intended to change the way an individual thinks. Though the effectiveness of a so-called 'truth serum' is debated, some argue that it is both morally more acceptable than physical coercion as well as being permitted under US law (Dershowitz 2002: 247–8 note 6). Mood-changing drugs can also be given, say in food, without the captive's knowledge. Also of interest is compelling the victim to take a drug which he believes to be a 'truth serum' but which is in fact a placebo. The result is that the prisoner may feel he has an acceptable 'excuse' to provide information (Bowden 2003: 15).

Of course, alcohol is another mood-changing drug that may lead a prisoner to provide information he did not intend to divulge. If taken voluntarily, however, this method might be better classified as 'kid gloves' treatment.

Velvet gloves

Here information is sought through deliberate threats of violence, whether implicit or explicit. Fear is created that the 'iron fist' hidden in the velvet glove could be used. The 'good cop, bad cop' routine often produces this uncertainty – what if the bad cop loses control or gets to interrogate me alone? Human rights and dignity are abused, and persistent or extreme threats of violence can cause severe psychological harm to the captive even if never actually carried out.

Another example is the threat of execution or arbitrary murder – as distinct from warnings that certain behaviour could lead to the death penalty through a legal process. In Russian roulette the threat is randomised in that life or death depends on a chance process rather than on a deliberate decision by the threatener. Russian roulette played without a bullet in the gun – a fact not known to the prisoner – is equally frightening but may be less morally objectionable. The presence of dogs also creates an uncertainty in the mind of the captive about what physical harm he might suffer.

A complex moral issue here is whether one may legitimately *threaten* to do something that is wrong in order to achieve a good outcome. Threats of physical pain, for example, may elicit information even if an interrogator has no intention of carrying them out. The same dilemma is found in other situations where the threatener prefers not to carry out the threat. In the Cold War, for example, some strategists argued that nuclear deterrence could succeed even if a state – secretly – had no intention of responding with nuclear weapons in the event of a first-strike by an opponent.

Boxing gloves

In what is sometimes called 'coercive interrogation' or 'torture lite' physical harm is inflicted (beatings, burns, suffocation, cutting, etc.), or psychological distress is sought by painful physical routines (stress positions, prolonged standing, etc.). Implicitly or explicitly there is a threat of more to come. Hurt is imposed directly by physical means – hence the analogy with boxing gloves which are designed to inflict pain without reaching the extreme (bare knuckles or torture). This category includes hurting a third party such as a relative or colleague in order to manipulate the prisoner. The latter is clearly more objectionable ethically in that pain is deliberately caused to a person known not to have the information desired, and perhaps known to be quite innocent.

There is room for much debate over whether measures of this kind short of torture are all permissible, all impermissible, or somewhere in-between. A critical issue is determining the point at which such measures do become torture (see below). US treatment of its detainees in Afghanistan, Iraq and Guantanamo Bay has been characterised by attempts to distinguish between what is acceptable and what is not. However, it is difficult to discern clear moral guidelines behind US practice apart from the idea that the shorter the time pain is inflicted and the shorter the period of recovery the better. In practice, the matter comes down to what decision-makers have considered reasonable, perhaps taking into account also the likely reaction of public opinion.

Given that in practice some techniques will be permitted, or at least not prohibited, much depends on the interrogators, their immediate superiors and the general atmosphere in an interrogation (and detention) centre. Individuals vary greatly in their attitudes. Some are keen to use violence, and Mackey cites a colleague: 'Just two minutes. Give me just two minutes alone with him' (Mackey 2004: 95). Others work out rules of thumb for what is acceptable. Mackey himself, for example, kept prisoners awake only for as long as he as an interrogator could stay awake. (Mackey 2004: 95; Yoo 2006: 191).[2] More homely rules mentioned include: 'what if my actions were reported on the front page of the newspapers?' and 'what would my mother think?' (Shane 2006).

In the same vein, it is sometimes suggested that methods used in training one's own soldiers are permissible (Mackey 2004: 350). Australian soldiers at risk of enemy capture, for example, are subjected to harsh Resistance To Interrogation training which includes being blindfolded and stripped naked, as well as stress positions, sleep deprivation, intense questioning and sexual humiliation. This particular argument, however, overlooks the fact that trainees are volunteers, that training is of limited duration and for the benefit of the trainee, and that it is carried out under strict controls.

Gloves off

Both critics and defenders of torture see it as an extreme, as something in a category of its own. Indeed, there is a clear parallel with terrorism which is also generally regarded as an extreme action – either never justifiable or permitted only in desperate circumstances (Holmes 2006: 129). The International Convention Against Torture of 1984, for example, distinguishes torture from other forms of cruel, inhuman and degrading treatment, outlawing it directly while enjoining signatories to prohibit lesser forms of brutality. It also denies states the right to resort to torture even in the extremities of war or public emergency. Decisions in British, European, Israeli and US courts have also drawn a line, albeit in varying places, between torture and other treatment that might still be cruel, inhuman or degrading.

Both terror and torture also encounter the problem of definition. Though a universally agreed general definition remains elusive, terrorism is outlawed in specific forms such as aircraft hijacking and bombing in public places. Torture has been defined in general terms but much uncertainty remains about its precise nature and scope. The Convention Against Torture refers to 'severe pain or suffering, whether physical or mental' that is 'intentionally inflicted'. But how severe must the pain be? Can lesser pain inflicted for a long period become severe? Are physical and mental suffering to be judged in the same way? Who is to judge severity – the torturer, the victim or a third party?

Torture has been employed for centuries for a variety of contentious purposes, including repression of political opponents, the saving of human souls, the extraction of confessions to secure punishment, the gaining of information for the public good as well as sheer cruelty. Debate about its moral value has revived since 9/11 as the desire of governments to prevent terrorist outrages has attracted attention to the interrogation of captives. There is no need here to go into the debate at length (Dershowitz 2002; Ignatieff 2004). The key dispute is between absolutists who argue that torture is inherently wrong and never justifiable (the deontological view), and pragmatists who argue that torture can be justified as a last resort when the ends are sufficiently great as to outweigh objections to the means (the consequentialist view).

The pragmatic approach has won a degree of support in recent years as the perceived threat of terrorism has grown. In earlier decades an attack might kill a few dozen people, at most a hundred or two on board an aircraft. Now, it is clear that a single terrorist act can kill 3,000 people or even more, perhaps 3 million if weapons of mass destruction are employed. The greater the evil to be prevented, it is argued, the greater the justification for extreme means in preventing it. The threat, moreover, is very real, coming from extremists and zealots prepared to stop at nothing and resistant to other methods of persuasion and deterrence.

A second leg of the ethical argument for torture is that it is a preventive measure for the public good. It envisages cases where information secured by torture genuinely allows authorities to prevent a looming atrocity, namely information can be secured, and sufficient time and suitable means are available, to disarm a 'ticking bomb'. In other words, the motives for torture are public-spirited, not political, punitive or personal. Safeguards can also be put in place – such as approval by an independent judiciary – in order to ensure that torture is only approved when pre-conditions are met and that it is only employed rarely and with reluctance.

A third type of defence focuses on the presumed character of the victim of torture. A captive known to be a terrorist who has no regard for ordinary law or morality has, some argue, lost the right to certain protections. Most 'deserving' of torture is the person who has actually placed a 'ticking bomb' or has committed outrages in the past. Perhaps he or she retains a right to life, but not necessarily the right to security from serious physical or psychological harm. Terrorists are 'at war' with society and hence lose their immunity (Paskins 1976: 141–2). On this view, terrorists are the modern equivalent of pirates, once deemed *hostes humani generis* – enemies of humankind who could be hunted down and killed by law-abiding citizens.

Finally, there are pragmatic arguments for permitting torture. One is that it is going to happen anyway, even if formally prohibited, so that setting up strict legal and political controls is more satisfactory than an ineffective ban that drives it underground (Dershowitz 2002). Moreover, if terrorists know that their captors will not use torture, they will be more likely to hold out against robust interrogation, especially if they have been trained to resist and know that interrogators are working within rules (MacDonald 2006: 85–6). The assumptions behind such arguments may be questioned but any rejection of torture in principle needs to at least consider the real-world consequences of such a position.

Among opponents of torture, the absolutist position argues that no human being is ever justified in deliberately inflicting extreme pain on another (save in emergency medical situations). Torture is always wrong, even if it actually prevents a greater evil. The lesser evil is not an option. Legalising torture, moreover, would produce what opponents see as an abhorrent consequence – society would in effect license certain people as torturers. Who would carry it out? How would they be trained? Any claim to protect human rights or to support the rule of law by the state concerned would lose all credibility.

A second type of argument against permitting torture is pragmatic. There is a 'slippery slope' in that once torture is permitted its use will naturally and inevitably widen even if well-intentioned safeguards are put in place (Luban 2006: 52–5; Yoo 2006: 193–4).[3] Torture will be carried out by agencies operating outside public scrutiny and there will be temptation to use it in the hope it will yield useful information. Once started, there is no natural time limit to torture – apart from death – for the torturer may well believe that more information can be gained, even if the victim has already talked. One success with torture, indeed, is likely to encourage more torture. There is also a slippery upward slope – if less painful interrogation techniques do not produce results, harsher treatment will follow and eventually torture will be employed. Only a total and unequivocal ban will keep coercive interrogation from crossing the boundary into torture.

A final criticism of torture challenges the assumptions underlying the 'ticking bomb' argument, arguing that they will rarely, if ever, obtain in practice. How can there be certainty in advance that a prisoner has the information concerned, that he or she will provide it in time, and that securing it will actually enable prevention of an atrocity? Arguments for torture often rely on extreme and hypothetical situations but 'artificial cases make bad ethics' (Shue 1978: 141).

Critics and supporters of torture take various positions on whether torture actually works. The former often argue that it simply does not work. Some individuals will simply not have the information sought. Some will resist even extreme pain indefinitely or to the death. Most likely, people under torture will provide information that is untrue or unreliable but which victims think the torturer wants to hear. By its nature torture seems designed to make victims confess to acts they have not committed. But even if torture occasionally produces results, the absolutist will remain opposed. For their part, supporters of torture claim that in some cases it has in fact saved innocent lives (Dershowitz 2002: 138). Yet even if this were not so, there is benefit in retaining the option against some future scenario when it may be needed.

Finally, one can take a wider view. Supporters of torture claim that it will send a powerful message to opponents, demonstrating determination to defend one's position and possibly deterring resort to terror. Critics of torture argue that even if it saves innocent lives, it will create more terrorists (Danchev 2007: 107). It may also provoke more intense opposition and a greater willingness among opponents to fight to the death.

Ethical guidelines

At the bottom of the scale, 'kid gloves' interrogation is unlikely to be seriously opposed on ethical grounds (though detention without charge may be). At the other end, torture has provoked strong and principled objection, though it does not lack defenders either. Can lines be drawn somewhere?

It is apparent that there are few, if any, 'bright lines' – the term used by John Yoo in defending US Department of Justice memoranda that sought to provide clear guidance about what was definitely torture. The aim was clarity even if blunt language was used and sensibilities offended (Yoo 2006: 175).[4] Clear rules also make it more difficult for those in authority to evade responsibility by claiming that subordinates engaging in torture broke the official guidelines. It is all too easy for those in authority to condemn practices in general terms without defining them closely and providing detailed rules.

Yet the benefits of clear lines can also be challenged, particularly if there is disagreement about the scope of an activity to be prohibited. Thus banning torture that is too widely defined invites widespread non-observance and encourages interrogators to keep dubious activities hidden from outside scrutiny, perhaps even from their superiors. On the other hand, defining an activity too narrowly will permit a great deal of undesirable behaviour or even encourage it because it is not expressly prohibited.

If the line between torture and coercive interrogation is slippery, so too is that between psychological pressure (surgical gloves) and physical pain (boxing gloves). There are certainly arguments that manipulation through, say, '[a]nxiety, humiliation, loneliness, and pride' is far more effective than physical pain (Perry 1995: 101). This goes to effectiveness, and suggests that physical pain is unnecessary. But is there any ethical distinction in principle between the two? A certain natural squeamishness causes many to react more strongly against physical coercion (perhaps because it can more easily be imagined) but both methods hurt the victim and both can cause long-lasting harm.

This points to the further problem in that individuals respond differently to pain, whether physical or mental. Identical treatment applied to different people could inflict very different levels of harm, both short and long term. Should rules of interrogation reflect the degree to which a prisoner can tolerate hurt? Is more permitted against someone who has had training to resist coercive methods? The difficulties in predicting a person's response are also evident, not least because an assessment must be made before coercion is applied. A further problem is that methods that might seem bearable for a short period of time could prove very harmful if used in the long term. Keeping a prisoner awake for two hours beyond normal bed-time is quite different from depriving him of sleep for two weeks.

If judgement by the impact on the victim offers no easy answers, nor does judgement by results. As already argued with regard to torture, success or failure cannot be known in advance for a number of reasons. Rules of conduct, however, are only useful if they provide guidance in advance on what can or cannot be done.

Perhaps, then, it comes down to the character or integrity of those seeking information – to what has been termed 'virtue ethics'. They alone know all or most of the circumstances and might be trusted to decide what methods are reasonable.

People with moral character will come up with defensible guidelines as to how far they can decently go. As a former CIA operative put it: 'Interrogation is such a dirty business that it should be done only by people of the cleanest character. Anyone with sadistic tendencies should not be in the business' (William Johnson cited in Perry 1995: 101).

But many would argue that those in the business of interrogation, especially the more coercive forms, cannot be relied on to make dispassionate judgements. Even practitioners disagree as to whether they can maintain their personal integrity while working in a job that requires lies and deception, threatening and harming (Perry 1995: 107). There are also obvious difficulties in creating a professional code of conduct and ethical principles for security agents along the same lines as established professions which rely on strongly internalised values and strict self-regulation.

For such reasons military professionals who live and die by rules and discipline normally reject torture or coercive interrogation as part of their duties and see it as simply incompatible with professionalism (James 2005: 27). Colin Powell, a former four-star general, insisted as Secretary of State that the US military must follow 'the highest standards of conduct' in the 'war on terror', a stance that prompted President Bush's order to treat prisoners 'humanely' even if the law of armed conflict did not apply (Yoo 2006: 40–1).

Other professions, notably doctors and psychologists, can also be drawn into the business of interrogation. Can or should a doctor help determine what is severe pain? Or whether a prisoner will suffer permanent injury or trauma as a result of coercive methods? Or actually help in devising such methods? There are also claims that doctors have falsified death certificates when prisoners in US custody have died as a result of coercive interrogation or brutal treatment by guards (Miles 2006). At the other extreme, many doctors would refuse to have any connection with practices that harm individuals, even if it is a matter of setting limits to such harm or undoing the harm already done (on the grounds that it encourages further mistreatment).

Ethics and responsibility

This analysis has focused on the interrogator, but responsibility for the treatment or mistreatment of detainees is always far wider. Abuse of prisoners at Abu Ghraib, for example, was primarily by jailers and not necessarily connected with interrogation. At worst, there may be a deliberate policy by guards of 'softening up' prisoners in advance of interrogation, but even at best detainees are likely to draw their own conclusion: cooperating with interrogators will reduce the risk of harsh treatment. Can interrogators ethically take advantage of this situation? Can interrogators avoid taking advantage of such a situation?

Ethical interrogation clearly needs more than just ethical interrogators. Governments bear overall responsibility for the actions of organisations and personnel involved directly and indirectly in interrogation. Many of the cases of mistreatment of detainees, an official US report conceded, were due to factors such as lack of planning, insufficient resources (especially interpreters), failure by superiors to respond to indications of problems and missed opportunities for detailed guidance on interrogation techniques (Church 2005).

In political, if not ethical, terms governments can seek to diffuse responsibility for mistreatment by employing private contractors rather than using their own agents. 'Failures' can then be blamed on the company or its employees – despite the supposed best efforts of government. It is fair to observe, however, that employees of private contractors may well be skilled and experienced interrogators, often ex-military, who do not need to rely on more coercive methods.

The most cynical device for shifting responsibility is that of 'extraordinary rendition' – transferring prisoners for interrogation in other states where it is possible, or even expected, that torture will be used. The practice is contrary to the Convention Against Torture but allows a government to deny (accurately) that it engages in torture. If the matter becomes public, blame can be placed on the receiving state. Similar considerations apply to states that agree to hand over battlefield detainees to another power as Australia did in relation to the wars in Afghanistan and Iraq (Muggleton 2006: 10–11). The law of armed conflict requires the transferring state to be satisfied that prisoners will be treated appropriately, an obligation that remains as long as their detention continues.

Information-gathering for intelligence purposes faces an environment unfavourable to the development of clear ethical principles and strong ethical practices. Lack of transparency and accountability, the high stakes involved, disparities of power, the difficulties of judgement about legitimate targets and legitimate methods – all conspire to starve ethical principles of oxygen. Is there any prospect for ethical rules and practices? Mark Bowden, for example, concludes that

> Candor and consistency are not always public virtues. Torture is a crime against humanity, but coercion is an issue that is rightly handled with a wink, or even a touch of hypocrisy; it should be banned but also quietly practiced.
>
> (Bowden 2003: 23)

Bowden also suggests that governments are wise to avoid public discussion of such matters. This is certainly a realist view but it is also perhaps too cynical a conclusion. Human conscience, a certain respect for human rights and a sense of professionalism, together with increased public interest during the 'war on terror', may help sustain some ethical principles in 'the great game'. Something can be expected, but not too much.

Notes

1 R.V. Jones identifies several ethical dilemmas but usually observes that he was fortunate not to have to face them himself.
2 US Secretary of Defense Rumsfeld took a similar line when he observed that since he stood for hours on end while working, there could be no objection to making prisoners stand.

3 Yoo argues that there is no evidence this occurs in the UK or Israel.

4 Yoo argues that an explicit definition of torture put forward by the Office of Legal Counsel in 2002, using a concept of 'severe pain' based on existing US law relating to 'health benefits for emergency medical conditions', had to be re-written in 2004 in much vaguer terms simply to avoid offence.

11 The international campaign to counter the financing of terrorism

J. C. Sharman

Immediately after the terrorist attacks of September 2001 President Bush declared: 'Money is the lifeblood of terrorist operations. We're asking the world to stop payment' ('Looking in the Wrong Places', *Economist*, 20 October 2005). The notion that terrorist organisations could be disrupted, or even defeated, by attacking their financial underpinnings has exercised a powerful hold on policy-makers' imaginations. Although the international effort to counter the financing of terrorism was born before September 2001, it was vastly expanded after the attacks on the United States.

Any expectations of a quick victory over al-Qaeda and related terrorist groups brought about by financial sanctions have now dissipated. But in Washington and other allied capitals the same ambitious goals remain: that terrorist organisations can and will be organisationally strangled, and thus their attacks prevented, by denying them monetary support. While the counter-terrorist measures affecting banks and the rest of the financial industry may have lacked the public profile of other developments, for example in airport security, they are regarded as being one of the few ways the United States and other governments can 'take the fight to the enemy'.

This chapter seeks to trace the development of the international campaign to block terrorist finance. It describes the important policy shifts that have taken place since 2001, the consequences for terrorists, but also the impact these developments have had on the legitimate financial services industry. It is argued that despite the scope and intensity of the response, the nature of terrorist financing means that it is largely invulnerable to the sort of counter-measures now being deployed.

In policy terms the effort to counter the finance of terrorism shows much more of a balance between US unilateralism and genuine multilateralism than has been the case in many other facets of the Bush administration's national security and foreign policies. There has certainly been a muscular assertion of United States (US) national power in the financial front of the 'War on Terror'. This can be seen in particular in the extra-territorial features included in the USA Patriot Act passed in October 2001. But the US has also worked within international organisations, and in important instances deferred to these bodies, rather than relying on *ad hoc* 'coalitions of the willing' familiar from the invasion and occupation in Iraq.

Furthermore, as much as the shock of September 11 threw open the policy agenda and radically broadened the scope of potential measures deemed acceptable, countering the financing of terrorism (CFT) is in some ways most notable for its generic nature and derivative solutions. The specific measures taken to interdict terrorists' money replicate almost exactly those put in place from the late 1980s onwards to combat money laundering as part of the 'War on Drugs'. Although the difficulty of amassing evidence makes a conclusive judgement impossible, it seems that the first set of policy instruments to hand, anti-money laundering regulations, are not especially well suited to tackle the distinct problem of terrorist finance.

The structure of this chapter is as follows. The first section presents an overview of international cooperation to counter the financing of terrorism, while the second section surveys the US response to the same problem, particularly as embodied in the USA Patriot Act. The third looks at the specifics of policies to counter the financing of terrorism, and in particular the almost complete similarity between current measures to disrupt terrorists' finance and standards earlier developed to attack the laundering of money derived from the international drug trade. The fourth section argues that despite this emphasis on the similarities between money laundering and terrorist finance in the policy response, there are important differences between the two. The last section gives a preliminary and necessarily tentative verdict on the success of efforts so far.

Overview of the international response

Efforts to strike at terrorism by 'following the money' were not born in 2001, although interest in the issue has increased exponentially since that point. Britain had a long running campaign to halt the flow of funds to the Irish Republican Army from sympathisers in the US. Often transferred through what were at least ostensibly charities, the United States authorities extended little cooperation in shutting down these flows. Similarly, the Liberation Tigers of Tamil Eelam have long raised funds amongst the Tamil diaspora, with the Sri Lankan government appealing to third countries to block this fund-raising activity.

The Council of Europe, one of the first international organisations to use the term 'money laundering', did so in 1980 in connection with the fight against left-wing terrorists in West Germany and Italy (Pieth 2002). The United Nations (UN) had even gone so far as to draw up an International Convention for the Suppressing of Financing Terrorism in 1999, though an indicator of the low priority accorded to this issue is the fact that only four countries had signed up previous to September 2001 (Rider 2004: 62); by April 2004 this number had increased to 117 (Council of Foreign Relations 2004: 9). Relating to al-Qaeda specifically UN Security Council Resolution 1267 (15 October 1999) obliged members to freeze assets of the organisation's members or individuals associated with it.

After the initial shock of the September 11 terrorist attacks, there was a stampede of international organisations looking to become involved in advancing international cooperation to stop terrorist finance. The G7 finance ministers' meeting issued a statement on the need to combat the financing of terrorism on 25 September 2001. Despite being barred from either a security or a criminal justice role, both the World Bank and International Monetary Fund began incorporating anti-money laundering and anti-terrorist finance components in their reviews of the adequacy of member states' financial supervision and regulation. Other bodies like the UN Office on Drugs and Crime, the Commonwealth and the Council of Europe began incorporating an anti-terrorist aspect into their existing anti-money laundering programmes. Indeed, it is almost easier to specify those international organisations that did *not* weigh in on the subject from September 2001 than listing all those that did.

On 28 September 2001 the UN Security Council passed Resolution 1373 which first created a Counter Terrorism Committee to oversee the UN's work on this topic. In turn, the Committee required all states to pass legislation making the finance of terrorism a crime in and of itself. It further required that all states set up Financial Intelligence Units or equivalent bodies to link law enforcement authorities with banks and other private financial intermediaries. States are asked to ensure that they have the legal mechanisms in place to freeze suspected terrorist funds. The Committee instituted regular reporting obligations to gauge members' progress in this area, which has elicited a highly unusual degree of almost perfect compliance. By mid-2004 the Counter Terrorism Committee had fielded requests for technical assistance in this area from 160 countries (Council for Foreign Relations 2004: 11).

However the institution that was able to lay the leading claim in standard setting and monitoring in this area was the Financial Action Task Force (FATF). The FATF was founded to co-ordinate the fight against money laundering with particular reference to the drug trade in the wake of the 1989 G7 heads of government summit. Its membership includes most of the OECD countries as well as certain 'strategically important' developing states. The FATF's small secretariat is hosted by the OECD in Paris. The most notable product of the FATF has been the 40 Recommendations, first released in 1990, and revised periodically since then. Reflecting the expanding scope of the anti-money laundering regime, from 1996 the FATF devoted itself to combating money laundering associated with all serious crimes, not just drug-related offences.

The FATF 40 Recommendations now constitute internationally-accepted best practice for the control of money laundering (see page 9 for details). Rather than working by binding international law, the FATF at first worked to raise standards among its members by a process of peer review and mutual evaluation (Levi and Gilmore 2002). Later, however, a more coercive approach was adopted, as from June 2000 the organisation created the Non-Cooperative Countries and Territories blacklist for non-member jurisdictions adjudged to be derelict in their anti-money laundering (AML) duties (Johnson 2001).

In October 2001 the FATF drew up the Eight Special Recommendations on the financing of terrorism, with an extra recommendation on bulk cash smuggling added shortly thereafter. However the June 2002 initial deadline for applying pressure against non-members who failed to comply had to be dropped after almost all FATF member states themselves, including the US, realised that they would not meet their own deadline ('Follow the Money', *Economist*, 30 May 2002). Since that time the FATF has included terrorist financing issues in its regular series of assessments of both member and non-member states.

The Special Recommendations call for states to ratify the UN convention against terrorist financing and to criminalise this practice, as well as extending the use of anti-money laundering measures like suspicious transaction reporting and mutual legal assistance to terrorist finance. Special Recommendations 6, 8 and 9 are the most ambitious.

Recommendation 6 calls for practitioners of alternative remittance systems to be brought within the coverage of existing AML procedures relevant to banks and other financial institutions. Alternative remittance systems such as the South Asian hawalah or Chinese chop are trust-based systems of cash transfer often used among ethnic diasporas. Being cheap and reliable, hawalah and its equivalents provide a highly economical means by which, for example, Indian workers in the Persian Gulf can remit money to their families at home. The fees for using these alternative systems are typically significantly lower than wire transfer companies such as Western Union, and in addition their coverage may extend to regions outside formal banking networks, like Somalia.

But because there is little formal accounting and no electronic transfers, the lack of a paper trail and consequent anonymity is seen as providing a means by which terrorists can compensate for being shut out of international banking networks. Given the informal nature of such operations, the weak government presence in countries where alternative remittance schemes are strongest, and the lack of affordable alternatives in the formal banking system, this recommendation poses serious implementation challenges. Although in the immediate aftermath of the 2001 attacks there was talk of trying to shut down alternative remittance systems completely, given their crucial legitimate economic role in the developing world this extreme response (which once more would have been very difficult to implement) was dropped. Currently the goal is to draw these schemes into the formal economy, and thus into official record-keeping and reporting systems.

Reflecting concerns about Islamic charities, Special Recommendation 8 calls for non-profit organisations to be regulated to ensure they are not abused as fronts for terrorist organisations. Once again this tends to presage a further expansion of the institutions subject to the reporting requirements drawn up initially to fight drug trafficking. Saudi Arabia in particular has been on the receiving end of strong US pressure in relation to this issue (Council of Foreign Relations 2002, 2004). But like alternative remittance systems, regulating charities represents a substantial implementation headache.

The last Special Recommendation seeks to halt the undeclared flow of bulk cash across borders. Cash smuggling has been a concern in Western countries in relation to drug traffickers (the weight and bulk of cash generated by drug sales may exceed the weight and bulk of the drugs themselves). But the recent emphasis on bulk cash transfers reflects the realisation that developing economies are far more cash-dependent than those of the average FATF member state, where electronic transfers are the norm.

The United States' unilateral response

The overall aim pronounced by President Bush after signing the executive order to freeze al-Qaeda assets was clear: 'We will starve the terrorists of funds' (*9/11 Investigations* 2004: 506). As noted earlier, although the fight against terrorist finance has to some extent been unusual in the degree to which the US has been willing to work through formal multilateral organisations, this has been complemented by a robust series of unilateral measures. The most important of these are contained in the USA Patriot Act. But rather than proceeding in parallel, there have been important intersections and complementarities in the US unilateral and multilateral efforts. International organisations like the FATF have benefited from the suspicion that compliance with its standards not only confers international legitimacy, but also provides some protection against the threat of being singled out for punitive action by the US government. Thus in defying the FATF the tiny Pacific state of Nauru ultimately came into conflict with the US. Conversely, the US has incorporated the language and standards of international organisations in its domestic legislation, as well as delegating important national policy prerogatives to such bodies.

The rather unlikely case of Nauru came to the attention of the FATF because of its shell banks. Desperate for a source of economic viability after the collapse of its phosphate industry, the government of Nauru turned to selling offshore banking licences with few if any checks on the customers. Though these banks had no physical presence beyond a plastic name plate on the wall of a small shed in Nauru, the licence did grant purchasers access to correspondent banking accounts through which money could be transferred all over the world. About 400 such licences were sold, though because a large proportion of the US$7,500 fee per bank was stolen by individual government employees, it is impossible to determine the exact number. From 1999 there were well-publicised accusations that these shell banks had been purchased by criminals in order to laundering money. The Russian Central Bank (no paragon of financial rectitude itself) claimed that up to US$70 billion had been laundered through Nauru's banks. As a result, Nauru was placed on the first issue of the FATF's Non-Cooperative Countries and Territories list in June 2000.

Nauru's government was unimpressed by international efforts to compel it to abolish its offshore sector. The Prime Minister demanded US$10 million as compensation, and when this sum was not forthcoming indicated that there was no prospect of compliance. Pressure mounted sharply in October 2002, however, when immediately after the Bali bombings US Secretary of State Colin Powell stated that Nauru's offshore banks and its practice of selling its passports both created a terrorist risk. It was alleged that members of an Islamic terrorist group had been apprehended in the possession of Nauruan passports. Citing the FATF's listing, the US placed Nauru under a financial embargo by unplugging it from the network used to process electronic banking transactions. Once this had happened, money could only be brought into or out of the country by physically carrying it. Because of the stigma of being on the FATF's blacklist, most foreign financial institutions had already decided that the reputational risk of processing transactions coming from, going to, or routed through Nauru were simply not worth it.

In March 2003 Nauru's government buckled, and abolished both the offshore banking licence regime and the economic citizenship programme (Van Fossen 2003). Third countries were quick to draw the lesson that rather than being an irrelevant talk shop, the FATF was backed by the financial power of the US. This realisation also extended to financial matters only tenuously related to the financing of terrorism, as many tax havens became distinctly more willing to exchange information on tax matters (Sharman 2006).

The USA Patriot Act (or to give it its full name, the Uniting and Strengthening America by Providing Appropriate Tools Required to Intercept and Obstruct Terrorism Act) contained a series of measures affecting US domestic institutions. Many of the clauses related to banks and other financial intermediaries collecting information on their customers for the benefit of the government had been unsuccessfully suggested by the Federal Deposits Insurance Commission as the Know Your Customer regulation from 1998. This earlier regulation had foundered after opposition based on privacy concerns, and complaints from the banking industry that the requirements would be excessively costly and burdensome. But it is the extra-territorial reach of the Act that is most noteworthy, allowing it to generate international 'cooperation', if of a less than spontaneous kind.

Section 311 of the Act empowers the Treasury Secretary to require all US institutions with correspondent relations with foreign banks in jurisdictions 'of primary money laundering concern' (with money laundering in this context including the financing of terrorism) to either collect more information on those using the correspondent accounts, or even sever these accounts altogether. US banks having correspondent relations with foreign banks have to establish the ownership of these foreign banks, and find out which other banks the foreign bank in question has correspondent accounts with. Furthermore, the Act prohibits relations with shell banks, i.e. those like in the case of Nauru that have no physical presence – no office and no employees. As a result of these changes, many US banks have simply refused to deal with transactions that come from foreign jurisdictions that, for one reason or another, have come under a cloud of suspicion, even when they are not formally listed as being of primary money laundering concern.

The most radical aspect, however, is section 319. This provision empowers US authorities to confiscate the assets of foreign banks maintained in the US if funds subject to seizure under American law are deposited with these banks anywhere in the world. There is no requirement that the actual money seized in the US be associated with the crime, or even that the bank was aware of the crime. Foreign banks sustaining correspondent relations with a US institution must also hand over information on foreign customers of interest to the US government, or else have those correspondent relations cut. This requirement applies even when the foreign bank would be breaking the laws of its home country to hand over such information (Preston 2002).

It is worth noting that the USA Patriot Act is by no means the only source of enhanced powers to collect information from foreign jurisdictions in contravention of local laws. From late 2001 the US Treasury's Office of Foreign Asset Control acting on behalf of the Central Intelligence Agency issued secret administrative subpoenas to the Society for Worldwide Interbank Financial Telecommunications (SWIFT) for details of inter-bank transactions. On an average day the Belgium-based SWIFT handles 10 million instructions on transfers worth US$6 trillion to and from almost every country in the world. After the programme was made public by the media in 2006 ('Bank Data is Sifted in Secret by US to Block Terror', *New York Times*, 22–23 June 2006), it was found to be illegal under Belgian and European Union law, as well as contravening privacy regulations in other third countries. As in the case of 'extraordinary renditions', however, it is unclear whether allied governments did not know or merely turned a blind eye to this use of SWIFT data.

If the example of Nauru shows how an international organisation benefited from the power of the US, there are also examples where the US has depended on the expertise of international organisations. The most important of these is in deciding which jurisdictions qualify as being 'of primary concern' in relation to money laundering and terrorist finance. In making this crucial judgement, the Patriot Act defers to the authority of 'credible international organizations or multilateral groups of experts'(section 5318A), in practice especially the FATF.

The US has so far been reluctant to use the full force of its new powers, instead preferring to rely on the potent threat these new legal prerogatives represent. Indeed, the mere possibility of ending up on the wrong side of the Patriot Act provisions has secured widespread cooperation from foreign jurisdictions. But the Council on Foreign Relations (2002, 2004) has been critical of the Bush administration for being too slow to use the punitive provisions, particularly against Saudi Arabia. These same critics seem oblivious to the very patchy record the US has itself on meeting international standards to counter money laundering and terrorist finance. It is now easier to establish anonymous corporate vehicles and associated bank accounts which obscure the true owner in certain US states than in almost any foreign tax haven (US Treasury 2005; Government Accounting Office 2006).

Anti-money laundering laws in the war on terror

The specific policy measures designed to counter the finance of terrorism are almost a direct copy of measures developed since the mid-1980s to counter money laundering. The relevant policy-making bodies at the national level, but even more so among international organisations active in the area, have explicitly acted on the assumption that money laundering and terrorist finance essentially share the same nature. Following from this logic, the dominant belief has been that the two problems demand essentially identical policy responses.

So closely have money laundering and terrorist finance been identified that they are generally known in combination by the unlovely acronym: AML/CFT (Anti-Money Laundering/Countering the Finance of Terrorism). Thus despite the way that terrorist financing burst onto the agenda as a policy problem in 2001, the regulatory regime drawn up as a result is remarkable for the degree of continuity exhibited with the global anti-money laundering regime that had evolved over the preceding two decades.

Money laundering occurs after a predicate offence has brought money into the hands of criminals. Predicate offences such as robbing a bank, selling heroin or people trafficking are motivated by criminals' desire for profits, but may leave the offenders with the problem of re-introducing large sums of money into the legitimate financial system without arousing the suspicions of law enforcement activities.

The first international institution founded specifically to counter money laundering, the FATF, once again grew out of a concern with the 'War on Drugs'. The organisation was founded after the 1989 G7 heads of government summit. An intensive process of meetings between government officials and regulators followed in late 1989 and early 1990. Aside from the G7 members, participation was soon extended to the other OECD member states, though the FATF has since been very reluctant to expand beyond a few more 'strategically important' developing countries.

Despite its tiny secretariat and its lack of formal legal standing, the FATF has had a far-reaching influence by way of its 40 Recommendations (Gilmore 1995; Sica 2000). Revised in 1996 and 2002, in combination the Recommendations place primary emphasis on requiring private financial intermediaries to collect information on their customers. Authorities must legislate in order that they can find, freeze and ultimately confiscate the illicit funds that are the proceeds of crime, as well as its working capital.

The most basic requirement of the Recommendations is that countries criminalise money laundering, following the lead of the US which was the first country to do so in 1986. Much of the burden of stripping away the veil of secrecy that aids criminal enterprises falls on private institutions which must adopt 'Know Your Customer' requirements. This refers to such practices as specifying that all new customers must provide photo identification before opening a bank account. Where more complex financial activity is involved, such as setting up a company or trust, financial intermediaries must search for information on their clients' backgrounds, and ensure they are not on any of the various national or international blacklists of terrorists. Intermediaries must establish the identity of the ultimate beneficial owners of all such corporate vehicles, possibly requiring a process of working back through a chain of corporations

Private firms must also report all instances of suspicious transactions to law enforcement authorities, or more usually a dedicated Financial Intelligence Unit linking the financial sector and law enforcement bodies. Suspicious transactions might include banking large amounts of cash, moving funds rapidly though a large number of accounts for no apparent purpose, or transacting with suspicious persons, firms or jurisdictions. At first limited to banks, the duty to report suspicious transactions has steadily been expanded to include accountants, stockbrokers, insurance providers, lawyers engaged in financial dealings and even casinos and jewellers. In each case these intermediaries face criminal prosecution if they either fail to report a suspicious transaction when they reasonably ought to have done so, or if they tip off their customer that they have submitted such a report.

In keeping with the borderless nature of the underlying problem, a key priority of the 40 Recommendations is to facilitate international cooperation in the pursuit of financial crime. Thus governments are enjoined to legislate to remove obstacles that may prevent the free flow of all this extra information from one country to another, usually via their Financial Intelligence Units. The key features that comprise the heart of AML measures ('Know Your Customer', suspicious transaction reporting obligations, freezing and confiscating funds, blacklists) now also define CFT standards in the same way.

Differences between money laundering and terrorist finance

Despite the tendency to adopt policies designed to counter money laundering almost unchanged in fighting the war against terrorist financing, there are important differences between the two activities. Recalling that AML policies themselves were created to stop drug trafficking, the logic was that money provides both the means (operational capital) and even more so the motive (profit) for crime. As such, it was calculated that efforts to disrupt criminal finance should be effective in reducing the incidence of crime over all. Yet both of these points are problematic when applied to terrorism. Although terrorists are sometimes sensitive to their pay and material rewards (Shapiro 2006), terrorism is clearly not a profit-driven activity in the way the illegal sale of drugs or arms is. Few terrorists live in luxury, if anything their illicit activity will make their lives much less, rather than more, comfortable.

Clearly there is a fundamental similarity between the two activities, in that both are premised on avoiding the gaze of law-enforcement and intelligence agencies. But it is not clear that this common imperative outweighs the other features that differentiate the role of money in terrorism from its role in drug trafficking and other criminal enterprises.

Terrorism is cheap. Even the September 11 attacks were funded on something like US$500,000, an essentially trivial sum of money. The coordinated bombings in Bali, Madrid and London cost only one-tenth of this amount. Suicide bombings like those in Israel and Iraq may cost as little as US$1000–3000. Terrorists only need very small sums of money to continue their activities, and thus they are generally insensitive to anything less than a near 100 per cent effective financial cut-off. Such a result is very unlikely to be achieved under current or any conceivable future AML/CFT laws.

The small sums of money also make detection particularly difficult, for the unsurprising reason that they have the same profile as most other kinds of financial transactions. Thus in the run-up to the September 11 attacks, the hijackers stayed in cheap motels, prepared their own food and washed their own clothes to save money (Naylor 2004). The major expenses were air travel and pilot training. Their funds came through the rather mundane channels of legal cheque and credit card accounts held with local US banks. Mohammed Atta did receive US$70,000 via wire-transfer from the United Arab Emirates (UAE), and a Suspicious Transaction Report was lodged but never read. Other funds from the UAE were sent via wire offices by al-Qaeda associates in Düsseldorf and Hamburg.

A further basic difference between money laundering and the financing of terrorism is that the former by definition involves the proceeds of a criminal offence, whereas the latter does not. Laundering money is hiding the criminal origins of that money. Although terrorist activities may also be funded by the proceeds of crime, much and perhaps most (there is a lack of evidence) of the money sustaining terrorist movements comes from legitimate sources. It is widely suspected that al-Qaeda and other Islamic terrorist groups are funded via donations to charities, though again conclusive evidence is lacking. The donors and charities may or may not be aware of the nature of the final recipients. Because the money is freely donated there is no predicate offence. Aside from donations by individuals and charitable foundations, Shapiro identities further legal sources of finance for terrorist groups in state sponsorship and profits from legitimate business activities (2006: 6).

Putting these differences between the two kinds of crime to one side, however, there are prominent concerns about the effectiveness of anti-money laundering techniques even on their own terms. A widely-cited UN report on the subject notes that money laundering is 'an area usually characterized by criminal successes and law enforcement failures' (Blum *et al.* 1998: 3). Judging by the small number of convictions, the meagre totals of assets confiscated, and the continuing problem of drug trafficking and other manifestations of organised crime, many other analysts have portrayed anti-money laundering policies as suffering from serious shortcomings at best, and at worst being entirely useless (Cuellar 2003; Naylor 2004; Pieth 2002; Rider 2004).

The results so far

In the second half of September 2001 some of the first responses from the US government to the attacks were financial, as assets belonging to or more usually associated with al-Qaeda and the Taliban were frozen. The UN's al-Qaeda and Taliban Sanctions Committee reported the freezing of $110 million worth of assets. However, the same committee also noted that as a response to this pressure al-Qaeda had largely moved out of the formal banking system and was instead relying on cash couriers and alternative remittance systems. Even though cash reporting requirements are an important component of the standard AML/CFT package of policies, in general these policies were drawn up with modern electronic banking systems in mind. Given that the OECD countries initially drew up these policies and standards, it is not surprising that they reflect the assumptions and features common to first world financial systems. But these same assumptions render AML/CFT regulations of dubious value when applied in the developing world, where credit cards and electronic transactions are rare, banks are distrusted, and transactions are generally conducted using cash or barter.

Aside from the inherently secretive nature of terrorists themselves, the selective nature of publicity concerning the campaign against the financing of terrorism is also an obstacle to assessing its effectiveness. There is a common tendency for more or less spectacular accusations to be made or reported, but the subsequent disconfirmations to be ignored. Arrests have often received widespread coverage, but when those taken into custody are prosecuted on lesser charges unrelated to terrorism (such as immigration violations), the media has moved on, and the authorities have little incentive to publicise their mistakes. Thus the median sentence of those convicted in 'international terrorism' cases in the United States since 2001 is only 20–28 days ('Study Finds Sharp Drop in Number of Terrorism Cases Prosecuted', *New York Times*, 4 September 2006). But because the initial sensational allegations have been cited back and forth so many times they are often then taken to be established facts.

Thus in the immediate aftermath of the September 11 attacks there was widespread speculation that al-Qaeda had profited from selling shares in airline and insurance companies only days before it struck, but these allegations turned out to be unfounded. Naylor details a long list of supposed al-Qaeda financing operations, said to involve diamonds, tanzanite, gold, cigarettes and other commodities, that generally turned out to be the product of unrelated crime, or were completely baseless (2004; compare with Ehrenfeld 2003: 33–70).

Further muddying the waters, governments all over the world have been keen to 'find' an al-Qaeda presence, financial or physical, to demonstrate their commitment to the cause and to smear domestic opponents. The ultimate example of such was the Macedonian government's admission in May 2004 that two years previously its police had kidnapped and executed seven refugees, framing the victims as al-Qaeda members in league with local ethnic Albanian separatists, in order to burnish the country's anti-terrorist credentials ('"Terrorists" Killed to Impress US', *Daily Telegraph*, 1 May 2004).

Meanwhile, in the West a massive private industry has grown up to assist firms in complying with the slew of new regulatory requirements in this area. Private firms have had to take on new staff to ensure compliance, as well as re-training existing staff. Firms must gather, store and exchange more information on their clients, as well as purchasing expensive new software. The author of a report on the impact of these new regulations for accounting firm KPMG holds that as a result: 'The cost to our global economy is so large, [terrorists have] already had the effect they wanted. The increasing costs of compliance and technology are a form of terrorism. We're damaging ourselves' ('Looking in the Wrong Places', *Economist*, 20 October 2005; see also KPMG 2004).

In this vein, there is a growing suspicion amongst both policy-makers and private banking and financial services firms that the regulations designed to make life harder for the financiers of terrorism are imposing disproportionate costs on the public purse, private firms and individual citizens. But the fear of being cast as 'soft on terrorism' has tended to stifle criticism that might otherwise have broken forth.

Small and developing states are increasingly adopting the same expensive CFT regulatory regime rushed through by OECD members from September 2001. These reforms entail hiring and training staff in central banks, Financial Intelligence Units, insurance supervisory offices, finance ministries, company registrars, and so on. Private sector firms also must acquire the necessary complement of Money Laundering Reporting Officers and data-monitoring processes. The combined public and private burden of this new apparatus imposes significant costs on countries whose resources are already stretched meeting other pressing challenges (Sharman and Mistry 2006).

One unequivocal result of the ratcheting up of requirements has been the greatly increased number of suspicious transactions reported. Yet this may create problems of information overload, as analysts seek to sift through the mountain of data to establish meaningful patterns. After all, it is worth remembering that the transactions to Mohammed Atta from the UAE in the lead up to the 2001 attacks were reported as suspicious, but such was the number of reports that this one was not processed until after the attacks.

Disappointing results in disrupting terrorist finance have conventionally been portrayed as necessitating a re-doubling of efforts. The basic model, however, has not been challenged in policy-making circles. Instead, the Financial Intelligence Units and other related bodies responsible for prosecuting this fight have received consistent and significant budget increases as well as expanded statutory powers. Financial counter-measures are still seen as being one of the few areas in which the West can take an offensive posture towards terrorists, rather than merely relying on passive counter-measures or responding to attacks.

All this is not to say that the effort expended by international organisations and state authorities has failed to yield any results. The extra information has proved very helpful in building up a picture of terrorist operations after attacks have occurred (Winer 2002: 276). Bank transfers and credit card receipts enable law enforcement bodies to discern the planning and preparation process in the lead-up to attacks. But this is still far from the goal of being able to prevent such attacks from being carried out in the first place. It is still the belief that the appropriate criterion for evaluating the success of CFT measures is in their pre-emptive effects, and only secondarily in aiding the apprehension and prosecution of terrorists after the fact. Yet it is probably unrealistic to hold CFT policies to such a demanding standard.

It is possible to venture some tentative predictions about the future shape of efforts to counter terrorism by starving terrorist groups of the funds they require to mount attacks against civilians and ensure organisational survival. Policy solutions designed in the West and imposed globally will continue to use the template of anti-money laundering to respond to the financing of terrorism, despite the important differences between the two activities described above. The key to fighting both sorts of crime is seen as being the collection of ever-greater quantities of information, though a more risk-based approach may lead to some kinds of data, involving certain countries, particular patterns of transactions, and specific individuals, receiving much higher priority than others. Increased financial transparency will continue to be the overarching aim. Despite only modest tactical and even less strategic success, anti-terrorist efforts in this areas will become increasingly costly, with most of the burden borne by the private sector and citizens rather than the state. Despite regulatory and technological advances in the US and across the globe, the modest financial flows that may constitute the lifeblood of terrorism are likely to continue to circulate for many years to come.

Conclusion

Sara E. Davies and Richard Devetak

This conclusion seeks to develop the various ideas about terrorism and the war on terror set out in the previous chapter by analysing how the security context that emerged in the 1990s has been altered again by the terrorist attacks of September 11, 2001. It will suggest that realist approaches at the end of the Cold War proved limited in their capacity to address the full range of security issues that arose at that time. This led to a greater appreciation of critical approaches that questioned why insecurity existed, who was most insecure, how those insecurities might be ameliorated and how best to understand and explain security and insecurity. We look at this period to demonstrate that, since 9/11, there has been a marked tendency to fall back on the assumptions that were made during the Cold War: that there is an 'us' fighting against a 'them', that what threatens us must threaten everyone else, and that the application of military force is the primary tool for mitigating the threat. As this book has demonstrated, the flaw with current conceptions of security in the 'war on terror' is that it is not clear what victory would look like. How would we achieve victory over this elusive 'enemy'? How do we know when victory is achieved? And, are the policies we produce improving or threatening our own security?

Classical realism, like liberalism, constructivism and critical security theory, provides a setting for powerful critical insights based on practical wisdom for understanding the relationships within international society. However, as the contributors to this volume have demonstrated only too well, the foreign and security policies of the US, UK and Australia post-9/11 has reflected more a pursuit of realist 'reactionism' rather than a critical reflection. September 11 and the tragedies since then have manifested a number of different social, political, legal and violent responses. Whether these responses were proportionate and whether we are safer today because of them was a core question that this book sought to explore. In profiling the responses and their consequences, we have sought to create a new impetus for those facing policy choices regarding terrorism and those in the academy seeking to explain and understand our current predicament.

This conclusion presents three positions based on observations drawn from this volume. First, the war on terror, as it is currently conceptualised, is flawed because of its inappropriate use of realist underpinnings and as a result will have further destabilising effects on global security. Second, the democratic 'fight for ideals' is emerging more as an 'ideological conquest' which could be taking the West into battles that it cannot win through the application of power. Finally, for every action there is a reaction. Foreign policy by powerful states influences the world at large and as a result there is a greater need for responsibility, leadership and prudence amongst those states. We conclude with Morgenthau's warning that powerful states cannot escape from the power that they wield or from the consequences that arise when it is not wielded wisely.

The changing security context: from the Cold War to September 11

The end of the Cold War and the rise of globalisation seemed to many, including US President George H. Bush, to herald a 'new world order', one that promised both peace and prosperity for more and more people around the globe. Prospects for international peace and security seemed bright as ideological enmity dissipated, leaving states to focus on wealth and welfare. The implosion of the Soviet Union left the US as the sole superpower, or, as coined by the then-French foreign minister Hubert Védrine, a 'hyperpower'. US power across the spectrum – from military and economic to political and cultural power – was unmatched. In the absence of the Soviet Union no other state could challenge the US, not even a rising China.

This new geopolitical context seemed to afford the US and its allies enhanced security. Having emerged triumphant from the Cold War, the West's territorial integrity and political institutions were now safer from serious threat than they had been for nearly a century. This at least was the more optimistic view propounded by liberals in the early 1990s (e.g. Fukuyama 1992). Realists of the time were still sceptical that the Cold War's end would enhance international security. Bipolarity, to their way of thinking, was one of the keys to stabilising the international system and containing security threats (e.g. Mearsheimer 1990). Unipolarity or multipolarity, depending on how you viewed the post-Cold War order, promised greater instability as rising and revisionist powers would, in seeking to improve their position in the international system, pose threats to neighbouring states and regions. Ultimately, the UN notwithstanding, responsibility for ensuring international peace and security would lie with the US and its willingness to lead. Realists have long held to the belief that hegemonic powers stabilised the international system through effective leadership, which would necessarily include coercive diplomacy and war as vital instruments. The fact that the Cold War ended without an actual engagement of military conflict between the two key enemies – US and USSR – did not deter realists from holding to their beliefs in the nature of war and states.

Though the 1990s bore witness to many bloody conflicts, Rwanda and Bosnia being only two of the most prominent, neither liberal nor realist perspectives seemed inclined to rethink their basic assumptions about security, particularly state-centrism and reliance on military force. Many of the conflicts, dubbed by Mary Kaldor as 'new wars', arose far away from Washington, London and Paris.

The dissolution of Yugoslavia and the protracted war in Bosnia posed a slightly different problem for the West, as they erupted on the fringes of Western Europe. Europe felt susceptible to the side-effects of these nearby conflicts – refugee flows, illicit arms trading, transnational criminal networks and so on. The imperative to intervene there was therefore more directly related to traditional security concerns but necessitated by 'non-traditional' security threats, and as a result the civil wars and genocides taking place further afield did not create an impetus to address the insecurity of those in Africa.

Two developments in security studies have taken place in response to this changing context. First, the security agenda was broadened to accommodate new or non-traditional threats. Second, 'critical security studies' emerged to reassess assumptions that underpinned 'traditional' security discourse.

The collapse of the bipolar system together with the rise of globalisation seemed to transform the international security agenda. A 'new security dilemma' was purported to exist, one where subnational and transnational flows of violence rendered interstate balances of power less effective mechanisms in regulating international relations (Cerny 1998). New threats arose that neither originated in states nor put the state's survival at risk. These included environmental degradation, economic instability and societal insecurity in the face of growing levels of transnational people movement. Critics questioned the appropriateness of forcing these concerns into the framework of security. Doing so restricted the terms of debate and led discussion away from the specifics of the issue and more generally away from normative issues. The problem, in short, was that turning all these issues into security problems tended towards 'depoliticisation' by searching for instrumental solutions where they were not always appropriate and emptying them of normative content.

The 9/11 terrorist attacks also forced a broadening of the security *agenda*, but it did not force a broadening of the White House *response* to this new form of insecurity. Though terrorism was by no means new, the scale and spectacular nature of al-Qaeda's devastating attacks on Washington and New York immediately led to its domination of Washington's security agenda. Research into the global networked, non-hierarchical character of the so-called 'new' terrorism was suddenly considered crucial to our very existence (Benjamin and Simon 2005); as has been research into the links between Islamism and terrorism (Sageman 2004; Holmes 2005; Barkawi and Laffey 2006).

Such is the level of anxiety amongst new terrorism experts and some western governments, 9/11 enshrined the moment where a new 'enemy' was defined that we all had to secure ourselves against – security became redefined as meaning 'safe from terrorism' rather than simply 'safe from threats'. In other words, the realist understanding of security – 'us' against 'them' – returned to the fore. In the immediate aftermath of the attacks it appeared to many, including President George W. Bush, that the world had changed. The 'age of terror' was said to be upon us, but we were to face it by mobilising the techniques and attitudes of Cold War. Most scholars and practitioners tended to be sceptical of such hyperbole, but agree that even if the world did not change, for the USA and its remaining allies the world *has* changed. As soon as September 12, 2001, the use of force was justified against anyone who was not 'with us' (Bush 2001). Dangers were to be squashed before they became real. 'Rogue states' would be transformed to make way for freedom, democracy and the rule of law so that regional and international security could be enhanced. All these ideas were enunciated before it was clear whether any state had actually directly assisted in the 9/11 attacks. Unilateralism, pre-emption and 'regime change' became the principal tenets of the highly controversial Bush Doctrine in the US-led 'war on terror'. They marked a deliberate departure from the traditional realist logic of containment which was alleged to be irrelevant to the new 'age of terror', but retained a realist understanding of threat and the belief that the source of threat could be traced to states seeking power, rather than a normative endeavour by radical fundamentalists that do not align themselves with or build their power through state-centred structures.

There can be no doubt that terrorism is a real and present danger, but there is a need to be much more specific about the scale and character of the threat if effective responses are to be devised. Greater clarification is therefore needed not just of terrorism's sources, but of the way that terrorism alters, or should alter, the way we think about security. This is not simply a matter of adding terrorism to a growing list of threats that states must deal with; and it is certainly not a matter of simplistically equating terrorism either with poverty or with Islam. In any case, the study of global terrorism requires examination of conventional security assumptions and with this entails inquiry into possible alternative approaches to seeking security.

The debates over the usefulness of subsuming various issue areas under the heading of security partly led to the rise of critical security studies (CSS). But a deeper spur was the tendency to leave certain fundamental assumptions unquestioned in security analysis. Krause and Williams (1996: 242) explain that critical approaches to security question the notions that security is an objective condition, that threats are simply material forces correctly perceived as dangerous, or that the referent (that is, the thing to be made secure) is historically fixed. Instead, CSS poses 'questions about *how* the object to be secured (nation, state, or other group) is constituted, and how particular issues (economic well-being, the risk of violence, environmental degradation) are placed under the "sign of security"' (Krause and Williams 1996: 242–3). That terrorism should be placed under the 'sign of security' is hardly controversial. But answers about how best to balance prevention with pre-emption, crime-fighting with war-fighting and intelligence-gathering powers with due process are far from self-evident.

Fighting the war on terror

The 'war on terror' has come to dominate security studies after 9/11. But from the outset it caused difficulties because it was a deterritorialised non-state actor unleashing the violence against states. Traditional security analysis, especially during the Cold War, assumed states as the primary protagonists. The problem, as revealed in the US's response to 9/11, was that America and its allies were ill-prepared to defend themselves against non-state threats. The only way that the US could conceptualise an 'enemy' that it could fight against was to very quickly shift its focus back to states. As Dick Cheney is reported to have said in National Security Council (NSC) meetings, it is much easier to target states than terrorists, which is why the President enlarged his target to include so-called 'rogue states' that harbour terrorists. That the White House and its closest allies saw the fight against terrorism in primarily military terms is clear in the very name '*war* on terror'.

Daniel Benjamin and Steven Simon (2005: 139–40) argue that the White House's perception of the terrorist threat through state-centric and militarist lenses represents a mistaken security policy, '[T]he Bush team's commitment to a worldview focused on states … and its determination to rely on military force in the fight against terror, have wrought lasting damage to America's strategic position'. Casting terrorism as a derivative problem of 'rogue states', they say, was a serious error, since state sponsorship of terrorism had declined markedly over the past several years (Benjamin and Simon 2005: 151). Nevertheless, the US focused its post-September 11 security strategy on states, rogue or failed (Bush 2002c). Failed and rogue states were placed at the centre of the US 'war on terror', but it was to be the 'rogue state' of Iraq that became the centrepiece of US strategy, and possibly its nadir.

Selling war: from Afghanistan to Iraq

The war against Afghanistan (which commenced in November 2001) became the first major episode of the open-ended 'war on terror'. The US military was able to topple the Taliban regime without much trouble, but they had greater difficulty trying to 'smoke out' and eliminate al-Qaeda. Nevertheless, the US was able to build on enormous and widespread international goodwill in the immediate aftermath of 9/11 to launch this war.

No such good will was to be extended to the US when it decided to invade Iraq – the second major episode in the 'war on terror'. After protracted and ill-tempered discussions amongst members of the UN Security Council (UNSC), it failed to deliver the resolution Bush and Blair were hoping for, but Iraq was invaded nonetheless. The war could not be 'sold' to France, Russia, China, nor several other UNSC members despite attempts by the US and the UK. First and foremost, the US and UK failed to persuade others that war against Iraq was justified. The US also oscillated between different justifications for war, including accusations of links between Iraq and al-Qaeda, and allegations that Iraq was continuing to develop weapons of mass destruction in defiance of various UNSC resolutions. In both cases, evidence was shaky to say the least. Moreover, the inspections, which were intended to provide certainty, were incomplete and inconclusive. By refusing to allow the inspections process to run its course the US appeared overzealous in its resort to war (Freedman 2004b).

Making a case for war on the basis of so much tendentious speculation is hardly conducive to accurate threat assessment which is central to good security strategy. But that was, in many respects, beside the point. The war's proponents were simply engaging in 'a classic case of *suppressio veri* and *suggestio falsi*' (Danchev 2004: 443) – withholding the truth and positing in its place something less than the full story – in order to strengthen the case for what they believed was necessary action, despite the lack of a compelling justification. Classic *raison d'état*, we might say. This same pattern of tendentious interpretation of intelligence to support a pre-determined policy was in evidence in the UK too. Alex Danchev (2004) notes the way Downing Street redrafted a memo from the Joint Intelligence Committee, deleting the word 'may' so as to heighten the sense of urgency. The final version read: 'The Iraqi military *is able to* deploy these [chemical and biological] weapons within 45 minutes of a decision to do so' (cited in Danchev 2004: 446, emphasis added).

The decision to invade Iraq and unseat Saddam Hussein must be seen in the context of 9/11. Even if it is true that neo-conservatives in Washington viewed deposing the Iraqi dictator as 'unfinished business' after the first Gulf War, it was the sense of post-9/11 fear that spurred the White House into action and imparted to it a veneer of legitimacy. After the terrorist attacks, neo-conservatives knew a more amenable domestic environment had been created to drum up support for war against Iraq. If Halper and Clark (2004: 230) are correct, it was a kind of post-9/11 'neurosis', which shaped the context in which these 'disparate and uncorroborated fragments of information about Iraq [were] formed into a mosaic of specific threats and dangers'. Here we see the reaction to 9/11 being mired in the need for a collective enemy to locate and defeat. The consequence has been that the identification of home-grown terrorists, such as we saw in the July 2005 London bombings, do not fit within this 'enemy' profile. In addition, as we have seen with the regrouping of Al-Qaeda on the Pakistan-Afghanistan borders, the chance to defeat an insidious organisation was lost when precious troops from the US and UK were deployed to Iraq rather than remaining in Afghanistan (ABC 2002).

Winning the war on terror?

In this section we review the state of play in the 'war on terror'. We argue that the 'war on terror' as presently understood in Washington, London and Canberra misconstrues the problem and consequently adopts a flawed strategy in dealing with global terrorism. Most prominently, it has led the 'coalition of the willing' into a complex war from which it will be difficult to extricate itself, and which has unwittingly exacerbated the problem of terrorism, both within Iraq and possibly beyond.

Forty-two days after the war against Iraq commenced, on 1 May 2003, President Bush stood aboard USS *Abraham Lincoln* in front of a massive banner declaring 'Mission accomplished'. 'The tyrant has fallen, and Iraq is free', he proudly announced. There can be no doubt that the removal of a brutal dictator like Saddam Hussein is a great political good, but this does not extinguish the normative and prudential doubts expressed over the war and future efforts to intervene to prevent human rights atrocities in other states.

Four years after Bush's confident pronouncement that 'Major combat operations in Iraq have ended', we may now be in a better position to judge the extent to which the Iraq war has assisted the 'war on terror'. Military operations to topple Saddam Hussein were indeed effective and swift. But the battle to establish the peace continues to be much more protracted and difficult. Iraq is now in chaos; violence is a daily reality. Over 3,000 US troops and tens of thousands of Iraqis have been killed.[1] The insurgency has progressively grown in regularity and deadliness.

Many also believe the Iraq war is fuelling global terrorism. Daniel Benjamin and Steven Simon (2005: 42) write that,

> Iraq has given violent Islamists more than an arena in which to dramatize their cause and bravery: It has provided them with a country-sized training ground and a laboratory for innovating the tactics and operations of the future. The loss of Afghanistan and its camps hurt the jihadists badly, but the on-the-job training they have received in Iraq has more than made up for that setback.

Declassified assessments from the National Intelligence Estimates reveal that America's intelligence agencies have arrived at the same conclusion. Their view is that 'the Iraq jihad is shaping a new generation of terrorist leaders and operatives', and that Iraq had 'become the "cause celebre" for jihadists, breeding a deep resentment of US involvement in the Muslim world and cultivating supporters for that global jihadist movement' (cited in Danner 2004: 84–5).

Conclusion

The academic mood since 9/11 has been as divided as the policy experts at the Pentagon, the State Department and the White House have been (Boyle 2007). To condemn the 'coalition of the willing' for their invasion into Iraq, their attempts at post-conflict reconstruction and call for troop withdrawal is, some allege, dangerous speculation that only fuels and justifies further terrorism (Howard 2007). Nevertheless, the political climate that international society finds itself in nearly six years since that tragic event on 9/11 deserves review. This book has unapologetically analysed the effects of a 'war on terror' being waged on a number of actors to assess whether security has been enhanced. Rather than demonstrating 'Western self-loathing', our analysis was born out of a desire to understand contemporary world politics and develop better ways of protecting Westerners and non-Westerners from further terror, mass violence and tragedy.

Hans Morgenthau (1962) remarked that the attempt to 'escape from power' can manifest in four different types of 'escape': scientism, dual moral standards, perfectionism and totalitarianism. The first, scientism, is born of a faith that the social world is susceptible to the same kind of analysis and control as the natural world. The second, dual moral standards, supposes that different moral standards apply to the private and public spheres. The last two, we conclude, are particularly relevant to today. Perfectionism and totalitarianism present two different ways of dealing with the gap between political ideals and political realities. Perfectionism acknowledges political realities as they exist, but holds the conviction that transformation is possible by determined acts of will. 'Once democracy, brought to all countries of the earth either by force of arms or preferably by education and exhortation, has been universally accepted, the evils of politics will have been made an end to, and reason will rule over domestic and international society' (Morgenthau 1962: 315). Perfectionism thus tries to close the gap between ideal and reality by bending reality to the ideal.

Totalitarianism moves in the opposite direction, 'tearing the ideal down to the level of the brutal facts of political life' (Morgenthau 1962: 317). As used by Morgenthau, totalitarianism refers to 'a state of mind', rather than the historical phenomenon (Morgenthau 1962: 316). 'What is, is good because it is, and power is to the totalitarian not only a fact of social life with which one must come to terms but also the ultimate standard for judging human affairs and the ideal source of all human values' (Morgenthau 1962: 316). Morgenthau (1962: 17) concludes that the totalitarian state of mind is the most dangerous mode of escapism,

> for, while here the political facts as facts are recognized, their moral significance is obscured. Power is glorified as the source of all material and moral good, and those transcendent concepts by which power must be tamed, restrained, and transformed are denied an independent existence.

It remains unclear whether the Bush Doctrine (as manifested in its 'war on terror') commits perfectionism or totalitarianism. Arguably, it is perfectionist in its attempt to lift political realities to the level of ideals in pursuing democratic transformation. Perfectionism would be applaudable if accomplished through means of distributive justice, rights-based approaches and cooperative enticements. But the laudable aspiration to spread democracy and the rule of law has been contradicted by means fundamentally at odds with democracy and the rule of law. The use of torture, extraordinary rendition and the denial of due process and other non-derogatory rights, together with dubious justifications for war in states unconnected to the event that triggered this 'escape' in the first place, may end up delivering more collective insecurity.

It is no doubt an uncomfortable thought to consider the Bush presidency's 'state of mind' as totalitarian, but on Morgenthau's definition, a strong case can be made for reaching just such a conclusion. The Bush Doctrine tends to equate US military might with moral superiority; and – as Sara E. Davies pointed out in relation to Guantanamo Bay – it has also worked hard to ensure that its war on terror is not judged against normal moral and legal standards. Indeed, the defence of moral and political ideals is often dismissed by Washington and its supporters in the press and the academy, as delusional. When fighting against an enemy who has dispensed with the rules, the only option is to be prepared to do the same when necessary, so it is argued.

What made 9/11 so truly terrifying, so devastating was that, as was noted in the Introduction, it shattered the security of citizens within Western states. Seeing death on a large scale in Africa, even Asia, is not beyond collective comprehension. These individuals live daily with the threat of death hanging over them due to disease, famine, disaster or war. In the West, there has been a feeling of security, of safety within its borders. September 11 removed that, and it changed how individuals understand and pursue security within a liberal democratic state. Ultimately this book sought to assess whether the United States and its allies have responded to the challenge of 9/11 in ways that have restored faith in the ability of states to secure the physical survival and deeply-held values of their citizens or further contributed – whether consciously or not – to many more experiencing greater levels of insecurity. Answers to these questions raised a number of troubling conclusions that point to the need for academics and policy makers to do better to respond to the challenge of 9/11.

Note

1   Iraq Body Count (IBC) estimates that somewhere between 55,794 and 61,507 Iraqis have been killed as of 9 February 2007. See www.iraqbodycount.net. As of the same date, the US Department of Defense has confirmed 3,102 US troop casualties. 54,910 'non-mortal casualties' are also reported. See www.icasualties.org/oif/.

References

Rasul v. Bush, 2004, Supreme Court of the United States.

Hamdan v. Rumsfeld, 2006, Supreme Court of the United States.

9/11 Commission (2004) *Final report of the National Commission on Terrorist Attacks upon the United States*, New York: Norton.

ABC 2002, *Al Qaeda regrouping in Afghanistan: UN*, The World Today, 19 December, viewed 26 March 2007 <http://www.abc.net.au/worldtoday/stories/s750864.htm>.

—— 2006, *Hicks' return not so simple, says Ruddock*, viewed 9 December 2006 <http://www.abc.net.au/cgi-bin/common/printfriendly.pl?http://www.abc.net.au/news/new>.

Abdela, L. 2005, *Iraq's war on women*, Open Democracy, 18 July, viewed 26 April 2007 <http://www.opendemocracy.net/conflict-iraqconflict/women_2681.jsp>.

Agamben, G. 1998, *Homo sacer: sovereign power and bare life*, Stanford University Press, Stanford, CA.

—— 2005, *State of exception*, University of Chicago Press, Chicago, IL.

Ahmed, S. 2004, *The cultural politics of emotion*, Edinburgh University Press, Edinburgh.

Alexandrov, S.A. 1996, *Self-defense against the use of force in international law*, Kluwer Law International, The Hague.

Alibek, K. 1999, *Biohazard*, Arrow, London.

—— and Bailey, C. 2004, 'Letter to the Editor: BioShield or BioGap', *Biosecurity and Bioterrorism*, vol. 2, no. 2, pp. 132–3.

Amnesty International 2005, *Iraq: decades of suffering, now women deserve better*, February, viewed 26 April 2007 <http://web.amnesty.org/library/Index/ENGMDE140012005>.

Amnesty International Australia 2006, *Hundreds of 'war on terror' detainees in US custody*, viewed 1 December 2006 <http://www.amnesty.org.au/Act_now/action_centre/featuredaction/guantanamo_bay_ac>.

Andres, R.B., Wills, C. and Griffith, T.E., Jr 2005, 'Winning with Allies: The Strategic Value of the Afghan Model', *International Security*, vol. 30, no. 3, pp. 124–60.

Anonymous 1998, *Military critical technologies List (MCTL), part 2: weapons of mass destruction technologies*, Office of the Under Secretary of Defense for Acquistion and Technology, Washington, DC.

—— 2002, 'The Scowcroft Memorandum', *CBW Convention Bulletin*, vol. 57, no. 2.

—— 2005, *Adherence to and compliance with arms control, nonproliferation and disarmament agreements and commitments*, US Department of State Online, viewed 22 December 2005 <http://www.state.gov/t/vci/rls/rpt/51977.htm>.

Anscombe, E. 1961, 'War and Murder', in W Stein (ed.), *Nuclear weapons and Christian conscience*, Merlin Press, New York.

Aquinas, T. (ed. Dyson, R.W.) 2002, *Aquinas: political writings*, Cambridge University Press, Cambridge.

Arendt, H. 1958, *The human condition*, University of Chicago Press, Chicago, IL.

Armon-Jones, C. 1991, *Varieties of affect*, Harvester Wheatsheaf, New York.

Aron, R. 1986, *Clausewitz: philosopher of war*, Simon and Schuster, New York.

Augustine, Bishop of Hippo 1998, *The city of God against the pagans*, Cambridge Texts in the History of Political Thought, Cambridge University Press, Cambridge.

—— 2001, 'Letter to Count Boniface', in E.M. Atkins and R.J .Dodaro (eds), *Augustine: –.political writings*, Cambridge University Press, Cambridge.

—— (ed. Dyson, R.W.) 2001, *Augustine: political writings*, Cambridge University Press, Cambridge.

Australian Government Law Reform Commission 2006, *Media release: are sedition laws necessary and affective*, viewed 20 March 2006 <www.alrc.gov.au>.

Ayres, T.E. 2005, '"Six Floors" of Detainee Operations in the Post-9/11 World', *Parameters*, vol. 35, no. 3, pp. 33–53.

Bailes, A.J.K. 2006, 'Introduction: The World of Security and Peace Research in 40-Year Perspective', in Stockholm International Peace Research Institute (SIPRI) (ed.), *SIPRI Yearbook 2006*, Oxford University Press, Oxford.

Barbalet, J.M. 2001, *Emotion, social theory and social structure: a macrosociological approach*, Cambridge University Press, Cambridge.

Barkawi, T. 2004, 'On the Pedagogy of "Small Wars"', *International Affairs*, vol. 80, no. 1, pp. 19–37.

Barkawi, T. 2006, *Globalization and war*, Rowman and Littlefield, Lanham, MD.

Barkawi, T. and Laffey, M. 2006, 'The Postcolonial Moment in Security Studies', *Review of International Studies*, vol. 32, no. 4, pp. 329–52.

BBC (2001) 'Cherie Blair Attacks Taleban "Cruelty"', 19 November, viewed 6 April 2007 <http://news.bbc.co.uk/1/hi/uk_politics/1663300.stm>.

BBC News Online 2004, *Bin Laden video threatens America*, viewed 6 March 2007 <http://news.bbc.co.uk/2/hi/middle_east/3966741.stm>.

—— 2004, *UK 'Spied on UN's Kofi Annan'*, viewed 15 March 2007 <http://news.bbc.co.uk/2/hi/uk_news/politics/3488548.stm>.

—— 2006, *Al Qaeda to avenge Israel deeds*, viewed 6 March 2007 <http://news.bbc.co.uk/2/hi/middle_east/5220162.stm>.

—— 2006, *Blair's concerns over face veils*, BBC News, 17 October, viewed 26 April 2007 <http://news.bbc.co.uk/1/hi/uk_politics/6058672.stm>.

BCDRC 2005, *Annual report*, Biological and Chemical Defence Review Committee Online, viewed 25 October 2006 <http://www.vcds.forces.gc.ca/bcdrc/annual_e.html>.

Beaumont, P. 2006, 'Hidden victims of a brutal conflict: Iraq's women', *The Observer*, 8 October, viewed 26 April 2007 <http://observer.guardian.co.uk/world/story/0,,1890260,00.html>.

Bellamy, A.J. 2002, 'The Great Beyond: Rethinking Military Responses to New Wars and Complex Emergencies', *Defence Studies*, vol. 2, no. 1, p. 25.50.

—— 2006, *Just wars: from Cicero to Iraq*, Polity, Cambridge, UK; Malden, MA.

Bendelow, G. and Williams, S.J. 1998, *Emotions in social life: critical themes and contemporary issues*, Routledge, London.

Benjamin, D. and Simon, S. 2005, *The next attack: the failure of the war on terror and a strategy for getting it right*, Hodder and Stoughton, London.

Bennett, B. 2006, *Stolen away*, Time, 23 April, viewed 26 April 2007 <http://www.time.com/time/magazine/printout/0,8816,1186558,00.html>.

Berdal, M. 2003, 'How "New" Are "New Wars"?' Global Economic Change and the Study of Civil War', *Global Governance*, vol. 9, no. 4, pp. 477–502.

Berezin, M. 2001, 'Emotions and Political Identity: Mobilizing Affection for the Polity', in J. Goodwin, J.M. Jasper and F. Polletta (eds), *Passionate politics: emotions and social movements*, University of Chicago Press, Chicago, IL, pp. 83–98.

—— 2002, 'Secure States: Towards a Political Sociology of Emotion', in J.M. Barbalet (ed.), *Emotions and sociology*, Blackwell Publishing/The Socological Review, Oxford; Malden, MA, pp. 33–52.

Bergen, P.L. 2006, *The Osama bin Laden I know: an oral history of al-Qaeda's leader*, Free Press, New York.

Berlant, L. 2000, 'The Subject of True Feeling: Pain, Privacy, Politics', in J Dean (ed.), *Cultural studies and political theory*, Cornell University Press, Ithaca, NY, pp. 42–312.

Best, G. 1994, *War and law since 1945*, Clarendon Press, Oxford.

Betts, R.K. 2002, 'The Soft Underbelly of American Primacy: Tactical Advantages of Terror', *Political Science Quarterly*, vol. 117, no. 1, pp. 19–36.

Biddle, S.D. 2005, 'Allies, Airpower, and Modern Warfare: The Afghan Model in Afghanistan and Iraq', *International Security*, vol. 30, no. 3, pp. 161–76.

Blair, T. 1993, 'Foreword', in C. Bryant (ed.), *Reclaiming the ground: Christianity and socialism*, Spire and the Christian Socialist Movement, London.

—— 2001, *Statement in response to terrorist attacks, 11 September 2001*, viewed 27 November 2006 <http://www.number-10.gov.uk/output/Page1596.asp>.

—— 2005, *Our Third term will be our best yet*, viewed 27 November 2006 <http://www. labour.org.uk/index.php?id=news2005&ux_news%5Bid%5D=tbnpf05&cHash=64dcd 1591a>.

Bleiker, R. 2000, 'We Don't Need Another Hero', *International Femininst Journal of Politics*, vol. 2, no. 1, pp. 30–57.

—— 2003, 'A Rogue Is a Rogue Is a Rogue: US Foreign Policy and the Korean Nuclear Crisis', *International Affairs*, vol. 79, no. 4, pp. 719–37.

Blum, Jack A., Levi, M., Naylor, R.T. and Williams, P. (1998) *Financial havens, banking secrecy and money laundering*. Prepared for the United Nations Office for Drug Control and Crime Prevention.

Blum, Y.Z. 1976, 'State Response to Acts of Terrorism', *German Yearbook of International Law*, vol. 19, pp. 223–33.

BMA 2004, *Biotechnology, weapons and humanity*, British Medical Association, London.

Booth, K., forthcoming, *Theory of world security*, Cambridge University Press, Cambridge.

Booth, K. and Dunne, T. (eds) 2002, *Worlds in collision: terror and the future of global order*, Palgrave, Basingstoke.

Bourke, J. 2005, *Fear: a cultural history*, Virago, London.

Bowden, M. 2003, 'The Dark Art of Interrogation', *Atlantic Monthly*, vol. 292, no. 3, pp. 51–76.

Bowker, D.W. 2006, 'Unwise Counsel: the War on Terrorism and the Criminal Mistreatment of Detainees in U.S. Custody', in K.J. Greenberg (ed.), *The torture debate in America*, Cambridge University Press, Cambridge; New York.

Bowett, D.W. 1958, *Self-defence in international law*, Manchester University Press, Manchester.

Boyle, M.J. 2007, 'America in Denial', *International Affairs*, vol. 83, no. 1, pp. 147–59.

Broad, W. 1998, 'Book says pre-Gulf War discovery raised germ warfare fears', *New York Times*, 7 June, p. A6.

Brown, S. 2003, *The illusion of control: force and foreign policy in the twenty-first century*, Brookings Institution Press, Washington, DC.

Brown, W. 1995, *States of injury: power and freedom in late modernity*, Princeton University Press, Princeton, NJ.

Brownlie, I. 1963, *International law and the use of force by states*, Oxford University Press, Oxford.

Buchanan, A. and Keohane, R.O. 2004, 'The Preventive Use of Force: A Cosmopolitan Institutional Proposal', *Ethics and International Affairs*, vol. 18, no. 1, pp. 1–22.

Bull, H. 1977, *The anarchical society: a study of order in world politics*, Columbia University Press, New York.

Burke, A. 2004, 'Just War or Ethical Peace? Moral Discourses of Strategic Violence after 9/11', *International Affairs*, vol. 80, no. 2, pp. 329–53.

—— 2005a, 'Against the New Internationalism', *Ethics and International Affairs*, vol. 9, no. 2, pp. 73–89.

—— 2005b, 'Iraq: Strategy's Burnt Offering', *Global Change, Peace and Security*, vol. 17, no. 2, pp. 191–213.

—— 2006, 'Critical Approaches to Security and Strategy', in D. Ball and R. Ayson (eds), *Strategy and security in the Asia Pacific*, Allen and Unwin, Sydney.

—— 2007, *Beyond security, ethics and violence: war against the other*, Routledge, London; New York.

Burkitt, I. 1991, *Social selves: theories of the social formation of personality*, Sage Publications, London.

Bush, G.W. 2000, *The first Gore–Bush presidential debate*, viewed 6 March 2007 <www.debates.org/pages/trans2000a.html>.

—— 2001, *Address to a joint session of Congress and the American people, 20 September*, viewed 27 November 2006 <www.whitehouse.gov/news/releases/2001/09/print/20010920-8.html>.

—— 2002a, *Speech at Cincinnati, 7 October*, viewed 2 February 2005 <www.whitehouse.gov/news/releases/2002/10/20021007-8.html>.

—— 2002b, *Speech at the West Point graduation ceremony, 1 June*, viewed 5 February 2005 <www.whitehouse.gov/news/releases/2002/06/print/20020601-8html>.

—— 2002c, *State of the union*, Office of the Press Secretary, 29 January, viewed 26 March 2007 <http://www.whitehouse.gov/news/releases/2002/01/20020129-11.html>.

—— 2003a, *President Bush announces major combat operations in Iraq Have Ended, 1 May*, viewed 27 November 2006 <http://www.whitehouse.gov/news/releases/2003/05/20030501-15.html>.

—— 2003b, *President delivers 'State of the union', 28 January*, viewed 27 November 2006 <www.whitehouse.gov/news/releases/2003/01/print/20030128-19.html>.

—— 2004, *Interview with President George W. Bush on NBC's 'Meet the press'*, viewed 20 February 2007 <http://msnbc.msn.com/id/4179618.>.

—— 2005, *President discusses Iraqi Constitution with press pool*, 23 August, viewed 26 April 2007 <http://www.whitehouse.gov/news/releases/2005/08/20050823.html>.

Bush, L. 2001, *Radio address by Laura Bush to the nation*, 17 November, viewed 26 April 2007 <http://www.whitehouse.gov/news/releases/2001/11/20011117.html>.

Butler, J. 2004, *Precarious life: the powers of mourning and violence*, Verso, London; New York.

Buzan, B. 1991, *People, states, and fear: an agenda for international security in the post-Cold War era*, 2nd edn, Lynne Rienner, Boulder, CO.

—— 2006, 'Will the "global war on terrorism" be the new Cold War?', *International Affairs*, vol. 82, no. 6, pp. 1101–18.

BWC 1991, *Annex to final declaration on confidence building measures*, Third Review Conference of the States Parties to the Convention on the Prohibition of the Development, Production and Stockpiling of Bacteriological (Biological) and Toxin Weapons and on Their Destruction, Geneva.

Byers, M. 2002, 'Terrorism, the Use of Force and International Law after 11 September', *International and Comparative Law Quarterly*, vol. 51, no. 2, pp. 401–14.

—— 2003a, 'Preemptive Self-Defense: Hegemony, Equality and Strategies of Legal Change', *The Journal of Political Philosophy*, vol. 11, no. 2, pp. 171–90.

—— 2003b, 'Letting the Exception Prove the Rule', *Ethics and International Affairs*, vol. 17, no. 1, pp. 9–16.

—— 2004, 'Policing the High Seas: The Proliferation Security Initiative', *American Journal of International Law*, vol. 98, no. 3.

—— 2005, *War law: international law and armed conflict*, Atlantic Books, London.

Calhoun, C.J. 2001, 'Putting Emotions in Their Place', in J. Goodwin, J.M. Jasper and F. Polletta (eds), *Passionate politics: emotions and social movements*, University of Chicago Press, Chicago, IL, pp. 45–58.

Campbell, D. 1994, 'The Deterritorialization of Responsibility: Levinas, Derrida, and Ethics after the End of Philosophy', *Alternatives*, vol. 19, no. 4, p. 455.

—— 1998, *National deconstruction: violence, identity, and justice in Bosnia*, University of Minneapolis Press, Minneapolis, MN.

—— 2005, 'Beyond Choice: The Onto-Politics of Critique', *International Relations*, vol. 19, no. 1, pp. 127–34.

Carr, E.H. 1946, *The twenty years' crisis, 1919–1939: an introduction to the study of international relations*, 2nd edn, Macmillan, Basingstoke.

Carter, P. 2004, *The road to Abu Ghraib*, Washington Monthly, November, viewed 26 April 2007 <http://www.washingtonmonthly.com/features/2004/0411.carter.html>.

Caruth, C. 1995, 'Recapturing the Past: Introduction', in C Caruth (ed.), *Trauma: explorations in memory*, Johns Hopkins University Press, Baltimore, MD.

Cassese, A. 1986, 'Return to Westphalia? Considerations on the gradual erosion of the charter system', in A. Cassese (ed.), *The current legal regulation of the use of force*, Martinus Nijhoff, Leiden.

Cassim, V., W, D, H, K and W, TT 1975, 'The Definition of Aggression', *Harvard International Law Journal*, vol. 16, no. 1.

CBDP 2005, *Chemical and Biological Defense Program Annual Report to Congress*, US Department of Defense.

—— 2006, *Chemical and Biological Defense Program Annual Report to Congress*, US Department of Defense.

CDC 2005, *List of select biological agents and toxins*, Centers for Disease Control and Prevention Online, viewed 5 July 2005 <http://www.cdc.gov/od/sap/docs/salist.pdf>.

Cerny, P. 1998, 'Neomedievalism, Civil War and the New Security Dilemma: Globalisation as Durable Disorder', *Civil Wars*, vol. 1, no. 1, pp. 36–64.

Cha, A.E. 2005, 'Computers simulate terrorism's extremes', *Washington Post*, p. A01.

Chan, S. 2005, *Out of evil: new international politics and old doctrines of war*, I.B. Tauris, London.

Church, A.A.T. 2005, *Executive Summary*, viewed 15 March 2007 <http://www.defenselink. mil/news/Mar2005/d20050310exe.pdf>.

Chyba, C.F. 2004, 'Biotechnology and Bioterrorism: An Unprecedented World', *Survival*, vol. 46, no. 2, pp. 143–62.

Chyba, C.F. and Greninger, A.L. (2004) 'Biotechnology and Bioterrorism: An Unprecedented World,' *Survival* vol. 46 no. 2 143–62.

Clark, I. 2005, *Legitimacy in international society*, Oxford University Press, Oxford; New York.

Clark, P.A. 2006, 'Medical Ethics at Guantanamo Bay and Abu Ghraib: The Problem of Dual Loyalty', *Journal of Law, Medicine and Ethics*, vol. 34, no. 3, pp. 570–80.

Clark, W.K. 2004, *Winning modern wars: Iraq, terrorism and the American Empire*, Public Affairs, New York.

Clarke, R.A. 2004, *Against all enemies: inside America's war on terror*, Free Press, New York.

Clausewitz, K. von, Howard, M.E. and Paret, P. 1976, *On war*, Princeton University Press, Princeton, NJ.

Cohen, H.W., Gould, R.M. and Sidel, V.W. 2004, 'The Pitfalls of Bioterrorism Preparedness: the Anthrax and Smallpox Experiences', *American Journal of Public Health*, vol. 94, no. 10, pp. 1667–71.

Cohn, C. 1987, 'Sex and Death in the Rational World of Defense Intellectuals', *Signs: Journal of Women in Culture and Society*, vol. 12, no. 4, p. 687.

Combacau, J. 1986, 'The exception of self-defence in UN practice', in A Cassese (ed.), *The current legal regulation of the use of force*, Martinus Nijhoff, Dordrecht, pp. 9–37.

Connolly, W.E. 1995, *The ethos of pluralization*, University of Minnesota Press, Minneapolis, MN.

—— 2002, *Neuropolitics: thinking, culture, speed*, University of Minnesota Press, Minneapolis, MN.

Cooper, R. 2004, *The breaking of nations: order and chaos in the twenty-first century*, revised and updated edn, Atlantic Books, London.

Coorey, P. 2006, 'Court grants urgent hearing on Hicks case', *Sydney Morning Herald*, 7 December 2006.

Cordesman, A.H. 2006, *Qana and the lessons for modern war*, Center for Strategic and International Studies, viewed 6 March 2007 <http://www.csis.org/media/csis/pubs/ 060731_qana_commentary.pdf>.

Council on Foreign Relations 2002, *Terrorist Financing*, Council on Foreign Relations Press, New York.

—— 2004, *Update on the global campaign against terrorist financing*, Council on Foreign Relations Press, New York.

Crawford, N.C. 2000, 'The Passion of World Politics: Propositions on Emotion and Emotional Relationships', *International Security*, vol. 24, no. 4, p. 116.

—— 2003a, 'The Slippery Slope to Preventive War', *Ethics and International Affairs*, vol. 17, no. 1, pp. 30–6.

—— 2003b, 'Just War Theory and the US Counterterror War', *Perspectives on Politics*, vol. 1, no. 1, pp. 5–25.

Cronin, A.K. 2006, 'How al-Qaida Ends: The Decline and Demise of Terrorist Groups', *International Security*, vol. 31, no. 1, pp. 7–48.

Cuellar, M.-F. 2003, *The tenuous relationship between the flight against money laundering and the disruption of criminal finance*, Research paper 64, Stanford Law School, Stanford.

Daalder, I.H. and Lindsay, J.M. 2003, *America unbound: the Bush revolution in foreign policy*, Brookings Institution, Washington, DC.

Dahlstrom, E.K. 2003, 'The Executive Policy Toward Detention and Trial of Foreign Citizens at Guantanamo Bay', *Berkeley Journal of International Law*, vol. 21, no. 3, pp. 662–82.

Danchev, A. (2004), 'The Reckoning: Official Inquiries and the Iraq War', *Intelligence and National Security*, vol. 19 no. 3, pp. 436–466.

—— 2005, 'Story Development, or, Walter Mitty, the Undefeated', in A. Danchev and J. MacMillan (eds), *The Iraq war and democratic politics*, Routledge, London.

—— 2006, 'Like a Dog: Humiliation and Shame in the War on Terror', *Alternatives: Global, Local, Political*, vol. 31, no. 3, pp. 259–83.

—— 2007, 'Human Rights and Human Intelligence', in S. Tsang (ed.), *Intelligence and human rights in the era of global terrorism*, Praeger, Westport, CT.

Danner, M. 2004, 'Torture and the truth', *New York Review of Books*.

Dannreuther, R. 2007, *International security: the contemporary agenda*, Polity Press, Cambridge.

Darby, P. 2006, 'Security, Spatiality and Social Suffering', *Alternatives: Global, Local, Political*, vol. 31, no. 4, pp. 453–73.

David, S.R. 2003, 'Israel's Policy of Targeted Killing', *Ethics and International Affairs*, vol. 17, no. 1, pp. 111–26.

Delbrück, J. 2002, 'The Fight Against Global Terrorism: Self-Defense or Collective Security as International Police Action? Some Comments on the International Legal Implications of the "War Against Terrorism"', *German Yearbook of International Law*, vol. 44, pp. 9–24.

Department of Foreign Affairs and Trade 2002, *Advancing the national interest: Australia's foreign and trade policy white paper*, viewed 20 February 2007 <http://www.dfat.gov.au/ani/>.

D'Esopo, M. and Nuzzo, J. 2004, 'Go Figure', *Biosecurity and Bioterrorism*, vol. 2, no. 2, pp. 134–5.

Der Derian, J. 2003, 'Decoding the National Security Strategy of the United States of America', *Boundary 2*, vol. 30, no. 3, pp. 19–27.

Derrida, J. 2005, *Rogues: two essays on reason*, Stanford University Press, Stanford, CA.

Dershowitz, A.M. 2002, *Why terrorism works: understanding the threat, responding to the challenge*, Yale University Press, New Haven.

Devetak, R., forthcoming, 'Globalization's Shadow: An Introduction to the Globalization of Political Violence', in R. Devetak and C. Hughes (eds), *The globalization of political violence: globalization's shadow*, Routledge, London.

Devetak, R. and Hughes, C. forthcoming, *The globalization of political violence: globalization's shadow*, Routledge, London.

DHS 2005, *Fact sheet: National Biodefense Analysis and Countermeasures Center*, US Department of Homeland Security Online, viewed 13 April 2005 <http://www.dhs.gov/dhspublic/display?content=4336>.

Dinstein, Y. 1988, *War, aggression and self-defence*, Grotius Publications, Cambridge.

Dodge, T. 2006, 'How Iraq Was Lost', *Survival*, vol. 48, no. 4, pp. 157-72.

Downer, A. 2004, *Meeting the challenges of a changing regional and global security outlook, speech to the World Affairs Council, Los Angeles*, viewed 20 February 2007 <http://www.foreignminister.gov.au/speeches/2004/040119_global_security.html>.

—— 2005a, *Interview-ABC 702 David Hicks, Cronulla Disturbances*, viewed 18 December 2006 <http://www.foreignminister.gov.au/transcripts/2005/051214_abc.html>.

—— 2005b, 'Securing Australia's Interests – Australian Foreign Policy Priorities', *Australian Journal of International Affairs*, vol. 59, no. 1, pp. 7–12.

Duffield, M. 2001, 'Governing the Borderlands: Decoding the Power of Aid', *Disasters*, vol. 25, no. 4, pp. 308–20.

—— 2002, 'War as a Network Enterprise: The New Security Terrain and Its Implications', *Journal for Cultural Research*, vol 6 no. 1, pp. 153–65.

Duffield, M. and Waddell, N. 2006, 'Securing Humans in a Dangerous World', *International Politics*, vol. 43 no. 1, pp. 1–23.

Duffy, H. 2005, *The 'war on terror' and the framework of international law*, Cambridge University Press, New York.

Dworkin, R. 2004, 'What the Court Really Said', *New York Review of Books*, vol. 51, no. 13.

—— 2005, 'Military Necessity and Due Process: The Place of Human Rights in the War on Terror', in D. Wippman and M. Evangelista (eds), *New wars, new laws? Applying the laws of war in 21st century conflicts*, Transnational Publishers, Ardley, NY, pp. 53–74.

Editorial 2005, 'An Acidic Message', *Washington Post*, 10 March, p. A20.

Edkins, J. 2002, 'Forget Trauma? Responses to September 11', *International Relations*, vol. 16, no. 2, pp. 243–56.

—— 2003, *Trauma and the memory of politics*, Cambridge University Press, Cambridge, UK; New York.

—— 2004, 'Ground Zero: Reflections on Trauma, In/distinction and Response', *Journal for Cultural Research*, vol. 8, no. 3, pp. 247–70.

Ehrenfeld, R. 2003, *Funding evil: how terrorism is financed-and how to stop it*, Bonus Books, Chicago.

Elshtain, J.B. 1992, *Just war theory*, Blackwell Press, Oxford.

—— 2002, 'How to Fight a Just War', in K. Booth and T. Dunne (eds), *Worlds in collision: terror and the future of global order*, Palgrave Macmillan, Basingsoke and New York.

—— 2004, *Just war against terror: the burden of American power in a violent world*, Basic Books, New York.

Elster, J. 1999, *Alchemies of the mind: rationality and the emotions*, Cambridge University Press, Cambridge, UK; New York.

Enserink, M. and Kaiser, J. 2005, 'Has Biodefense Gone Overboard?' *Science*, vol. 307, no. 5714, pp. 1396–8.

Euben, R.L. 1999, *Enemy in the mirror: Islamic fundamentalism and the limits of modern rationalism*, Princeton University Press, Princeton, NJ.

—— 2002, 'Killing (for) Politics: Jihad, Martyrdom and Political Action', *Political Theory*, vol. 30, no. 1, pp. 4–35.

Falk, R. 1963, *Law, morality and war in the contemporary world*, Paeger, New York.

FAS 2002, *Draft recommendations for a code of conduct for biodefense programs*, Federation of American Scientists Online, available at <http://www.fas.org/bwc/papers/code.pdf> (accessed 30 May 2005).

—— *Draft Recommedations for a code of conduct for biodefense programs*, Federation of American Scientists Online, viewed 30 May 2005 <http://www.fas.org/bwc/papers/code.pdf>.

Feinstein, L. and Slaughter, A-M. 2004, 'A Duty to Prevent', *Foreign Affairs*, vol. 83, no. 1, pp. 136–50.

Ferejohn, John, and Pasquino, Pasquale 2004, 'The Law of the Exception: A Typology of Emergency Powers', *International Journal of Constitutional Law*, vol. 2, no. 2, pp. 210–39.

Fierke, K. 2004, 'Whereof We Can Speak, Thereof We Must Not Be Silent: Trauma, Political Solipsism and War', *Review of International Studies*, vol. 30, no. 4, pp. 471–91.

—— 2007, *Critical approaches to international security*, Polity, Cambridge.

Fiorill, J. 2005, *US Plans to defend against engineered bioattack*, Global Security Newswire Online, viewed 1 July 2005 <http://www.nti.org/d_newswire/issues/2005/6/15/F1EB5240-6C65-41F5-A24E-DFD8EFF6C642.html>.

Fisher, L. 2005, *Military tribunals and presidential power: American revolution to the war on terrorism*, University Press of Kansas, Kansas.

Fletcher, G.P. 2006, 'The *Hamdan* Case and Conspiracy as a War Crime: A New Beginning for International Law in the US', *Journal of International Criminal Justice*, vol. 4, no. 3, pp. 442–7.

Foer, J.S. 2005, *Extremely loud and incredibly close*, Houghton Mifflin Company, Boston.

Foreign Policy and Fund for Peace 2005, 'The Failed States Index', *Foreign Policy*, vol. 149, no. July–August, pp. 56–65.

Foucault, M. 1978, *The history of secuality: volume 1, The will to knowledge*, Penguin, Harmondsworth.

Franck, T.M. 2002, *Recourse to force: state action against threats and armed attacks*, Cambridge University Press, Cambridge.

Freedman, L. 2001/2, 'The Third World War?' *Survival*, vol. 43, no. 4, pp. 61–87.

—— 2002, 'The Coming War on Terrorism', *Political Quarterly*, vol. 73, no. 1, pp. 40–56.

—— 2004a, *Deterrence*, Polity Press, Malden, MA.

—— 2004b, 'War in Iraq: Selling the Threat', *Survival*, vol. 46, no. 2, pp. 7–49.

—— 2005, 'The Age of Liberal Wars', *Review of International Studies*, vol. 31, no. Special Issue, pp. 93–107.

—— 2006, 'The Transformation of Military Strategy', *Adelphi Papers*, vol. 379, pp. 61–71.

Frum, D. and Perle, R. 2004, *An end to evil: how to win the war on terror*, Random House, New York.

Fukuyama, F. 1992, *The end of history and the last man*, Sage Press, New York.

—— 2002, 'History and September 11', in K. Booth and T. Dunne (eds), *Worlds in collision: terror and the future of global order*, Palgrave, London; New York.

Fullinwinder, R.K. 1975, 'War and Innocence', *Philosophy and Public Affairs*, vol. 5, no. 1, pp. 90–7.

Garamone, J. 2006, *Bush says military commissions act will bring justice*, viewed 1 December 2006 <http://www.defenselink.mil/News/NewsArticle.aspx?id=1633>.

Gaudioso, J. and Salerno, R.M. 2004, 'Biosecurity and Research: Minimizing Adverse Impacts', *Science*, vol. 304, no. 5671, p. 687.

Gazit, S. 2004, Interview with author, 25 August.

Geisbert, T.W., Hensley, L.E., Jahrling, P.B., Larsen, T., Geisbert, J.B., Paragas, J., Young, H.A., Fredeking, T.M., Rote, W.E. and Vlasuk, G.B. 2003, 'Treatment of Ebola Virus Infection With a Recombinant Inhibitor of Factor VIIA/Tissue Factor: a Study in Rhesus Monkeys', *The Lancet*, vol. 362, no. 9400, pp. 1953–8.

George, J. 2005, 'Leo Strauss, Neoconservatism and US Foreign Policy: Esoteric Nihilism and the Bush Doctrine', *International Politics*, vol. 42, no. 2, pp. 174–202.

Gilmore, W.C. 1995, *Dirty money: the evolution of money laundering counter-measures*, Council of Europe, Strasbourg.

Glennon, M.J. 2002, 'The Fog of Law: Self-Defense, Inherence, and Incoherence in Article 51 of the United Nations Charter', *Harvard Journal of International Law and Public Policy*, vol. 25, no. 2, pp. 541–9.

—— 2003, 'Why the Security Council Failed', *Foreign Affairs*, vol. 82, no. 3, pp. 16–35.

Godfrey, E.D. 1978, 'Ethics and Intelligence', *Foreign Affairs*, vol. 56, no. 3, pp. 624–42.

Goldenbeg, S. 2006a, *Five US soldiers in Iraq rape and murder inquiry*, Guardian Unlimited, 1 July, viewed 26 April 2007 <http://www.guardian.co.uk/Iraq/Story/0,,1810326,00.html>.

—— 2006b, *Woman soldier refuses return to Iraq, claiming sexual harassment*, Guardian Unlimited, 21 June, viewed 26 April 2007 <http://www.guardian.co.uk/international/story/0,,1802178,00.html>.

Goldgeier, J.M. and McFaul, M. 1992, 'A Tale of Two Worlds: Core and Periphery in the Post-Cold War Era', *International Organization*, vol. 46, no. 2, pp. 467–91.

Goldie, P. 2002, *The emotions: a philosophical exploration*, Clarendon Press, Oxford.

Gore, A. 2004, 'The Politics of Fear', *Social Research*, vol. 71, no. 4, pp. 779–98.

Government Accounting Office 2006, *Company formation: minimal company ownership information is collected and available*, Government Accounting Office, Washington, DC.

Gray, C.D. 2000, *International law and the use of force*, Oxford University Press, Oxford; New York.

Gray, C.H. 2005, *Peace, war and computers*, Routledge, London; New York.

Greenberg, K.J. 2006, 'Introduction', in K.J. Greenberg (ed.), *The torture debate in America*, Cambridge University Press, Cambridge; New York.

Greener-Barcham, Beth K., and Barcham, Manuhuia 2006, 'Terrorism in the South Pacific? Thinking Critically About Approaches to Security in the Region', *Australian Journal of International Affairs*, vol 60, no. 1, pp. 67–82.

Greenwood, C. 2002, 'International Law and the "War Against Terrorism"', *International Affairs*, vol. 78, no. 2, pp. 301–17.

—— 2003, 'International Law and the Pre-emptive Use of Force: Afghanistan, Al-Qaida, and Iraq', *San Diego International Law Journal*, vol. 7, pp. 7–37.

Gross, O. 2000, 'The Normless and Exeptionless Exception: Carl Schmitt's Theory of Emergency Powers and the "Norm-Exception" Dichotomy', *Cardozo Law Review*, vol. 21, no. 5–6, pp. 1825–68.

—— 2006, 'What "Emergency" Regime?' *Constellations*, vol. 13, no. 1, pp. 74–88.

Grotius, H. 1913, *De jure belli ac pacis libri tres*, Carnegie Council, Washington, DC.

—— 2005, 'The rights of war and peace', in K. Haakonssen and J. Barbeyrac (eds), *Natural law and enlightenment classics*, Liberty Fund Press, Indianapolis, IN.

Gugliotta, G. 2002, 'Still No Arrests in Anthrax Probe, But "Progress" is Noted', *Washington Post*, 4 August, p. A08.

Guillemin, J. 2005, *Biological weapons: from the invention of state-sponsored programs to contemporary bioterrorism*, Columbia University Press, New York.

Hafetz, J. 2006, 'Hamdan and the Guantanamo Detainees', *Jurist Forum,* 12 July 2006. http://jurist.law.pitt.edu/forumy/2006/07/hamdan-and-guantanamo-detainees.php (accessed 1 December 2006).

Halliday, F. 2005, *The Middle East in international relations: power, politics and ideology*, Cambridge University Press, Cambridge, UK; New York.

Halper, S.A. and Clarke, J. 2004, *America alone: the neo-conservatives and the global order*, Cambridge University Press, Cambridge.

Hamilton, B. 1963, *Political thought in sixteenth century Spain: a study of the political ideas of Vitoria, De Soto, Suárez, and Molina*, Clarendon Press, Oxford.

Hammer, R. 2003, 'Militarism and Family Terrorism: a Critical Feminist Perspective', *The Review of Education, Pedagogy and Cultural Studies*, vol. 25, pp. 231–56.

Harding, L. 2004a, 'Focus Shifts to Jail Abuse of Women', *Guardian*, 12 May, viewed 26 April 2007 <http://www.guardian.co.uk/print/0,,4921772-103550,00.html>.

—— 2004b, 'The Other Prisoners', *Guardian*, 20 May, viewed 26 April 2007 <http://www.guardian.co.uk/print/0,,4928134-103691,00.html>.

Harré, R. 1986, *The Social construction of emotions*, Basil Blackwell, Oxford.

Hibbitts, B. 2006, *US assures Australia that Hicks will not face death penalty in new military trial*, viewed 7 November 2006 <http://jurist.law.pitt.edu/paperchase/2006/08/us-assures-australia-that-hicks-will.php>.

Hill, R. 2005, *Terrorism and the new global security environment, speech at Murdoch University, Perth, 18 May*, viewed 20 February 2007 <http://www.defence.gov.au/minister/HillSpeechtpl.cfm?CurrentId=4874>.

Hills, A. 2004, *Future war in cities: rethinking a liberal dilemma*, Frank Cass Publishers, London.

Hills, A. 2006, 'Fear and Loathing in Falluja', *Armed Forces and Society*, vol. 32, no. 4, pp. 623–39.

Hindess, B. 2001, 'The Liberal Government of Unfreedom', *Alternatives*, vol. 26, no. 2, pp. 93–111.

Hochschild, A.R. 1998, 'The Sociology of Emotions as a Way of Seeing', in G. Bendelow and S.J. Williams (eds), *Emotions in social life: critical themes and contemporary issues*, Routledge, London, pp. 3–15.

Hoffman, P. 2004, 'Human Rights and Terrorism', *Human Rights Quarterly*, vol. 26, no. 4, pp. 932–55.

Holmes, S. 2005, 'Al Qaeda, September 11, 2001', in D. Gambetta (ed.), *Making sense of suicide missions*, Oxford University Press, Oxford.

—— 2006, 'Is Defiance of Law a Proof of Success? Magical Thinking in the War on Terror', in K.J. Greenberg (ed.), *The torture debate in America*, Cambridge University Press, Cambridge; New York.

Homes, S. 1995, *Passions and constraint: on the theory of liberal democracy*, University of Chicago Press, Chicago, IL.

Hoskins, A. 2006, 'Temporality, Proximity and Security: Terror in a Media-Drenched Age', *International Relations*, vol. 20, no. 4, pp. 453–66.

Hovell, D. 2005, *Justice at Guantanamo? The Paradox of David Hicks*, viewed 7 November 2006 <http://jurist.law.pitt.edu/forumy/2005/11/justice-at-guantanamo-paradox-of-david.php>.

Howard, J. 2005, 'Australia in the World', Address by the Prime Minister, the Hon John Howard MP to the Lowy Institute for International Policy, available at http://www.lowyinstitute.org/Publication.asp?pid=396.

—— 2007, *Interview: John Howard*, Sunday, 11 February, viewed 26 March 2007 <http://sunday.ninemsn.com.au/sunday/political_transcripts/article_2124.asp>.

Howard, M. 2002, 'What's in a Name? How to Fight Terrorism', *Foreign Affairs*, vol. 81, no. 1, pp. 8–13.

Howard, M.E. 1978, *War and the liberal conscience*, Temple Smith, London.

Howeidy, A. 2004, *Balfour to Bush*, Al-Ahram Weekly, viewed 6 March 2007 <http://weekly.ahram.org.eg/2004/686/fr3.htm>.

Hoyt, K. and Brooks, S.G. 2004, 'A Double-Edged Sword: Globalization and Biosecurity', *International Security*, vol. 28, no. 3, pp. 123–48.

Humphrey, M. 2000, 'From Terror to Trauma: Commissioning Truth for National Reconciliation', *Social Identities*, vol. 6, no. 1, pp. 7–27.

—— 2002, *The politics of atrocity and reconciliation: from terror to trauma*, Routledge, London; New York.

Humphreys, S. 2006, 'Legalizing Lawlessness: On Giorgio Agamben's State of Exception', *European Journal of International Law*, vol. 17, no. 3, pp. 677–87.

Hunt, S. and Posa, C. 2004, 'Iraq's Excluded Women', *Foreign Policy*, vol. 143, pp. 40–5.

Huntington, S.P. 1996, *The clash of civilizations and the remaking of world order*, Simon and Schuster, New York.

Hurrell, A. 2002, ''There Are No Rules' (George W. Bush): International Order after September 11', *International Relations*, vol. 16, no. 2, pp. 185–204.

ICRC 2005, *US detention related to the events of 11 September 2001 and its aftermath – the role of the ICRC*, viewed 1 December 2006 <http://www.icrc.org/web/eng/siteeng0.nsf/iwpList454/541ACF6DC88315C4C125700B004FF643>.

Ignatieff, M. 1997, *The warrior's honor: ethnic war and the modern conscience*, Metropolitan Books, New York.

—— 2003, *Empire lite: nation building in Bosnia, Kosovo and Afghanistan*, Vintage, London.

—— 2004, *The lesser evil: political ethics in an age of terror*, Edinburgh University Press, Edinburgh.

Ikenberry, J.G. 2004, 'The End of the Neo-Conservative Moment', *Survival*, vol. 46, no. 1, pp. 7–22.

Iraq Study Group 2006, *The way forward – a new approach*, Vintage, New York.

IRIN 2006a, *Iraq: focus on increasing domestic violence*, IRINnews.org, 24 November, viewed 26 April 2007 <http://www.irinnews.org/report.asp?ReportID=37204&SelectRegion=Iraq_Crisis&SelectCountry=IRAQ>.

—— 2006b, *Iraq: widow numbers rise in wake of violence*, IRINnews.org, 26 April, viewed 26 April 2007 <http://www.irinnews.org/report.aspx?reportid=26320>.

—— 2006c, *Iraq: lawyers killed for defending cases 'against Islam'*, IRINnews.org, 6 November, viewed 25 November 2006 <http://www.irinnews.org/print.asp?ReportID=55146>.

—— 2006d, *Sex traffickers target women in war-torn Iraq*, electronicIraq.net, 26 October, viewed 26 April 2007 <http://electroniciraq.net/news/2569.shtml>.

Jackson, R. 2005, *Writing the war on terrorism: language, politics and counter-terrorism*, Manchester University Press, Manchester; New York.

Jackson, R.J., Ramsay, A.J., Christensen, C.D., Beaton, S., Hall, D.F. and Ramshaw, I.A. 2001, 'Expression of Mouse Interleukin-4 by a Recombinant Ectromelia Virus Suppresses Cytolytic Lymphocyte Responses and Overcomes Genetic Resistance to Mousepox', *Journal of Virology*, vol. 75, no. 3, pp. 1205–10.

Jaggar, A.M. 1989, 'Love and Knowledge: Emotion in Feminist Epistemology', in S. Bordo and A.M. Jaggar (eds), *Gender/body/knowledge: feminist reconstructions of being and knowing*, Rutgers University Press, New Brunswick, NJ, pp. 145–71.

James, F. 2004, 'Anti-bioterror Labs Raise Risk to US, Critics Say', *Chicago Tribune*, 5 December, p. 9.

James, N. 2005, 'Torture: An Unwarranted Case', *Defender*, vol. 22, no. 2, pp. 25–7.

Jamieson, K.H. 1992, *Dirty politics: deception, distraction, and democracy*, Oxford University Press, New York.

Jeleniewski Seidler, V. 1998, 'Masculinity, Violence and Emotional Life', in G. Bendelow and S.J. Williams (eds), *Emotions in social life: critical themes and contemporary issues*, Routledge, London; New York, pp. 193–210.

Johns, F. 2005, 'Guantanamo Bay and the Annihilation of the Exception', *European Journal of International Law*, vol. 16, no. 4, pp. 613–35.

Johnson, J. 2001, 'Blacklisting: Initial Results, Responses and Repercussions', *Journal of Money Laundering Control*, vol. 4, no. 2, pp. 211–25.

Johnson, J.T. 1975, *Ideology, reason, and the limitation of war: religious and secular concepts, 1200–1740*, Princeton University Press, Princeton, NJ.

—— 1981, *Just war tradition and the restraint of war: a moral and historical inquiry*, Princeton University Press, Princeton, NJ.

—— 1996, 'The Broken Tradition', *The National Interest*, vol. 45, pp. 27–37.

—— 1999, *Morality and contemporary warfare*, Yale University Press, New Haven, CT.

—— 2005, *The war to oust Saddam Hussein: just war and the face of new conflict*, Rowman and Littlefield, Lanham, MD.

—— 2006, 'Humanitarian Intervention after Iraq: Just War and International Law Perspectives', *Journal of Military Ethics*, vol. 5, no. 2, pp. 114–27.

Johnstone, I. 2004, 'US–UN Relations after Iraq: The End of the World (Order) as We Know It?' *European Journal of International Law*, vol. 15, no. 4, pp. 813–38.

Jones, R.V. 1989, *Reflections on intelligence*, Heinemann, London.

—— 1995, *Some Lessons in Intelligence*, Studies in Intelligence, viewed 15 March 2007 <https://www.cia.gov/csi/studies/95unclass/Jones.html>.

Jones, S.G. 2006, 'Averting Failure in Afghanistan', *Survival*, vol. 48, no. 1, pp. 111–27.

Kagan, R. 2003, *Of paradise and power: America and Europe in the new world order*, 1st Vintage Books with a new afterword, Atlantic Books, London.

Kaiser, J. 2004, 'Citizens Sue to Block Montana Biodefense Lab', *Science*, vol. 305, no. 5687, p. 1088.

Kaldor, M. 1999, *New and old wars: organized violence in a global age*, reprinted with a new afterword, Polity Press, Cambridge.

—— 2003, *Global civil society: an answer to war*, Polity Press, Cambridge.

—— 2006, *New and old wars: organized violence in a global era*, 2nd edn, Polity Press, Cambridge.

Kaplan, A. 2005, 'Where is Guantanamo?' *American Quarterly*, vol. 57, no. 3, pp. 831–58.

Karoubi, M.T. 2004, *Just or unjust war?: international law and unilateral use of armed force by states at the turn of the 20th century*, Ashgate, Aldershot; Burlington, VT.

Kaufman, M. 2006, 'Bush sets defense as space priority', *The Washington Post*, p. A01.

Kaufman, W. 2005, 'What's Wrong with Preventive War? The Moral and Legal Basis for the Preventive Use of Force', *Ethics and International Affairs*, vol. 19, no. 3, pp. 23–38.

Keenan, T. 2004, 'To Speak in a Language that Needs no Translation', unpublished paper.

Keene, E. 2002, *Beyond the anarchical society: Grotius, colonialism and order in world politics*, Cambridge University Press, Cambridge; New York.

Kelley, M. and Coghlan, J. 2003, 'Mixing Bugs and Bombs', *Bulletin of the Atomic Scientists*, vol. 59, no. 5, pp. 24–31.

Kellogg, F.B. 1928, 'Address of the Hon. Frank B. Kellogg, 28 April 1928', *Proceedings of the American Society of International Law*, vol. 22, pp. 141–3.

Kelsen, H. 1948, 'Collective Security and Collective Self-Defense Under the Charter', *American Journal of International Law*, vol. 42, no. 3.

Kilcullen, D. 2006, 'Counter-insurgency *Redux*', *Survival*, vol. 48, no. 4, pp. 111–30.

Kissinger, H.A. 1969, *National Security Decision Memorandum (NSDM) 35, United States Policy on Chemical Warfare Program and Bacteriological/Biological Research Program, from National Security Advisor Henry A Kissinger to the Vice President, the Secretary of State, the Secretary of Defense, etc.*, George Washington University National Security Archive Online, viewed 27 May 2005 <http://www.gwu.edu/~nsarchiv/NSAEBB/NSAEBB58/RNCBW8.pdf>.

Klusmeyer, D. and Suhrke, A. 2002, 'Comprehending "Evil": Challenges for Law and Policy', *Ethics and International Affairs*, vol. 16, no. 1, pp. 27–42.

Koh, H.H. 2005, 'America's Jekyll-and-Hyde Exceptionalism', in M. Ignatieff (ed.), *American exceptionalism and human rights*, Princeton University Press, New Jersey, pp. 111–43.

Komp, C. 2006, *Domestic abuse in military families growing 'systemic'*, The New Standard, 6 June, viewed 26 April 2007 <http://newstandardnews.net/content/index.cfm/items/3271>.

Korch, G. 2004, *Leading edge of biodefense: The National Biodefense Analysis and Countermeasures Center, Lecture to the Department of Defense Pest Management Workshop, Jacksonville Naval Air Station*, Bioweapons and Biodefense Freedom of Information Fund Online, viewed 26 May 2005 <http://www.cbwtransparency.org/archive/nbacc.pdf>.

Koskenniemi, M. 2005, *From apology to Utopia: the structure of international legal argument*, 2nd edn, Cambridge University Press, Cambridge.

KPMG 2004, *Global Anti-Money Laundering Survey 2004: how banks are facing up to the challenge*, KPMG International.

Krasner, S.D. and Pascual, C. 2005, 'Addressing State Failure', *Foreign Affairs*, vol. 84, no. 4, pp. 153–63.

Krause, K. and Williams, M.C. 1996, 'Broadening the Agenda of Security Studies: Politics and Methods', *Mershon International Studies Review*, vol. 40, no. 2, pp. 229–54.

Kumar, D. 2004, 'War Propaganda and the (Ab)uses of Women, Media Constructions of the Jessica Lynch story', *Feminist Media Studies*, vol. 4, no. 3, pp. 297–313.

Kunz, J.L. 1947, 'Individual and Collective Self-Defence in Article 51 of the Charter of the United Nations', *American Journal of International Law*, vol. 41, no. 4, pp. 872–9.

LaFeber, W. 2002, 'The Bush Doctrine', *Diplomatic History*, vol. 26, no. 4, pp. 543–58.

Lam, C., Franco, C. and Schuler, A. 2006, 'Billions for Biodefense: Federal Agency Biodefense Funding, FY2006-FY2007', *Biosecurity and Bioterrorism*, vol. 4, no. 2, pp. 113–27.

Lang, A.F. 2004, 'The Illegality of Punishing States – from Grotius to the ILC', paper presented to International Studies Association, Montreal.

Lasky, M.P. 2006, *Iraq women under siege*, Cope Pink/Global Exchange, viewed 26 April 2007 <http://www.codepinkalert.org/downloads/IraqiWomenReport.pdf>.

Lawrence, B. 2005, *Message to the world: the statements of Osama Bin Laden*, Verso, London; New York.

Leighton, S.R. 2003, *Philosophy and the emotions: a reader*, Broadview Press, Peterborough, Ont.

Leitenberg, M. 2003, 'Distinguishing Offensive From Defensive Biological Weapons Research', *Critical Reviews in Microbiology*, vol. 29, no. 3, pp. 223–57.

Leitzau, W. 2005, 'Combating Terrorism: The Consequences of Moving from Law Enforcement to War', in D. Wippman and M. Evangelista (eds), *New wars, new laws?:*

applying the laws of war in 21st century conflicts, Transnational Publishers, Ardley, NY, pp. 31–52.

Letter 2005, 'An Open Letter to Elias Zerhouni (multiple authors)', *Science*, vol. 307, no. 5714, pp. 1409–10.

Levi, M. and Gilmore, W.C. 2002, 'Terrorist Finance, Money Laundering and the Rise and Rise of Mutual Evaluation: A New Paradigm for Crime Control', *European Journal of Law Reform*, vol. 4, no. 2, pp. 337–64.

Levinas, E. 1969, *Totality and infinity: an essay on exteriority*, Duquesne University Press The Hague; M. Nijhoff, Pittsburgh, PA.

—— 1987, *Time and the other [and additional essays]*, Duquesne University Press, Pittsburgh, PA.

—— 1996, 'Peace and Proximity', in A.T. Peperzak, S. Critchley and R. Bernasconi (eds), *Emmanuel Levinas: basic philosophical writings*, Indiana University Press, Bloomington, IN.

Levinson, S. 2006, 'Preserving Constitutional Norms in Times of Permanent Emergencies', *Constellations*, vol. 13, no. 1, pp. 59–73.

Lisle, D. 2004, 'Gazing at Ground Zero: Tourism, Voyeurism and Spectacle', *Journal for Cultural Research*, vol. 8, no. 1, pp. 3–21.

Lowe, V. 2003, 'The Iraq Crisis: What Now?' *International and Comparative Law Quarterly*, vol. 52, no. 4, pp. 859–71.

Luban, D. 2005, 'The War on Terrorism and the End of Human Rights', in M.V. Tushnet (ed.), *The constitution in wartime: beyond alarmism and complacency*, Duke University Press, Durham, NC.

—— 2006, 'Liberalism, Torture, and the Ticking Bomb', in K.J. Greenberg (ed.), *The torture debate in America*, Cambridge University Press, Cambridge; New York.

Lucas, G.R. 2003, 'The Role of the "International Community" in Just War Tradition – Confronting the Challenges of Humanitarian Intervention and Preemptive War', *Journal of Military Ethics*, vol. 2, no. 2, pp. 122–44.

Lukes, S. 2005, 'Liberal Democratic Torture', *British Journal of Political Science*, vol. 36, no. 1, pp. 1–16.

Lustgarten, L. and Leigh, I. 1994, *In from the cold: national security and parliamentary democracy*, Clarendon Press, Oxford.

Lutz, C.A. and Abu-Lughod, L. 1990, *Language and the politics of emotion*, Cambridge University Press, Cambridge; Paris: Éditions de la maison des sciences de l'homme, New York.

MacDonald, H. 2006, 'How to Interrogate Terrorists', in K.J. Greenberg (ed.), *The torture debate in America*, Cambridge University Press, Cambridge; New York.

McAlea, D. 2005, 'Post-Westphalian Crime', in D. Wippman and M. Evangelista (eds), *New wars, new laws: applying the laws of war in 21st century conflicts*, Transnational Publishers, Ardley, NY, pp. 111–34.

McClintock, A. 1995, *Imperial leather: race, gender, and sexuality in the colonial conquest*, Routledge, New York.

McCormack, T.L.H 1996, *Self-defence in international law: the Israeli raid on the Iraqi nuclear reactor*, St Martin's Press, Oxford.

McDougal, M.S. 1963, 'The Soviet-Cuban Quarantine and Self-Defence', *American Journal of International Law*, vol. 57, no. 2, pp. 597–604.

McDougal, M.S. and Feliciano, F.P. 1961, *Law and minimum world public order: the legal regulation of international coercion*, Yale University Press, New Haven, CT.

McKelvey, T. 2005, *A soldier's tale: Lynndie England*, Marie Claire, viewed 26 April 2007 <http://www.marieclaire.com/world/news/lynndie-england-1>.

Mackey, C. 2004, *The interrogator's war: inside the secret war against Iraq*, John Murray, London.

Mackinlay, J. 2002, 'Globalisation and Insurgency', *Adelphi Papers*, vol. 352, November, pp. 5–116.

McNally, N. 2004, 'Illegal Imprisonment at Guantanamo Bay', *Law Society Journal*, vol. 42, no. 3, pp. 78–82.

Marcus, G.E. 2000, 'Emotions in Politics', *Annual Review of Political Science*, vol. 3, pp. 21–50.

Marks, S. 2006, 'State-Centrism, International Law, and the Anxieties of Influence', *Leiden Journal of International Law*, vol. 39, no. 2, pp. 339–47.

Marqusee, M. 2005, 'A Name that Lives in Infamy: the Destruction of Falluja was an Act of Barbarism that Ranks Alongside My Lai, Guernica and Halabja', *Guardian*, 10 November, p. 32.

Martyn, A. 2005, *Progress of the military trial of David Hicks*, viewed 7 November 2006 <http://www.aph.gov.au/library/pubs/rn/2004-05/05rn33.htm>.

Matsumoto, G. 2003, 'Anthrax Powder: State of the Art?' *Science*, vol. 302, no. 5650, pp. 1492–7.

Mearsheimer, J.J. 1990, 'Why We Will Soon Miss the Cold War', *The Atlantic*, vol. 266, no. 2, pp. 35–50.

Megret, F. 2002, ''War''? Legal Semantics and the Move to Violence', *European Journal of International Law*, vol. 13, no. 2, pp. 361–99.

Menkhaus, K. 2004, 'Somalia: State Collapse and the Threat of Terrorism', *Adelphi Papers*, vol. 364, no. Mar, pp. 7–92.

—— 2005, 'Somalia and Somaliland', in R.I. Rotberg (ed.), *Battling Terrorism in the Horn of Africa*, Brookings Institution Press, Washington, DC.

Mercer, J. 1996. 'Approaching Emotion in International Politics', paper presented and the International Studies Association Conference, San Diego, California, 25 April.

Mercer, J. 2005, 'Rationality and Psychology in International Politics', *International Organization*, vol. 59, no. 1, pp. 77–106.

Miami Herald 2005, *Timeline of legal and judicial events related to Guantanamo Bay*, viewed 3 March 2006 <http://www.miami.com/mld/miamiherald/news/special_packages/archive/11276706.html>.

Miles, D. 2006, *Bush Reacts to Supreme Court ruling on military tribunals*, viewed 1 December 2006 <http://www.defenselink.mil/news/Jun2006/20060629_5543.html>.

Miles, S.H. 2006, *Oath betrayed: torture, medical complicity, and the war on terror*, Random House, New York.

Miller, J. 1998, *To Terror's Source*, ABC news.com, viewed 6 March 2007 <http://www.freerepublic.com/focus/news/833647/posts>.

—— 2003, 'Scientist Files Suit Over Anthrax Inquiry', *New York Times*, 27 August, p. A13.

Miller, J., Engelberg, S. and Broad, W. 2001, 'US Germ Warfare Research Pushes Treaty Limits', *New York Times*, 4 September, p. A1.

Minca, C. 2005, 'The Return of the Camp', *Progress in Human Geography*, vol. 29, no. 4, pp. 405–12.

Moïsi, D. 2007, 'The Clash of Emotions', *Foreign Affairs*, vol. 86, no. 1, p. 8.

Monbiot, G. 2005, 'Behind the Phosphorous Clouds are War Crimes within War Crimes', *Guardian*, viewed 17 January 2006 <http://www.guardian.co.uk/Columnists/Column/0,5673,1647998,00.html>.

Montgomery, A.H. 2005, 'Ringing in Proliferation: How to Dismantle an Atomic Bomb Network', *International Security*, vol. 30, no. 2, pp. 153–87.

Morgenthau, H.J. 1962, 'The Escape From Power', in H.J. Morgenthau (ed.), *The decline of democratic politics*, University of Chicago, Chicago, IL.

Mori, M. 2006, 'Lecture for the Australian Lawyers', paper presented to Australian Lawyers Alliance, Brisbane Convention Centre, Australia, 3 November.

Morris, D.B. 1993, *The culture of pain*, University of California Press, Berkeley, CA.

Mueller, J. 2004, 'A False Sense of Insecurity', *Regulation*, vol. 27, no. 3, pp. 42–6.

Muggleton, P. 2006, *Certain legal and ethical aspects of contemporary ADF operations*, Command Papers, Centre for Defence Leadership Studies, Australian Defence College, Canberra.

Mullerson, R. 1991, 'Self-defense in the contemporary world', in D.J. Scheffer and L.F. Damrosch (eds), *Law and force in the new international order*, Westview Press, Boulder, CO, pp. 13–15.

Myjer, E.P.J. and White, N.D. 2002, 'The Twin Tower Attack: An Unlimited Right to Self-Defence', *Journal of Conflict and Security Law*, vol. 7, no. 1, pp. 5–17.

NAS 2004, *Biotechnology research in the age of terrorism*, National Academy of Sciences, Washington, DC.

Nash, K. 2003, 'Cosmopolitan Political Community: Why Does It Feel So Right?' *Constellations*, vol. 10, no. 4, pp. 506–18.

National Commission on Terrorist Attacks Upon the United States 2004, *9/11 investigations*, National Commission on Terrorist Attacks Upon the United States (9-11 Commission), New York.

National Security Council (NSC) 2002, *National security strategy of the United States of America*, viewed 20 February 2007 <http://www.whitehouse.gov/nsc/nss/2002/nss.pdf>.

—— 2003, *National strategy for combating terrorism*, The White House, Washington. DC.

—— 2006a, *National security strategy of the United States of America*, viewed 20 February 2007 <http://www.whitehouse.gov/nsc/nss/2006/nss2006.pdf>.

—— 2006b, *National strategy for combating terrorism*, The White House, Washington, DC.

Naylor, R.T. 2004, *Wages of crime: black markets, illegal finance and the underworld economy*, revised edn, Cornell University Press, Ithaca,NY.

Neiman, S. 2003, *Evil in modern thought: an alternative history of philosophy*, Scribe Publications, Melbourne.

Nelson, R. 2004, 'Biosafety Laboratories Proliferate Across the USA', *The Lancet Infectious Diseases*, vol. 4, no. 10, p. 596.

Neocleous, M. 2006, 'The Problem with Normality: Taking Exception to "Permanent Emergency"', *Alternatives*, vol. 31, no. 2, pp. 191–213.

Netanyahu, B. 2002, 'How Terror Feeds on Hope', *The Age*.

Newman, E. 2004, 'The "New Wars" Debate: A Historical Perspective Is Needed', *Security Dialogue*, vol. 35, no. 2, pp. 173–89.

Newton, M. 2005, 'Unlawful Belligerency After September 11: History Revisited and Law Revised', in D. Wippman and M. Evangelista (eds), *New wars, new laws?: applying the laws of war in 21st century conflicts*, Transnational Publishers, Ardley, NY, pp. 75–110.

NIH 2003, *NIAID funds construction of biosafety laboratories*, National Institutes of Health Online, viewed 10 May 2005 <http://www2.niaid.nih.gov/newsroom/releases/nblscorrect21.htm>.

—— 2005, *NIAID awards first $27 million using new bioshield authorities*, National Institutes of Health Online, viewed 9 June 2005 <http://www.nih.gov/news/pr/may2005/niaid–09.htm>.

Nussbaum, M.C. 1990, *Love's knowledge: essays on philosophy and literature*, Oxford University Press, New York.

—— 1995a, 'Rational Emotions', in M.C. Nussbaum (ed.), *Poetic justice: the literary imagination and public life*, Beacon Press, Boston, MA, pp. 53–78.

—— 1995b, 'Emotions and Women's Capabilities', in M.C. Nussbaum and J. Glover (eds), *Women, culture, and development: a study of human capabilities*, Oxford University Press, New York, pp. 360–95.

—— 2001, *Upheavals of thought: the intelligence of emotions*, Cambridge University Press, Cambridge.

Ober, J. 1994, 'Classical Greek Times', in M.E. Howard, G.J. Andreopoulos and M.R. Shulman (eds), *The laws of war: constraints on warfare in the Western world*, Yale University Press, New Haven, CT, pp. 12–26.

O'Brien, W.V. 1981, *The conduct of just and limited wars*, Praeger, New York.

O'Donovan, O. 2003, *The just war revisited*, Cambridge University Press, Cambridge.

O'Driscoll, C. 2006, 'Re-negotiating the Just War: The Invasion of Iraq and Punitive War', *Cambridge Review of International Affairs*, vol. 19, no. 3, pp. 405–20.

Office of Force Transformation 2003, *Military transformation: a strategic approach*, Office of the Secretary of Defense, Washington, DC.

O'Malley, S. 2006, *Bush promises trial for Hicks*, viewed 1 December 2006 <http://www.news.com.au/story/0,10117,20774567-1702,00.html?from=public_rss>.

Online, B.N. 2001, *Cherie Blair attacks Taliban cruelty*, BBC News, 19 November, viewed 26 April 2007 <http://news.bbc.co.uk/2/hi/uk_news/politics/1663300.stm>.

Osgood, R.E. 1957, *Limited war: the challenge to American strategy*, University of Chicago Press, Chicago, IL.

—— 1979, *Limited war revisited*, Westview Press, Boulder, CO.

Osgood, R.E. and Tucker, R.W. 1967, *Force, order and justice*, Johns Hopkins University Press, Baltimore, MD.

Pantesco, J. 2006, *Australia repeats intent to seek Hicks return if charges not laid soon*, viewed 14 November 2006 <http://jurist.law.pitt.edu/paperchase/2006/11/australia-repeats-intent-to-seek-hicks.php>.

Paskins, B. 1976, 'What's Wrong with Torture?' *British Journal of International Studies*, vol. 2, no. 2, p. 141.

Patrick, S. 2006, 'Weak States and Global Threats: Fact or Fiction?' *Washington Quarterly*, vol. 29, no. 2, pp. 27–53.

PBS 2001, *Looking for Answers*, 9 October.

Perry, D.L. 1995, '"Repugnant Philosophy": Ethics, Espionage, and Covert Action', *Journal of Conflict Studies*, vol. 15, no. 1, pp. 92–115.

Pettman, J.J. 2004, 'Feminist International Relations after 9/11', *Brown Journal of World Affairs*, vol. 10, no. 2, pp. 85–96.

Pew Forum on Religion and Public Life 2002, *Just war tradition and the new war on terrorism*, viewed 27 February 2007 <http://pewforum.org/events/print.php?EventID=15>.

Pfaff, T. and Tiel, J.R. 2004, 'The Ethics of Espionage', *Journal of Military Ethics*, vol. 3, no. 1, pp. 6–10.

Philp, C. 2005, *Iraq's women of power who tolerate wife-beating and promote polygamy*, TimesOnline, 31 March, viewed 26 April 2007 <http://www.timesonline.co.uk/tol/news/world/iraq/article440798.ece>.

Pieth, M. 2002, 'Financing of Terrorism: Following the Money', *European Journal of Law Reform*, vol. 4, no. 2, pp. 365–76.

Pillar, P.R. 2006, 'Intelligence, Policy, and the War in Iraq', *Foreign Affairs*, vol. 85, no. 2, pp. 15–28.

Port Villa Presse 2004, *Pacific a soft terror target: US*, viewed 20 February 2007 <http://www.news.vu/en/news/RegionalNews/pacific-a-soft-terror-tar.shtml>.

Preston, E. 2002, 'The USA Patriot Act: New Adventures in American Extraterritoriality', *Journal of Financial Crime*, vol. 10, no. 2, pp. 104–16.

Pufendorf, S. 1994, 'On the Law of War', in C.L. Carr (ed.), *The political writings of Samuel Pufendorf*, Oxford University Press, Oxford, p. 285.

Quirk, M. 2004, 'Boost to US National Security With Signing of Bioshield', *The Lancet Infectious Diseases*, vol. 4, no. 9, p. 540.

Read, T.D., Salzberg, S.L., Pop, M., Shumway, M., Umayam, L., Jiang, L., Holtzapple, E., Busch, J.D., Smith, K.L., Schupp, J.M., Solomon, D., Keim, P. and Fraser, C.M. 2002, 'Comparative Genome Sequencing for Discovery of novel Polymorphisms in Bacillus Anthracis', *Science*, vol. 296, no. 5575, pp. 2028–33.

Record, J. 2003, *Bounding the war on terrorism*, US Army War College Strategic Studies Institute, Carlisle, PA.

Reinhart, T. 2006, *Road map to nowhere*, Verso, London; New York.

Rengger, N. 2004, 'Just a War against Terror? Jean Bethke Elshtain's Burden and American Power', *International Affairs*, vol. 80, no. 1, pp. 107–16.

Rentoul, J. 2001, *Tony Blair: prime minister*, Little, Brown, and Company, London.

Reus-Smit, C. 2005, 'Liberal Hierarchy and the Licence to Use Force', *Review of International Studies*, vol. 31, no. Special Issue, pp. 71–92.

—— 2005, 'Constructivism', in S. Burchill (ed.), *Theories of international relations*, 3rd edn, Palgrave Macmillan, London.

Reveron, D.S. 2006, 'Old Allies, New Friends: Intelligence-Sharing in the War on Terror', *Orbis: a journal of world affairs*, vol. 50, no. 3, pp. 453–68.

Richardson, L. 2006, *What terrorists want: understanding the terrorist threat*, John Murray, London.

Rider, B.A.K. 2004, 'Law: the War on Terror and Crime and the Offshore Centres: the "New" Perspective', in D. Masciandaro (ed.), *Global financial crime: terrorism, money laundering, and off shore centres*, Ashgate, Aldershot; Burlington, VT, pp. x, 256.

Roberts, A. 2004, 'Righting Wrongs or Wronging Rights? The United States and Human Rights Post-September 11', *European Journal of International Law*, vol. 15, no. 4, pp. 721–49.

—— 2005, 'The "War on Terror" in Historical Perspective', *Survival*, vol. 47, no. 2, pp. 101–30.

Roberts, G. 1999, 'The Counterproliferation Self-Help Paradigm: A Legal Regime for Enforcing the Norm Prohibiting the Proliferation of Weapons of Mass Destruction', *Denver Journal of International Law and Policy*, vol. 27, no. 3, pp. 483–518.

Robin, C. 2004, *Fear: the history of a political idea*, Oxford University Press, Oxford.

Rogers, P. 2006, *Iraq and the war on terror: twelve months of insurgency 2004/2005*, I.B. Tauris, London.

Rorty, R. 1989, *Contingency, irony, and solidarity*, Cambridge University Press, Cambridge; New York.

Ross, A.A.G. 2005, *Affective states: rethinking passion in global politics*, John Hopkins University Press, PhD dissertation.

—— 2006, 'Coming in from the Cold: Constructivism and Emotions', *European Journal of International Relations*, vol. 12, no. 2, pp. 197–222.

Ross, K. 2003, 'Globalization, Governance and Guns: Some Reflections on the South Pacific in the 1990s', *The Round Table*, vol. 92, no. 372, pp. 687–96.

Rossiter, CL 1949, 'Constitutional Dictatorship in the Atomic Age', *The Review of Politics*, vol. 11, no. 4, pp. 395–418.

Rotberg, R.I. 2002, 'Failed States in a World of Terror', *Foreign Affairs*, vol. 81, no. 4, pp. 127–40.

Rothwell, D. 2006, *David Hicks and the US military commissions process: next steps*, viewed 7 November 2006 <http://jurist.law.pitt.edu/forumy/2006/10/david-hicks-and-us-military.php>.

Rumsfeld, D. 2001, *Remarks at stakeout outside ABC TV studio, 28 October*, viewed 3 February 2005 <www.defenselink.mil/news/Oct2001/t10292001_t1028sd3.html>.

Safran Foer, J. 2005, *Extremely loud and extremely close.* Boston, MA: Houghton Mifflin Company.

Sagan, S.D. 2006, 'How to Keep the Bomb From Iran', *Foreign Affairs*, vol. 85, no. 5, pp. 45–59.

Sageman, M. 2004, *Understanding terror networks*, University of Pennsylvania Press, Philadelphia.

Sartre, J.-P. 2002, *Sketch for a theory of the emotions*, Routledge, London.

Saurette, P. 2006, 'You Dissin Me? Humiliation and Post 9/11 Global Politics', *Review of International Studies*, vol. 32, no. 3, pp. 495–522.

Scarry, E. 1985, *The body in pain: the making and unmaking of the world*, Oxford University Press, New York.

Schaap, Andrew. 2005. *Political reconciliation*. London: Routledge.

Scheff, T.J. 1994a, 'Emotions and Identity: A Theory of Ethnic Nationalism', in C.J. Calhoun (ed.), *Social theory and the politics of identity*, Blackwell, Oxford, pp. 277–303.

—— 1994b, *Bloody revenge: emotions, nationalism and war*, Westview Press, Boulder, Colorado.

Schelling, T.C. and Affairs, HUCfI 1966, *Arms and influence*, Yale University Press, New Haven, CT.

Scheuerman, W.E. 1994, *Between the norm and exception: the Frankfurt School and the rule of law*, MIT Press, Cambridge, MA

—— 2006, 'Carl Schmitt and the Road to Abu Ghraib', *Constellations*, vol. 13, no. 1, pp. 108–24.

Schmitt, C. 1985, *Political theology: four chpaters on the concept of sovereignty*, MIT Press, Cambridge, MA.

Schmidt, S. and Leob, V. 2003, "'She Was Fighting to the Death"; Details Emerging of W. Va. Soldier's Capture and Rescue', *Washignton Post*, 3 April.

—— 1996, *The concept of the political*, University of Chicago Press, Chicago, IL.

Schwarzenberger, G. 1955, 'The Fundamental Principles of International Law', in G. Schwarzenberger (ed.), *Recueil des Cours*, A.W. Sijthoff, Leiden, pp. 195–383.

Schwellenbach, N. 2005, 'Biodefense: a Plague of Researchers', *Bulletin of the Atomic Scientists*, vol. 61, no. 3, pp. 14–16.

Scott, J.B. 1934, *The Spanish origins of international law: Francisco De Vitoria and his law of nations*, Clarendon Press, Oxford.

Shane, S. 2004, *Bioterror fight may spawn new risks*, Baltimore Sun Online, viewed 29 June 2004 <http://www.baltimoresun.com/news/nationworld/bal–te.biodefense27jun27, 0,6098679.story>.

—— 2006, 'An Exotic Tool for Espionage: Moral Compass', *The New York Times*, 28 January.

Shapiro, J. 2006, 'Terrorist Organizations Inefficiencies and Vulnerabilities', paper presented to International Studies Association, San Diego, 22 March.

Shapiro, M.J. 1997, *Violent cartographies: mapping cultures of war*, University of Minnesota Press, Minneapolis, MN.

Sharman, J.C. 2006, *Havens in a storm: the struggle for global tax regulation*, Cornell University Press, Ithaca, NY.

—— and Mistry, P.S. 2006, *Developmental Implications of Recent International*

Sheehan, M. 2005, *International security: an analytical survey*, Lynne Rienner Publishers, Boulder, CO.

Shehadi, N. 2004, Interview with author, 30 July.

Shilling, C. 1997, 'Emotions, Embodiment and the Sensation of Society', *Sociological Review*, vol. 45, no. 2, pp. 195–219.

Shklar, J.N. 1984, *Ordinary vices*, Belknap Press of Harvard University Press, Cambridge, MA; London.

Shlaim, A. 2000, *The iron wall: Israel and the Arab world*, London: Penguin

Shue, H. 1978, 'Torture', *Philosophy and Public Affairs*, vol. 7, no. 2, pp. 124–43.

Shulsky, A.N. 1993, *Silent warfare: understanding the world of intelligence*, Brassey's, Washington, DC.

Shumway, C. 2005, 'Rise of Extremism, Islamic Law Threaten Iraqi Women', *The New Standard*, 30 March, viewed 26 April 2007 <http://newstandardnews.net/content/index. cfm/items/1600>.

Sica, V. 2000, 'Cleaning the Laundry: States and the Monitoring of the Financial System', *Millennium*, vol. 29, no. 1, pp. 47–72.

Sidel, V. 2002, 'Defense Against Biological Weapons: Can Immunization and Secondary Prevention Succeed?' in S. Wright (ed.), *Biological warfare and disarmament: new problems, new perspectives*, Rowman and Littlefield, Lanham, MD.

Silke, A. 2005, 'Fire of Iolaus: The Role of Countermeasures in Causing Terrorism and What Needs to be Done', in T. Bjørgo (ed.), *Root causes of terrorism: myths, reality, and ways forward*, Routledge, London; New York.

Simma, B. 2002, *The charter of the United Nations: a commentary*, Oxford University Press, Oxford.

Singer, P. 2004, *The president of good and evil: the ethics of George W. Bush*, Dutton, New York.

Slaughter, A.-M. 1995, 'International Law in a World of Liberal States', *European Journal of International Law*, vol. 6, no. 3, pp. 503–38.

—— 2000, 'A Liberal Theory of International Law', *Proceedings of the American Society of International Law*, vol. 94, pp. 240–9.

—— 2003, 'Leading Through Law', *The Wilson Quarterly*, vol. 27, no. 4, pp. 37–44.

—— 2005, 'A Brave New Judicial World', in M. Ignatieff (ed.), *American exceptionalism and human rights*, Princeton University Press, Princeton, NJ, pp. 277–303.

Smith, R. 2005, *The utility of force: the art of war in the modern world*, Allen Lane, London.

Smith, S. 2005, 'The Contested Concept of Security', in K. Booth (ed.), *Critical security studies and world politics*, Lynne Rienner Publishers, Boulder, CO, pp. 47–63.

Snow, T. 2006, *Interview with the Vice-President by Tony Snow, 29 March*, March 2007 <http://www.whitehouse.gov/news/releases/2006/03/20060329–2.html>.

Snyder, J. 2003, 'Imperial Temptations', *National Interest*, vol. 71, no. spring, pp. 29–40.

Sofaer, A.D. 1986, 'Terrorism and the Law', *Foreign Affairs*, vol. 64, no. 5, p. 901.

—— 2003, 'On the Necessity of Pre-Emption', *European Journal of International Law*, vol. 14, no. 2, pp. 209–26.

Solomon, R.C. 1993, *The passions: emotions and the meaning of life*, 2nd edn, Hackett, Indianapolis.

—— 2003, *Not passion's slave: emotions and choice*, Oxford University Press, Oxford.

Stabile, C.A. and Kumar, D. 2005, 'Unveiling Imperialism: Media, Gender, and the War on Afghanistan', *Media, Culture and Society*, vol. 27, no. 5, pp. 765–82.

Stalenheim, P., Fruchart, D., Omitoogun, W. and Perdomo, C. 2006, 'Military Expenditure', in Stockholm International Peace Research Institute (SIPRI) (ed.), *SIPRI yearbook 2006*, Oxford University Press, Oxford.

Stephens, A. and Connery, D. 2006, 'Defence Transformation', in D. Ball and R. Ayson (eds), *Strategy and security in the Asia Pacific*, Allen and Unwin, Sydney.

Stephens, P. 2004, *Tony Blair: the price of leadership*, Politico's, London.

Stevens, K.R. 2004, *Border diplomacy: the Caroline and McLeod affairs in Anglo-American-Canadian relations*, University of Alabama Press, Montgomery, AL.

Stewart, J.G. 2006, 'Rethinking Guantanamo: Unlawful Confinement as Applied in International Criminal Law', *Journal of International Criminal Justice*, vol. 4, no. 1, pp. 12–30.

Steyn, J. 2004, 'Guantanamo Bay: The Legal Black Hole', *International and Comparative Law Quarterly*, vol. 53, no. 1, pp. 1–15.

Stiehm, J.H. 1982, 'The Protected, the Protector, the Defender', *Women's Studies International Forum*, vol. 5, no. 3/4, pp. 367–76.

Suárez, F. 1944a, *Selections from three works: De triplici virtute theologica, fide, spe, et caritate*, Carnegie Classics on International Law, New York.

—— 1944b, 'On war', in G. Williams (ed.), *Selections from three works*, Oxford University Press, Oxford.

Sullivan, N.J., Geisbert, T.W., Geisbert, J.B., Xu, L., Yang, Z., Roederer, M., Koup, R.A., Jahrling, P.B. and Nabel, G.J. 2003, 'Accelerated Vaccination for Ebola Virus Haemorrhagic Fever in Non-Human Primates', *Nature*, vol. 424, no. 6949, pp. 681–4.

Supreme Court of the United States (2006) 'Hamdan v. Rumsfeld, Secretary of Defense, et al.', Bench Opinion. Cited as: 548 US 2006.

Sydney Morning Herald 2005, 'How Habib Became one of the "Worst of the Worst"', viewed 1 December 2006 <http://www.smh.com.au/news/Anti-Terror-Watch/How-Habib-became-one-of-the-worst-of-the-worst/2005/01/12/1105423542199.html>.

—— 2006, 'Hicks' Lawyers in Bid to Bring Him Home', viewed 6 December 2006 <http://www.smh.com.au/news/national/hicks-lawyers-in-bid-to-bring-him-home/2006/12/06/1165081013265.html>.

Takacs, S. 2005, 'Jessica Lynch and the Regeneration of American Identity and Power Post 9/11', *Feminist Media Studies*, vol. 5, no. 3, pp. 297–310.

Taylor, S.A. and Snow, D. 1997, 'Cold War Spies: Why They Spied and How They Got Caught', *Intelligence and National Security*, vol. 12, no. 2, pp. 101–25.

Tesón, F.R. 1998, *A philosophy of international law*, Westview Press, Boulder, CO.

—— 2005, 'Ending Tyranny in Iraq', *Ethics and International Affairs*, vol. 19, no. 2, pp. 1–20.

The Age 2004, *The charges against David Hicks*, viewed 1 December 2006 <http://www.theage.com.au/articles/2004/06/13/1087065029888.html?from=storylhs>.

Travalio, G. and Altenburg, J. 2003, 'Terrorism, State Responsibility, and the Use of Military Force', *Chicago Journal of International Law*, vol. 4, no. 1, pp. 97–119.

Tucker, J.B. 2004, 'Biological Threat Assessment: Is the Cure Worse Than the Disease?' *Arms Control Today*, vol. 34, no. 8, pp. 13–9.

Tucker, R.W. 1960, *The just war: a study in contemporary doctrine*, Johns Hopkins University Press, Baltimore, MD.

Tushnet, M.V. 2005, 'Emergencies and the Idea of Constitutionalism', in M.V. Tushnet (ed.), *The constitution in wartime: beyond alarmism and complacency*, Duke University Press, Durham NC, pp. 39–54.

United Nations 1998, *Financial havens, bank secrecy and money laundering*, United Nations Office on Drug Control and Crime Prevention, Vienna.

United Nations High-level Panel on Threats Challenges and Change 2004, *A more secure world our shared responsibility: report of the High-level Panel on Threats, Challenges, and Change*, United Nations <http://www.un.org/secureworld/>.

United Sates Department of Defense 2004, *Charge sheet – David Hicks*, viewed 7 November 2006 <http://www.defenselink.mil/news/Jun2004/d20040610cs.pdf>.

—— 2005a, *JTF-GTMO information on detainees*, viewed 7 November 2006 <http://www.google.com.au/search?hl=en&q=jtf-gtmo+Information+on+detainees&meta=>.

—— 2005b, *The national defense strategy of the United States of America*, viewed 26 March 2007 <http://www.defenselink.mil/news/Mar2005/d20050318nds1.pdf>.

—— 2006a, *Quadrennial defense review report*, viewed 1 March 2007 <http://www.globalsecurity.org/military/library/policy/dod/qdr-2006-report.pdf>.

—— 2006b, *Detainee transfer announced*, viewed 1 December 2006 <http://www.defenselink.mil/Releases/Release.aspx?ReleaseID=10081>.

—— 2006c, *Military commissions fact sheet*, viewed 1 December 2006 <http://www.defenselink.mil/news/Oct2006/d20061016factsheet.pdf>.

—— 2006d, *Commission transcripts, exhibits, and allied papers – David Hicks*, viewed 1 December 2006 <http://www.defenselink.mil/news/commissions_exhibits_hicks.html>.

US 2002, *The national security strategy of the United States of America*, Washington, DC, September.

US Department of State 2005, *Victims of trafficking and violence protection act of 2000: trafficking in persons report*, US Department of State, Washington.

US Treasury 2005, *Money laundering threat assessment*, US Treasury, Washington, DC.

USAID 2005, *Fragile states strategy*, USAID, Washington, DC.

Van Creveld, M.L. 1991, *The transformation of war*, Free Press; Collier Macmillan Canada; Maxwell Macmillan International, New York; Toronto.

Van Evera, S. 1990, 'Why Europe Matters, Why the Third World Doesn't: American Grand Strategy After the Cold War', *Journal of Strategic Studies*, vol. 13, no. 2, pp. 1–51.

—— 2006, 'Bush Administration, Weak on Terror', *Middle East Policy*, vol. 13, no. 4, pp. 28–38.

Van Fossen, A. 2003, 'Money Laundering, Global Financial Instability and Tax Havens in the Pacific Islands', *Contemporary Pacific*, vol. 15, no. 2, pp. 237–75.

Vattel, E. 1916, *The law of nations and the principles of natural law applied to the conduct and to the affairs of nations and sovereigns*, Carnegie Institution, Washington, DC.

Vernant, J-P. 1982, *The origins of Greek thought*, Cornell University Press, Ithaca, NY.

Vitoria, F.D. 1991, *Vitoria: Political writings* edited and translated by Anthony Pagden , Cambridge: Cambridge University Press.

Walt, S.M. 2006, *Taming American power: the global response to US primacy*, W.W. Norton, New York.

Walzer, M. 1973, 'Political Action: the Problem of Dirty Hands', *Philosophy and Public Affairs*, vol. 2, no. 2, pp. 160–80.

—— 1977, *Just and unjust wars: a moral argument with historical illustrations*, Basic Books, New York.

—— 1992, *Just and unjust wars: a moral argument with historical illustrations*, 2nd edn, Basic Books, New York.

—— 2004, *Arguing about war*, Yale University Press, New Haven, CT; London.

Warrick, J. 2006, 'The Secretive Fight Against Bioterror', *Washington Post*, 30 July, p. A01.

Webster, D. 1983, 'Letter to Sir Henry Stephen Fox', in K.E. Shewmaker (ed.), *The Papers of Daniel Webster: Diplomatic Papers, Volume 1: 1841–1843*, University of New England Press, Armidale.

Wechsler, W. 2001, 'Follow the Money', *Foreign Affairs*, vol. 80, pp. 40–57.

Weeks, L. 2007, *Silence no longer an option, says Fonda*, The Sydney Morning Herald, 29 January, viewed 26 April 2007 <http://www.smh.com.au/news/world/fonda-speaks-out-on-iraq/2007/01/28/1169919213371.html>.

Weisman, S.R. 2003, 'Pre-emption Evolves from an Idea to Official Action', *New York Times*, 23 March, p. B1.

Wheeler, N.J. 2000, *Saving strangers: humanitarian intervention in international society*, Oxford University Press, Oxford; New York.

White House 2003, *Statement of the Atlantic Summit: A vision for Iraq and the Iraqi people*, 16 March, viewed 25 March 2007. <http://whitehouse.gove/news/releases/2003/03/20030316-1.html>

—— 2006a, *President Bush Signs Military Commissions Act of 2006*, Office of the Press Secretary, viewed 1 December 2006 <http://www.whitehouse.gov/news/releases/2006/10/print/20061017-1.html>.

—— 2006b, *President discusses creation of military commissions to try suspected terrorists*, Office of the Press Secretary, viewed 15 March 2007 <http://www.whitehouse.gov/news/releases/2006/09/20060906-3.html>.

Wilkinson, M. and Pearlmann, J. 2004, *Military trial only option for Hicks, says Ruddock*, viewed 18 December 2006 <http://www.smh.com.au/articles/2004/01/22/1074732544937.html>.

Williams, C. 2006, 'Terrorism', in D. Ball and R. Ayson (eds), *Strategy and security in the Asia Pacific*, Allen and Unwin, Sydney.

Williams, S.J. 2001, *Emotion and social theory: corporeal reflections on the (ir)rational*, Sage, London; Thousand Oaks, CA.

Winer, J.M. 2002, 'Globalization, Terrorist Finance, and Global Conflict: Time for a White List?' *European Journal of Law Reform*, vol. 4, no. 2, pp. 255–90.

Wippman, D. 2005, 'Introduction: Do New Wars Call for New Laws?' in D. Wippman and M. Evangelista (eds), *New wars, new laws?: applying the laws of war in 21st century conflicts*, Transnational Publishers, Ardley, NY, pp. 1–28.

Wolff, C. 1934, *Jus gentium*, Carnegie Classics on International Law, New York.

Woods, N. 2005, 'The Shifting Politics of Foreign Aid', *International Affairs*, vol. 81, no. 2, pp. 393–409.

Woodward, B. 2004, *Plan of attack*, Simon and Schuster, New York.

Wroe, D. 2005, 'Iraq was motive for bombing: suspect', *The Age*, 2 August, p. 1.

Yoch Jr, J.M. 2006, *Hicks to challenge US military commissions law*, viewed 7 November 2006 <http://jurist.law.pitt.edu/paperchase/2006/10/hicks-to-challenge-us-military.php>.

Yoo, J. 2004, 'Using Force', *The University of Chicago Law Review*, vol. 71, no. 3.

—— 2006, *War by other means: an insider's account of the war on terror*, Atlantic Monthly Press, New York.

Young, I.M. 2003, 'Feminist Reactions to the Contemporary Security Regime', *Hypatia*, vol. 18, no. 1, pp. 223–31.

Zoya 2006, *Five years later, Afghanistan still in flames*, 7 October, viewed 26 April 2007 <http://www.rawa.org/zoya_oct7-06.htm>.

Zylinska, J. 2004, 'Mediating Murder: Ethics, Trauma and the Price of Death', *Journal of Cultural Research*, vol. 8, no. 3, pp. 232–35.

Index

abaya (full length Islamic dress) 50, 51
Abbasid Caliphate 22
Abdel-Kader, Salah 51
Abu Ghaith, Suleiman 33–4
Abu Ghraib 40, 43, 48, 53, 103, 174
Abu Sayyaf 21
Acton, Lord 157
Afghanistan: al-Qaeda 14, 21, 22, 23,
    195; cause and effects of of military
    intervention 27, 28, 31, 32; detention of
    Hicks 81, 83; as failed state generating
    terrorism 136–7; invasion by US and
    allies (2001) 71, 119; policies for
    reconstruction 16–17; prisoners moved
    to Guantanamo Bay from 71, 72, 74;
    war of response to terrorism 3, 61, 194
Afghan women 42, 43, 44–5, 53
Africa 15, 28, 127, 192, 198
African National Congress 20
Agamben, Giorgio 77–9, 87, 89, 91, 125,
    130, 131–2
Ahmed, Sara 63
Albright, Madeleine 134
Algeria 21
Alibek, Ken 144, 153
Amnesty International 76
ancient Greek philosophy: approach to
    emotions 64; distinction betwen natural
    and political life 131
Annan, Kofi 2
anthrax: envelope attacks (2001) 142, 148;
    use of *B anthracis* in Iraq 154
Aquinas, St Thomas 97, 100, 101
Arab states: al Qaeda's objectives 21
Arafat, Yasser 36
Arendt, Hannah 131
Aristotle 131
armed attack: and pre-emptive action
    109–10, 111, 117

armed conflict *see* law of armed conflict
Armitage, Richard 32
Ashcroft, John 148
Asia 198; *see also* Northeast Asia;
    Southeast Asia
asymmetric warfare 29
Athenian empire 3
Atta, Mohammed 186, 188
Augustine of Hippo, St 4, 94–5, 97, 100,
    101
Australia: agreement to hand over
    detainees 175; assumptions about
    failed states 137; debates surrounding
    women's wearing of veil 43;
    experiment with mousepox virus
    144; good governance as focus of aid
    programme 140; government's refusal
    to seek release of Hicks 73, 83, 90; part
    in invasion of Iraq (March 2003) 36;
    post-9/11 foreign and security policies
    190; Resistance to Interrogation
    Training of soldiers 170
Australian Defense Forces (ADF) 81
Australian Law Commission 67
authoritarian governments 11
'axis of evil' states 19–20, 133, 135

Baader-Meinhof group 20
Baghdad 22
Bailey, Charles 144
Bali bombings 2, 27, 32, 60, 181, 185
Balkans 127; *see also* Bosnia; Macedonia
banks: measures to counter terrorist
    finance 177, 182–3, 186–7
Barcham, Manuhuia 138
Basque Homeland and Freedom 21
Beirut 34, 35
Benjamin, Daniel 194, 196
Berra, Yogi 161

Best, Geoffrey 158

Bin Laden, Osama: alliance with al-Zarqawi 22; business properties 15; Clinton's failure to act against 114; declaration of war against US 35; downplaying of own importance 21; on fatwa against Americans 33; idea of international tribunal to try 40; impact of Israeli invasion of Lebanon 34; on language of force 134; power of the example in speeches 39; and Salim Ahmed Hamdan 84; statement during 2004 US election campaign 25–6, 36

biodefence programmes 142, 143, 150–4, 154–5; research 145–9, 154

biological weapons (BW) 142, 147; threat assessments 150–2, 155

Biological Weapons Convention (BWC) (1972) 150–1, 153

biopolitics 132, 139

biosecurity 147–9

Biosecurity and Bioterrorism 144

bioterrorism 142–3; pharmaceutical defence 142, 143–5, 154

Black, Cofer 164

Blair, Cherie 45, 53

Blair, Tony 1, 194; rhetoric on war on terror 97, 99, 100, 102–3

Bleiker, Roland 134, 135

Bosnia 28, 134, 191, 192

Bowden, Mark 175

Bowett, D.W. 120

Bowker, D.W. 164

Bragg, Rick 46

Bremmer, Paul 18

Britain: bugging of French embassy (1960–3) 159; campaign to block US funds to IRA 178; freeing of citizens detained in Guantanamo 72, 81, 83; invasion of Iraq (March 2003) 31, 36; support for Israel's 2006 invasion of Lebanon 38; *see also* United Kingdom (UK)

British Institute of International and Comparative Law 71

British Medical Association (BMA) 145, 153

Bryant, Christopher 98

Burkitt, Ian 63

Bush, George H.W. 35

Bush, George W.: alignment of failed states with terrorist threat 136, 137; 'Bush doctrine' 11–12, 197; declaration of campaign against terrorist finance 177, 181; declaration on fall of Saddam 195; and detention of prisoners in Guantanamo Bay 71, 81; on imminence of terrorist threat 113; justifications for war in Iraq 4, 51, 60, 118; Netanyahu's praise of 33; order to treat prisoners 'humanely' 174; rhetoric on war on terror 93, 97–8, 100, 102–3, 117–18, 129; on rogue states 117–18, 133, 193, 194

Bush, Laura 42, 45, 53

Bush administration: arguments for non-proliferation strategy 19–20; attempts to defend Lynndie England and colleagues 49; biodefence programmes 143; claim of right to act pre-emptively 106; defiance of international law regarding Guantanamo Bay 73, 75–6, 78; gendered politics 47–8; macho foreign policy 135; military response to 9/11 attacks 36; policies for reconstruction of Iraq 17–19, 23–4; presentation of Islamist threat 1

Buzan, B. 12

Bybee, Jay 80

Byers, M. 120–1

Campbell, David 66

Canada 112, 154

Canberra 129

Caroline, dispute over sinking of 107, 111–13, 117

Carr, E.H. 1, 117

Caruth, Cathy 59

Center for Disease Control (CDC) 146

Centre for Constitutional Rights 81

Chalabi, Ahmed 18

Chechnya 21

Cheney, Richard 37, 118, 194

China 12, 152, 194

Christianity: Blair's values 98

CIA (Central Intelligence Agency) 35, 164, 174, 183

civil liberties: curtailment in name of state security 11, 13

Clarke, Jonathan 135, 195

Clark, W.K. 3

classical realism 190

Clausewitz, K. von 26, 27–8, 30, 41, 127

Clinton, Bill 114, 133, 154

Cold War: defectors 162; dualistic thinking 3, 5, 60, 61, 190; end of 2, 125, 126, 140, 190, 191; exchange of captured spies 158; intelligence gathering 161,

163, 164; nuclear deterrence 169;
policy analyses of threats 67
Combatant Status Review Tribunal (CSRT)
86
Commonwealth 179
communism: Cold War 61, 162; limited
wars against 29
Communist Party of Nepal-Maoists 21
community: development of belligerent
forms 58–9; emotions linked with 57,
61–2, 64–7; impact of terrorist attack
on 59–62; importance in rethinking
security policy 68
conflict zones: new paradigm of war 28
Connery, David 29, 30
Connolly, William 58, 64, 66
Cordesman, Anthony 38–9
Council of Europe 178, 179
Council on Foreign Relations 183
countering financing of terrorism (CFT):
anti-money laundering laws 183–5;
international campaign 177, 179–81;
results and outlook 186–9; US response
181–3, 186
counter-insurgency 22
counter-terrorism 13, 15, 27, 31–2
Covenant of the League of Nations 97, 99
Crawford, Neta 58, 64
Creveld, Martin van 28
criminal activities: al Qaeda 21
critical security studies (CSS) 193
Cronin, Audrey Kurth 14, 20–1, 23
Cuba: Guantanamo Bay 74
Czechoslovakia 109

Dahlstrom, Elizabeth 79, 80
Danchev, Alex 195
Darby, Philip 66
Dar es Salaam 35
Darfur 1
Daschle, Tom 142
Davies, Sara E 197
defence transformation 29, 38–9
Democratic Republic of Congo (DRC) 1
derogation: historical right 77, 78–80,
87–8
Derrida, Jacques 133
detention without charge 172
deterrence: Cold War nuclear threat 169;
limited ability to constrain terrorism
114; posture of US Office of Force
Transformation 31
development: fusion with security 139–40
difference: relationship with identity 66–7

Dodge, T. 17
Downer, Alexander 137–8
drug trafficking: measures against 180; al
Qaeda's engagement in 21; 'War on
Drugs' 178, 184
Duffield, Mark 139–40
Duffy, Helen 79
Düsseldorf 186
Dylan, Bob 103

Economist 177, 187
effects-based operations (EBO) 29, 30, 31,
38–9
Egypt 111, 119
Elshtain, Jean Bethke 93, 94–5, 96, 97, 98,
99, 100, 102
emotions: links with identity and
community 57, 58–62; manipulation to
justify policies 57, 60, 67–8; scholarly
views 62–4; security's linkage with 57,
58–9, 61–2, 65–9; triggered by terrorist
attacks 57, 58–9, 62–4, 66–7
England, Lynndie 43, 48–9, 53
ethics: arguments for and against
intelligence gathering 156–8;
arguments for and against torture
171–2; guidelines for intelligence
gathering 172–4; issues in interrogation
of prisoners 174–5; issues in security
policy decisions 65–6
ethnic cleansing 127
Euben, R.L. 3
Europe: security concerns over Balkan
conflicts 192
extraordinary rendition 175

failed states 125; alignment with terrorist
threat 129, 136–8, 140, 194; move to
centre of global politics post-9/11
128–9; North's response to 132–3,
139–40; in spaces of exception 132
Falluja 18–19, 75, 103
fatwa: Bin Laden's declaration (1998) 33,
35
Fauci, Anthony 146
fear, politics of 60, 61, 68
Federation of American Scientists (FAS)
152
Feinstein, L. 115
Feith, Douglas 17–18
Feliciano, F.P. 119–20
feminism: analysis of war on terror's effect
on women's security 42, 43, 49, 52–3
Ferejohn, John 130

finance *see* countering financing of
   terrorism
Financial Action Task Force (FATF)
   179–81, 184–5
Fiorill, J. 144
First Gulf War (1991) 96, 195
First World War 45, 98–9
Food and Drug Administration (FDA) 143
force: Clausewitzian concept 27–8, 31,
   41; in just wars 95–6, 97; language of
   134–5; new concepts 28–9; new US
   strategies 31, 117–18, 134; and right of
   pre-emption 121; right to use in self-
   defence 106; *see also* military force
Foreign Affairs 58
foreign policy: Bush administration's
   macho approach 135; post-9/11 realist
   reactionism 190; powerful states 191
Forsyth, John 112
Foucault, Michel 131
France 83, 159, 194
Freedman, L. 12, 102
Frum, D. 116
Fukuyama, Francis 33, 128, 191

G7 members 178–9, 184
Garner, Jay 18
Gaza 26, 31, 35
Gazit, Shlomo 27
gendered identities 43, 44, 45, 47–8, 49, 53
Geneva Conventions 40, 80; issues
   regarding Guantanamo detainees 72,
   73, 84, 85, 86, 88–9; liberal states'
   ability to create legal excepions to 75;
   US deviations from 73, 85, 103
genocides 127, 192
Germany 4, 112, 117, 186; *see also* West
   Germany
Gilpin, Robert 127
Glennon, M.J. 116
'global commons' 31
global war on terror (GWoT): Bush
   doctrine 11–12, 103; effects on security
   and international relations 10–11;
   Pentagon's agenda for transformation
   30–1; problematic nature of term 1–2,
   12–13; in Sharon's justification of force
   against Palestinians 36
Godfrey, E.D. 161
Goldgeier, James 127
good and evil: Bush and Blair's rhetoric
   60, 98; Manichean narratives 10, 19,
   134
Gore, Al 61

Graner, Charles 48–9
Gray, Chris Hables 28
Greece 110
Greek civilisation *see* Athenian empire
Greenberg, Karen 164
Greener-Barcham, Beth 138
Greenwood, C. 80
Gross, O. 75
Grotius, Hugo 93, 100, 101–2, 104, 108
Guantanamo Bay: Agamben's view as
   zone of anomie 78, 79, 87, 89; Camp
   X-Ray 40, 103; case of David Hicks
   72–3, 81–4, 87, 89, 90, 91; case of
   Salim Ahmed Hamdan 84–6, 89;
   conditions of detention 71–2; goals
   pursued by US 165, 197; key points
   regarding legal status 86–91, 167;
   legalist challenge 79–81, 89; legal
   status of detainees 72, 73–5, 87

Hague Conventions 85
Haitian refugees 74
Halliday, F. 1
Halper, Stefan 135, 195
Hamas 31, 35, 40
Hamburg 186
Hamdan, Salim Ahmed 84–5, 88, 89
Hamdan v. Rumsfeld case 83, 84–6, 87
Harman, Sabrina 48
Hatfill, Steven 148
Herat 17
Hezb-i-Islami 17
Hezbollah 34–5, 40
Hicks, David 72–3, 81–4, 87, 89, 90, 91
hijab (veil) 43, 51
Hills, Alice 18–19
Hindess, Barry 132
Hiroshima 39
Hobbes, Thomas 68, 132, 135, 158
Hoffman, Paul 76, 79
homeland defense 14
homo sacer 131–2, 140
honour killings 51
Howard, John 136, 137
humanitarian interventions 127, 128, 129,
   140
human rights: issues in intelligence
   gathering 167, 175
human rights abuses: against Guantanamo
   Bay detainees 71–2, 74; in interrogation
   of suspected terrorists 164
Humphreys, S. 77
Huntington, Samuel 61
Hunt, S. 52

Hussein, Saddam 35, 47, 133; overthrowing of 40, 195–6; women's rights
  under 51, 52
Huxsoll, David 151

identity: emotions linked with 57, 59–60,
  61–2, 63, 64–7; importance in approach
  to security policy 66–7, 68
Ignatieff, Michael 128
Ikenberry, J.G. 106
India 12, 19, 117
Indonesia 2, 16
industrial warfare: First World War 98–9;
  outdated concept 28; weapons of 9/11
  attack 12
Indyk, Martin 133
information technology 15, 22
insurgency 22–3
intelligence gathering 156; before war on
  terror 158; ethical guidelines 172–4;
  ethical objections and justifications
  156–8; methods of collection 160–3;
  pressures to expand means of 164–5;
  since 9/11 163–4; those targeted for
  158–60; in war on terror 166,
  167–72
International Atomic Energy Agency 20
International Committee of the Red Cross
  (ICRC) 71
International Convention Against Torture
  (1984) 158, 170, 175
International Court of Justice (ICJ) 110,
  110–11, 119
International Covenant on Civil and
  Political Rights (ICCPR) 79, 80
International Institute of Strategic Studies
  32
international law: concerns regarding
  Guantanamo Bay 73, 75–6, 79, 80, 87,
  88; illegality of Bush's pre-emptive
  self-defence 11; new liberal arguments
  for re-ordering of 113, 115; new
  realists' view of 113, 115–17; right to
  use self-defence 109–14
International Monetary Fund (IMF) 179
international relations: effect of global war
  on terrorism on 11; North–South divide
  in post-Cold War analyses 129
International Security Assistance Force
  (ISAF) 16
Iqbal, Asif 81
Iran 19, 20
Iraq: alleged program for WMD 2; current
  state of chaos and fuelling of terrorism

138, 196; as failed state 138; Israel's
  air strike against nuclear reactor 111;
  Muslims killed by US and Israel in
  past decade 33–4; new constitution
  51–2; policies for reconstruction
  17–19; al Qaeda 22, 23; as rogue state
  133; suicide bombings 58; US non-
  proliferation strategy 19; US strategies
  of force 31
Iraqi Lawyers Association 51
Iraqi women: worsening of security
  situation 49–52
Iraq war: as anticipatory war 97; attempts
  to justify 98, 194–5; dramatic rescue
  of Private Jessica Lynch 46–9; final
  economic cost to US 10; new paradigm
  of war 28; as response to terrorism 3,
  4, 27, 36, 61, 194; worsening security
  situation of women 49–52
Irgun/Stern Gang 20
Irish Republican Army (IRA) 178;
  Provisional IRA 20; Real IRA 20, 21
Islamic charities 180, 186
Islamic fundamentalism: Afghanistan 46;
  post-invasion Iraq 51
Islamism: arguments for killing of civilians
  34; interpretations of Western actions
  39; linked with terrorism 1, 192;
  in new Iraqi constitution 52; prime
  importance of religious identity 33; rise
  of movements 14
Israel: Hezbollah's guerilla war with
  35; killing of Muslims in Iraq and
  Palestine 33–4; military operations
  against Palestinians 27, 31, 36; policies
  of causal importance to 9/11 26–7;
  possession of nuclear weapons 19;
  pre-9/11 Islamist terrorism against 2;
  pre-emptive attacks by 111, 119; war
  on Lebanon (2006) 26, 31, 38
Italy 178
Al Itihad Al Islamiya 15

Jackson, Richard 40
Jakarta: bombing of Australian embassy
  36, 37
James, William 64
Al Jazeera 25
Jemaah Islamiyah 36
The Jerusalem Post 32–3
jihad 21, 34–5, 40, 196
Johns, Fleur 79
Johnson, James Turner 4, 93, 95–6, 97, 98,
  99–100, 102

Johnson, William 174
Jones, R.V. 159, 160
Jones, Seth 16–17
Jordan 50
just war: contemporary theories 93–7, 102, 103–4; importance of *Caroline* case 107, 113, 118; and notion of vindictive justice 100–2; in self-defence 99–100, 106, 108–9

Kabul 16
Kaldor, Mary 28, 127, 191
Kandahar 17, 82
Kant, Immanuel 131, 157
Karprinski, Colonel Janis 49
Karzai, Hamid 16
Keenan, Tom 135
Keene, Edward 128
Kellogg-Briand Pact (1928) 99, 109
Kelsen, Hans 110
Kenya 16
Kerry, John 25
Khan, A.Q. 19
Khan, Ismail 17
Khmer Rouge 21
Kilcullen, David 22
Kissinger, Henry 120, 150–1
Klein, Dale 144
Kollar-Kotelly, Colleen 84
Korch, George 151, 152
Kosovo 28, 116, 134
Kosovo Liberation Army (KLA) 81
KPMG (accounting firm) 187
Krasner, Stephen 136–7, 140
Krause, K. 193
Kumar, D. 46, 47
Kurdistan Workers Party 20, 21

Lashkar e Tayyiba (LET) 81
Lasky, M.P. 52
lawlessness: and collapse of Iraqi state 18; in situations of state collapse 15–16
law of armed conflict 165–6, 175
Lawrence, Bruce 25
lawyers: murdered and attacked in post-invasion Iraq 51
Leahy, Patrick 142
Lebanon: Israel's 1982 invasion 34–5; Israel's 2006 war on 26, 31, 38; Israel's new offensive against (1996) 35; US strategies of force 31
Leob, V. 47
Levinas, Emmanuel 66

liberal democracy: and counter-insurgency 22–3; justification of use of torture 76; US promotion of 13, 23, 39–40
liberal states: abandoning of principles in state of emergency 75–7, 87; North–South divide in international relations theory 129; suspension of principles regarding rogue states 134
Liberation Tigers of Tamil Eelam 178
Libya 19, 103
Lietzau, W. 73
limited wars 29, 38–9
London bombings (2005) 32, 37, 60, 76, 98, 185, 195
long war ideology 13–20, 23–4
Los Alamos National Laboratory, New Mexico 150
Luban, David 76
Lukes, Steven 76
Lynch, Jessica 43, 46–9, 53

McClintock, Anne 127–8
McDougal, M.S. 110, 119–20
Macedonia 187
McFaul, Michael 127
Machiavelli, Niccolò 157–8, 158
Mackey, C. 167, 167–8, 170
Madrid bombings 32, 37, 185
Maghreb 14
Makiya, Kanan 18
Marcus, G.E. 64
Marks, Susan 79, 80
Martyn, A. 82, 83
media: context of new paradigm of war 28; coverage of plight of Afghan women 44, 45–6; coverage of rescue of Private Jessica Lynch 46
Menkhaus, Ken 15–16, 138
Mercer, J. 58, 64
Middle East: Bush's arguments for promoting democracy in 39–40; terrorist threat 2
Military Commissions/Tribunals: to try Guantanamo detainees 72, 73, 81, 82, 84–5
Military Commissions Act (MCA) 90
military force: Bush administration's preference for 19; Clausewitzian reasoning 28; in Cold War mentality 5; Cordesman's concerns 39; post-9/11 response to terrorism 11, 27; strategic and moral issues 3; *see also* force
'military transformation' 29–30
Miller, Jon 33

Milosevic, Slobodan 134
Mohammed, Khaled Sheikh 35
Moïsi, Dominique 58
money laundering: anti-money laundering (AML) measures 178, 179, 183–5; differences with terrorist finance 185–6
morality: dual standards (Morgenthau's 'escape from power' theory) 196–7; framework of Bush-Blair rhetoric 100, 103; issues regarding mehtods of interrogation 167–8, 169; role of fear in foundations of 68
Morgenthau, Hans 117, 191, 196–7
Mori, Michael Dan 83, 84

Nagasaki 33, 39
Nairobi: bombing of US embassy 35
Nassiriya 46
National Biodefense Analysis and Countermeasures Center (NBACC) 151
National Institute for Allergy and Infectious Diseases (NIAID) 146, 148
National Institutes for Health (US) 146–7, 148
National Intelligence Estimates (US) 196
National Security Strategy (US government, 2002) 107, 114, 117–18
National Strategy for Combating Terrorism (NSC) (US government, 2006) 37
NATO (North Atlantic Treaty Organization) 12, 17, 40, 116, 134
Nature 145
Nauru 181–2, 183
Naylor, R.T. 187
NBC Nightly News 142
Neiman, Susan 5
neo-conservatives 32, 33, 195
Netanyahu, Benjamin 33
net-centric warfare 38–9
new liberals 113, 114–15
new realists 113, 115–17
'new wars: in post-Cold War underdeveloped world 127, 191–2
New York 59, 128
New York Post 142
New York Times 152, 187
Nicaragua v. US case 110–11
Nijaf 52
9/11 attacks: Bin Laden's admission of responsibility 25–6; and campaign against terrorist financing 177, 178; causal importance of US and Israeli policies 26; effects on North–South divide 126, 128, 129, 140; funding of

185–6; generation of culture of fear 60; impact on security of Western states 10, 190, 192–3, 198; as justifying exceptional acts by liberal states 76; potential as turning point for US foreign policy 36; significance for international politics 1–5; subsequent rhetoric of good versus evil 57, 60, 98; traumatic emotions triggered by 59, 67; US response 1, 3, 4, 11, 60, 192, 193–4
9/11 Commission Report (2004) 33
Nixon, Richard 153
non-state actors: complicating of non-proliferation strategy 20; as instruments of violence 127; al Qaeda 20, 75; *see also* terrorist movements/organisations
Northeast Asia 2
Northern Alliance 16, 81, 82, 83
Northern Ireland 28
North Korea: Bush's perception 135; nuclear test (October 2006) 2, 20; US non-proliferation strategy 19, 20
North–South divide 125; and changing strategic cartographies 126, 128; core and periphery states 127, 139; widening after end of Cold War 126–8
Norway: German invasion 112
Nuclear Non-Proliferaion Treaty 19
Nuclear Posture Review (2002) 20
nuclear weapons: advent 99; and limited war doctrines 29; US partnerships with states in possession of 19; *see also* weapons of mass destruction (WMD)
Nuremburg International Military Tribunal 85, 99, 112
Nussbaum, Martha 63–4

O'Brien, William V. 99
O'Donovan, Oliver 93, 96–7, 98, 99, 100, 102
OECD (Organization for Economic Cooperation and Development) 179, 186–7, 188
Office of the Coordinator for Reconstruction and Stabilization (S/CRS) 139
Operation Defensive Shield 40
Operation Enduring Freedom 12, 16, 23, 31, 44–5, 111
Operation Grapes of Wrath 35
Operation Infinite Justice 103
Operation Iraqi Freedom 23, 103
Operation Vigilant Justice 18–19
opium production 17

Organisation for Women's Freedom in
  Iraq 50
Osgood, Robert 29

Pacific Islands 138; *see also* Nauru
Pakistan: as base for terrorist organisations
  16, 17, 138; citizens detained in
  Guantanamo 72; Hicks's visit 81,
  82; possession of nuclear weapons
  19; prisoners moved to Guantanamo
  Bay from borders of 71, 74; al Qaeda
  contacts 21, 22, 195; ungoverned zones
  137
Palestine Liberation Organization (PLO)
  20, 34, 35
Palestinians: Intifada 35, 36; Islamic Jihad
  35; Israeli counter-terrorist strategy 27;
  Israelis' operations against authority
  of 31, 36; massacred during Lebanon
  war (1982) 34; Muslims killed by US
  and Israel in past decade 33–4; US
  strategies of force against 31
Pascual, C. 136–7
Pasquino, Pasquale 130
Patrick, Stewart 138
Paul, St 95, 96, 100–1
peace movements 99
Pearl Harbor 157
Pentagon: central role in Iraqi project
  17–18; gendered politics 47–8; Office
  of Transformation's new strategic
  concepts 29–31
People's Will 21
perfectionism (Morgenthau's 'escape from
  power' theory) 197
Perle, R. 116
Perry, D.L. 162, 173
Philippines 2, 16, 21, 31
Philp, C. 51–2
political life: distinction with 'bare' or
  natural life 131
Posa, C. 52
Powell, Colin 118, 174, 181
power: dynamics of abuse of Abu Ghraib
  prisoners 48; possessional and
  relational perspectives 18–19; Schmitt's
  view of sovereignty 130
powerful states: foreign policy 191
pre-emptive self-defence: ambiguity in
  UN Charter 106; approach permitting
  application against terrorism 107,
  118–21; Bush-Blair presentation of
  Iraq war as 98; Bush doctrine 11,
  106; in just war thinking 108–9, 113;

and legitimisation of war on terror
  61; reconceptualised to respond to
  terrorism 114, 118–21; US *Strategy*
  way of re-thinking 117–18
preventive attacks: Bush administration's
  strategy of 107, 118; forbidden in right
  of self-defence 111; labelled as pre-
  emptive by *Strategy* 117–18
prisoners of war: law of armed conflict
  165–6
Proliferation Security Initiative (PSI) 19
prostitution: Iraqi women 50
public health issues: biodefence 144–5,
  154
Public Health Security and Bioterrorism
  Preparedness Act 2002 147
Pufendorf, Samuel 108

Al Qaeda: in Afghanistan 16, 194, 195;
  allegations of Hicks's membership
  81, 82, 83; American targets in
  Iraq 5; campaign and ideology 26;
  development and organisation 14–15;
  financing of 186, 187; founding of
  (1988) 35; freezing of assets 178,
  181, 186; grievances and justification
  of attacks on the West 33–4; human
  consequences of Afghan wars as fuel
  for 27; idea of war against the West
  before 9/11 12; increased support since
  wars of response 4, 21; as non-state
  actor 20, 75; possible strategies for
  defeating 20–3; 'state of war' against
  14, 31–2, 88; strategies that could have
  weakened 40
Qana 35, 38
al-Qushtaini, Zeena 50
Qutb,... 40

Ramsey, Paul 95
Rasul, Shafiz 81
Rasul v. Bush case 81, 86
RAWA (Revolutionary Association of the
  Women of Afghanistan) 45–6
Reagan, Ronald 103
reconciliation 66–7, 68–9
Record, Jeffrey 30, 31–2, 33
Red Brigades 20
Red Cross 159, 161
regime change 116
responsibility: and idea of 'vindictive
  justice' 97; in interrogation of prisoners
  174–5; issues in security policy
  decisions 65–6

Reus-Smit, Christian 26
Revolutionary Armed Forces of Columbia
    21
revolution in military affairs (RMA) 29
Richardson, Louise 31
Roberts, A. 21, 23
Rogers, Paul 22
rogue states 125; Bush's rhetoric
    on 20, 117–18, 133, 193, 194;
    characterisations 133–4; identification
    of sources of terrorism with 129, 133,
    140, 194; imminence of threat from
    113, 121; North's response to 132, 134,
    140; role of deterrence 114; in spaces
    of exception 132
Roman antiquity: *homo sacer* 131–2
Ross, Andrew 58, 64
Rossiter, Clinton 130
Ross, Ken 138
Rotberg, Robert 136
Rumsfeld, Donald 13, 17–18, 29, 117
Russia 2, 117, 194
Rwanda 191

Safran Foyer, Jonathan 67
Sagan, Scott 20
satellite spy systems 161, 164
Saudi Arabia: al-Qaeda 14, 22; basing of
    US troops in 35; regulation of non-
    profit organisations 180, 183
Schaap, Andrew 66
Scheff, Thomas 63
Schelling, Thomas 29
Scheuerman, W.E. 75–6
Schmidt, S. 47
Schmitt, Carl 75, 76–7, 79, 86–7, 91,
    130–1, 132, 134
scientism: (Morgenthau's 'escape from
    power' theory) 196
Scott, James Brown 101
Scowcroft, Brent 151
Second World War 75
security: alternative approaches regarding
    terrorism 5–6, 193; changing
    context since Cold War 191–3;
    clusters of threats identified by UN
    9–10; definitions and conceptions 9;
    deterioration in Afghanistan 16–17;
    effect of narrowing of North–South gap
    129; fusion with development 139–40;
    linkage with emotions 57, 58–9, 61–2,
    65–9; need to rewrite Clausewitzian
    formulae 41; realist reactionism of
    policy responses 190, 191; regulation

of biotechnology sector 147–9; role
    of intelligence gathering 157–8, 159;
    significance of 9/11 attacks for West
    2–5, 10, 190, 192–3, 198; US policy's
    state-centric policy 194; 'war on terror'
    and worsening situation of women
    42–3
security agencies/organisations 165, 166
security studies: analyses of war on terror
    193–4; need to place terrorism in
    appropriate contexts 24
self-defence: in international law 109–14;
    and just war 99, 106, 108–9; right of
    106–7; *see also* pre-emptive self-
    defence
September 11 attacks *see* 9/11 attacks
Serbia 134
sexual abuse: of Abu Ghraib prisoners 48
sexual slavery: Iraqi women 50
Shapiro, J. 186
Shapiro, Michael 66
Shari'a 51, 52
Sharm El Sheikh 37
Sharon, Ariel 34, 35, 36
Shehadi, Nadim 39–40
Shi'a 51
Shining Path 20, 21
Shirzai, Gul Agha 17
Short, Clare 159
Sidon 35
Simma, B. 110
Simon, Steven 194, 196
Slaughter, Anne-Marie 115, 129
Smith, James 150
Smith, General Rupert 28, 29
Society for Worldwide Interbank Financial
    Telecommunications (SWIFT) 183
Sofaer, Abraham 106
Solomon, Robert 63–4
Somalia 15, 16, 138
South America 2
Southeast Asia 2, 14
sovereignty: Agamben's idea 131;
    Schmitt's view 130; US power to
    decide use of force 134
Soviet Union: biological weapons
    programme 153; collapse 126, 191;
    'evil empire' during Cold War 61;
    intervention in Czechoslovakia (1948)
    109; responses to spy-planes over 161
special forces operations 31
Srebrenica 1
Sri Lanka 178
state collapse 15–16

state of emergency: and derogation from ratification of international treaties 77; response of liberal states 75–6, 77
state of exception (SOE): ideas of Schmitt and Agamben 130–2; Iraq 138; legal 74–7, 91; North's view of South 125–6, 140–1; political 77–9, 91
state terrorism 13
Stephens, Alan 29, 30
Stevens, Justice 87, 88–9
Stevens, K.R. 112
Stevens, Robert 142
Stewart, James G. 79
Steyn, J. 71
Stiehm, J.H. 44
Stimson, Henry L. 156–7
strategic thought: Clausewitzian concept of force 27–8; new paradigm of war 28–9, 38; new western concepts 29–31; questioning traditional tenets 26–7
Strategy see National Strategy for Combating Terrorism
Suárez, Francisco 100, 101, 108
Sudan 14, 21
suicide bombings 35, 36, 58, 185
Sunnis 14
Syria 50, 137

Tajikistan 17
Takacs, S. 47
Taliban 16–17, 22, 31, 81, 186; claims about Afghan women suffering under 42, 44, 45, 46; overthrowing of regime by US 16, 111, 194
terrorism: alignment of failed states with 136–8, 140; alignment of rogue states with 129, 133, 140; emotions associated with 57, 58–9, 62–4, 65–6, 67; examination of cause and effect 26–7; globalisation and collapsing of distance 128; Gore's characterisation of 61; governments' application of label 13, 76; increase in attacks since start of war on terror 5; interdisciplinary approaches to dealing with 5–6, 24; nature of threat 2; and need to change way of thinking about security 5, 193; need to understand grievances behind 32–3, 34; notion of 'imminence' 113–14, 118–19; potential for mass destruction 171; pre-emptive self-defence to meet threat of 107, 118–21; problem of definition 170; small cost of attacks 185–6; as threatening as ever

today 61; trauma caused by 57, 59–62; *see also* 9/11 attacks; countering financing of terrorism; global war on terrorism; war on terrorism
terrorist movements/organisations: alternative strategies against 40–1; difficulties of intelligence gathering on 159; explanations for decline or end of 20–1; operation in weak states 16; recruitment of disenchanted individuals 3–4; use of force against 28
Tesón, Fernando 114
Thailand 2
Third World: post-Cold War decline in strategic significance 126
Thompson, Tommy 146
Tokyo Criminal Tribunal 99
torture: of Abu Ghraib prisoners 48; acts in war against terrorism 5, 164; debates about value 170–1; ethical arguments for and against 172–3; international law prohibiting 158, 170; in interrogation of prisoners 167, 169–70; problem of definition 170; used on Guantanamo detainees 76
totalitarianism (Morgenthau's 'escape from power' theory) 197
trauma 59–60; caused by terrorism 57, 62; need for security policy to address 65–6, 68
treason 162
Tucker, R.W. 29, 99

Al Ubaedey, Jenan 51–2
UN Charter 71, 97, 99, 100, 103, 106; Article 51 on right of self-defence 109–11, 116, 120
underdeveloped world: post-Cold War crises 126
Uniform Code of Military Justice (UCMJ) 72
United Arab Emirates (UAE) 186, 188
United Kingdom (UK): debates surrounding women's wearing of veil 43; deployment of troops to Iraq 195; dispute with US over sinking of *Caroline* 107, 111–12; engagement in spying on UN 159; post-9/11 foreign and security policies 190; redrafting of JIC memo regarding WMD 195; *see also* Britain; London bombings
United Nations (UN): Counter Terrorism Committee 179; General Assembly 111; High Level Panel

on Threats, Challenges, and Change
9; International Convention for the
Suppressing of Financing Terrorism
178, 180; Office on Drugs and Crime
179; al Qaeda and Taliban Sanctions
Committee 186; recent conflicts fought
by members 116; report on money
laundering 186; Security Council 20,
40, 98, 109, 111, 115, 118, 178, 194;
UK's engagement in spying on 159; *see
also* UN Charter
United States (US): agenda for
representation of Jessica Lynch 47; aid
committed to development 140; dispute
with UK over sinking of *Caroline*
107, 111–12; effect of Bin Laden's
communication on elections 25; funds
for IRA 178; global perspective on
intelligence gathering 163; human
rights abuses of Guantanamo detainees
74; invasion of Iraq (March 2003) 36,
194, 195; killing of Muslims in Iraq
and Palestine 33–4; and language of
force 134, 136; limited war doctrines
29; long war ideology 13–14, 23–4;
National Security Strategy 11–12, 15,
129, 137; new realists' thinking on self-
defence 115–16; policy on bioterrorism
142–55; post-9/11 foreign and security
policies 190; post-9/11 view of world
politics 10; post-Cold War hegemony
30–1, 126, 191; promotion of liberal
democratic values 13, 23; 'protection
myth' framework of war on terror
44; response to 9/11 attacks 1, 3, 11,
60, 192, 193–4; risk of undermining
international order 3; slogan 'global
war against terrorism' 12–13; strategies
of force in war on terror 31, 134;
strategies to combat al-Qaeda 15;
support for Israel's 2006 invasion of
Lebanon 38; treatment of detainees in
war on terror 169; Uniform Military
Code of Justice (UMCJ) 85, 86, 90;
unilateral response against financing
of terrorism 181–3, 186; *see also* Bush
administration
US Agency for International Development
(USAID) 128–9, 137
USA Patriot Act 2001 177, 181, 182–3
US Army: reservists charged with Abu
Ghraib prisoner abuses 48; sexual
harassment towards women 42–3

US Army Edgewood Chemical Biological
Center 152
US Army Medical Research Institute for
Infectious Diseases (USAMRIID)
145–6, 149
USA Today 45
US Department of Defense (DOD):
allegations against David Hicks 82–3;
Chemical and Biological Defense
Program (CBDP) 144; creation of S/
CRS 139; on 'military transformation'
29–30; *National Defense Strategy* 133;
Quadrennial Defense Review (QDR)
February 2006) 13–14, 14, 19, 23; on
threat from failed states 137; use of
Guantanamo Bay detention camp 71,
72
USS *Abraham Lincoln* 195
USS *Cole* 35
US State Department: *Future of Iraq*
project 17–18, 18; report on people
trafficking 50–1
US Supreme Court: findings on
Guantanamo Bay detainees 81, 83,
84–5, 87; neglect of issue of derogation
80; rulings on Guantanamo Bay 72, 73,
74, 78, 83–4, 88–9, 90
Uzbekistan 17, 140

Van Evera, Stephen 135, 136, 137
Vattel, E. 4, 108, 108–9, 114
Védrine, Hubert 191
veil *see hijab*
Vietnam war 29, 39
'vindictive justice' 97–8, 100–2
violence: Bin Laden's attempt to
communicate about causes and effects
25; breaking cycles of 66; daily
reality in Iraq 196; in interrogation
of prisoners 168–9; Islamist ideology
of 39; long-term consequences for
society 4; movement from grievance
to use of 32; in 'new wars' discourse
127; spiralling cycle generated by
wars of response 61; state of exception
allowing justification of 77–8
Vitoria, Francisco de 97, 100, 101

Waldock, Sir Humphrey 110
Walt, Stephen 136
Walzer, Michael 99
war: Clausewitz's first strategic question
on 41; new paradigm 28–9, 38; zones

of chaos 127–8; *see also* just war; 'new wars'

Warren, Earl 156

wars of response to terrorism 3–5; generation of further hatred and violence 61

war on terror: actions at individual level 164; anti-money laundering laws 183–5; Bush's rhetoric 97–8, 99, 100, 102, 129; concept of force in 28; current state of play 195–6; as defining present age 93; establishment of spaces of exception 130; flawed conception of 190, 195–6; gendered identities 43, 44, 45, 47–8, 49, 53; Geneva Conventions as applicable to 73; impact of emotions 61–2; intelligence gathering 156, 163–4, 175; justification and legitimisation 61; problem of categorising as war or crime 165; questioning of idea of 31, 40; role of Jessica Lynch narrative 47; and use of Guantanamo detention facilities 71; US rhetoric to justify 57; and worsening security of women 42–3, 49–53; *see also* global war on terror

Washington, DC 59, 128, 129

Washington Post 147, 150

weapons of mass destruction (WMD): and intelligence gathering 163; Iraq's alleged program 2, 194; and legitimisation of pre-emptive attack on Iraq 61, 98; threat from nations suspected of 115; US priority of preventing proliferation 14, 19–20

Weather Underground 20

Webster, Daniel 111–13, 117, 119

the West: development of grievances against 32; justification of violence against those outside state system 75; significance of 9/11 attacks for security 2–5, 10, 198

West Bank 26, 31, 35, 36

West Germany 178

Williams, Clive 31

Williams, M.C. 193

Williams, Paul 3–4

Wippman, D 80

Wolff, C. 108

Wolfowitz, Paul 17–18

women: historical linkage of emotions with 62; worsening security situation due to war on terror 42–3, 49–53

Woodward, Bob 98

World Bank 179

World Islamic Front for Jihad against Crusaders and Jews 35

World Trade Center 35

World Wide Web 161

Yemen 16, 50, 83

Yoo, John 80, 173

Yousef, Ramsi 35

Yugoslavia *see* Bosnia; Serbia

al-Zarqawi, Abu Musah 22

Zerhouni, Elias 146

zones of chaos 127–8, 129, 136, 139, 140

'zones of indistinction' 132

Zoya 46